# LAW, LAWYERS AND LITIGANTS IN EARLY MODERN ENGLAND



Written in memory of Christopher W. Brooks, this collection of essays by prominent historians examines and builds on the scholarly legacy of the leading historian of early modern English law, society and politics. Brooks's work put legal culture and legal consciousness at the centre of our understanding of seventeenth- and eighteenth-century English society, and the English common law tradition. The essays presented here develop a number of strands found in his work and take them in new directions. They shed new light on central debates in the history of the common law, exploring how law was understood and used by different communities in early modern England, and examining how and why people engaged (or did not engage) in litigation. The volume also contains two hitherto unpublished essays by Christopher Brooks, which consider the relationship between law and religion and between law and political revolution in seventeenth-century England.

MICHAEL LOBBAN is the author of a number of works on eighteenth- and nineteenth-century English legal history. He was a colleague of Christopher Brooks at Durham University and co-edited the volume *Community and Courts in Britain 1150–1900* (1997) with him.

JOANNE BEGIATO has published widely in the history of emotions, material culture, masculinities, family, parenting and marriage. Her PhD was supervised by Christopher Brooks at Durham University.

ADRIAN GREEN studies the history of buildings – especially the relationship between architecture and society in England and English America between the Reformation and the Industrial Revolution. His PhD in Archaeology and History was supervised by Matthew H. Johnson and Christopher W. Brooks at Durham University.

# LAW, LAWYERS AND LITIGANTS IN EARLY MODERN ENGLAND

## Essays in Memory of Christopher W. Brooks

Edited by

MICHAEL LOBBAN

*London School of Economics and Political Science*

JOANNE BEGIATO

*Oxford Brookes University*

ADRIAN GREEN

*Durham University*

CAMBRIDGE
UNIVERSITY PRESS

**CAMBRIDGE**
**UNIVERSITY PRESS**

University Printing House, Cambridge CB2 8BS, United Kingdom

One Liberty Plaza, 20th Floor, New York, NY 10006, USA

477 Williamstown Road, Port Melbourne, VIC 3207, Australia

314-321, 3rd Floor, Plot 3, Splendor Forum, Jasola District Centre, New Delhi - 110025, India

79 Anson Road, #06-04/06, Singapore 079906

Cambridge University Press is part of the University of Cambridge.

It furthers the University's mission by disseminating knowledge in the pursuit of education, learning and research at the highest international levels of excellence.

www.cambridge.org
Information on this title: www.cambridge.org/9781108740647
DOI: 10.1017/9781108666862



First published 2019
First paperback edition 2021

*A catalogue record for this publication is available from the British Library*

*Library of Congress Cataloging in Publication data*
Names: Brooks, C. W., honouree. | Begiato, Joanne, editor. | Green, Adrian (Adrian Gareth), editor. | Lobban, Michael, editor.
Title: Law, lawyers, and litigants in early modern England : essays in memory of Christopher W. Brooks / edited by Joanne Begiato (Oxford Brookes University), Adrian Green (University of Durham), Michael Lobban (London School of Economics and Political Science).
Description: Cambridge, United Kingdom ; New York, NY : Cambridge University Press, [2019] | Includes bibliographical references.
Identifiers: LCCN 2018058899 | ISBN 9781108491723
Subjects: LCSH: Brooks, C. W. | Practice of law – England – History. | Law – England – History. | Lawyers – England – History. | Religion and law – England – History.
Classification: LCC KD474 .L39 2019 | DDC 349.4209/03–dc23
LC record available at https://lccn.loc.gov/2018058899

ISBN 978-1-108-49172-3 Hardback
ISBN 978-1-108-74064-7 Paperback

# CONTENTS

# FIGURES

# TABLES

# CONTRIBUTORS

JOANNE BEGIATO is Professor of History at Oxford Brookes University.

MICHAEL J. BRADDICK is Professor of History at the University of Sheffield.

ADRIAN GREEN is Associate Professor in Early Modern British and American History at Durham University.

STEVE HINDLE is W. M. Keck Foundation Director of Research at the Huntington Library, San Marino, California.

R. A. HOUSTON is Professor of Early Modern History at the University of St Andrews.

R. W. HOYLE is Visiting Professor of Economic History in the Centre for Economic History at the University of Reading.

MICHAEL LOBBAN is Professor of Legal History at the London School of Economics and Political Science.

GWENDA MORGAN is a teaching assistant at the University of Newcastle, having retired as Reader in American History at the University of Sunderland.

CRAIG MULDREW is Professor of Early Modern Economic and Social History at the University of Cambridge.

PETER RUSHTON is Professor of Historical Sociology at the University of Sunderland.

DAVID SUGARMAN is Emeritus Professor of Law at the Law School of Lancaster University.

JOHN WALTER is Emeritus Professor of History at the University of Essex.

PHIL WITHINGTON is Professor in Social and Cultural History at the University of Sheffield.

1

# Introduction*

MICHAEL LOBBAN, JOANNE BEGIATO
AND ADRIAN GREEN

When Christopher W. Brooks died of a heart attack, on 19 August 2014, he was at the height of his intellectual powers.[1] Since 2010, he had been able to devote himself full-time to researching his volume of the *Oxford History of the Laws of England* thanks to being awarded two prestigious fellowships from the Leverhulme Trust and the Huntington Library. He planned to retire the following October from his chair in the History Department at Durham University – where he had been since 1980 – and was about to embark on writing up the great 350,000-word project of the *Oxford History*, as well as another book on 'Law and Religion in Early Modern England'. At the same time, he had a number of other projects on the go: preparing papers on law and literature, and law and the people in early modern England;[2] and preparing an exhibition on law and life in Shakespeare's England for the Folger Shakespeare Library in Washington, DC.[3] Chris Brooks had established a firm reputation as the most important and influential historian of law and society in early modern England – but he still had a great deal more to say. He was in many ways uniquely placed to write the history of English law from Charles I to James II for the *Oxford History* – a project he had been working on for twenty years – and his untimely death robbed the

* The editors would like to thank Sharyn Brooks for her help, particularly in making available the two hitherto unpublished pieces by her husband, which are included in this volume.

1 For an appreciation, see Adrian Green, 'Christopher W. Brooks, 1948–2014: a tribute', *The Seventeenth Century* 29 (2014), 403–409.

2 The first of these was originally given as a lecture to the Centre for Mediaeval and Early Modern Law and Literature, St Andrews University, October 2013. It was published posthumously as Christopher W. Brooks, 'Paradise lost? Law, literature, and history in Restoration England', in Lorna Hutson (ed.), *The Oxford Handbook of English Law and Literature, 1500–1700* (Oxford University Press, 2017), pp. 198–218. The second, intended for Keith Wrightson (ed.), *A Social History of England, 1500–1750* (Cambridge, 2017), was never completed.

3 This exhibition, entitled 'Age of Lawyers: The Roots of American Law in Shakespeare's Britain', was held at the Folger Shakespeare Library between 12 September 2015 and 3 January 2016.

scholarly community of the knowledge and insights he would have brought to this subject.[4]

This volume derives from a conference on Law and Society in Early Modern England held in Durham in Chris Brooks's memory in March 2016.[5] Alongside the scholars whose work is included in this volume, there were contributions at the conference from friends and colleagues including Jonathan Barry, Bernard Capp, Alan Cromartie, Henry French, Cynthia Herrup, Lorna Hutson, Judith Spicksley, Tim Stretton and Andy Wood. The aim of the conference was to explore the implications of Chris's work for the wider historiography of seventeenth- and eighteenth-century England, in terms of both his distinctive interpretations and his wider approach in bringing together the tools of legal history and social history. As is more fully explained in the discussions of his work in this volume by Michael J. Braddick (see Chapter 2) and David Sugarman (see Chapter 3), a hallmark of this approach was the combination of painstaking, detailed archival research with a focus on contributing to our understanding of the major topics in the historiography (and taking them in new directions). Chris's first book, *Pettyfoggers and Vipers of the Commonwealth: The 'Lower Branch' of the Legal Profession in Early Modern England*, might at first glance look like a narrow study of a specialised topic: the history of attorneys. But both its thesis and its data established how pervasive and important the law and lawyers were in early modern England – a point that had important ramifications for our understanding of the political, constitutional, social and economic history of the era. These themes would be developed in even greater depth in *Law, Politics and Society in Early Modern England*. In the light of his scholarship bridging legal history and early modern historiography as a whole, historians of early modern England can no longer afford to ignore the impact of law, its languages or law-mindedness.

The chapters in this volume each explore how law was understood or used in early modern England. The volume begins with three historiographical chapters, two (by Braddick, in Chapter 2, and Sugarman, in Chapter 3) focusing on Chris Brooks's own work, and one (by R. A. Houston, in Chapter 4) on the significance for early modern history of F. W. Maitland. Often seen as a key figure for the history of medieval legal doctrines and institutions, Maitland is also recognised by Houston

[4] The task of completing this volume has now passed to a younger generation of scholars.

[5] The conference, which was co-organised by Professor John O'Brien, was hosted by Durham University's Institute for Medieval and Early Modern Studies, with support from the Selden Society and the Huntington Library.

as an important forerunner of the kind of approach taken by Brooks and as a vital influence on the historiography on the early-modern social history of law. Two chapters follow that shed new light on some central debates relating to the early seventeenth-century common law. In Chapter 5, R. W. Hoyle explores the question of the king's power to decide legal cases – a question much debated among contemporaries in the well-known controversy of the case of prohibitions. Hoyle looks at an aspect that has not hitherto received the attention it deserves: the king's intervention as an arbitrator, making decisions in disputes that might then be enforced by order of court. Phil Withington's contribution (Chapter 6) considers a question much debated since Maitland's time: the impact of the Renaissance on English law. By tracing the use of the language of 'modernity' in the legal literature of the early seventeenth century, Withington shows that English lawyers were much less impervious to the influence of the European Renaissance than is sometimes assumed.

The subsequent chapters focus on the local uses and knowledge of law in early modern England. Steve Hindle's fine-grained study, in Chapter 7, of a Warwickshire tithe dispute from 1657 shows how a close study of the documents generated by litigation can tell us a great deal not only about the means used by seventeenth-century communities in settling their disputes, but also about the wider social and spatial dynamics in which these disputes were played out. As he shows, 'law' did not simply supplant 'love' as a means of dispute resolution in this era; rather, litigation was one strategy that might be used alongside agreement, mediation or arbitration. In his contribution (Chapter 8), John Walter explores the nature and extent of popular knowledge of law. He shows both how ordinary folk came to obtain knowledge of the law and how they then used that knowledge, for instance in the way in which they protested against perceived infringements of their rights, such as enclosures. Peter Rushton's chapter (Chapter 9) explores the paradoxical relationship between central and local authorities in early modern England, showing that, as the early modern state developed and became stronger, so it required local authorities to take on more responsibilities. This raises the question of how far there might be local legal cultures that were distinct and how far local practice deviated from what national 'law' demanded.

Our next set of chapters explores aspects of law in the eighteenth century. In Chapter 10, Joanne Begiato takes up the theme of how far popular uses of law deviated from its letter, looking at marriage practices in the early eighteenth century. Although recent work by Rebecca Probert has suggested that there were few 'clandestine' marriages in the eighteenth century (and that almost all couples married formally in a church),[6] Begiato shows that a greater diversity might exist at local levels, where legal forms might be manipulated and moulded to ensure that, although couples might not have followed the strict forms of the law, they might nonetheless be regarded as 'wed enough'. In his chapter (Chapter 11), Craig Muldrew takes up a question explored in one of Chris Brooks's most influential articles and in Muldrew's own earlier work on litigation:[7] why did litigation rates, which had been so high in the seventeenth century, decline so rapidly in the eighteenth? Muldrew addresses this problem by noting the changing way in which credit was negotiated in the later era. In the early seventeenth century, most credit was unsecured, resting on reputation and one's ability to pay the debts one had contracted verbally. By the eighteenth century, however, credit was becoming ever more securitised, in the form of written notes and bonds, as well as mortgages. Lawyers were heavily involved in the creation and maintenance of this credit network, which did not require litigation. Thus, although litigation declined, the role of law and lawyers certainly did not. Gwenda Morgan's contribution (Chapter 12) looks to compare the lives and careers of two justices of the peace, Landon Carter of Virginia and Edmund Tew of County Durham, as reflected in their personal diaries, which shed important light on their different experiences of life on the bench.

Adrian Green's chapter (Chapter 13) takes us back to the city in which Chris spent more than thirty years of his life in exploring a theme central to his concerns: the relationship between law and society as a lived experience, seen through the architecture of the courts and legal offices in early modern Durham. Green demonstrates the variety of courts and jurisdictions on the peninsula between the cathedral and the castle, and how they were housed and operated. He also takes us into the life of the lawyers in this city. It is, perhaps, rather satisfying to discover that the office that Chris occupied on the North Bailey for so many years was

[6] Rebecca Probert, *Marriage Law and Practice in the Long Eighteenth Century: A Reassessment* (Cambridge, 2009).

[7] Craig Muldrew, 'Interpersonal conflict and social tension: civil litigation in England 1640–1830', in A. L. Beier, David Cannadine and James M. Rosenheim (eds), *The First Modern Society: Essays in Honour of Lawrence Stone* (Cambridge, 1989), pp. 357–399. See also Craig Muldrew, *The Economy of Obligation: The Culture of Credit and Social Relations in Early Modern England* (Basingstoke, 1998), pp. 216–236.

home to law offices in the eighteenth century, with architectural detail modelled to imitate those of fine chambers in London.

The collection is rounded off with two hitherto unpublished pieces by Christopher W. Brooks himself. The editors have chosen to include them with some sense of caution, for he was a very meticulous scholar who did not rush into print, but was always keen to work out his ideas thoroughly and fully before publishing them. Readers are therefore asked to bear in mind that these pieces were very much works in progress on topics that he was still developing. The two pieces are snapshots of his thinking about two projects, which Chris envisaged as growing into books, rather than articles.

The first of these is entitled 'Law and Revolution: The Seventeenth-Century English Example'. This paper grew out of the project with which Chris was engaged at the time of his death – that is, the volume of *The Oxford History of the Laws of England* covering the period 1625–1688. A number of versions of the paper were delivered at various institutions during the academic year 2012/13, which he spent as Fletcher Jones Distinguished Fellow in British History at the Huntington Library, in California. The version published here was delivered at the University of Southern California (USC) in November 2012.[8] Another shorter version, entitled 'Through the Looking Glass: Law and Revolution in England 1640–1650', was delivered in April 2013 as part of USC's Early Modern British History Seminar series, under the aegis of the USC–Huntington Early Modern Studies Institute.

The aim of the paper was to explore some of the larger questions concerning the nature of legal change in the era Chris was studying for the *Oxford History*, to help him to make sense of the period as a whole. Part of his concern was to address questions about the nature of legal change over time that he felt had not hitherto been asked very vigorously. Working, as he was, on a history of law in the seventeenth century, he was interested in exploring both the impact of the short-term changes that occurred in the turbulent period of the civil war and its aftermath, and also the long-term changes that he saw emerging from the interaction of legal ideas and economic and social changes over the century before the civil war (and which could be seen reflected in the long-term fluctuations in litigation that he had explored in earlier work). Looking at the longer

[8] An earlier version was also given in October 2011 at the 'Law and Governance in Pre-Modern Britain' conference at the University of Western Ontario and subsequently at Yale Law School.

term, he saw this period as a remarkable phase in the history of the common law, in which a legal system that was much more accessible to the middling sorts was forged by judges and lawyers. Looking at the common law as a working system that had penetrated into the daily lives and consciousness of the people of England, the shorter-term crisis of the civil war did not prove to be revolutionary. The system of law survived, at a time when the Church of England collapsed, and proposals for radical legal reform went nowhere. However, as Chris saw it, if the civil war was not a watershed for the legal system as a system of *law*, the years down to 1689 did see significant change in the role of the common lawyers as political actors – for, as he explains in the second part of this paper (and more fully in the second paper on 'Religion and Law in Early Modern England', which is published here as Chapter 15), after the Restoration, the political centrality of common law discourse was dislodged, partly as a result of the dynamic between religion and law in this era. As he put it in his comments to his audience in 2012:

> [W]hen parliamentary legislation of the 1660s and 1670s was countered by royal declarations of indulgence to dissenters, the common law and its judges became hopelessly caught up in openly political partisanship, which undermined their independence, their credibility, and their authority. At the same time, the decline of the learning exercises at the inns of court seems to have deprived common law thought of its vitality and its confidence. The intellectual life of the law and its role in English politics was never the same thereafter.[9]

In the shorter version of this paper, 'Through the Looking Glass', these issues are explored from the narrower perspective of the 1640s and 1650s. In this paper, Chris takes up an argument made in *Law, Politics and Society* – that is, that 'the advent of civil war represented the failure rather than the success of the political use of legal discourse and ideas'.[10] In the

[9] The text of 'Through the Looking Glass' ends thus: 'Conscientious judges, like Henry Rolle insisted that they should maintain the fundamental laws of the land, but the profession itself was divided by politics, and [the] institutional infrastructure that had helped to shape those laws, the learning exercises and student culture at the inns of court[,] was severely atrophied in the 1650s, and, arguably, has never recovered. No distinctive view of the new polity was developed at the inns. Law became plumbing, social and economic infrastructure that kept the paperwork flowing in the right direction, and the direction was determined largely by the state, whatever form that might take. Medieval community of the realm mediated by law was replaced by a notion that someone had to be in charge and then law becomes instrumental' (Christopher W. Brooks, 'Through the Looking Glass: Law and Revolution in England 1640–1650', ts, ff. 24–25).

[10] Ibid., f. 4.

decades before the civil war, it was disagreements over the nature of the ecclesiastical polity that led lawyers to make their most important interventions. One of these was Edward Bagshaw's 1640 reading on the ecclesiastical legislation of Edward III, which articulated a vision that had been maturing among common lawyers for a century, denying the bishops any secular political authority (an issue discussed at greater length in 'Religion and Law in Early Modern England', published here as Chapter 15). This, Chris asserts, 'can probably be described as the last really controversial and significant law lecture to be given for the next two hundred years'; it was also 'the first reading at the inns of court ever to have been suppressed by the government'.[11] However, if, in the event, it was the church that came off worst in the conflict, it was also the case that the common lawyers did not know what to replace it with: '[H]aving undermined the existing church, lawyers were much more ambivalent about what to put in its place.'[12]

Chris's explorations of the relationship between temporality and spirituality link the two papers published here, for, as he explained on one occasion, 'it is the relationship between religion and municipal law which constitutes the single most important dynamic of the period'.[13] This was the topic more fully explored in 'Religion and Law in Early Modern England' (see Chapter 15). An early version of this paper was delivered at the University of Southampton in February 2008.[14] A fuller version, the one produced here, was drafted in the autumn of 2010 and refined over the next few months. Chris contemplated submitting it to a leading journal, but in the end decided not to do so, since he felt that he had much more to say on this topic. In the next couple of years, he increasingly thought of developing it into another book. He did, however, air some of the ideas he was working on during his year at the Huntington Library, presenting papers under the title 'Providence versus Prudence: Law and Religion in Early Modern England' at the Huntington in February 2013 and at the Triangle Legal History Seminar/Triangle Global British Studies Seminar in Durham, North Carolina, in September 2013.

[11] Ibid., f. 9.

[12] Ibid., f. 12.

[13] Brooks's notes for presenting 'Law and Revolution' at USC in 2012.

[14] In the version given here (see Chapter 15), he observed that he had come to the conclusion '(which some might describe as a no brainer arrived at after years of study) ... that what Sir John Neale described in the 1950s as the "nationalisation" of religion raised a number of serious problems for the English polity, many of which were worked out in the language of secular legal and constitutional thought'.

One of the points that Chris made at these seminars was that while religion and religious ideas were clearly central to the lives of all seventeenth-century Englishmen and women – who were, at the very least, expected by statute law to attend church on Sunday – there was much to be learned about the ideas and assumptions that drove interpersonal relations on the other six days of the week. In turning one's attention to those questions, the historian was led pretty quickly into the territory of the other major profession, the law. What also struck him was the fact that lawyers before the civil war had an 'unexpected capacity' to 'compartmentalize their professional discourse from that of the evangelical Protestantism of the later sixteenth and seventeenth centuries, even though there is absolutely no doubt that they often knew a great deal about it'.[15] While lawyers like Sir Matthew Hale were undoubtedly very pious and thought a good deal about religion, 'theology or divinity of the kind engaged in by university-trained clergymen, which was based largely on readings of the scriptures and the early Church Fathers, figured hardly at all in every-day professional legal thought or in the political discourse associated with it'.[16] Both in form and content, secular legal thought differed from religious thought. The kind of works men such as Hale put together for their 'day-job' – such as the commonplace book he called his 'Black Book of the New Law' – saw law as an inductive science in which 'the general rules were "discovered" by a consideration of a large number of particular circumstances'.[17] These circumstances came to the lawyer's attention in cases brought by ordinary people into court, which reflected their experiences and predicaments. The kinds of cases and issues digested in Hale's book reflected the social relations that people experienced in the six days of the week when they did not go to church, and which were 'usually dealt with in ways that had very little to do (at least on a formal level) with the teachings of Christianity or the interpretation of scripture, not to mention the book divinity of the more learned clergymen'.[18]

Part of the interest in this paper was therefore to stress the importance of the notion of the rule of law in seventeenth-century minds. As Chris put it in the seminar paper:

[15] Christopher W. Brooks, 'Providence versus Prudence: Religion and Law in Seventeenth-Century England', ts, ff. 1–2.
[16] Ibid., f. 11.
[17] Ibid., f. 13.
[18] Ibid.

> [L]egal discourse contained spaces for more reflective thought about the nature of society and the polity. And in speeches, arguments, briefs and lectures we learn about contracts and kings being limited by the rule of law rather than of divine right or the obligations associated with patriarchy, concepts that that come largely out of clerical writing. Subjects could be described as citizens, and obedience to established authority is not so much a religious precept as a legitimate expression of how best to look out for one's best interests in what would otherwise be a Hobbesian state of nature where the strong might easily subdue the weak.[19]

It was with this in mind that he turned to the broader debates among common lawyers about the nature of the ecclesiastical polity and about the sources of authority for all human law, which he saw as so central to seventeenth-century political thought. In both the seminar paper and the fuller draft article published here, Chris elaborated on some of the themes touched on in the 'Law and Revolution' paper – in particular, the problem faced by common lawyers once the bishops had been removed from the House of Lords and the Church of England had been undermined. Common lawyers remained uncertain during the interregnum about what kind of church settlement they wanted, which created dilemmas for them after the Restoration. Problems concerning the ecclesiastical polity were seen most sharply in the debates over the Declarations of Indulgence, in which there was sufficient room for lawyers to differ in opinion that it was possible for kings to play musical chairs with the judiciary, to secure compliant judges. In a context in which the lawyers were no longer able to give clear answers to the most pressing questions concerning the relationship between temporality and spirituality, the matter ultimately had to be left to Parliament for resolution. The triumph in 1688 of parliamentary authority was therefore in no small part the outcome of the inability of common lawyers to resolve the political and legal problems concerning the ecclesiastical polity.

These unfinished pieces give us some insight into the development of Chris's thinking, as his new research took him further into the second half of the eighteenth century. Had he lived to complete his projected *Oxford History* and *Law and Religion* volumes, the scholarly community would have received the same kind of benefits that it reaped from his earlier works. What is given here can be only a small glimpse into those larger projects. Nonetheless, his legacy remains a great one. The scholarly concerns that drove his work – the need to understand how people

[19] Ibid., f. 14.

worked with the law, and how the law informed and constituted so much of English social agency – are ones that are increasingly regarded as part of the mainstream of seventeenth-century historiography. As the contributions in this volume show, Chris's erudite scholarship was, in many ways, only a starting point; there is much work still to be done, and his own interpretations remain open to challenge and contestation. It is our hope that the chapters in this volume will contribute to moving the field forward, as well as offer a fitting tribute in his memory.

# 2

# Christopher Brooks's Contribution to Early Modern History

MICHAEL J. BRADDICK

Discussion of Chris Brooks's work almost invariably involves reference (often in reverential terms) to the Herculean archival effort and austere scholarship that underlay it. What has become perhaps his headline finding, about steepling levels of litigation in England during the sixteenth and seventeenth centuries followed by an apparently precipitate decline, rested on months, probably years, of unenviable labour in the archives; his work on legal history proper, and on legal thought, was equally scholarly, but in a different way, depending on patient close reading of technically difficult texts. We can see in this the imprint of J. P. Cooper, Brooks's PhD supervisor. But I think the Lawrence Stone influence was equally important in the questions Brooks asked – big questions about societal transformations of one kind or another – and also perhaps in the way he answered them – with analytic acuity, but also a whiff of whiggery, or at least an overt commitment to modern liberal values and a critical interest in the narratives set out before revisionism. He certainly refers to Stone more often and more visibly than to Cooper. This gives Brooks's work as a whole a cutting edge partly because it sets it slightly at odds with the mainstream of both social and political history; it also puts him at a tangent with some of the main traditions of legal history and scholarship (on which, see David Sugarman's essay in this volume, at Chapter 3).

## Lawyers, Litigation and English Society

Brooks's own account of himself, in the preface to his collected essays, states that his starting point, in the early 1970s, was 'an interest in the role of lawyers and legal ideas in parliamentary debates during the early seventeenth century, the age of Sir Edward Coke'.[1] His first publication

[1] C. W. Brooks, 'Preface', in *Lawyers, Litigation and English Society since 1450* (London and Rio Grande, 1998), p. ix.

was a comment on an article in *Past and Present* by Donald Kelley, co-authored with Kevin Sharpe (a friend and student in Oxford at the same time) and published in 1976.[2] Kelley had contrasted the liveliness of historical and legal scholarship in Renaissance France with the timelessness, complacency and insularity of common law thought. The jointly authored reply is notable for the roundedness of the consideration of legal thought – its connection with large themes in contemporary understandings of the past, not least the feudal past, but also with constitutional thinking and the possibilities for political change. This hints at the kind of hinterland that underpinned Brooks's rather modestly titled DPhil thesis on 'Some aspects of attorneys in England during the late sixteenth and early seventeenth centuries', accepted two years later.[3]

The aspects of attorneys that most preoccupied Brooks in the coming years were social and professional, rather than intellectual or political. Again, as he puts it himself, this was really a way to clear the decks for the main action:

> I soon became convinced that the kind of understanding I wanted of the political history of the period could only be achieved by trying to gain a better appreciation of what social life, more broadly defined, was like. Since I was interested in the political ideas expressed by lawyers, an examination of lawyers and what lawyers did seemed a logical place to start. What began as a digression became an ongoing preoccupation.[4]

As he had put it in an earlier essay, despite the obvious place of lawyers and legal argument in early Stuart political controversy, 'we know all too little about the structure of the legal profession, its aims, or the way in which the judicial system it operated touched on the lives of those who used it'.[5]

Having lighted on the docket rolls and the rolls of warrants of attorney in King's Bench and Common Pleas, Brooks was able to begin to reconstruct the profile of the lower branch of the legal profession and its development, set fully in the context of its interaction with, on the one hand, the clients and, on the other, the courts. The central theme, of course, became the relationship between the development of the legal

[2] C. W. Brooks and K. M. Sharpe, 'History, English law and the Renaissance: a comment', *Past and Present* 72 (1976), 133–146.

[3] DPhil thesis, University of Oxford (1978).

[4] 'Preface', in *Lawyers, Litigation and English Society*, p. ix.

[5] 'Litigants and attorneys in the King's Bench and Common Pleas, 1560–1640' (first published 1978), reprinted in *Lawyers, Litigation and English Society*, pp. 9–25, quotation at p. 9.

profession and the rising levels of litigation in early modern English society. The numbers of attorneys grew at a much faster rate than did the population at large, as did litigation, and much of that litigation related to debt. At the same time, trespass – usually a cause related to violence – declined. In all, it seems likely that 'the late sixteenth and early seventeenth centuries were the most litigious periods in English history'; a later decline in the use of the law to resolve differences 'has meant a corresponding decline in the general influence of lawyers in political life and social planning'.[6]

These findings probably represented Brooks's most influential intervention in the field: that part of his monograph on *Pettyfoggers and Vipers* which related to the themes of the earlier article on litigants and attorneys in King's Bench and Common Pleas, as well as his article in the Festschrift for Stone, are probably his most widely cited writings.[7] By 1989, contributing to a Festschrift for Lawrence Stone was a potentially career-limiting move, at least in the United Kingdom, although Stone continued (and continues) to enjoy a much higher reputation in the United States. Although the theme of the book was the *First Modern Society*, by then an increasingly unfashionable thing to write about, and although Brooks was interested in long-term trends, his account was not conventionally Whiggish.

At that point, of course, the new social history had been seriously engaged with legal records for some time. Keith Wrightson's use of quarter sessions records to recover measures of social control helped to inspire a wave of work that sought access to the lives of the poor through the records of their encounters with authority.[8] In my own case, it was my

[6] Ibid., p. 12.

[7] C. W. Brooks, *Pettyfoggers and Vipers of the Commonwealth: The 'Lower Branch' of the Legal Profession in Early Modern England* (Cambridge, 1986); C. W. Brooks, 'Interpersonal conflict and social tension: civil litigation in England, 1640–1870', first published in A. L. Beier, D. Cannadine and J. M. Rosenheim (eds), *The First Modern Society: Essays in Honour of Lawrence Stone* (Cambridge, 1989), pp. 357–399, reprinted in *Lawyers, Litigation and English Society*, pp. 27–62. For a sense of the impact of this aspect of Brooks's work, see T. Stretton, 'The people and the law', in K. E. Wrightson (ed.), *A Social History of England 1500–1750* (Cambridge, 2017), pp. 199–220.

[8] K. E. Wrightson, 'The Puritan reformation of manners with special reference to the counties of Lancashire and Essex, 1640–1660', PhD thesis, University of Cambridge (1978); K. E. Wrightson and D. Levine, *Poverty and Piety in an English Village: Terling, 1525–1700* (2nd edn, Oxford, 1995); K. E. Wrightson, *English Society 1580–1680* (London, 1982). Other influential works of this kind included J. Brewer and J. Styles (eds), *An Ungovernable People? The English and Their Law in the Seventeenth and Eighteenth Centuries* (London, 1980); J. A. Sharpe, *Crime in Seventeenth-Century England: A County*

interest in the development of those structures of authority, and the clash of social interests that lay behind it, that led me to Brooks's work. But I (and, I think, others) tended to treat the law as a framework within which social history happened, or in the records of which social relations could be detected.[9] The real power of Brooks's findings about litigation levels, however, was the insight that the rise of lawyers and litigation helped actually to constitute social relations, and was a causal factor in their development. This insight was powerfully and influentially developed by Craig Muldrew, or at least provided the backdrop to his innovative work on credit, contract and trust.[10]

More broadly, though, Brooks was arguing that we should see the law and the legal profession as a social phenomenon in its own right – one that existing scholarship was ill-equipped to address. As he put it himself, there was no 'analytical perspective capable of doing justice to the complex and multi-faceted role of law in society'.[11] Historical practice increasingly licensed routine specialization that almost gives Brooks's approach an interdisciplinary quality.

Understanding the history of the legal profession was central to understanding the development of a society that was both a litigious and – by the same token, rather than by contrast – a law-abiding society. During the eighteenth century, critics lamented that, in a period of very low levels of litigation, ordinary people were denied access to the law. Elizabethan and Stuart critics had, by contrast, tended to say that high levels of litigation were a symptom of a broken society. Brooks clearly took an eighteenth-century view. The rise of debt and decline of trespass in the earlier period reflected the triumph of orderly dispute resolution, and litigation was, for him, a positive aspect of interpersonal relations. As a consequence, he had interpreted the decline of litigation as

*Study* (Cambridge, 1983); J. A. Sharpe, *Crime in Early Modern England* (Harlow, 1984); C. Herrup, *The Common Peace: Participation and the Criminal Law in Seventeenth-Century England* (Cambridge, 1987); M. Ingram, *Church Courts, Sex and Marriage in England, 1570–1640* (Cambridge, 1987). Brooks noted that scholars were beginning to take an interest in the criminal law as he began his doctoral work and he cited a number of these works as the fruits of that interest: 'Introduction', in *Lawyers, Litigation and English Society*, p. 2; 'Law, lawyers and the social history of England, 1500–1800', in *Lawyers, Litigation and English Society*, pp. 179–198, at pp. 179–180, nn. 2–4. Much of it was informed, of course, by the earlier work of E. P. Thompson, Douglas Hay and Peter Linebaugh.

[9] On this point, see the essay by Sugarman, at Chapter 3 in this volume.

[10] C. Muldrew, *The Economy of Obligation: The Culture of Credit and Social Relations in Early Modern England* (Basingstoke, 1998).

[11] 'Law, lawyers and social history', p. 179.

a potentially damaging thing: those who could not access the law in the eighteenth century had recourse, in unknown numbers, to arbitration or 'suffered the frustration of having to lose what they considered their just causes'.[12]

There seems to have been a biographical aspect to this, for the native of Maryland 'who grew up . . . during the civil rights campaigns of the 1950s and 1960s'.[13] But there was, too, a more narrowly historiographical point: that the law cannot be considered simply a tool of class domination, but instead should be seen as a 'cultural resource'. Brooks took the idea from the final chapter of Thompson's *Whigs and Hunters* (1975), citing it as a 'characterisation which I have always found particularly thought-provoking'.[14] Brooks's analysis of levels of litigation from 1660 to 1830 ended on this point: that those patterns reflected, to a considerable degree, the choices of the users of the law – for example the preference of urban middling sorts for promissory notes over the relatively inflexible machinery of debt litigation, or the local pressure for the establishment of courts of requests. He concluded that it 'is clearly no longer tenable to think of English law in the eighteenth century as simply a matter of gentry hegemony over the rest of the population'.[15] This reinforced the sense that a decline of litigation was a bad thing, in so far as it reflected reduced access to the cultural resource for ordinary people, rather than a good thing because there was less legal dispute in English society. He extended this analysis over the very *longue durée*, too, arguing that there was never a full recovery from the eighteenth-century nadir of engagement with the courts and that, in the twentieth century, the law was less accessible than at any time since 1700.[16]

This stress on the law as a resource informed the successful conference held in Durham in 1995, some of the fruits of which appeared in a volume co-edited with Michael Lobban.[17] It is an interest that sits very well with

12 'Interpersonal conflict and social tension', p. 60. See also C. W. Brooks, 'A law-abiding and litigious society', in J. Morrill (ed.), *The Oxford Illustrated History of Tudor and Stuart England* (Oxford, 1996), pp. 139–155.

13 'Introduction', p. 2.

14 Ibid., p. 5, n. 16.

15 'Interpersonal conflict and social tension', p. 62.

16 'Litigation and society in England, 1200–1996', in *Lawyers, Litigation and English Society*, pp. 63–128. These arguments are brought out very fully in C. W. Brooks, 'The longitudinal study of civil litigation in England 1200–1996', in W. Prest and S. Roach Anleu (eds), *Litigation: Past and Present* (Sydney, 2004), pp. 24–42.

17 C. W. Brooks and M. Lobban (eds), *Communities and Courts in Britain, 1150–1900* (London, 1997). Many of these themes are summarized succinctly in C. W. Brooks,

much recent work in social history, although much of that history has been more concerned with clarifying the ways in which class power *did* inflect the use of the law, rather than with demonstrating that it was not *simply* a tool of class domination: exploring the scope for subordinate groups to limit the effects of the power held by their social superiors and of the place of the law in what is sometimes referred to as the negotiation of power.[18]

## The Middling Sort, the Professions and English Social History

The history of the legal profession that underpinned this analysis was Brooks's entrée into the history of the middling sort – another theme central to writing about social history during the 1990s. In 1981, his findings about the profession were trailed in an essay on 'The common lawyers in England 1560–1640'.[19] The great growth in numbers of attorneys, who were suspected by contemporaries of cooking up the business that was flooding the courts, was followed by decline in the profession and its institutions in the eighteenth century. Fees deterred clients from litigation and there was a greater resort to arbitration, so that it became a much less attractive, or lucrative, profession. Numbers fell sharply so

'Lawyers as intermediaries between people and courts: some reflections on the English experience (c. 1450–1800)', in C. Dolan (ed.), *Les auxiliaires de la justice: intermédiaires entre justice et les populations de la fin du Moyen Âge à la période contemporaine* (Sainte-Foy, 2005), pp. 279–299.

18 M. J. Braddick, *State Formation in Early Modern England* (Cambridge, 2000); S. Hindle, *The State and Social Change in Early Modern England, c. 1550–1640* (Basingstoke, 2000); M. J. Braddick and J. Walter (eds), *Negotiating Power in Early Modern Society: Order, Hierarchy and Subordination in Britain and Ireland* (Cambridge, 2001). This is also a prominent theme in, for example, Andy Wood's work. Like some others, Wood has been critical of the utility of the notion of negotiated power for understanding these relationships: A. Wood, 'Fear, hatred and the hidden injuries of class in early modern England', *Journal of Social History* 39 (2006), 803–826; A. Wood, 'Subordination, solidarity and the limits of popular agency in a Yorkshire valley, c. 1596–1615', *Past and Present* 193 (2006), 41–72.

19 C. W. Brooks, 'The common lawyers in England, c. 1558–1642', in W. R. Prest (ed.), *Lawyers in Early Modern Europe and America* (London, 1981), pp. 42–64. He also contributed to work on notaries and reflected on the different access that archives gave to early modern English life by comparison with France, with its more active and well-documented notaries: C. W. Brooks, R. H. Helmholz and P. G. Stein, *Notaries Public in England since the Reformation* (London, 1991); C. W. Brooks, 'Les actes juridiques, le cycle de vie, et les relations sociales dans l'Angleterre de la période moderne', in S. Beauvalet-Boutouyrie, V. Gourdon and F.-J. Ruggiu (eds), *Liens sociaux et actes notariés dans le monde urbain en France et en Europe: XVIe–XVIIIe siècles* (Paris, 2004), pp. 77–86.

that access to lawyers in the provinces was greatly reduced. Forms of apprenticeship and training had been sustained, however, and formed the basis of legal education in the nineteenth century; in this sense, the profession as it was constituted in 1880 was remarkably like that of the 1660s.

Here, Brooks was taking on deeply embedded teleologies and strongly institutional approaches.[20] His account of the lawyers stood in contrast to these approaches, exploring the social and intellectual formation of lawyers, and how that explained their actions and social role. His key observation – that, in terms of numbers, education and social formation, there was little to separate the lawyers of the 1880s from those of two centuries earlier – undercut dominant narratives linking the development of professions and the emergence of industrial society: narratives emphasizing specialization of function and monetization as hallmarks of modernity and its economic roles. *Pettyfoggers and Vipers* did pay full attention to the institutional features of the life of the lower branch, of course, but also to the life that a lawyer might lead: their wealth, intellectual formation, the extent of social mobility through the law, their practical role in mediating between their clients and the courts, and the place they held in their local society.[21] All of this offered a fuller and very satisfying context for understanding the litigation boom and the roots of pressure for law reform throughout the period.

This was thoroughly empirical work, but with the intent to inform and reflect upon big debates. Brooks's reflections – not speculations, given the depth of learning on which they are based – were of general significance, problematizing the emphasis on the nineteenth-century origins of professionalization and middle-class culture, and of the close connection between both and modernity. Instead, he traced the powerful influence of professional groups on the development of associational life, and middling-sort culture, in the eighteenth century – an extension of the fully rounded history of the profession that his monograph represented.

His empirical findings also cast nineteenth-century reform in a different light. It now appeared to be restoring a practical, vocational, education that had atrophied during the eighteenth century. However, something had been lost: the atrophy of the institutions of legal life during the eighteenth century had led to a greater emphasis on practical,

[20] For a fuller discussion of the relations between history and legal history, see Sugarman, Chapter 3 in this volume.

[21] 'Common lawyers'; *Pettyfoggers*.

vocational education as opportunities and rewards for a more theoretical and liberal education reduced. As a result, and rather unusually, nineteenth-century England maintained a separation between largely vocational legal education and the liberal education offered in the universities.[22]

'Exorcising professionalisation is liberating', Brooks declared in an expansive moment, clearing space for other ways of thinking about lawyers and their place in the social structure.[23] He was interested here not only in 'conceptualising the past on its own terms', but also in 'charting change over time'.[24] This interest was timely, intersecting with a rising appreciation of the importance of the 'middling sort' and informing the publication of a very influential volume co-edited with Jonathan Barry.[25] In that context, Brooks explored the wider significance of apprenticeship and the legal profession to English society. Writing about apprenticeship more broadly, and lawyers alongside other professionals, he developed a view of a society in which key and numerically important groups played a critical role in diffusing ideas that shaped a wider consciousness. Learned professions 'depended very largely on the cultivation of work for people from a surprisingly broad social range' and, as a consequence:

> Neither the common law nor the Protestant religion were simply hegemonic ideologies which descended from London outwards and downwards to the rest of the population. Common access to the scriptures and notions of spiritual equality promised the literate middling sort some control over their religious lives, just as the ideal of the rule of law in theory guaranteed a certain degree of protection from arbitrary power in social and economic relationships.[26]

These professional groups, positioned between the rich and the poor, had access to the professional discourses of the church and the law, and to

[22] 'The decline and rise of the English legal profession', in *Lawyers, Litigation and English Society*, pp. 129–147; 'Apprenticeship and legal training in England, 1700–1850', in *Lawyers, Litigation and English Society*, pp. 149–178. For the discussion of Giddens and Perkin, see 'Law, lawyers and the social history of England'. For reform of legal education, see also C. W. Brooks and M. Lobban, 'Apprenticeship or academy? The idea of a law university, 1830–1860', in J. A. Bush and A. Wijffels (eds), *Learning the Law: Teaching and Transmission of Law in England, 1150–1900* (London, 1999), pp. 353–382.

[23] 'Law, lawyers and social history', p. 186.

[24] Ibid., p. 198.

[25] J. Barry and C. W. Brooks (eds), *The Middling Sort of People: Culture, Society and Politics in England, 1550–1800* (Basingstoke and London, 1994).

[26] 'Professions, ideology and the middling sort in the late sixteenth and early seventeenth centuries', first published in Barry and Brooks, *The Middling Sort*, pp. 113–140, reprinted in *Lawyers, Litigation and English Society*, pp. 231–258, quotations at pp. 240, 248.

their texts. This was thought to – and clearly sometimes did – offer them a source of independent critique of both church and Crown. Brooks's target was partly influential work that emphasized how law facilitated social control, trying to elucidate 'ways in which a broad range of social and economic interests were mediated and expressed'.[27] More broadly, he was giving political life a social context and social change a place in explaining political conflict, but on very different terms from those set out by Whigs or Marxists.

His reflections on apprenticeship were the basis for comment on a different, but equally large, historical issue: the development of class society. Following the broad trend he had first discerned in relation to legal training, apprenticeship as a social institution reached a heyday in the sixteenth and seventeenth centuries, before a decline from which it never recovered in the eighteenth century. In Brooks's eyes, this had implications for the inculcation of the social values that apprenticeship had promoted, alongside a specific trade or skill. By the nineteenth century, it was routine to think of those values as inculcated in the household and family, and not through working relationships, with the result that a more separate middle-class world developed, marked off more clearly from the manners and values of the working class than had been the case in the early modern period.[28]

As all this suggests, the dialogue Brooks pursued between energetic archival work and some of the very big modernization stories of historical sociology reflects the influence of Stone, to whom these essays make frequent reference – but it also reflects an interest in currents in sociology and allied disciplines. For example, this work on the middling sort and associational life was a conscious engagement with Habermas, and Brooks was among a number of historians to enter into that productive critical encounter. Others sought to locate the actual origins of the bourgeois public sphere – notably, Steve Pincus – or to reconceptualize the public sphere as a post-Reformation form of political engagement a line developed very influentially by Peter Lake. Others have tried to move beyond Habermas, to try to discuss the role of print in terms of public politics – for example as Jason Peacey has done – or to explore associational life and company as a distinctively early modern conception

27 Ibid., p. 234.

28 'Apprenticeship, social mobility and the middling sort, 1550–1800', in Barry and Brooks, *The Middling Sort*, pp. 52–83.

of society – here, thinking of Phil Withington.[29] Brooks's broader work, on legal culture as a resource for the construction and ordering of social relations, and the currency of political debate, perhaps links better to this broader strand of work on forms of associational life and political engagement than to work on the public sphere.

## Among the Revisionists

Brooks's analysis of the law as a means through which individuals and groups asserted and established their agency was taking him back to where he started – the place of legal argument in political debate – although, in the course of his long digression, his interests had moved much beyond the role and arguments of lawyers simply in parliamentary debate. In his article on Magna Carta, Brooks turned again to this issue, which had been at stake in his comment on Kelley, arguing that the seventeenth-century interpretation of Magna Carta had to be understood in the light of a much broader European jurisprudential tradition.[30]

It is a theme more fully developed in his monograph *Law, Politics and Society*, which might be characterized in this context as dealing with legal culture and its political charge.[31] Kevin Sharpe's revisionism had led him in the direction of cultural history – to a greater concern with contemporary consciousness and subjectivity, in opposition to the schematics of socio-economic and teleological analyses of early modern politics. Sharpe was fully capable of large stories, but they were not those of the giants of modernization histories with which he had grown up. Brooks clearly shared some of this methodological ground, but, by contrast, retained a fascination with those older grand narratives about social and political development. He retained more affection for the questions posed by

[29] P. Lake and S. Pincus (eds), *The Politics of the Public Sphere in Early Modern England* (Manchester, 2007); J. Peacey, *Print and Public Politics in the English Revolution* (Cambridge, 2013); P. Withington, *Society in Early Modern England: The Vernacular Origins of Some Powerful Ideas* (Oxford, 2010).

[30] 'The place of Magna Carta and the "Ancient Constitution" in sixteenth-century English legal thought' (first published 1993), reprinted in *Lawyers, Litigation and English Society*, pp. 231–258.

[31] C. W. Brooks, *Law, Politics and Society in Early Modern England* (Cambridge, 2008). These themes of participation and agency are also strongly developed in two later essays: Brooks, 'Longitudinal study of civil litigation'; C. W. Brooks, 'Litigation, participation and agency in seventeenth- and eighteenth-century England', in D. Lemmings (ed.), *The British and Their Laws in the Eighteenth Century* (Woodbridge, 2005), pp. 155–181.

Whig narratives than his more self-consciously revisionist contemporaries did.

Brooks did, however, clearly share with the revisionists a strong empiricist instinct and a desire to understand the culture from the inside – the kind that might prompt a powerfully productive digression such as that leading through his early essays and *Pettyfoggers and Vipers*. This taste for detailed and sensitive archival work is manifest in some of his asides, too: Stone's observation that eighteenth-century England might have been a relatively pacified society raised questions, Brooks remarked, of almost 'unlimited scope' – an invitation to intense study and thought.[32] In the same essay, reporting on painstakingly assembled data presented in a beguilingly simple table, he urged the reader that a 'glance' at the results might be all that the evidence would bear – a broad pattern, suggestive, but not to be trusted in detail.[33]

Brooks's treatment of feudalism reveals these characteristics of his work. He addressed the phenomenon as a matter of actual practice – the legal protection offered to base tenures by the common law courts – but in dialogue with historical and legal thought. His arguments were subtle and perhaps among his most elusive, but he was explicit in acknowledging that he was turning to a question posed by Stone: that 'the idea that the early modern period was one in which feudalism was somehow undone and replaced by something else, usually capitalism, is a commonplace'.[34] He argued that the view of seigneurialism and feudalism that prevailed in the late sixteenth and early seventeenth centuries reflected a broader European historiography – in the English case, associating feudal tenures with the Norman conquest and royal authority. As an imposition on native rights, it was closely allied to the critical account of Popery, as a jurisdictional invasion of the English church and English life. Scholarly research that sought to locate secure forms of copyhold in the Anglo-Saxon past, and the contemporary experience that copyholds were protected in common law and that manors were held by non-nobles, undermined feudalism both as a legal system and a matter of social and economic practice. For contemporaries, then, there was a debate about the origins and trajectory of feudalism, and a chronology

32 'Interpersonal conflict and social tension', p. 49.

33 Ibid., p. 50.

34 C. W. Brooks, 'Contemporary views of "feudal" social and political relationships in sixteenth and early seventeenth-century England', in N. Fryde and P. Monnet (eds), *Die Gegenwart des Feudalismus – Présence du féodalisme et présent de la féodalité – The Presence of Feudalism* (Göttingen, 2002), pp. 109–135, quotation at p. 110.

for its decline, which closely mapped onto the arguments of twentieth-century historians.

In fact, the term had taken flight at exactly the moment when the phenomenon was being observed to be in decline, and it carried a significant political charge in the criticism of both Crown and exorbitant clergy. Court records again reveal that the political debate was not simply an abstract one: there are plenty of cases of lords trying to enforce tenurial obligations, and it was not outlandish to make a connection between that and the policies of the Crown in relation to its own rights, forest fines or distraint for knighthood, for example. While such fiscal feudalism was arguably legal, 'it was not popular, and it may be that historians have failed to consider the full significance of the fact that fiscal feudalism was introduced onto a population that from bottom to top had been engaged in similar conflicts for at least seventy or eighty years previously'.[35] This approach is characteristic: an interest in established grand narratives, explored on the basis of broad archival knowledge – the latter acquired by following his nose, but always with the intention of returning to those questions. In a later essay, Brooks's observation of this common law resistance to seignurialism, the recognition of copyhold tenures, the benefit this held for smaller holders and the associated atrophy of manorial courts all formed the basis for a critique of Tawney's famous argument about *The Agrarian Problem of the Sixteenth Century* (1912).[36] Brooks's empirical work often made him critical of received grand narratives, but keen to offer better answers to the same questions.

## Law, Politics and Society

Brooks's second major monograph, on *Law, Politics and Society*, certainly sits at an angle to established lines of argument in intellectual and political history. It reviews the development of legal institutions and legal doctrine from the early Tudors to the outbreak of the civil war, offering a notably broad view of what was entailed in the rule of law for Tudor and Stuart people, those living in England's most litigious age and perhaps in the greatest intimacy with the courts in English history. His interests had also broadened from a largely Thompsonian interest in class, power and agency, and the role of the law as both a resource and an

[35] Ibid., p. 130.
[36] Considered in more detail in the section 'Law, Religion and Revolution'.

instrument of domination. At this point, Brooks's interest in law and social relations took him into the household, and led him to embrace the history of women's encounters with the law, as well as the constitutional controversies.[37]

Resting on a huge research effort, the book reveals a subtle understanding of the substantive law and of legal discourse, and of their complex interactions with a highly varied set of institutions. It traces these relationships across England, Scotland, Ireland and Wales, as well as the complex entanglement of legal with religious thought and with the canon law. A key element is the sensitive account of the mosaic of lower jurisdictions and their use; a key finding is that this use inflected thinking about law and legal institutions at the highest level. The law and its principles, like religion, held the potential to forge connections between quotidian experience and abstract principles of the most profound importance. His early critique of Kelley is more fully developed, as Brooks demonstrates how those interpreting the law were fully grounded in Renaissance readings of the classics and in European jurisprudence.

Brooks's main theme is the 'law-mindedness' that developed in this complex social, professional and institutional context, and how that gave rise to a language of liberty. He opens his conclusion with Francis Ashley, writing then primarily about lower polities and ecclesiastical jurisdictions, although he was later to become interested in the *Five Knights' case* (1627). In this earlier text, then, Ashley 'was expressing a version of early modern "rights speak" associated as much with ordinary subjects going about their daily business as with the predicament of country squires imprisoned at the will of the crown'.[38]

There was then a strong demotic element to the use of the law – its practices and concepts were deeply ingrained in early modern life, so that there were not many areas of social relations that were not mediated by legal discourses and institutions – and that meant that the shaping of legal culture reflected the actions and interests of a broad social group, much beyond the elite. So, for example, the penetration of the law into early modern households made available, to ordinary people, claims about their rights in other areas: 'While the king might be described as the head of a commonwealth in the same way that fathers were the heads

[37] For his influence in this area, see, among many examples: A. Erickson, *Women and Property in Early Modern England* (Oxford, 1995); J. Bailey, *Unquiet Lives: Marriage and Marriage Breakdown in England, 1660–1800* (Cambridge, 2003); T. Stretton, *Women Waging Law in Elizabethan England* (Cambridge, 2005).

[38] *Law, Politics and Society*, p. 423.

of households, everyone knew that in cases where there was abuse by a father or a master, even servants were obliged to bring the disorder to the attention of the magistrates.'[39]

This was not, in Brooks's judgement, a modern rights view, because it was grounded on the assumption that individual interests and those of the polity were coterminous: an absolute right in property, for example, was qualified by a notion of the public good, which might restrict enclosers – 'rights to landed property were seen ultimately as a consequence of human laws rather than an inherent natural right'. The roots of this lay in the 'Aristotelian teleology of the state [which] implied that since the polity had been created for the good of the subjects and civil society as a whole, it was logically impossible that any of its acts should be detrimental to an individual member of it'. Thus individual rights had to be weighed against the 'common good'. It was not inconsistent, therefore, that Magna Carta could be qualified by customary right as established in local jurisdictions.[40]

These jurisdictions embraced many aspects of the lives of ordinary people. The rise of litigation in central courts did not extinguish these lower jurisdictions and there is little evidence of a 'folk justice' outside this complex web of courts. As a result, this legal culture impinged on the lives of a very broad slice of the population, and was shaped by their use of available jurisdictions and principles. The complex intersection of jurisdictions, and the need to think about the intertwining of systems of law in Wales, Scotland and Ireland, meant that English common law thought was not at all immune to external influences. Coke responded to this complexity by resting the authority of the common law in the past, but mid-century figures tended instead to emphasize its dependence on a sovereign authority. This located its authority ultimately in the community, although clearly also limited by royal prerogative. As a result, and despite all these complexities, common law-mindedness provided a language for securing freedom from interference in particular circumstances, as well as, in that sense, a source of arguments about rights that was quite open to the understanding and use of relatively humble people. It was widely understood, for example, that: 'Local privileges ought not to prohibit anyone from exercising their common-law right to earn a living. It was wrong that trade should

[39] Ibid., p. 384.
[40] Ibid., p. 423.

be impeded by excessive tolls levied for passing through towns or crossing bridges.'[41]

This approach framed Brooks's view of the English revolution of the mid-seventeenth century:

> Prior to the civil wars . . . English law was in a state of ongoing contestation within a long-established and reasonably widely accepted set of conventions. Constituting social relationships and providing much of the language that described them, it might even be described as a 'public transcript' that prescribed behavior over a range of human interactions. The institutions and processes of English law made it subject to an ongoing process of negotiation participated in by a broad cross-section of the population.[42]

By contrast, '[i]t is likely that the principal impact of the two mid-century decades of civil war and political turmoil was to drive the lawyers in the direction of a greater reliance on legal formalism and a stress on known and established rules'.[43] This returned him to some of his earliest conclusions about the relative disengagement of the people from the law in the centuries after this high point of practical and ideological engagement.

This was a central theme in a late essay in which Brooks revisited the findings of his earlier work on the rise and decline of litigation, and its relationship with the changes in the profession. But, here, he was more explicitly engaging with work in social history on issues of agency and participation. Prior to 1700, 'Easy access to courts was a source of both individual agency and, possibly, a high degree of political consciousness that was diffused more widely than we might expect from considering other kinds of sources.'[44] This had directly political implications too:

> Legal discourse (rhetoric), some of which had a noticeable populist thrust, and most of which emphasized legally protected self-interest as a primary reason for an individual adhering to authority, was exchanged regularly

[41] Ibid., p. 422.

[42] Ibid., p. 431. The public transcript is a reference to J. C. Scott, *Domination and the Arts of Resistance: Hidden Transcripts* (New Haven, 1990). The notion has been influential in English social history. See, for example, the essays in Braddick and Walter, *Negotiating Power*; J. Walter, '"The pooremans joy and the gentlemans plague": a Lincolnshire libel and the politics of sedition in early modern England', *Past and Present* 203 (2009), 29–67; J. Walter, 'Gesturing at authority: deciphering the gestural code in early modern England', in M. J. Braddick (ed.), *The Politics of Gesture: Historical Perspectives* (Oxford, 2009), pp. 96–127.

[43] *Law, Politics and Society*, p. 431.

[44] 'Litigation, participation and agency', p. 158.

> with the wider public and formed the common currency of political debate at least up until the outbreak of Civil War in 1642.[45]

The period 1720–1770, by contrast, saw a decline in the use of the law and in a wide range of local jurisdictions, and a much-reduced role for lawyers in a wide range of social and economic relationships. This represented 'a distinctive phase in the history of the relationship between the person, the community, and the law' to which nineteenth-century reform responded, in rapidly changing demographic, political and economic circumstances.[46]

## Law, Religion and Revolution

Brooks's previously unpublished essay on law and revolution points to some of the ways in which he might himself have developed these ideas about the place of the English revolution in this long-term history.[47] His unpublished trailer for the *Oxford History of the Laws of England* was primarily concerned with the consequences of the revolution, rather than its causes – with what the revolution did for legal culture rather than the other way around. He starts with Tawney, presumably with deliberate provocation, and the way in which revolutionary culture did or did not open up economic relations to the fuller development of capital. While dismissive of almost every aspect of Tawney's conclusions, Brooks was drawn to the question of the place of the revolution in securing gentry hegemony – specifically, the place of legal change in that development. In an earlier essay, developing his arguments about the trajectory of 'feudalism', Brooks had explored the impact of the civil war on legal titles, concluding that, in fact, the common law had been progressively recognizing copyhold titles in the decades before the revolution and that the completion of this process by around 1680 reflected the continuities of legal practice rather than any dramatic rupture. Moreover, those changes reflected in part the interests of small landholders themselves. The result was 'something like a social revolution', which saw the emergence of a class of smaller holders alongside the gentry who were fully capable of 'vigorously exercis[ing] their "rights"': by the 1680s, 'all land, including copyhold, had

[45] Ibid.
[46] Ibid., p. 180.
[47] See Chapter 14 in this volume.

become caught up in a broader market for both property and credit'.[48]

While Tawney's account of the relationship between the courts, landowners and the revolution did not bear scrutiny, there was nonetheless a story to be told about the relationship between the lawyers and patterns of landholding. Similarly, there was a story to be told about the relationship between law and revolution, approached on a very broad basis and as an 'example', presumably of something still larger. Brooks argued that the crisis reveals the connection between legal rhetoric and rights claims; the importance and logic of law reform; and the effects on legal argument of the very radical suggestion that human law might simply be replaced by divine law – that the country might be governed by religious conscience rather than established constitutional and common law principles. But the result was survival: 'To cut a long story short', and despite the abolition of some jurisdictions and the undercutting of the ecclesiastical courts, 'the structure of the system as a whole, and the volume and general nature of the business in the courts in the 1680s, were so similar to what they had been before 1640 that it is hard to see a compelling reason for describing the civil wars as a watershed'.[49]

This was because so much had been done to shape and establish legal culture prior to 1640. A key factor here, traced in a number of essays, was the clash between common law and canon law, particularly over the *ex officio* oath, which was plausibly claimed to be in conflict with Magna Carta. 'As intellectual disciplines, law and divinity were remarkably incommensurate. Common lawyers were hard-wired with a type of anticlericalism that transcended personal religious beliefs' at a time when prominent bishops were often influential with the monarch, and '[m]uch of the language of liberty that emerged from this same period was generated in connection with conflicts between ecclesiastical and temporal courts'.[50]

In his fuller paper on the relationship of legal and religious thought, also previously unpublished, Brooks argued that this conflict led lawyers to compartmentalize their thought, creating the origins of the firewall in US constitutional thought between church and state.[51] Here, his

[48] C. W. Brooks, 'The agrarian problem in "revolutionary" England 1640–1689', in J. Whittle (ed.), *Landlords and Tenants in Britain 1440–1660: Tawney's Agrarian Problems Revisited* (Woodbridge, 2013), pp. 183–199, at pp. 198, 199.

[49] See Chapter 14 in this volume.

[50] Ibid.

[51] See Chapter 15 in this volume.

intellectual ambition is particularly evident, seeking to frame political argument over a long period in terms of the definition of an ecclesiastical polity: at the heart of much political thinking over two centuries, he argued, was the relationship between common law and ecclesiastical law – between prudence and providence. In the centuries after the Reformation, defenders of the ecclesiastical courts 'plausibly defended them as institutions that had existed for so long that they enjoyed a customary role in the polity no less venerable then that of the common law itself'. However, 'it was easy enough to retort that all English ecclesiastical law had been introduced against the prerogative of the king and the will of the people. Since God never explicitly gave the clergy power to make laws within the realm, those in existence were based on the usurped authority of the Bishop of Rome.'[52]

Brooks placed Selden's *History of Tithes* (1618) directly in this context. Despite Selden's own 'perhaps disingenuous' protestations, it was read by 'the clergy and lay readers ... to be a refutation of the proposition that tithes were due to the church according to divine right'. Selden insisted that the subject should be addressed on the basis of European legal history and not through the scriptures or the writings of the Church Fathers, and argued further that '[i]f tithes were the subject of municipal law, there was no conceivable reason why their nature and history should not be interrogated by a common lawyer'. This underpinned his claim that common lawyers were part of a larger European cadre of legal professionals with a role in the articulation of the legal and constitutional relationships of the states in which they lived, including those involving the church. He was brought before High Commission and became the subject of a polemical campaign, which seemed to confirm Selden's thought that the 'divine right' theories clergymen were applying to the monarchy, and in defence of their own customs, were fundamentally at odds with the secular rights enshrined in the common law. This was a prominent issue in the revolutionary decades, of course, and one of considerable quotidian importance, but Brooks thinks the controversy over the *ex officio* oath was a more powerful influence on the dissemination of these arguments. James Morice's collection of examples of relatively humble laypeople, caught in the snares of ecclesiastical jurisdiction and forced to respond in ways that contravened Magna Carta, made

[52] Ibid. See also C. W. Brooks, 'A Puritan collaboration in defence of the liberty of the subject: James Morice, Robert Beale, and the Elizabethan campaign against ecclesiastical authority', in P. Scott (ed.), *Collaboration and Interdisciplinarity in the Republic of Letters: Essays in Honour of Richard G. Maber* (Manchester, 2010), pp. 3–16.

a powerful case. Ashley, already referred to, 'seems to have been predominately interested in the ways in which the common law, and the writ of habeas corpus in particular, could be used by individual subjects to resist all kinds of "oppressions". Nevertheless he was particularly vehement in celebrating the protection that the great charter offered against the "exorbitant pretensions of the clergy".'[53]

This long history, and the professional development and legal practice that it reflected, meant that common lawyers were natural opponents of the authority of the church, and lawyers were prominent in attempts to exclude bishops from the House of Lords in the early 1640s. Against this background, it is also no surprise that the common lawyers did not lament the reduced influence of the ecclesiastical courts after 1660. In the end, though, Brooks argues, this did not serve the interests of the cultural authority of the law, which claimed no abstract or fundamental underpinning to match the claims of divine or natural law.

These arguments are potentially very important for emerging themes in writing about the English revolution. Brooks notes in his paper on law and revolution that his arguments were pushing towards the claim that 'the legal culture of the pre-civil war years contributed significantly to the political idiom in which the mid-century conflicts were argued, nor was it in any obvious way out of touch with the interests of aspirations of most sections of the population'.[54]

This insight has great potential to open up discussion of political culture and popular politics in the mid-century crisis. Recent work on the Levellers and on John Lilburne, for example, has revealed the importance of the practical experience of the legal system (and urban associational life) for the development of radical politics, as well as the mix of ideas that Brooks associates with law-mindedness.[55] John Morrill's claim that the civil wars were wars of religion prompted a lot of work on print

[53] See Chapter 15 in this volume.

[54] See Chapter 14 in this volume.

[55] M. J. Braddick, *The Common Freedom of the People: John Lilburne and the English Revolution* (Oxford, 2018); P. Baker, '*London's Liberty in Chains Discovered*: the Levellers, the civic past, and popular protest in civil war London', *Huntington Library Quarterly* 76 (2013), 559–587; J. Peacey, 'The people of the *Agreements*: the Levellers, civil war radicalism and political participation', in P. Baker and E. Vernon (eds), *The Agreements of the People, the Levellers and the Constitutional Crisis of the English Revolution* (Basingstoke, 2012), pp. 50–75; P. Baker, 'The Levellers, decentralisation and the Agreements of the People', in Baker and Vernon, *The Agreements of the People*, pp. 97–116; P. Withington, 'Urban citizens and England's civil wars', in M. J. Braddick (ed.), *The Oxford Handbook of the English Revolution* (Oxford, 2015), pp. 312–329.

as a way of understanding how the rhetoric of religious debate was made available to, and mobilized support among, broader sections of the population and the extent to which it can be considered, in a narrow sense, 'religious'.[56] There really is no comparable work on legal polemic:[57] although Alan Cromartie, following Pocock's lead, has written very penetratingly about the intersection of legal thought and political debate in this period, the intersection of the fuller legal culture and the mainsprings of political action in the 1640s remains to be explored.[58]

## Conclusion

Chris Brooks's early empirical work revealed, in the litigation boom and the history of the legal profession, a social phenomenon of major importance of which we were previously largely unaware. In his subsequent work on that phenomenon, he was doing for law and lawyers almost single-handedly what an army of scholars were doing for the post-Reformation clergy and religion. Intrigued by the grand narratives of a previous generation, he made major contributions to the social history of the professions and the middling sort, the transformation of agrarian relations, and our understanding of social relations, and he offered a fruitful starting point from which to reconsider the roots and consequences of the English revolution. It is quite a legacy: a product both of an interest in those – often unfashionable – grand narratives and of a profound commitment to detailed scholarship. A strong theme of all this work is the role of legal history in academic life. During the nineteenth century, it was, like divinity, central to the development of the historical profession and it exerted a foundational influence, for example, in medieval historiography. Law departments, Brooks complained, had tended to focus on vocational education, however, while social history tended to take the law as a given – an instrument in the hands of the powerful.[59] And his entire career had been prompted, of course, by the

[56] For an overview and critical discussion, see C. W. A. Prior and G. Burgess (eds), *England's Wars of Religion, Revisited* (Farnham, 2011).

[57] For a recent contribution in this area, see A. Hitchman, '"They themselves will be the Judges what commands are lawfull": legal pamphlets and political mobilisation in the early 1640s', PhD thesis, Sheffield (2017).

[58] J. G. A. Pocock, *The Ancient Constitution and the Feudal Law: A Study of English Historical Thought in the Seventeenth Century – A Reissue with a Retrospect* (Cambridge, 1987); A. Cromartie, *The Constitutionalist Revolution: An Essay on the History of England, 1450–1642* (Cambridge, 2006).

[59] *Lawyers, Litigation and English Society*, pp. 4–6.

perception that the political role given to lawyers was not matched by an understanding of who they were and what they did. In Brooks's hands, the history of the law, its practitioners and its users, was at once a window onto aspects of social, political, intellectual and constitutional history, *and* the history of a phenomenon of fundamental interest itself. It was quite an ambition – and it underpinned a very significant achievement.

# 3

# Law, Law-Consciousness and Lawyers as Constitutive of Early Modern England

## Christopher W. Brooks's Singular Journey

DAVID SUGARMAN*

During the last half-century, Christopher W. Brooks (1948–2014) established himself as the foremost historian of law in early modern English society. Through his scholarship, his teaching and the generations of students he advised and supervised, and as a friend and colleague, Brooks exercised, from the early 1990s onwards, an increasingly significant influence on writing about early modern English history. He was the leading exponent of a history of early modern England that transcended the boundaries of social, political and legal history, and which placed law and lawyers centre stage. In doing so, he challenged major premises of the dominant vision of law-in-history in writing about English history. This chapter brings a critical, if friendly, eye to Brooks's work, focusing on how Brooks beat his own path through the methodological thickets to create a distinctive vision of law in history, and on the strengths and weaknesses of that vision.

### From Princeton to *Pettyfoggers* (1967–1986)

Born in Maryland, Brooks grew up in 1950s and 1960s America during the advancement of civil rights.[1] This 'rights revolution' owed much to the democratization of access to the courts, the vitality of the support systems for rights litigation, liberal judicial activism and the large

* I would like to thank Sharyn Brooks, for supplying me with details concerning her late husband's life, and Michael Lobban, for his advice on the framing of this chapter. I benefited greatly from Wilfrid Prest's comments and suggestions, and owe him a special acknowledgement. As always, I am indebted to Léonie Sugarman, who made many valuable points about the way in which this chapter was expressed.

[1] Christopher W. Brooks, *Lawyers, Litigation and English Society since 1450* (London, 1998), p. 2.

numbers of lawyers scrambling for business.[2] The centrality of law and lawyers in American society had long been noted. Tocqueville famously observed that '[t]here is almost no political question in the United States that is not resolved sooner or later into a judicial question'.[3] Indeed, Americans appeared to be quite conscious of their rights, and many viewed going to court as a respectable and viable way of engaging in disputes.[4] Brooks brought this awareness of the centrality of law and lawyers in society and the popular imagination to bear on the history of early modern England.

As an undergraduate at Princeton, Brooks was inspired by Lawrence Stone, who remained a key influence throughout his life. It was Stone who first taught Brooks the value of adopting the *longue durée* in social and cultural history; that historians can be both expansive *and* focused; that they should address big questions, postulate bold ideas and strive to address the diverse facets of society – intellectual, economic, moral, cultural and social – as a totality; that they should be prepared to inform their work with concepts derived from other disciplines; that they should open up fresh territories and new bodies of evidence; and that history should be interesting and exciting.[5] That Brooks identified himself, first and foremost, as a social historian of early modern England and made social history his vocation was probably in no small measure due to Stone.

Following Princeton, Brooks began postgraduate study at Johns Hopkins,[6] where several historians were undertaking pioneering work on the history of the professions – notably, law – which transcended the confines of institutional history, combining quantitative and qualitative analyses to produce histories that were both institutional *and* social.[7] In his first PhD supervisor, Wilfrid Prest, Brooks found a lifelong mentor,

[2] Charles R. Epp, *The Rights Revolution: Lawyers, Activists and Supreme Courts in Comparative Perspective* (Chicago and London, 1998), pp. 1–70.

[3] Alexis de Tocqueville, *Democracy in America*, ed. and trans. Harvey C. Mansfield and Delba Winthrop (Chicago and London, 2000 [1835]), p. 257.

[4] Paul W. Kahn, *The Reign of Law: Marbury v. Madison and the Construction of America* (New Haven, 1997); cf. David M. Engel, *The Myth of the Litigious Society* (Chicago, 2016).

[5] Brooks acknowledged that Stone stimulated his interest in English social history: A. L. Beier, David Cannadine and James M. Rosenheim (eds), *The First Modern Society: Essays in English History in Honour of Lawrence Stone* (Cambridge, 1989), p. xvi.

[6] Brooks entered the History programme at Johns Hopkins University in September 1970.

[7] Leonard R. Berlanstein, *The Barristers of Toulouse in the Eighteenth Century, 1740–1793* (Baltimore, 1975); R. L. Kagan, *Lawsuits and Litigants in Castile, 1500–1700* (Chapel Hill, 1981); Daniel Duman, *The Judicial Bench in England 1727–1875: The Reshaping of a Professional Elite* (London, 1982); Daniel Duman, *The English and Colonial Bars in the Nineteenth Century* (London, 1983).

friend and interlocutor. Prest's research on barristers was a vital role model.[8] It suggested that barristers and their institutional home, the Inns of Court, were more important than historians had often assumed. Prest argued that the history of the Inns of Court (and, by implication, lawyers) needed to be saved from 'the domain of antiquaries and domestic chroniclers'.[9] Rather than treating lawyers and the Inns of Court as 'isolated from society at large', Prest placed them '. . . firmly in their historical context, based on a thorough examination of the surviving evidence', over a sufficiently lengthy period of time so as to challenge the conventional wisdom that the history of the Inns (and, by implication, the profession) was essentially one of continuity, thereby producing '. . . a telescoped view of their later development'.[10]

Prest subsequently critiqued the functionalist assumptions of much historical and sociological writing on the professions – notably, that the history of the profession did not really begin until the Industrial Revolution. Pointing to the paucity of historical research on the professions in medieval and early modern England, Prest argued that the Bar assumed many of the characteristics of a profession, and was so regarded, prior to industrialization.[11] Brooks's research would subsequently demonstrate that, in the case of the lower branch of the profession, Prest was right.[12]

Several of the hallmarks associated with Brooks's scholarship gelled early in his career (although this is perhaps more apparent with the benefit of hindsight, rather than indicative of Brooks's self-consciousness at the time). Certainly, his impressive first-year graduate paper, 'The Common Lawyers in the House of Commons of 1621',[13] presages it:

[8] See, e.g., Wilfrid R. Prest (ed.), *Lawyers in Early Modern Europe and America* (New York, 1981); Wilfrid R. Prest, *The Rise of the Barristers: A Social History of the English Bar* (Oxford, 1986).

[9] Wilfred R. Prest, *The Inns of Court under Elizabeth I and the Early Stuarts, 1590–1640* (London, 1972), p. vii.

[10] Ibid., p. 4.

[11] Wilfrid R. Prest, 'Why the history of the professions is not written', in G. R. Rubin and D. Sugarman (eds), *Law, Economy and Society: Essays in the History of English Law, 1750–1914* (Abingdon, 1984), pp. 300–320.

[12] Christopher W. Brooks, *Pettyfoggers and Vipers of the Commonwealth: The 'Lower Branch' of the Legal Profession in Early Modern England* (Cambridge, 1986); Brooks, *Lawyers*, p. 181.

[13] Christopher W. Brooks, 'The common lawyers in the House of Commons of 1621', First-year graduate paper, Johns Hopkins University, 14 April 1971. My thanks to Wilfrid Prest for sharing this paper with me.

> This essay . . . will study the role of lawyers in one House of Commons – that of 1621 – asking . . . were the lawyers leaders in the House, and for which side did they speak? Secondly, how and when did the lawyers use the law? That is, did they uphold it dispassionately or did they conscientiously distort its meaning to suit their own and the Commons' ends? The inquiry will begin with a statistical analysis of the lawyers' leadership, and a presentation of various educational and social facts which might account for their behavior. The last part of the paper will consist of a close evaluation of the most important events in the Parliament and the lawyers' place in them.
>
> I hope to demonstrate that the lawyers were leaders both to the opposition and court parties, but that whether they spoke for or against the Crown seems to make little difference in their very strict constructionalist use of the law.[14]

Brooks's analysis of the quantitative and qualitative evidence challenged the historical orthodoxy. Confidently, but carefully, he disputed the claims of Christopher Hill, Eric Ives and Lawrence Stone.[15] According to Brooks, the lawyers in the House were not an undifferentiated bloc, either defenders of the common law against Stuart absolutism or self-interested opportunists bent on royal preferment and therefore hostile to reform (especially that which might affect their purses). Rather:

> As the statistics demonstrate . . . the [legal] profession divid[ed] between support for the Crown and for the 'country' or 'popular' party. However, both the opposition and Court factions were characterized by their self-conscious role of professional upholders of the law of the land.[16] . . . The lawyers opinions were [distinguished] by legal baggage such as precedents, which had a significant effect on the way they saw and handled a problem.[17]

Brooks concluded that '[t]he lawyers were leaders in the House of Commons of 1621',[18] that they wielded 'great' influence[19] and that they

[14] Ibid., ff. 1–2.

[15] Ibid., f. 71, challenging views disparaging the role of lawyers (citing Christopher Hill, *The Century of Revolution, 1603–1714*, New York, 1966, pp. 62–66); ibid., ff. 14–15, repudiating Ives' suggestion that, for some lawyers, self-interest was a motive for opposition (E. W. Ives, *The English Revolution, 1600–1660*, London, 1968, p. 122); ibid., f. 12, n. 23a, rejecting '. . . the commonly made error of using the opposition of Sir Edward Coke as an example of the entire legal profession' (exemplified by Lawrence Stone, 'The English Revolution', in Robert Forster and Jack P. Greene (eds), *Preconditions for Revolution in Early Modern Europe* (Baltimore, 1971), pp. 55–108).

[16] Ibid., f. 69.

[17] Ibid., f. 20.

[18] Ibid., f. 69.

[19] Ibid., f. 70.

'contributed greatly to the general development of the Commons'.[20] Brooks's emphasis on the importance of lawyers and the inner world of the law, including how it mediated the agency of lawyers and helped to explain their power and influence, was unusual for the times. Equally striking are the means with which he addressed these issues. This paper heralded what would become Brooks's abiding interests: the role of law and legal ideas in the seventeenth century – the political ideas expressed by lawyers, and the political significance of law, legal ideas and lawyers.[21] It shows how Brooks made significant strides in forging his own vision of law in history prior to his move to England.

With Prest's encouragement, Brooks transferred to Oxford, where his doctoral supervisor was J. P. Cooper, who became another important formative influence, shaping Brooks's conception of the vocation of the historian, with its careful attention to archival sources, its emphasis on precision and presenting the right evidence, its erudition and its breadth of interests.[22] As Brooks recalled: 'Since I was interested in the political ideas expressed by lawyers, an examination of lawyers and what lawyers did seemed a logical place to start. What began as a digression became an ongoing preoccupation.'[23] His newfound love of archival research was facilitated by a junior research fellowship at Brasenose College, Oxford. He deepened his knowledge of early modern English history, and he began to develop friendships with several leading historians of English law, including John Baker, and to acquire a detailed knowledge of the law, its institutions and the sources for researching them.

Fortunately for Brooks, English legal history was at a turning point, in terms of both the numbers of people involved and the range of subjects and approaches adopted. Brooks was in at its beginning, testing and refining his work through participation in the first conferences of what would become the bi-annual British Legal History Conference (BLHC), the stimulation and advice that he received, and the contacts he developed.[24] C. A. F. Meekings guided Brooks on how best to locate

[20] Ibid.

[21] Brooks, *Lawyers*, p. ix.

[22] Christopher W. Brooks, *Law, Politics and Society in Early Modern England* (Cambridge, 2008) was dedicated to J. P. Cooper (see ibid., p. viii). On Cooper, see G. E. Aylmer, 'J. P. Cooper as a scholar', in J. P. Cooper, *Land, Men and Beliefs: Studies in Early-Modern History*, ed. G. E. Aylmer and J. S. Morrill (London, 1983), pp. ix–xiii, at p. ix.

[23] Brooks, *Lawyers*, p. ix.

[24] Brooks attended the inaugural Legal History Conference, Aberystwyth, July 1972, and attended fairly regularly until the early 1990s.

the King's Bench files.[25] Another BLHC attendee, J. S. Cockburn, then undertaking pioneering work applying quantitative and qualitative methods to the history of crime, shared his experience of the possibilities and pitfalls of counting cases.[26] It was at the inaugural conference that John Baker issued a clarion call to join him in the enterprise of illuminating 'the dark age of English legal history' (the legal history of Tudor and Stuart England), one of the most important periods in the history of the common law.[27] And it was three years later, at the BLHC of 1975, that Brooks presented a paper that would mark an important milestone both in his career and for the history of early modern England.[28] Based on the research conducted for his Oxford PhD thesis, Brooks's statistical and descriptive analysis outlined several of the key insights with which he is most associated. Litigation in the courts of King's Bench and Common Pleas began to soar from 1560. By 1640, there was three times more litigation than in 1580 – perhaps fifteen times more than there had been in the 1490s.[29] If the increase in population is allowed for, the data 'implies that there was more litigation per head of population under Elizabeth I and the early Stuarts then there was in the early nineteenth century ... Thus, it is very likely that the late sixteenth and early seventeenth centuries were the most litigious periods in English history.'[30] Brooks claimed that the early modern common law courts were not the sole preserve of the landed classes; rather, they were surprisingly cheap and accessible. That there were more lawyers than ever before, 'made the law a weapon which could be put into the hands of ordinary men'.[31]

These findings challenged those historians – notably, Christopher Hill – and some contemporary puritan and other seventeenth-century literature critical of the common law, which saw English law as an

[25] On Meekings, see David Crook, 'Introduction', in C. A. F. Meekings, *Studies in 13th Century Justice and Administration* (London, 1981), pp. ix–xix, at p. ix.

[26] Brooks, *Pettyfoggers and Vipers*, p. xi.

[27] J. H. Baker, 'The dark age of English legal history, 1500–1700', in Dafydd Jenkins (ed.), *Legal History Studies 1972* (Cardiff, 1975), pp. 1–27.

[28] Brooks's paper was delivered at the Cambridge legal history conference, July 1975, and published as Christopher W. Brooks, 'Litigants and attorneys in the King's Bench and Common Pleas, 1560–1640', in J. H. Baker (ed.), *Legal Records and the Historian* (London, 1978), pp. 41–59.

[29] Brooks, 'Litigants and attorneys', p. 43. Much of this great rise in cases comprised actions of debt and suits for breach of contract.

[30] Ibid., p. 44.

[31] Ibid., p. 59.

oppressive tool of the ruling elite.[32] But there was a degree of commonality too: Hill and Brooks (at least during the latter's Oxford period, up to and including *Pettyfoggers and Vipers*) tended, like other historians, to regard legal history as excessively concerned with the internal development of law. Under this optic, the history of law and legal institutions was separate from, but connected to, social history. Brooks sought to transcend what he termed legal history's preoccupation with 'tracing the genealogies of doctrine';[33] rather, he gave law and its institutions a social context, and explored law's place within the socio-political firmament.

Brooks's concern to address the social context of law paralleled contemporary American scholarship and the contextual turns in English legal education and legal history that gained fresh impetus from about the mid-1960s.[34] Law, legal history and history were all turning outward. The boundaries separating 'social' and 'legal' history, and the 'social' and the 'legal', were blurring, although the long-standing tendency to treat them as distinct, and the abiding competition between them, remained. Occasional references to the new contextualist literature on lawyers and legal services in England appear in Brooks's work.[35] In a limited sense, then, Brooks was probably influenced by the changing nature of legal-historical scholarship in law faculties.

Brooks's first book, *Pettyfoggers and Vipers of the Commonwealth*, both developed his 1975 lecture and reached out into new areas. It examined

[32] See, e.g., Brooks, *Lawyers*, pp. 5–6. Sadly, Hill never altered his views about the role of seventeenth-century law and lawyers by taking account of Brooks and allied research: see Christopher Hill, *Liberty against the Law: Some Seventeenth-Century Controversies* (London, 1996).

[33] Brooks, *Pettyfoggers and Vipers*, p. 9.

[34] Bryant Garth and Joyce Stirling, 'From legal realism to law and society: reshaping law for the last stages of the social activist state', *Law and Society Review* 32 (1998), 409–471; William Twining, *Blackstone's Tower: The English Law School* (London, 1994), ch. 2. Much of the contextual turn in legal history concerned civil law, lawyers and the civil justice system: Brian Abel-Smith and Robert Stevens, *Lawyers and the Courts* (London, 1967); P. S. Atiyah, *The Rise and Fall of Freedom of Contract* (Oxford, 1979); A. W. B. Simpson, 'Legal liability for bursting reservoirs: the historical context of *Rylands* v. *Fletcher*', *Journal of Legal Studies* 13 (1984), 209–264; G. R. Rubin and D. Sugarman (eds), *Law, Economy and Society: Essays in the History of English Law, 1750–1914* (Abingdon, 1984); K. J. M. Smith and J. P. S. McLaren, 'History's living legacy: an outline of "modern" historiography of common law', *Legal Studies* 21 (2001), 251–324.

[35] For example, Brooks, *Pettyfoggers and Vipers*, pp. 28, n. 69, 107, n. 179, 191, n. 43, 264, n. 3 and 341, n. 65. Abel-Smith and Stevens, *Lawyers and the Courts*, probably played an early and important role in shaping Brooks's view of law, lawyers, access to justice and legal culture in England, 1750–1965.

the social history of the lower branch of the legal profession – attorneys, solicitors and minor legal officials – who were much larger in number and spread more widely around the country than their more prestigious counterparts. Reconstructing their lives was a formidable undertaking. It is hard now to recapture the experimental nature of this research, for which there was then no training and scant expertise. Its vision of law in history brought together the social history of lawyers, the interplay between civil litigation and society, the social context of civil litigation and the history of ideas. Most notably, perhaps, it addressed a key issue that social historians had only begun to consider and which would continue to be at the heart of Brooks's subsequent work – namely, the ways in which the law and its institutions affected and were used by ordinary people. It was argued that the vast majority (up to 70–80 per cent) of plaintiffs and defendants in the common law courts were neither very rich nor very poor and that early modern England 'was deeply imbued with the importance of the idea of the rule of law'.[36] *Pettyfoggers* exhibited the scholarship, professionalism and high standards for which Brooks's work became a byword. As Geoffrey Elton observed, 'Dr Brooks ... has done so much ... patiently wearisome work as any man [*sic*] can be asked to do. One can only feel admiration for the way in which he avoided inflicting the tedium of research upon the reader.'[37]

In sum, through his work on his Oxford doctoral dissertation and its progression to a book, Brooks had already found his way into law and legal history. The vision of law in history that he forged was constituted against:

- the pure intellectual history of Pocock, and the presentation of the common law mind in oversimplified terms and in isolation from other modes of political discourse;[38]
- Hill's depiction of the common law and its practitioners as mere tools of the ruling elite that had nothing to offer to the bottom 80 per cent of

[36] Brooks, *Pettyfoggers and Vipers*, p. 265.

[37] G. R. Elton, 'Book review of *Pettyfoggers and Vipers*', *Historical Journal* 30 (1987), 239–246, p. 241.

[38] J. G. A. Pocock, *The Ancient Constitution and the Feudal Law: A Study of English Constitutional Thought in the Seventeenth Century* (Cambridge, 1987) – a criticism Pocock acknowledged: ibid., p. xi. See further Christopher W. Brooks and Kevin Sharpe, 'History, English law and the Renaissance: a comment', *Past and Present* 72 (1976), 133–146; Brooks, *Lawyers*, pp. 6, 188 and ch. 8.

the population, and of legal institutions as frequently corrupt and subject to lax standards;[39]

- the reductionist interpretation of the law as class rule, of the rule of law as purely fictional, of the social structure of early modern England as exclusively based on deference and hierarchy, and of a two-class (patrician/plebeian) model;[40]
- the dominant tradition within social theory, the sociology of professions and modern history that assumed that the professions were a modern phenomenon and that professionalization, and the growth and importance of the professions, was associated with the Industrial Revolution, and with the needs of the aristocracy and gentry, or capitalism or professional self-interest;[41] and
- a legal history that treats law as a biologically closed system, detaching law and legal institutions from their wider context, and over-representing the experiences of the wealthier sections of society.

In important respects, Brook's vision of law in history was framed by the new thinking about social history that emerged in the 1960s and 1970s.[42] He shared assumptions implicit and sometimes explicit in much social history – that 'the answers to the big questions could be found only in empirical historical research, much of it closely focused'[43] – and that archival mastery and more rigorous processes of verification were essential, as well as that quantification, allied to systematic research across multiple archival sources, was necessary for reconstructing the past. This approach also entailed a concentration on the lived experience of the people, rather than the ruling elite; a preoccupation with agency over structure; an engagement with a much wider range of subjects,

[39] While echoing Hill's emphasis on the power of ideas, rather than brute economics.

[40] An interpretation associated with some forms of social history, including elements within the new histories of crime, criminal law, policing and punishment. See Gareth Stedman Jones, 'Class expression versus social control?' *History Workshop Journal* 4 (1977), 162–170; Michael Ignatieff, 'State, civil society and total institutions: a critique of recent social histories of punishment', in David Sugarman (ed.), *Legality, Ideology and the State* (London, 1983), pp. 183–211; David Phillips, 'A just measure of crime, authority, hunters and blue locusts', in S. Cohen and A. Scull (eds), *Social Control and the State* (Oxford, 1983), pp. 50–74.

[41] Brooks, *Pettyfoggers and Vipers*, pp. 263–264.

[42] Steve Hindle, Alexandra Sheppard and John Walter, 'The making and remaking of early modern English social history', in *Remaking English Society: Social Relations and Social Change in Early Modern England* (Woodbridge, 2013), pp. 1–27.

[43] Ibid., p. 19.

many of which traversed conventional disciplinary boundaries; and demythologization.

And yet Brooks's vision of law in history deviated from the mainstream of social history. Its originality resulted partly from the ways in which he deployed legal history, social history, and law and society scholarship to pursue his distinctive agenda and to challenge conventional wisdom. Underlying his vision was the belief that not only the poor and inarticulate needed rescuing from the enormous condescension of posterity; lawyers – particularly those practitioners of the lower branch who were, in comparison with the likes of Coke, 'very largely uncelebrated and unknown', and those middling groups in society to which professions such as the lower branch belong – also warranted rescuing.[44] This was underpinned by the notion that lawyers, and the middling sort, were pivotal in early modern society and in ways that had not been fully appreciated. According to Brooks, 'even rather obscure lawyers such as country attorneys made important contributions to local administration, politics and society'.[45]

Studies of civil litigation, and of the criminal justice system, were usually limited by county, region or a specific field of litigation.[46] *Pettyfoggers and Vipers* quantified civil litigation on a scale that was unprecedented.[47] A part of its audacity lay in its claim to be a national study and in the considerable ingenuity with which it sought to rebuff potential concerns that the construction of judicial statistics distorted, concealed or omitted relevant detail to the analysis, as well as the serious problems of definition and methodology arising from sampling. Moreover, its counterintuitive findings challenged conventional conceptions of early modern England and modernity.

Of course, those findings built upon the work of other scholars.[48] In addition to the authors and sources already mentioned, Brooks

[44] Brooks, *Pettyfoggers and Vipers*, p. 2.

[45] Ibid, p. 3.

[46] For example, Joel Samanha, *Law and Order in Historical Perspective: The Case of Elizabethan Essex* (London, 1974); J. A. Sharpe, *Crime in Seventeenth-Century England: A County Study* (Cambridge, 1983).

[47] Cf. J. A. Sharpe, *Crime in Early Modern England, 1550–1750* (London, 1984), p. 19: 'Early modern records do not permit the type of analysis of national trends which some historians have attempted for the nineteenth and early twentieth centuries. Both the current state of research and the sheer problem of record survival would make such analysis impossible for our period.'

[48] Marjorie Blatcher, *The Court of King's Bench, 1450–1550* (London, 1978); W. J. Jones, *The Elizabethan Court of Chancery* (Oxford, 1967); Ronald A. Marchant, *The Church*

acknowledged, for example, the work of law and society scholars on the measurement of court usage, and its potential for enlarging our understanding of law in society and, in particular, his reliance on legal historians.[49] *Pettyfoggers and Vipers* is also telling for what is omitted: nothing is said about criminal proceedings, which, while they clearly do not belong within the category it defined as litigation, nevertheless affected the amount of business handled by the courts. The new social history, including the history of crime and criminal law, had a brief, but critical, mention possibly reflecting the distance Brooks then perceived between this work and his own.[50]

Given the amount of time already devoted to the research that culminated in *Pettyfoggers*, it was probably unrealistic to expect the book to include anything more than a brief discussion of the relationship between civil and criminal proceedings or, perhaps, the relevance of the new history of crime. But this neglect of the criminal justice system and the new history of crime had consequences. The new history of crime raised important questions about the relationship between law, power, domination, exclusion, structure, totality and society, and the way in which the legal system can be routinely manipulated to serve those privileged by property and position, problematizing the nature and extent of popular belief in the rule of law – issues that Brooks tended to de-emphasize.[51]

*under the Law: Justice, Administration and Discipline in the Diocese of York, 1560–1640* (Cambridge, 1969); Ralph Houlbrooke, *Church Courts and the People During the English Reformation, 1520–1570* (Oxford, 1979); J. A. Sharpe, *Defamation and Sexual Slander in Early Modern England* (York, 1980). The most frequently referenced author was probably John Baker. Other frequently referenced authors include J. S. Cockburn, Eric Ives, Lawrence Stone and Wilfrid Prest.

49 'Special issue on litigation and dispute processing: part one', *Law and Society Review* 91 (1974), 1–160; 'Special issue on litigation and dispute processing: part two', *Law and Society Review* 9 (1975), 163–391.

50 Brooks, *Pettyfoggers and Vipers*, pp. 279–280. The new social history of crime, criminal law, punishment and policing (hereafter, the 'new history of crime') that emerged and quickly established itself as a distinct branch of social history in the 1970s and early 1980s reflected the growing recognition within social history that the exploitation of court records offered a vital window on the history of society: J. A. Sharpe, 'The history of crime in late medieval and early modern England: a review of the field', *Social History* 7 (1982), 187–203; Victor Bailey (ed.), *Policing and Punishment in Nineteenth-Century Britain* (London, 1981), Ignatieff, 'State, civil society and total institutions'.

51 Douglas Hay, Peter Linebaugh, John G. Rule, E. P. Thompson and Cal Winslow, *Albion's Fatal Tree; Crime and Society in Eighteenth Century England* (London, 1975); Douglas Hay, 'War, dearth and theft in the eighteenth century: the record of the English courts', *Past and Present* 95 (1982), 117–160; E. P. Thompson, *Whigs and Hunters: The Origins of the Black Act* (London, 1975); John Brewer and John A. Styles, *An Ungovernable People: The English and Their Law in the Seventeenth and Eighteenth*

While some historians overlooked or minimized the agency of middling and ordinary people, and the use they made of the law, social historians were increasingly challenging the reductionist interpretation of the law as class rule and, in several respects, adopting a similar view of the justice system and the juridical as that advanced by Brooks.[52]

## From Law and Litigation in Context to Law and the Constitution of Society, 1987–2014

Brooks subsequently reconfigured his vision of law in history by deepening his treatment of a number of topics addressed previously, extending the range of subjects that he tackled, the sources that underpinned them and the period that he traversed.[53] He was encouraged to persist with his

*Centuries* (London, 1980); J. S. Cockburn (ed.), *Crime in England, 1550–1800* (Princeton, 1977); V. A. C. Gatrell, Bruce Lenman and Geoffrey Parker (eds), *Crime and the Law: The Social History of Crime in Western Europe since 1500* (London, 1980).

[52] In addition to the works by Cockburn, Crime in England, and Brewer and Styles, An Ungovernable People, see David Phillips, *Crime and Authority in Victorian England: the Black Country, 1835–1860* (London, 1977); J. A. Sharpe, 'Enforcing the law in a seventeenth-century English village', in V. A. C. Gatrell, Bruce Lenman and Geoffrey Parker (eds), *Crime and the Law: The Social History of Crime in Western Europe since 1500* (London, 1980), pp. 97–119; J. A. Sharpe, 'The people and the law', in Barry Rea (ed.), *Popular Culture in Seventeenth-Century England* (London, 1985), pp. 244–270; Cynthia B. Herrup, 'Law and morality in seventeenth-century England', *Past and Present* 106 (1985), 102–123; Peter King, 'Decision makers and decision making in the English criminal law, 1750–1800', *Historical Journal* 27 (1984), 25–58. The absence of any reference to the work of E. P. Thompson – especially his conclusion to *Whigs and Hunters*, which contains several key arguments subsequently advanced and developed by Brooks – is striking. As will be seen in the next section, Brooks would later acknowledge the importance of Thompson's influence. I suspect that Brooks came to appreciate Thompson's significance for his own work subsequent to the completion of *Pettyfoggers*. Compare David Sugarman, 'Promoting dialogue between history and socio-legal studies: the contribution of Christopher W. Brooks and the "legal turn" in early modern English history', *Journal of Law and Society* 44 (2017), S44, which erred in claiming that Brooks's doctoral research was influenced by Thompson.

[53] He deepened his work on the lower branch, examining the relationships between notaries and scriveners, and between notaries and solicitors (Christopher W. Brooks, Richard H. Helmholz and Peter G. Stein, *Notaries Public in England since the Reformation*, London, 1991), comparing the professional history of barristers and solicitors, 1750–1850 (Brooks, *Lawyers*, ch. 5), and apprenticeship and legal education, 1700–1860 (Christopher W. Brooks and Michael Lobban, 'Apprenticeship or academy? The idea of a law university 1820–1860', in Jonathan A. Bush and Alain A. Wijffels (eds), *Learning the Law* (London, 1999), pp. 353–382), while tackling new subjects, such as feudalism, and attitudes thereto in sixteenth- and seventeenth-century England (Christopher W. Brooks, 'Contemporary views of "feudal" social and political relationships in sixteenth- and early seventeenth-century England', in Natalie Fryde and Pierre Monnet (eds), *Die Gegenwart*

own research by the small, but growing, number of historians who were researching early modern litigation, and the relationship between law and agency (some inspired by him), and whose studies confirmed the importance of going to court for ordinary men and women, a considerable renaissance in legal history, and signs of improved communication between social and legal history.[54] Contemporary developments in social history and the study of law in society, Brooks's deepening association with the legal history community and his collaboration with legal historian Michael Lobban also proved important.

Brooks's second book, *Lawyers, Litigation and English Society since 1450*, is a collection of larger and smaller-scale work, juxtaposed with historiographical and programmatic reflections. For example, Brooks extended his survey of rates of litigation and their likely impact on the social and political history of the country to cover seven-and-a-half centuries.[55] This prodigious research was sustained by legal, socio-legal, law and society, and legal history scholarship, social, political and economic history, and a smattering of social theory. Brooks considered both immediate causal factors and the *longue durée*, conjecturing that the legal

*des Feudalismus – Présence du féodalisme et présent de la féodalité – The Presence of Feudalism* (Göttingen, 2002), pp. 109–135).

[54] Brooks, *Lawyers*, pp. ix–x, 189–198. For example, Amy Louise Erickson, *Women and Property in Early Modern England* (London, 1993); Laura Gowing, *Domestic Dangers* (Oxford, 1996); Henry Horwitz and Patrick Polden, 'Continuity or change in the court of Chancery in the seventeenth and eighteenth centuries?', *Journal of British Studies* 35 (1996), 24–57; W. A. Champion, 'Recourse to law and the meaning of the great litigation decline, 1650–1750', in Christopher W. Brooks and Michael Lobban (eds), *Communities and Courts in Britain 1150–1900* (London, 1997) pp. 179–198; Craig Muldrew, *The Economy of Obligation* (Basingstoke, 1998). Others whose scholarship offered similar encouragements included David Lemmings, Wilfrid Prest and Tim Stretton. See further the material in fn. 86.

[55] Brooks, *Lawyers*, ch. 4, which builds on and much expands the material contained in Brooks, 'Litigants and attorneys', and Christopher W. Brooks, 'Interpersonal conflict and social tension: civil litigation in England, 1640–1830', in A. L. Beier, David Cannadine and James M. Rosenheim (eds), *The First Modern Society: Essays in English History in Honour of Lawrence Stone* (Cambridge, 1989), pp. 357–399. Wilfrid Prest pointed to some problems with the nature of Brooks's statistics and the conclusions drawn from them: Wilfrid Prest, 'Law tricks', *Journal of British Studies* 39 (2000), 372–382, p. 375; Wilfrid Prest, 'The experience of litigation in eighteenth-century England', in David Lemmings (ed.), *The British and Their Laws in the Eighteenth Century* (Woodbridge, 2005), pp. 135–144; cf. Christopher W. Brooks, 'Litigation, participation and agency in seventeenth- and eighteenth-century England', in David Lemmings (ed.), *The British and Their Laws in the Eighteenth Century* (Woodbridge, 2005), pp. 151–181; Christopher W. Brooks, 'The longitudinal study of civil litigation in England 1200–1996', in Wilfrid Prest and Sharyn R. Anleu (eds), *Litigation: Past and Present* (Sydney, 2004), pp. 24–42.

culture of early modern England was more inclusive and vibrant, and that the institutional participation of laypersons in the legal system, access to the law, and political and social participation in civil society through the law, locally and nationally, were much greater than has been seen since. He concluded that ordinary people subsequently became more isolated from the legal system, and that 'legal culture was arguably less significant in eighteenth- and-nineteenth-century England than it had been before 1700'.[56] Under this optic, the divide between early modern and modern England was great indeed – but not necessarily in the ways that modern historians and social theorists had assumed.

The key to understanding Brooks's scholarly agenda and the development of his vision of law in history is a manifesto lying at the heart of *Lawyers*. This twenty-page call-to-arms argued that the promise of 'socio-legal history' was largely unfulfilled, that much remained to be done to turn that promise into a reality, and that conventional treatments of some of the core concerns of early modern England were, and would continue to be, flawed until law, legal institutions and legal history are taken more seriously and actively integrated within social history. Brooks proposed a number of measures, which amounted to a long-term plan of collective action that, if implemented, could significantly enrich our historical understanding of England, 1500–1800.

Specifically, Brooks claimed that whilst much had been achieved in the history of crime and criminal law, and the history of those who serviced legal institutions:

> ... there are also grounds for concern about the apparent failure of these branches ... either to communicate much with each other or to make a significant impact on the general social and political history of England between 1500 and 1800. The root of the problem is that we still lack an analytical perspective capable of doing justice to the complex and multi-faceted role of law in society.[57]

[56] Brooks, *Lawyers*, p. 109. This was, in part, a consequence of the deprofessionalization experienced by the legal profession throughout the eighteenth century: Brooks, *Lawyers*, pp. 29–62 and ch. 5; Brooks, 'Litigation, participation and agency', pp. 160–168. See also David Lemmings, *Gentlemen and Barristers* (Oxford, 1990); David Lemmings, *Professors of the Law* (Oxford, 2000); David Lemmings, *Law and Government in England during the Long Eighteenth Century: From Consent to Command* (Basingstoke, 2011).

[57] Brooks, *Lawyers*, pp. 179–180. Henceforth, Brooks began to address the relationship between civil and criminal justice: see, e.g., Brooks, 'Litigation, participation and agency', pp. 160–181.

Brooks now focused on law as discourses that inscribed social, political and economic relationships, and which constituted a formal set of values.[58] This opened the door to a consideration of lawyers as 'a diverse group of people who are at the centre of the creation and exchange of one of the major social discourses of the day: the set of norms, practices and ideologies known collectively as "the law"'.[59] This was a perspective that was increasingly adopted within the sociology of law, law and society, and critical legal scholarship, legal anthropology and the study of lawyers in society.[60] Brooks noted that while this proposition may seem novel when applied to lawyers, it had long been a commonplace in the study of theology and the clerical profession. The implication was clear: what was good for religion was also good for law. Concerning the diverse influences driving legal discourse, Brooks sought to transcend those approaches that treated legal discourse as exclusively or largely the product of top-down (elite, the state) or professional influences; rather, he emphasized the need to investigate the biggest customers of the law – that is, the middling 70 per cent of the population – and the role of lawyers and legal discourse in facilitating and legitimating their concerns, as well as the extent to which the middling sort were a dynamic force shaping legal ideas and values.[61]

Brooks conceded that the sources for investigating the new possibilities opened up by a legal discourse perspective were mainly those produced by lawyers. This largely unexamined lawyerly material (such as readings and law lectures at the Inns of Court) was uncongenial, being mostly in manuscript, 'written in barbarous law French and sometimes diabolically obscure' – but, '. . . with a little digging', he said, it could 'produce gems'.[62]

Brooks continued:

> This list of material could be expanded to include printed law texts, speeches in parliament or at state trials, unpublished treatises, and the addresses which were regularly used to preface charges delivered to quarter sessions and assizes – public utterances which often dilated on

[58] Ibid., pp. 180–181, 189, 198.

[59] Ibid., p. 186.

[60] For example, Maureen Cain, 'The general practice lawyer and client', *International Journal of the Sociology of Law* 7 (1979), 331–354.

[61] See further Jonathan Barry and Christopher W. Brooks (eds), *The Middling Sort of People* (Basingstoke, 1994), which owed something to Jürgen Habermas, *The Structural Transformation of the Public Sphere* (Cambridge, MA, 1989).

[62] Brooks, *Lawyers*, p. 188.

> the role of law in society. Sources such as these enable us to broaden the scope of legal ideology beyond the rather narrow and precedent ridden 'common law mind' formulated by Professor Pocock.[63] They illustrate the ways in which it was exchanged with the wider public. They offer the prospect of a history of generalised legal ideas about the state and society which can be traced over time and compared with that of other strands of thought.[64]

Brooks encouraged social historians to study systematically the case law of civil courts to establish what they might tell us about 'whole categories of social relationships: economic transactions; husband-and-wife; landlord and tenant; judge and defendant; urban oligarch and freeman; community and person ... [Legal] discourse always includes assumptions about the nature of the person, social relations and knowledge.'[65] Brooks outlined how the development of juristic ideas and substantive law can offer new perspectives, while also contributing to areas already addressed in the study of early modern social history, such as the relationship between law and the community, and between class power, discretion and deference.[66] And he briefly highlighted the importance of juristic thought – notably, the rule of law – for ideas about the state, obedience to authority and its promised protection against the oppression of the individual.[67] To this, he added that the relationship between law and religion had not received a systematic treatment on anything like the scale it deserved.[68] Elsewhere, Brooks threw down the gauntlet on the relative significance of criminal and civil law: '[T]he civil law is even more important than the criminal law in maintaining the social and economic relationships in any society.'[69]

Again, Brooks noted that the abiding problem was '[o]ur continuing ignorance of the details of legal thought, and of its interaction with the

[63] By taking insufficient allowance for the impact of juristic humanism on English legal thinking and the common currency of Aristotelian and natural-law modes of thought: Brooks, *Lawyers*, pp. 6–7, and ch. 8; Brooks, *Law, Politics and Society*, pp. 11–29, 41, 58, 67, 81.

[64] Brooks, *Lawyers*, p. 188.

[65] Ibid., p. 189, citing at n. 46 Sally Humphreys, 'Law as discourse', *History and Anthropology* 1 (1985), 239–264, p. 252.

[66] Brooks, *Lawyers*, pp. 191–193.

[67] Ibid., pp. 193–195.

[68] Ibid., p. 197.

[69] Ibid., p. 28, reiterating J. H. Langbein, 'Albion's fatal flaws', *Past and Present* 98 (1983), 96–120, p. 118.

population at large'.[70] In his final book, *Law, Politics and Society*, Brooks set out to dispel this ignorance, to test his belief in the centrality of the law and generally to put his manifesto into practice. He undertook a large-scale investigation of the nature and extent of law-consciousness, and of the inscription of law in politics and society, within England, Scotland, Wales and Ireland, from the later Middle Ages until the outbreak of the English civil war.[71] Drawing on a host of sources, including those championed in his manifesto, Brooks concluded that law permeated almost all levels of society and that, like religion, it was a principal discourse through which the English understood their world. Indeed, he aimed to 'reintegrate the history of law, legal institutions and the legal professions within the general political and social history of the period'.[72] Brooks also set out to persuade early modern historians that they should take the social history of law itself more seriously and to show how they might do so. Brooks delineated the constitutive and penetrative character of law throughout society by mapping the creation, transmission and reception of legal thought. He lavished particular attention on the thousands of local courts whose trials involved the presentation of oral testimony in a public forum. Brooks found that these local courts impacted on legal thinking in the central courts sustained by a legal world with 'an enduring tendency to privilege customary practices'.[73] He investigated both elite and popular law-consciousness on an almost unparalleled scale, adopting top-down and bottom-up approaches that revealed the trickle-up, as well as trickle-down, diffusion of legal ideas.

This daunting project gained traction in light of the cultural turn in history and cognate developments in the treatment of law in society. While historians and lawyers have long anchored English exceptionalism in the rule of law and legal institutions, they have tended to treat 'law' and 'society' as separate spheres, each independent of the other, although related through various mechanisms of causal linkage.[74] For historians, 'economy' or 'society' are the primary realms of experience, and the 'law' and its institutions are secondary phenomena that merely channel or

[70] Christopher W. Brooks, 'Review: Pocock, *The Ancient Constitution and the Feudal Law*', *English Historical Review* 105 (1990), 733–735, p. 734.

[71] Brooks, *Law, Politics and Society*. Brooks's acknowledgements included Paul Halliday, Cynthia Herrup, Henry Horwitz, James Oldham, Tim Stretton and Keith Wrightson, as well as those whom he had acknowledged in his previous work: ibid., pp. vii–viii.

[72] Ibid., p. 10.

[73] Ibid., p. 425.

[74] Robert W. Gordon, 'Critical legal histories', *Stanford Law Review* 36 (1984), 57–125.

facilitate social relations. 'Law' served as evidence for social and economic history;[75] it was merely a means by which 'economy' and 'society' might be illuminated.[76]

But change was under way. While traditional Marxist and other leftist work had largely focused on the coercive and hypocritical character of the law, new strands within criminology, legal anthropology, social history, the sociology of law, the socio-legal studies movement, feminist legal studies and American critical legal studies (CLS) progressively investigated and elevated law's non-coercive legitimating functions.[77] This turn to 'law as ideology' led to legal ideas being taken more seriously, paralleling earlier and concurrent developments in the history of ideas, and the 'cultural turn'.[78] Importantly, this intellectual and political movement – a movement that was both interdisciplinary and transnational – challenged the separation of 'law' and 'society' and the one-directional causality that frequently accompanied such notions. According to this new paradigm, law not only classified, simplified and specified, but also played a significant role in constituting social relations, identity formation,[79] and the minds and practices of individuals.[80]

The social historian who best articulated this new understanding of law-in-society was E. P. Thompson, who concluded that law was:

> ... deeply imbricated within the very basis of productive relations, which would have been inoperable without this law ... The rules and categories of law penetrate every level of society, effect ... and contribute to ... [an individual's] sense of identity. Productive relations themselves are, in part,

[75] Brooks, *Law, Politics and Society*, p. 2.

[76] Although this is usually associated with the base/superstructure model of Marxism, it is equally evident in much law-in-history writing of a conservative, liberal and leftist hue, albeit that it is rarely articulated so explicitly: see Gordon, 'Critical legal histories'.

[77] See, e.g., Ian Taylor, Paul Walton and Jock Young (eds), *Critical Criminology* (London, 1975); Humphreys, 'Law as discourse'; Mark Kelman, *A Guide to Critical Legal Studies* (Cambridge, MA, 1987), pp. 242–268. On constitutive approaches to law, see Roger Cotterrell, 'Law as constitutive', in Neil J. Smelser and Paul B. Baltes (eds), *International Encyclopedia of the Social & Behavioral Sciences* (Amsterdam, 2001), vol. 12, pp. 84–97.

[78] Geoff Eley, *A Crooked Line: From Cultural History to the History of Society* (Ann Arbor, 2005).

[79] For example, gender, race, class and ethnicity.

[80] For example, Clifford Geertz, 'Local knowledge', in *Local Knowledge* (New York, 1983), pp. 167–234, at pp. 232–233; Pierre Bourdieu, 'The force of law', *Hastings Law Journal* 38 (1987), 805–853, pp. 838–839; Jürgen Habermas, *Between Facts and Norms* (Cambridge, MA, 1996).

> only meaningful in terms of their definitions at law: the serf, the free labourer; the cottager with common rights, the inhabitant without . . .[81]

Thompson emphasized that the law could sometimes be appropriated and used by the politically and economically dispossessed; that socio-economic relations in early modern England were not simply the product of the decisions of the elite, but involved an ongoing process of negotiation in which a broad cross-section of the population participated; and, controversially, that the rule of law was an unqualified human good.[82] In the hands of Robert W. Gordon, a leading American historian of legal ideas and advocate of CLS, Thompson's notion of law's imbrication in society was allied to the idea of law as constitutive of consciousness: '[In] practice, it is just about impossible to describe any set of "basic" social practices without describing the legal relations among the people involved – legal relations that don't simply condition how the people relate to each other but to an important extent define the constitutive terms of the relationship.'[83] While many social historians were influenced by Thompson's revisionism, his impact on Brooks was distinctive.[84] In the first place, Brooks was the only social historian of England of whom I am aware whose internalization of Thompson was mediated and intensified by allied work in legal and cultural anthropology and CLS – notably, Gordon's critique of evolutionary teleologies and the law/society divide, as well as his claim that law was constitutive of consciousness.[85] In the second, while most of the historical work triggered by Thompson's new thinking was concerned with crime and

[81] Thompson, *Whigs and Hunters*, pp. 261 and 267; see also E. P. Thompson, *The Poverty of Theory* (London, 1978), p. 288.

[82] Thompson, *Whigs and Hunters*, pp. 259–269; E. P. Thompson, *Customs in Common* (London, 1993), pp. 97–351.

[83] Gordon, 'Critical legal histories', p. 103.

[84] Brooks wrote that he found Thompson's final chapter of *Whigs and Hunters* 'particularly thought-provoking' (Brooks, *Lawyers*, p. 5, n. 16) and that it 'partly' inspired his attempt to 'reintegrate the history of law, legal institutions and the legal profession with ... general political and social history ...' (Brooks, *Law, Politics and Society*, p. 1). Brooks described Thompson's *Customs in Common* as 'magisterial' and 'brilliant' (Brooks, 'Litigation, participation and agency', pp. 173 and 178, respectively).

[85] Brooks singled out 'Critical legal histories' as a key work that helped to shape his views about law, lawyers and the social history of England (Brooks, *Lawyers*, p. 186, n. 33), and he quoted an extract in which Gordon elaborated the constitutive role of law (Brooks, *Law, Politics and Society*, p. 5). Although it was not cited extensively, Brooks referenced other works, mostly on the anthropology of law, that also advanced the notion that law was constitutive of consciousness (see, e.g., Brooks, *Lawyers*, p. 186, n. 33, p. 189, n. 43, and p. 189, n. 46). In short, the claim that law constitutes society increasingly pervades Brooks's post-*Pettyfoggers* work – in particular, Brooks, *Law, Politics and Society*.

criminal justice, Brooks's explored the wide-ranging impact of legal discourse and the civil side of the legal system.[86]

Brooks challenged that vein of social history which juxtaposed law (being the law of the elite and of the state) against the community (the easier-going neighbourly relations typical of customary village life):

> [There] is much that is convincing in this formulation, but it . . . does not confront the question of when, if ever, lawyers and the law were not so intimately involved in village life that social relations might be discussed without reference to them . . . Even a casual glance at the [manorial court] records . . . reveals village life to have been anything but ideally peaceful and devoid of contention . . . The significance of the manorial courts is that they throw into bold relief, indeed problematize . . . the relationship between custom and the generalised values of local communities versus the formal legal ideas on processes, such as those which were enshrined in Parliamentary statutes or enforced by the courts (a classic example of our obsession with the distinction between elite and popular culture).[87]

The point was not that knowing something about manorial courts would solve the problem of defining popular justice, but that it would be misleading to talk about local communities, custom and justice without considering the ways in which they were constituted by the law.[88]

[86] Brooks's vision of law in history was further enriched by other research, concerning: the prominence of legal thought within early modern political culture, and the interplay between legal, religious and philosophical discourses (A. Cromartie, *The Constitutionalist Revolution: An Essay on the History of England, 1450–1642*, Cambridge, 2006); how the law constituted and policed marriage and patriarchy, and how women attenuated and circumvented coverture using law and lawyers (see, e.g., Erickson, *Women and Property in Early Modern England*; Gowing, *Domestic Dangers*; Tim Stretton, *Women Waging Law in Elizabethan England*, Cambridge, 1998; Joanne Bailey, *Unquiet Lives: Marriage and Marriage Breakdown in England, 1660–1800*, Cambridge, 2003; Garthine Walker, *Crime, Gender and Social Order in Early Modern England*, Cambridge, 2003; Tim Stretton and Krista J. Kesselring, *Married Women and the Law*, Montreal and London, 2013); the interplay between litigation, governance, state formation and the agency of subaltern groups (Steve Hindle, *The State and Social Change in Early Modern England*, Basingstoke, 2000; Michael J. Braddick, *State Formation in Early Modern England 1550–1700*, Cambridge, 2000; Michael J. Braddick and John Walter (eds), *Negotiating Power in Early Modern Society*, Woodbridge, 2001). Much of this research acknowledged its debt to Brooks's scholarship. Additionally, Brooks's frequent visits to the United States (perhaps not least his year-long fellowship at the National Humanities Center in the early 1990s) helped to keep him in touch with trans-Atlantic intellectual developments and scholarship on the law and history/society/culture interface, as did his membership of the editorial board of *Law and History Review*.

[87] Brooks, *Lawyers*, p. 191.

[88] Ibid., pp. 191–192.

Similarly, the social and political pluralism that social historians had discerned in early modern society and, to some extent, counterposed against the law were, in important respects, connected to and sustained by legal pluralism.[89]

In sum, Brooks's intellectual development reveals a scholarly metamorphosis from the late 1990s onwards. From an 'externalist' (social and intellectual history) perspective on law, consciously complementing 'internalist' legal history's preoccupation with institutional and doctrinal evolution, he moved to embrace an approach that married 'externalist' and 'internalist' perspectives on law – integrating social and political history with the history of law, legal institutions and the legal professions.

Always careful and rigorous, Brooks acknowledged the pitfalls involved in deciphering court usage and law-mindedness. While conveying a strong sense of the complexity of the phenomena he investigated, the sweep and ambition of his scholarship raises challenging evidential and conceptual questions. Was litigation always a good thing, both as an ideal and in practice?[90] Was litigation equally good for all social groups in a society that was grossly unequal?[91] And how did the significant increase in litigation that extended from the 1580s until the 1670s (with occasional minor fluctuations) impact on personal relations and contemporary notions of 'neighbourliness'?[92]

Brooks's partiality for things 'legal' extended to lawyers, whom he usually held in high regard. He was especially smitten with Coke.[93] He rebutted, perhaps overenthusiastically, contemporary criticisms of attorneys (namely, that they cheated and exploited their clients, and that they were poorly regulated), the inequities of the legal system, the adequacy of

[89] Brooks, *Law, Politics and Society*, especially chs 2, 5, 6, 9 and 13. This emphasis on legal pluralism was echoed in contemporary legal anthropology and law-and-society scholarship.

[90] Brooks acknowledged that arbitration was a popular means of resolving disputes in the fifteenth and seventeenth centuries: Brooks, *Pettyfoggers*, p. 91.

[91] Research on contemporary America and elsewhere emphasizes that the 'haves' tend to come out ahead: Marc Galanter, 'Why the "haves" come out ahead', *Law and Society Review* 9 (1974), 95–160.

[92] Tim Stretton has suggested that litigation may have been one of the causes of the corrosion of personal relations in early modern England: Tim Stretton, 'Written obligations, litigation and neighbourliness, 1580–1680', in Steve Hindle, Alexandra Sheppard and John Walter, *Remaking English Society: Social Relations and Social Change in Early Modern England* (Woodbridge, 2013), pp. 189–210, at p. 189.

[93] Brooks, 'The common lawyers in the House of Commons of 1621', in *Pettyfoggers*, pp. 45, 94, 100, 120, 121, 128, 129, 131, 134, 146, 148, 150, 163, 177, 198–199, 204, 210, 218 and 219.

the Inns of Court's provision for professional regulation and education, and persistent demands for law reform.[94]

Brooks's claims that adherence to, and respect for, the rule of law was widespread, and that the law and law-consciousness penetrated, and in vital respects, constituted much of early modern England, run into the problem that apparent use and conformity with the law, or knowing the law, may obscure non-conformity and a lack of legitimacy.[95] That people justified their action by reference to the law does not in itself confirm the legitimacy of the rule of law. Individuals who appeal to the rule of law may do so differently in different contexts and times, and such appeals are as likely to be motivated by short-term or self-interested sentiment as by a belief in the legitimacy of the law.[96] It is also likely that the idea of the 'rule of law' meant different things to, say, landowners and the poor, and that these differences were compounded by the existence of overlapping and sometimes competing systems of governance. Indeed, the motives and beliefs of individuals when they appeal to legality are almost invariably mixed. It may not be possible to differentiate those motives and beliefs (such as pragmatism, Christian morality, a desire to protect one's family, possessions and livelihood, or acquiescence in law's power) – especially given the stark social and economic inequalities and disadvantages of the age – and to establish their relative importance.

Brooks recognized that the relationship between the legal ideas discussed in Parliament, or famous state trials, and the everyday legal life of the mass of the population was problematic; he acknowledged that 'it is not easy to measure the practical impact of' law.[97] But this sits uneasily with some aspects of his analytical framework – notably, that law was 'deeply imbricated' throughout society and supremely 'constitutive of consciousness'. These assumptions confirmed Brooks's long-standing belief that '[l]aw, and the sources of authority for lawmaking, were central features of seventeenth-century discourse' and an essential part of the mentality of most people of the age.[98] When taken too literally,

[94] Prest, 'The experience of litigation'; Paul Raffield, 'A discredited priesthood: the failings of common lawyers and their representation in seventeenth century satirical drama', *Law and Literature* 17 (2005), 365–395. Brooks was probably reacting to easy acceptance by historians of contemporary complaints about law and lawyers.

[95] However, individuals' legal consciousness may be framed by ideas about law even when they are actively resisting it.

[96] Brooks acknowledged that self-interest may have had a good deal to do with the acceptance of political authority: Brooks, *Lawyers*, p. 6.

[97] Brooks, *Law, Politics and Society*, pp. 61, 241, 383, 426 and 432.

[98] Brooks, 'Review: Pocock', p. 734.

however, these assumptions become trans-historical relational statements, rather than working hypotheses, akin to the reversal of the hitherto dominant base–superstructure polarities, switching one directionality and causality for another, rendering law wholly autonomous, and thereby exaggerating the range and depth of law-consciousness, and law's legitimacy, and marginalizing 'alternative' discourses, such as antinomianism and popular constitutionalism.[99]

Also, what makes 'law-mindedness' or a promise to perform a contract 'legal', as distinct from 'religious', 'moral', 'economic', 'political' and so on (all of which may be partly shaped by 'law')?[100] Of course, law matters – but 'everyday life has its own battery of normative ideas and habits, which interact with law, even when law is at its most constitutive'.[101]

This suggests that, until we know how individuals such as defendants judged their engagement with the law, claims about law-mindedness and legitimacy are best kept modest and circumspect. It also points towards the need for greater discussion of the complex and diverse definitions of law-mindedness, law-consciousness, legitimacy, imbrication, ideology, negotiation and other key concepts explicitly and implicitly employed in such research, and the possible locations of their empirical referents.

99 'Eighteenth-century law ... existed in its own right': Thompson, *Whigs and Hunters*, p. 262. See further Christopher Tomlins, 'How autonomous is law?' *Annual Review of Law and Society* 3 (2007), 45–68, pp. 49–52, 57–59. For criticisms of Thompson's treatment of the rule of law see, e.g., Adrian Merritt, 'The nature and function of law', *British Journal of Law and Society* 7 (1980), 194–214; for a defence of Thompson, see Daniel H. Cole, 'An unqualified human good', *Journal of Law and Society* 28 (2001), 177–203. For a critique of law as constitutive of consciousness, see Anthony Woodiwiss, *Rights v. Conspiracy* (New York, 1990), pp. 141–173. These criticisms are elaborated and extended in Tomlins, 'How autonomous is law?' Robert Gordon has emphasized that his claim that law was, in significant respects, constitutive was a hypothesis: see, generally, Robert W. Gordon, 'Critical legal histories revisited', *Law & Social Inquiry* 37 (2012), 200–215. Did Brooks's increasing embrace of lawyer's law and legal history accentuate a tendency to be 'too lawyerly'? Apparently, Lawrence Stone thought so: Adrian Green, 'Christopher W. Brooks, 1948–2014', *The Seventeenth Century* 29 (2014), 403–409.

100 See further Hendrik Hartog, 'Introduction to symposium on "critical legal histories"', *Law & Social Inquiry* 37 (2012), 147–154, p. 153; S. L. Blumenthal, 'Of Mandarins, legal consciousness, and the cultural turn in US legal history', *Law & Social Inquiry* 37 (2012), 178–179.

101 Austin Sarat and Thomas R. Kearn, 'Beyond the great divide: forms of legal scholarship and everyday life', in Austin Sarat and Thomas R. Kearns (eds), *Law in Everyday Life* (Ann Arbor, 1993), pp. 21–62, at pp. 54–55. Brooks was sensitive to differences of legal penetration and import across regions, localities and time, and this has become an important way of problematizing some of the larger claims made about the import of law in early modern Britain.

The problems posed by Brooks's larger conclusions reflect, to some extent, the problems of social history and the wider study of law-in-society.[102]

The claim that legal culture was less important after c. 1700 than in the period c. 1560–1700 is difficult to access in any general sense, at least without much more research, and is likely to elicit a complex response.[103] To some extent, it depends where you look. While the decline of legal culture in the eighteenth century has been persuasively canvassed,[104] for those engaged in modern history, the story may not be straightforward. Lawyers and legal thinkers such as Bentham, Fitzjames Stephen, Maine, Dicey and Bryce were, in varying degrees, public intellectuals who supplied ideological rationales for the character of English society or for social reform, staking claims to represent certain cultural practices and ideas, or certain groups, such as the middle classes. More generally, law and lawyers were active in both the construction of the British state and the British Empire – with lawyers playing key roles as administrators, the drafters of comprehensive codes of law, the authors of legal textbooks that reconstituted the law, and as members of Parliament, judges and jurists.[105] The close involvement of lawyers and professional bodies such

[102] Historians may find recent contemporary research on law-consciousness suggestive: see, e.g., Sally Engle Merry, *Getting Justice and Getting Even: Legal Consciousness among Working-Class Americans* (Chicago, 1990); Austin Sarat, '"... The Law Is All Over": Power, Resistance and the Legal Consciousness of the Welfare Poor', *Yale Journal of Law and the Humanities* 2 (1990), 343–379; Patricia Ewick and Susan Silbey, *The Common Place of Law* (Chicago, 1998).

[103] Brooks, *Lawyers*, p. 109.

[104] Brooks, 'Litigation', pp. 160–176; Lemmings, *Gentlemen and Barristers*; Lemmings, *Professors of the Law*; Lemmings, *Law and Government in England*.

[105] Christopher Harvie, *The Lights of Liberalism* (London, 1976); Robert Stevens, *Law and Politics: The House of Lords as a Judicial Body, 1800–1976* (London, 1979); Duman, *The English and Colonial Bars*; Stefan Collini, Donald Winch and John Burrow, *That Nobel Science of Politics* (Cambridge, 1983), chs 7 and 9; David Sugarman, 'Legal theory, the common law mind and the making of the textbook tradition', in William Twining (ed.), *Legal Theory and Common Law* (Oxford, 1986), pp. 26–61; David Sugarman, 'Simple images and complex realities: English lawyers and their relationship to business and politics', *Law and History Review* 11 (1993), 257–301; Leonore Davidoff and Catherine Hall, *Family Fortunes* (London, 1987); R. C. J. Cocks, *Sir Henry Maine* (Cambridge, 1988); Stefan Collini, *Public Moralists* (Oxford, 1991), chs 5 and 7; Lauren Benton, *Law and Colonial Cultures* (Cambridge, 2001); Philip Schofield, *Utility and Democracy: The Political Thought of Jeremy Bentham* (Oxford, 2006); Duncan Bell, *The Idea of Greater Britain* (Cambridge, 2007); Karuna Mantena, *Alibis of Empire: Henry Maine and the Ends of Liberal Imperialism* (Princeton, 2010); Shaunnagh Dorsett and John McLaren (eds), *Legal Histories of the British Empire* (London, 2014).

as the Law Society in the formulation of legislation, law reform and legal practice suggests that they exercised an important influence on the available normative languages, on the contemporary definitions of the public and the private, and therefore on the presuppositions of the legislative and decision-making process.[106] Moreover, the law was far from absent in contemporary fiction.[107]

None of this, however, challenges the importance of Brooks's scholarship. Brooks's achievement was to systematically integrate law, politics and society, and legal, social and political history, and to demonstrate the considerable increase in historical knowledge that is likely to ensue from this fusion. He took law out of the law courts and lawyers' offices and brought it into society. Brooks, probably more than any other social historian of early modern England, appreciated and internalized the significance of legal history, legal doctrine and legal culture – the law from the 'outside' and the 'inside'.[108] This substantiated their importance, providing valuable guidance on how they might be understood and on the sources for researching them. He demonstrated that law and lawyers warranted at least the same attention as that traditionally lavished on religion and clerics.[109] While his larger conclusions may be contested, it is hard to see how his emphasis on the centrality of law to so many aspects of early modern England will ever be overturned.

Brooks was clear that his was the first, not the last, word on the subject.[110] Like most original, cutting-edge scholarship, his raises as many questions as it answers, but in so doing it highlights important

106 David Sugarman, 'Bourgeois collectivism, professional power and the boundaries of the state: the private and public life of the Law Society, 1825–1914', *International Journal of the Legal Profession* 3 (1996), 81–135.

107 Tim Dolin, *Mistress of the House: Women of Property in the Victorian Novel* (London, 1997); Kieran Dolin, *Fiction and the Law* (Cambridge, 1999); Jan-Melissa Schramm, *Testimony and Advocacy in Victorian Law, Literature, and Theology* (Cambridge, 2000); Catherine O. Frank, *Law, Literature and the Transmission of Culture in England, 1837–1925* (London, 2010).

108 Brooks's increasingly positive attitude towards legal history, and his emphasis on its centrality to the writing of early modern social and political history, was perhaps, in part, connected to the counsel and works of Sir John Baker (Brooks, *Pettyfoggers*, p. ix; Brooks, *Law, Politics and Society*, p. viii), and Brooks's collaboration with, and the advice and encouragement that he received from, Michael Lobban (Brooks, *Lawyers, Law, Politics and Society*, p. viii), as well as Brooks's election to, and service on, the Council of the Selden Society.

109 Brooks's 'blind spot', when it came to religion, may explain his tendency to downplay the religious and perhaps exaggerate the importance of the secular (including secular courts and their law) in early modern England: see Green, 'Christopher W. Brooks', p. 403.

110 Brooks, *Lawyers*, p. 8.

themes and issues for future scholarship to consider. More generally, Brooks's manifesto and his stress on the need for an analytical framework capable of doing justice to the complex and multifaceted role of law in society remain both important visionary prescriptions and challenges for historians. This is especially so in this age of constant pressure for quick returns on university budgets, and the increasingly limited ability of universities in general and the humanities in particular to undertake long-term research and to foster sustained interdisciplinary collaboration of the kind advanced by Brooks.[111] Likewise, the lack of institutional commitment to bringing together history and law in the United Kingdom relative to, say, Canada and the United States, may inhibit his impact. Is there, for example, sufficient support to enable and encourage historians to acquire the requisite skills necessary for working on lawyer's materials? It would be regrettable if Brooks's reach were to fail to extend beyond social history and law and literature into the realms of general history, the history of politics and socio-legal studies.

By describing and analysing in such exceptional detail what he conceived as the golden age of English law and society, and by arguing against any kind of linear or progressive evolution over time, Brooks reminds us why the questions that were at the forefront of his attention – lay participation in law and governance, access to justice, the recognition of the public interest and moral imperatives, as well as private interest, within legal discourse and legislative authority, and the rule of law as a bulwark against authoritarianism and the abuse of power – remain so compelling.

[111] See, generally, Jo Guldi and David Armitage, *The History Manifesto* (Cambridge, 2014).

4

# 'The Hard Rind of Legal History'

## F. W. Maitland and the Writing of Late Medieval and Early Modern British Social History

R. A. HOUSTON*

The greatest English legal historian of all time and arguably one of the most important historians of any kind, F. W. Maitland has had surprisingly little coverage in historiographical writings about late medieval and early modern England, from the 1940s to the present. Michael Bentley's monumental *Companion to Historiography*, for example, contains no more than a handful of references.[1] The late Geoffrey Elton, in an appreciation of Maitland's place in historical writing, said simply that his work was done 'well, conscientiously, circumspectly, methodically'.[2] Yet Maitland has pride of place in many historiographical studies by legal historians, some of whom see him as the creator of their subject – even if they may rely on stating how important he was rather than explaining precisely why.[3] Among these historians, his work 'has been regarded, and

* I am grateful to Michael Bentley and John Hudson for reading earlier drafts of this piece.

1 M. Bentley (ed.), *Companion to Historiography* (London, 1997).

2 G. R. Elton, *F. W. Maitland* (Cambridge, 1985), p. 100. Elton's brief appreciation concentrated mainly on Maitland's work on the 1305 Parliament; cf. C. H. S. Fifoot, *Frederic William Maitland: A Life* (Cambridge, MA, 1971).

3 R. S. de Montpensier, 'Maitland and the interpretation of history', *American Journal of Legal History* 10 (1966), 259–281; F. B. Weiner, 'Maitland the incomparable', *American Journal of Legal History* 16 (1972), 177–191; D. Jenkins, 'English law and the Renaissance: eighty years on – in defence of Maitland', *Journal of Legal History* 2 (1981), 107–142. See also R. W. Southern, 'Review essay of C. H. S. Fifoot (ed.), *The Letters of Frederic William Maitland*', *History and Theory* 6 (1967), 105–111; P. B. M. Blaas, *Continuity and Anachronism: Parliamentary and Constitutional Development in Whig Historiography and in the Anti-Whig Reaction between 1890 and 1930* (The Hague, 1978), ch. 4; J. Hudson (ed.), *The History of English Law: Centenary Essays on 'Pollock and Maitland'* (Oxford, 1996); J. Hudson, *F. W. Maitland and the Englishness of English Law* (London, Selden Society Lecture, 2007), pp. 9–16; B. R. O'Brien, 'Maitland, Frederic William (1850–1906)', in D. R. Woolf (ed.), *A Global Encyclopaedia of Historical Writing*

still is, almost as revelation'.[4] Writing after Maitland is arguably one of most difficult things about being an English medievalist, legal or otherwise. He was perhaps the first, and certainly the most distinguished, of a new breed of professional legal historians who imbibed some of the ideas concerning the writing and teaching of history developed in early and mid-nineteenth-century Germany. Christopher W. Brooks was one of his most worthy successors.

To some extent, the neglect among mainstream historians may be the result of Maitland's distance in time and the apparently esoteric nature of his work. Furthermore, his sources and methods seem uncongenial to modern historians of a cultural bent, who are interested more in discourses and representations than in what he called the 'hard rind of legal history'.[5] Maitland went on: 'Legal documents, documents of the most technical kind, are the best, often the only evidence that we have for economic and social history, for the history of morality, for the history of practical religion.'[6] Because of this view – that history's materials are mostly the products of law – Maitland's influence fades the further forward in time we move from the later Middle Ages. After this, other, apparently more promising (certainly less technical and probably more tractable), sources begin to become more abundant. Maitland himself seems to have been less at home in the sixteenth and seventeenth centuries than he was in the twelfth and thirteenth; his writings, less assured.[7] In spite of this, Alan Macfarlane believes that Maitland's

(London, 1998), pp. 584–585; A. Brundage and R. A. Cosgrove, *The Great Tradition: Constitutional History and National Identity in Britain and the United States, 1870–1960* (Stanford, 2007), pp. 215–227; J. Rose, 'Studying the past: the nature and development of legal history as an academic discipline', *Journal of Legal History* 31 (2010), 101–128; M. Lobban, 'The varieties of legal history', *Clio@Themis* 5 (2014).

4 S. F. C. Milsom, 'F. W. Maitland', *Proceedings of the British Academy* 66 (1980), 265–281, p. 266. Toby Milsom also wrote the *Oxford Dictionary of National Biography* (ODNB) entry 'Maitland, Frederic William (1850–1906)'.

5 For a devastating critique of this trend at its worst, see M. Bentley, 'Victorian politics and the linguistic turn', *Historical Journal* 42 (1999), 883–902.

6 F. W. Maitland, 'Why the history of English law is not written', in *The Collected Papers of Frederic William Maitland*, ed. H. A. L. Fisher, three vols (Cambridge, 1911) (hereafter *Collected Papers*), vol. I, p. 486; Elton, *Maitland*, p. 23. Contemporary continental thinkers agreed on the centrality of law to understanding society and some, like Weber, had trained as lawyers: M. Rheinstein, *Max Weber on Law in Economy and Society* (Cambridge, MA, 1954 [1925]); D. R. Kelley, *The Human Measure: Social Thought in the Western Legal Tradition* (Cambridge, 1990), pp. 270–274.

7 C. H. S. Fifoot (ed.), *The Letters of Frederic William Maitland* (London, 1965) (hereafter *Letters*, vol. I), no. 233. This was despite recognizing the time of Coke and Hale as 'the heroic age of English legal scholarship': *Collected Papers*, vol. III, pp. 447, 453.

'profound sociological and philosophical analysis was covered over with a veneer of technical legal history which has deceived subsequent historians into thinking of him just as a historian or legal historian'.[8] Best exemplified in Macfarlane, Maitland's effect on late medieval and early modern history is far from slight. Despite the tag 'legal historian', the reason is precisely because '[w]hat interested Maitland was the society behind the legal concepts'.[9]

This chapter's aim is not, as Macfarlane has done, to assess whether Maitland (and thus Macfarlane) was right. Nor is it designed to be hagiographical, for Maitland does not lack admirers. Instead, the intention is to explore the influence of his methodology and preoccupations, his soaring speculations and grand (if compressed and complex) generalizations, on subsequent generations of scholars.[10] As Michael Postan pointed out nearly half a century ago and as Stephen White has reiterated more recently, Maitland did not anticipate all of the most important trends in twentieth-century historical writing – notably, research on demography, the family and gender – although he had important things to say about the last two and he did write of the 'deepening' of history by subjects that 'have burst the political barrier'.[11] In spirit, if not always in interpretation, his impact nevertheless remains strong, albeit sometimes overlooked. His approach, his probing questions (uncovering, if not always explaining) and his preoccupation with society mean that he still has much to offer late medieval and early modern social historians. More than this, many of the best early modern social historians cite his work and some, like Brooks, explicitly acknowledge his influence.

[8] A. Macfarlane, *The Making of the Modern World: Visions from the West and East* (Basingstoke, 2002), p. 120.

[9] Southern, 'Review essay', p. 107. This was not his sole sphere and his later works show a developing interest in political theory.

[10] Macfarlane, *Making*, pp. 121–135; P. Vinogradoff, 'Frederic William Maitland', *English Historical Review* 22 (1907), 280–289; Elton, *Maitland*, pp. 20–26, 97–98.

[11] M. M. Postan, *Fact and Relevance: Essays on Historical Method* (Cambridge, 1971), p. 53; S. D. White, 'Maitland on family and kinship', in J. Hudson (ed.), *The History of English Law: Centenary Essays on 'Pollock and Maitland'* (Oxford, 1996), pp. 91–92. R. Houlbrooke, *The English Family, 1450–1700* (London, 1984), p. 5, notes the seminal importance of Maitland's work on family law, clear even in his own age. A. Macfarlane, *The Origins of English Individualism* (Oxford, 1978), pp. 132–133, 159–160, 192, used Maitland to argue for the strong legal position of women in historic England. For a more nuanced approach to women and the law (and one closer to Maitland), see A. L. Erickson, *Women and Property in Early Modern England* (London, 1993); T. Stretton, *Women Waging Law in Elizabethan England* (Cambridge, 1998), especially pp. 21–24, 36–37.

The boldest of those who follow in Maitland's footsteps have sought to bring out the peculiarities of the English. J. G. A. Pocock argued for Edward Coke's contribution to the 'common-law mind' – an inward-looking, empiricist tradition based on the antiquity of law and custom, which permeated political thought and helped to form English national identity.[12] Others have expanded analysis of the role of common-law thinking on political thought.[13] Maitland cared about origins, but his main interest in comparing was to highlight what England was not. His approach was nevertheless the exact opposite of 'the proud, defensive insularity' of many Victorian scholars, breaking down assumptions about what was normal, natural or even normative, by drawing comparisons with alternative ways of doing things.[14] Maitland modestly recognized 'that fatal disease of contented insularity which so easily besets' the English, and concluded that 'there is nothing that sets a man thinking and writing to such good effect about a system of law and its history as an acquaintance however slight with other systems and their history'.[15] He openly acknowledged the German influence, seeing the history of early English law as part of '*die germanische Rechtsgeschichte*'.[16]

Curious about German roots, Maitland directed his comparative method primarily at illuminating what made England special. Patriotic, rather than nationalist, he also observed: 'I am always feeling that neither Scotland nor England can be known in severalty, and that a great many points will become clear when the Scotch [*sic*] and English stories are properly correlated.'[17] He went so far as to express to one of his correspondents, Glasgow magistrate George Neilson, a wish to spend

[12] J. G. A. Pocock, *The Ancient Constitution and the Feudal Law* (Cambridge, 1957), chs 2 and 3; cf. *Collected Papers*, vol. I, p. 491; F. W. Maitland, *English Law and the Renaissance* (Cambridge, 1901). Maitland broke new ground by seeing the civilians as the progressive tendency in sixteenth- and early-seventeenth-century English law. For critiques of Pocock's views, see J. W. Tubbs, *The Common Law Mind: Medieval and Early Modern Conceptions* (Baltimore, 2000); C. W. Brooks, 'The place of Magna Carta and the ancient constitution in sixteenth-century English legal thought', in E. Sandoz (ed.), *The Roots of Liberty: Magna Carta, Ancient Constitution, and the Anglo-American Tradition of Rule of Law* (Columbia, 1993), pp. 75–114.

[13] G. Burgess, *The Politics of the Ancient Constitution* (Basingstoke, 1992); A. Cromartie, *The Constitutionalist Revolution: An Essay on the History of England, 1450–1642* (Cambridge, 2006).

[14] J. W. Burrow, *A Liberal Descent: Victorian Historians and the English Past* (Cambridge, 1981), p. 109.

[15] *Collected Papers*, vol. III, p. 460; *Collected Papers*, vol. I, p. 489.

[16] *Collected Papers*, vol. III, p. 457; P. N. R. Zutshi (ed.), *The Letters of Frederic William Maitland* (London, 1995) (hereafter *Letters*, vol. II), no. 175.

[17] *Letters*, vol. II, nos 175, 178.

a hypothetical second life 'among your Scotch documents, and this for the sake of England'.[18] Earlier, Maitland had told Neilson: 'I am always wishing that I knew Scotland. I believe that he who knew it would be able to speak some decisive words about English affairs.'[19] Maitland offered tentative comparisons with Scotland alongside reflections on the distinctive legal and administrative history of the north of England, which alert us to the importance of regions in both English and British history. He sponsored, but never contributed to, the *Scottish Historical Review* when Neilson launched it in 1903.[20]

Maitland's aspirations towards a comparative history have guided my own research since I wrote my doctoral thesis and the book partly based on it.[21] More specifically, it was one of Maitland's observations about the similarity between Scotland and the north of England that inspired me:

> [I]t is most curious, Scotch [*sic*] medieval law is to me so French, so Norman – and the change from English to Scottish is not sudden at the border, but is 'mediated' by the condition of our four northern counties, which seem to me the Frenchest part of England. As you travel northward, the hundreds and frank-pledge and murder-fine drop off and the county court changes its character. The further he gets from his lord at Westminster the more Norman, the more French the baron becomes. It seems as if the later infusion of French jurisprudence met a kindred element in Scotland that had been there for a very long time . . . I have long had the dream that Scotland is the link between England and Normandy.[22]

18 *Letters*, vol. II, no. 187. Lack of knowledge of Scotland meant that Maitland had blind spots: J. W. Cairns and G. McLeod, 'Thomas Craig, Sir Martin Wright, and Sir William Blackstone: the English discovery of feudalism', *Journal of Legal History* 21 (2000), 54–66.

19 *Letters*, vol. II, no. 145.

20 *Letters*, vol. II, nos 254, 310. An excellent example of Maitland's 'British' approach is H. L. MacQueen, *Common Law and Feudal Society in Medieval Scotland* (Edinburgh, 1993). Here and elsewhere, MacQueen qualifies Maitland's claims about the similarity of laws north and south of the Tweed. Maitland also wrote (sketchily) about the role of the Scottish Reformation in creating an incipiently British identity: F. W. Maitland, 'The Anglican Settlement and the Scottish Reformation', in A. W. Ward, G. W. Prothero and S. Leathes (eds), *The Cambridge Modern History: The Reformation* (Cambridge, 1903), vol. II, p. 550, which was drawn on in Gordon Donaldson, 'The relations between the English and Scottish Presbyterian movements to 1604', PhD thesis, University of London (1938), f. ii.

21 R.A. Houston, 'Aspects of society in Scotland and north-east England, 1550–1750: social structure, literacy and geographical mobility', PhD thesis, University of Cambridge (1981); R. A. Houston, *Scottish Literacy and the Scottish Identity: Literacy and Society in Scotland and England, 1600–1850* (Cambridge, 1985). See also the debt acknowledged by G. W. S. Barrow, *The Kingdom of the Scots: Government, Church and Society from the Eleventh to the Fourteenth Century* (Edinburgh, 2003 [1973]), pp. 7–8.

22 *Letters*, vol. II, no. 164.

Other historians of Scotland have been influenced by these and comparable insights. Historical geographer Robert Dodgshon is one of the most original contributors of the last generation to understanding late medieval and early modern Scottish agriculture and society. He used Maitland's idea of a shift 'from the vague to the definite' when it came to understanding the development of landholding.[23] Open fields were 'not incompatible with a very perfect individualism, a very complete denial that the village community had any proprietary rights whatever'.[24] Looking at Scottish 'runrig', Dodgshon argued that communalism's significance for landownership had been overstated; Maitland had described community as a 'slippery' and 'nebulous' concept – a product of what Donald R. Kelley terms 'the enthusiasms of Celticists'.[25] Dodgshon also followed Maitland when discussing elsewhere the legally amorphous Highland concept of *duthchas* ('heritage') whereby tacksmen linked to their lord (notionally, at least) by kinship expected a customary right to the hereditary possession of their land. This right was ill-defined and, because it was based on an appeal to fictive kinship and emotion, it was 'antithetical to being prescribed or redacted'.[26] Community might have lacked substance, but it remained significant – as we shall see when discussing the limits on individualism, exploring regionalism and analysing association.

Despite this influence, and partly because of its small historical establishment and focus on specific national issues, Scotland (like Wales) has been less touched by Maitland's ideas than England. He bemoaned the insularity of its historians, which seemed to condemn Scottish history to irrelevance: 'Scotch [*sic*] historians writing about the history of Ecclesiastical Polity are apt to leave unsaid just the very thing that the ignorant southron wants to know – it is all so very trite north of the Tweed, but so very untrite here.'[27] As Colin Kidd has observed, from the time of Maitland until late in the twentieth century, 'Scottish history became a scene of romantic escapism and local color, fenced off from a Whig saga of state formation and constitutional evolution in which the wider experience of the British peoples was collapsed into

[23] *Collected Papers*, vol. II, p. 363.

[24] *Collected papers*, vol. I, p. 361, quoted in R. A. Dodgshon, 'Runrig and the communal origins of property in land', *Juridical Review* 20 (1975), 189–208, p. 191.

[25] F. W. Maitland, *Township and Borough* (Cambridge, 1898), p. 84; D. R. Kelley, *Fortunes of History: Historical Inquiry from Herder to Huizinga* (New Haven, 2003), p. 239.

[26] R. A. Dodgshon, *From Chiefs to Landlords: Social and Economic Change in the Western Highlands* (Edinburgh, 1998), p. 45.

[27] *Letters*, vol. II, no. 165.

the history of England.'[28] Maitland was, in contrast, curious about Scottish law and society, as shown in his correspondence with Neilson.[29] Their friendship arose from Neilson's work on the ordeal and Maitland's interest (among other things) in changing methods of proof by this means and by oaths, as well as the contrast between the development of the jury in English courts and the inquisitorial processes of late medieval justice elsewhere in Europe.

Dodgshon's remarks about *duthchas* come out of another of Maitland's observations. While identifying individualism in early England (if mainly to deny more categorically the existence of communalism), Maitland recognized that 'the influence of groups made itself felt, to a certain extent, in a loose and extra-legal way'.[30] This quotation comes from 'The Laws of Wales' and is perhaps more broadly relevant to what he termed 'the Celtic fringe' in the late Middle Ages and beyond than it is to the English heartland.[31] Yet it applies there too because manorial custom is unintelligible if we ignore social practice and attitudes.[32] Historians have recognized, even for early modern England, the power of a merely moral obligation to take account of the interests of family, 'friends' and other community members in what appears to be legally unlimited economic decision-making by individuals.[33] Lords too exerted important constraints on the development of abstract rights of property,

[28] C. Kidd, 'Scottish historiography', in D. R. Woolf (ed.), *A Global Encyclopaedia of Historical Writing* (London, 1998), p. 822; Elton, *Maitland*, pp. 92–93.

[29] Fifoot, *Maitland*, pp. 101–102; G. Neilson, *Trial by Combat* (Glasgow, 1890).

[30] Maitland, 'The laws of Wales: the kindred and the blood feud', in *Collected Papers*, vol. I, p. 209; Vinogradoff, 'Maitland', p. 286; R. A. Dodgshon, 'The landholding foundations of the open-field system', *Past and Present* 67 (1975), 3–29; R. A. Dodgshon, *Land and Society in Early Scotland* (Oxford, 1981), pp. 110–112.

[31] F. W. Maitland, *Domesday Book and Beyond: Three Essays in the Early History of England* (Cambridge, 1897), p. 16; F. Pollock and F. W. Maitland, *The History of English Law before the Time of Edward I*, two vols (London, 1968), vol. II, pp. 240–248; *Letters*, vol. II, no. 84. It is important to note that, despite this categorization, Maitland eschewed the racial interpretations of both Germanists and some of his Victorian compatriots. He seems to have taken less interest in Ireland, but see *Collected Papers*, vol. II, pp. 81–83, and his lucid summary of similarities and differences between England, Scotland, Ireland and the dominions, with respect to nineteenth-century legal processes, in F. W. Maitland, *Justice and Police* (London, 1885), pp. 3–10.

[32] Stephen D. White and Richard T. Vann, 'The invention of English individualism: Alan Macfarlane and the modernization of pre-modern England', *Social History* 8 (1983), 345–363, p. 356.

[33] G. Sreenivasan, 'The land–family bond at Earls Colne (Essex), 1550–1650', *Past and Present* 131 (1991), 3–37; J. Whittle, 'Individualism and the land–family bond: a reassessment of land transfer patterns among the English peasantry, c. 1270–1580', *Past and Present* 160 (1998), 25–63.

prior to the active intervention of the king's courts in the fifteenth and sixteenth centuries.[34] Individualism existed, but it remained 'rough and rude' in early modern England, as in Scotland and Wales.[35]

Despite his determination to show the relevance of the history of law to English (and British) history as a whole, we may overlook Maitland precisely because of his label as a legal historian. He thought training in modern law 'almost indispensable' for doing good legal history.[36] Historians may, in contrast, perceive the law as dry and impersonal – the largely impenetrable preserve of pettyfoggers.[37] Authority too is different. For historians, it is provided by evidence and context; for lawyers, by texts and judgments. Thus Maitland observed: 'What the lawyer wants is authority and the newer the better; what the historian wants is evidence and the older the better.'[38] Few objected to his analysis until after the Second World War, when history became a larger (and more exclusive) discipline.[39] Since then, historians have become more willing to learn, led by Brooks and others who were adamant that, to interpret (and not to over-interpret) any topic in social history, it was vital to understand its legal aspects. Understanding the law is not, after all, so different from learning a foreign tongue or statistics; it just involves a different language of enumeration and categorization, and, like any language, it helps to create the society it purports to describe or mediate. Maitland himself recognized that 'language is no mere instrument that we can control at will; it controls us'.[40]

Nor is the law necessarily uninteresting. Paul Vinogradoff acknowledged Maitland's extraordinary ability to transform the dry into

[34] Milsom, 'Maitland', pp. 278–279; White and Vann, 'Invention of English individualism', pp. 361–363; R. A. Houston, *Punishing the Dead? Suicide, Lordship, and Community in Britain, 1500–1830* (Oxford, 2010).

[35] Pollock and Maitland, *History of English Law*, vol. I, p. 616; vol. II, p. 247. Vinogradoff later called this 'Maitland's antiquarian individualism': Vinogradoff, 'Maitland', p. 285.

[36] *Collected Papers*, vol. I, p. 493.

[37] C. Holmes, 'G. R. Elton as a legal historian', *Transactions of the Royal Historical Society* 7 (1997), 267–279. As we shall see, Elton's strictures did not prevent him from appreciating the value of legal documents.

[38] *Collected Papers*, vol. I, p. 491.

[39] T. F. T. Plucknett, 'Maitland's view of law and history', *Law Quarterly Review* 67 (1951), 179–194.

[40] Pollock and Maitland, *History of English Law*, vol. I, p. 87; J. G. A. Pocock, 'The concept of language and the *métier d'historien*: some considerations on practice', in A. Pagden (ed.), *The Languages of Political Theory in Early-Modern Europe* (Cambridge, 1987), pp. 19–40, stresses the importance of semantics and properly contextualized meanings in historical analysis.

something 'curiously attractive through the reflexion of a kind of organic process in the mind of the scholar creating order and sense in the midst of confusion'.[41] As Marc Bloch put it: '[S]een in Maitland's way, could the history of law be anything other than a particularly vivid chapter of social history?'[42] Maitland focused closely on the individual and the particular: '[W]hat he wanted most was to trace ideas to their embodiment in facts' – to 'transform abstract analysis into the living experience of real people'.[43] Part of his success in doing so lay in his sense of place – of landscape as narrative – which is another area of influence. His concern with 'that marvellous palimpsest ... the testimony of our fields and walls and hedges' inspired important mid-twentieth-century historians such as W. G. Hoskins and M. W. Beresford to get mud on their boots.[44] Hoskins, in particular, wrote of 'trying to enter into the minds of the first men to break into a virgin landscape' by picking away 'the cultural humus of sixty generations'.[45] Hoskins' methods – including getting the landscape to speak to him – were central to the emergence of English local history in the 1940s and 1950s, and to its subsequent influence on the 'new social history' from the 1960s onwards.[46]

One might even argue that knowledge of the law is essential to understanding early modern people, because it was so deeply imbricated in day-to-day life as to make society almost law-bound.[47] To take just

41 Vinogradoff, 'Maitland', p. 287.

42 M. Bloch, 'Review of *Collected Papers*', *Annales* 10 (1938), 138–139 (author's translation).

43 Vinogradoff, 'Maitland', p. 282; Elton, *Maitland*, p. 31.

44 Maitland, *Domesday Book*, pp. 15–16. Maitland used the manorial and fiscal geography of Domesday Book to get at the 'physical and villar geography': ibid., p. 1. See also H. M. Cam, 'Introduction', in H. M. Cam (ed.), *Selected Historical Essays of F. W. Maitland* (Cambridge, 1957), pp. xii–xiii; W. G. Hoskins, *The Making of the English Landscape* (London, 1955); W. G. Hoskins, *Local History in England* (London, 1959), p. 38; W. G. Hoskins, *Fieldwork in Local History* (London, 1969), pp. 17, 117; M. W. Beresford, *History on the Ground: Six Studies in Maps and Landscapes* (London, 1957); M. W. Beresford, *Time and Place: An Inaugural Lecture* (Leeds, 1961), pp. 21–22.

45 Hoskins, *Making*, pp. 18, 235. See also the parallel influence of geographers such as H. C. Darby: H. C. Darby, *The Draining of the Fens* (Cambridge, 1940); H. C. Darby, 'On the relations of geography and history', *Transactions and Papers (Institute of British Geographers)* 19 (1953), 1–11; H. C. Darby, *Domesday England* (Cambridge, 1977).

46 C. P. Lewis, 'The great awakening of English local history, 1918–1939', in C. Dyer, A. Hopper and E. Lord (eds), *New Directions in Local History since Hoskins* (Hatfield, 2011), pp. 47–48; D. Matless, 'Doing the English village, 1945–90: an essay in imaginative geography', in P. J. Cloke, M. Doel, D. Matless, M. Phillips and N. J. Thrift, *Writing the Rural: Five Cultural Geographies* (London, 1994), pp. 7–88.

47 J. A. Sharpe, '"Such disagreement betwyx neighbours": litigation and human relations in early modern England', in J. Bossy (ed.), *Disputes and Settlements: Law and Human Relations in the West* (Cambridge, 1983), pp. 172–187; J. A. Sharpe, 'The People and the

three, Martin Ingram, Laura Gowing and Garthine Walker, none of them formally trained in the law, exemplify how the best scholars have transcended Maitland's worry about the 'large and fertile tracts of history which the historian has to avoid because they are too legal'.[48] These three are, of course, historians of crime, broadly construed as analysing what dysfunction within communities tells us about the normal workings of society. Of the three, only Ingram can be said to work on the social history of the law, as opposed to using legal records to study social and cultural topics.[49] Yet Brooks more closely followed Maitland's lead, by focusing on the civil law, which worked at the heart of economic and social relationships to exert a direct influence on everyday mentalities and material life.

Leaving aside Fitzjames Stephen's Victorian outline of the origins and development of the criminal law, court procedures and punishment, modern work on the administration of English criminal justice, in whose footsteps our last three examples follow, started at Cambridge in the 1930s and 1940s through alliances between historically informed lawyers (most notably, Leon Radzinowicz) and those with a background in criminal law (such as Cecil Turner).[50] This field did not, however, become mainstream for early modernists until the 1970s, with the work

Law', in B. Reay (ed.), *Popular Culture in Seventeenth-Century England* (London, 1985), pp. 244–270; C. W. Brooks, *Pettyfoggers and Vipers of the Commonwealth: The Lower Branch of the Legal Profession in Early Modern England* (Cambridge, 1986); C. W. Brooks, *Lawyers, Litigation, and English Society since 1450* (London, 1998); C. W. Brooks, *Law, Politics and Society in Early Modern England* (Cambridge, 2008).

48 *Collected Papers*, vol. I, p. 486; M. Ingram, *Church Courts, Sex and Marriage in England, 1570–1640* (Cambridge, 1987); J. Kermode and G. Walker (eds), *Women, Crime and the Courts in Early Modern England* (London, 1994); L. Gowing, *Domestic Dangers: Women, Words and Sex in Early Modern London* (Oxford, 1996).

49 Ingram and Gowing work mainly on church courts, the first set of judicial records to receive attention from social historians of the law in the mid-twentieth century: B. L. Woodcock, *Medieval Ecclesiastical Courts in the Diocese of Canterbury* (London, 1952); R. A. Marchant, *The Church under the Law: Justice, Administration and Discipline in the Diocese of York, 1560–1640* (London, 1969).

50 J. F. Stephen, *A History of the Criminal Law of England*, three vols (London, 1883); L. Radzinowicz, *A History of English Criminal Law and Its Administration from 1750*, five vols (vol. 5 with R. Hood) (London, 1948–1986); B. P. Smith, 'English criminal justice administration, 1650–1850: a historiographic essay', *Law and History Review* 25 (2007), 604–608; J. Innes and J. Styles, 'The crime wave: recent writing on crime and criminal justice in eighteenth-century England', in A. Wilson (ed.), *Rethinking Social History: English Society, 1570–1920, and Its Interpretation* (Manchester, 1993), pp. 201–265.

of James Sharpe, Keith Wrightson and others.[51] Perhaps the brightest flowering was among what some now term 'the Warwick school', including Douglas Hay and Peter Linebaugh. Enthusiasm, imagination and ideological commitment marked out its members, but those who come under its umbrella did learn from, and in turn stimulate, others more in the mould of Maitland, such as John Beattie.[52] Elite North American law schools, to one of which Beattie latterly belonged, are more likely to teach comparative and interdisciplinary courses of the kind that spawned those who would have pleased Maitland than are many modern English and Welsh (although not Scottish) university law departments, which take a largely vocational approach.[53] Law schools in North America teach graduates, whose first degrees cover many disciplines, whereas legal education in England and Wales is mainly undergraduate. We might also observe that, for much of the last century, North American scholars were more open to interdisciplinary influences from the human sciences, broadly construed, than were their British counterparts.[54]

Among those associated with Warwick (and perhaps more broadly in this field), the closest follower of Maitland was, perhaps surprisingly, E. P. Thompson, whose thoughts on 'the rule of law' at the end of *Whigs and Hunters* echoed those of his political polar opposite, G. R. Elton. What united them (apart from respect for Maitland) was a belief in the accessibility and potential impartiality of the law – although, for Thompson, its broadly political dimension, 'both as ideology and as

[51] When writing an early synthesis, Sharpe likened the state of his subject to what Maitland said about legal history in 'Why the history of English law is not written': J. A. Sharpe, *Crime in Early Modern England 1550–1750* (London, 1984), p. 14.

[52] Douglas Hay, Peter Linebaugh, John G. Rule, E. P. Thompson and Carl Winslow, 'Preface', in *Albion's Fatal Tree: Crime and Society in Eighteenth-Century England* (London, 1975), pp. 1–13, at p. 13; J. M. Beattie, *Crime and the Courts in England, 1660–1800* (Oxford, 1986). See also the reaction to the arguments of *Albion's Fatal Tree* in J. H. Langbein, 'Albion's fatal flaws', *Past and Present* 98 (1983), 96–120; P. King, *Crime, Justice, and Discretion in England, 1740–1820* (Oxford, 2000).

[53] C. Donahue, 'Comparative legal history in North America', *Tijdschrift voor Rechtsgeschiedenis* 65 (1997), 1–17; J. W. Cairns, 'National, transnational and European legal histories: problems and paradigms – a Scottish perspective', *Clio@Themis* 5 (2014).

[54] For example, Maitland corresponded with Charles Gross about social and economic history, starting in 1893: *Letters*, vol. I, no. 124; C. Gross (ed.), *Select Cases from the Coroners' Rolls A.D. 1265–1413* (London, 1896). It is also significant in this context that Christopher W. Brooks was an American and his first PhD supervisor, Wilfrid Prest, an Australian: see C. W. Brooks, 'Introduction', in *Lawyers, Litigation, and English Society*, pp. 2, 5; W. R. Prest, 'Legal history in Australian law schools: 1982 and 2005', *Adelaide Law Review* 27 (2006), 167–177; H. Lücke, 'Legal history in Australia: the development of Australian legal/historical scholarship', *Australian Bar Review* 34 (2010), 109–148.

actuality', was also important and its practical workings were subject to manipulation and abuse.[55] While nodding towards rule *by* law, rather than the rule *of* law, Thompson averred that 'the history of law does matter and is a very subtle and complex question'.[56] His 'moral economy' was, for example, founded on custom and practice, but it was also based on shared understandings and uses of the law; protest was a (lower) part of English constitutionalism.[57] Subsequent work on English juries – and on topics such as the changing criteria of trust and proof – builds on Maitland's remark that the common law accepted 'the rough verdict of the countryside, without caring to investigate the logical processes, if logical they were, of which that verdict was the outcome'.[58] This development was the basis of an early shift in England from private criminal appeals towards a more centralized public system of criminal prosecution.[59]

Far more of Maitland's work was about the civil law than the criminal. From the premise that '[l]aw was the point where life and logic met', he sought to unravel medieval society by understanding how people gained access to land, studying 'the interdependences of law and economic

55 Hay et al., 'Preface', p. 13; E. P. Thompson, *Whigs and Hunters: The Origin of the Black Act* (London, 1975), p. 266 (pronouncing the rule of law to be 'an unqualified human good'); E. P. Thompson, 'The poverty of theory: or an orrery of errors', in *The Poverty of Theory, & Other Essays* (London, 1978), pp. 193–397, at p. 288; G. R. Elton, 'The rule of law in sixteenth-century England', in A. J. Slavin (ed.), *Tudor Men and Institutions: Studies in English Law and Government* (Baton Rouge, 1972), pp. 265–294; H. J. Kaye, *The British Marxist Historians: An Introductory Analysis* (Cambridge, 1984), pp. 194–197, 203–205.

56 M. Merrill, 'Interview with E. P. Thompson', in H. Abelove, B. Blackmare, P. Dimock and J. Schneer (eds), *Visions of History* (Manchester, 1976), pp. 3–26, at p. 9; Thompson, *Whigs and Hunters*, pp. 266–268. Thompson also distanced himself from Christopher Hill, who regarded the law as a crude instrument of oppression and exploitation: C. Hill, *Liberty against the Law: Some Seventeenth-Century Controversies* (London, 1996), p. 338.

57 E. P. Thompson, 'The moral economy of the English crowd in the eighteenth century', *Past and Present* 50 (1971), 76–136; E. P. Thompson, *The Making of the English Working Class* (London, 1963), pp. 62–76.

58 Pollock and Maitland, *History of English Law*, vol. II, pp. 660–661; T. A. Green, *Verdict According to Conscience: Perspectives on the English Criminal Trial Jury, 1200–1800* (Chicago, 1985); J. W. Cairns and G. MacLeod (eds), *The Dearest Birth Right of the People of England: The Jury in the History of the Common Law* (Oxford, 2002).

59 Pollock and Maitland, *History of English Law*, vol. I, pp. 137–144. The contrast with the 'Celtic fringe' has prompted studies of the continuing role of private direct action there: R. R. Davies, 'The survival of the bloodfeud in medieval Wales', *History* 54 (1969), 338–357; J. Wormald, 'Bloodfeud, kindred and government in early modern Scotland', *Past and Present* 87 (1980), 54–97; K. M. Brown, *Bloodfeud in Scotland, 1573–1625: Violence, Justice and Politics in Early Modern Society* (Edinburgh, 1986).

fact'.[60] From R. H. Tawney until the 1980s, much of the history of early modern society and economy was likewise an analysis of tenures.[61] Progressivists such as Tawney and Eileen Power were especially important in pushing forward this agenda. Realizing the potential of legally informed study, they moved fifteenth- and sixteenth-century history towards society and its institutions.[62] Like Maitland, Power 'heard the people [s]he was writing about' and her efforts carried into the early generations of 'new social historians'.[63] Others influenced by Maitland contributed strongly to manorial, tenurial and broader legal history, not only in the United Kingdom, but also in North America. Helen Cam, for example, was devoted to Maitland (and to William Stubbs and Vinogradoff), first during her time at Cambridge and then at Harvard.[64] A year working with Maitland at Cambridge, while he was writing *Domesday Book and Beyond*, influenced Nellie Neilson's work on Ramsey Abbey, as it did her wider studies of land use, and of the relationship between diverse local custom and the development of common law.[65]

Maitland's work was, however, far from exclusively about 'law and economic fact'. He implicitly rejected the nominalist reductionism inherent in Marxism – that is, the idea that all human action can ultimately be

[60] F. W. Maitland, 'Introduction', in F. W. Maitland (ed.), *Year Books of Edward II* (London, 1903), vol. I, p. xxxiii. He meant the use of language by lawyers who 'mediated between the abstract Latin logic of the schoolmen and the concrete needs and homely talk of gross, unschooled mankind' (ibid., p. xxxvii). The latter phrase in the body of the text describes Vinogradoff, but applies equally to Maitland: D. P. Heatley, *Studies in British History and Politics* (London, 1913), p. 140.

[61] See, e.g., *Letters*, vol. II, no. 361, about why Scotland had no copyhold: R. H. Tawney, *The Agrarian Problem in the Sixteenth Century* (London, 1912); M. Spufford, *Contrasting Communities: English Villagers in the Sixteenth and Seventeenth Centuries* (Cambridge, 1974). The Marxist account of 'rent' as an economic category in Keith Tribe, *Land, Labour and Economic Discourse* (London, 1978), pp. 27–34, is based largely on Maitland.

[62] Maxine Berg, 'The first women economic historians', *Economic History Review* 45 (1992), 308–329, p. 322; Maxine Berg, *A Woman in History: Eileen Power, 1889–1940* (Cambridge, 1996), pp. 112–113, 202–205; E. Power, *Medieval People* (London, 1924).

[63] ODNB.

[64] J. Sondheimer, 'Helen Maud Cam, 1885–1968', in E. Shils and C. Blacker (eds), *Cambridge Women: Twelve Portraits* (Cambridge, 1996), pp. 93–112, at pp. 102, 104; E. Taylor and G. Weaver, 'Helen Cam, 1885–1968', in J. Chance (ed.), *Women Medievalists and the Academy* (Madison, 2005), pp. 255–272; H. M. Cam, *Law-Finders and Law-Makers in Medieval England: Collected Studies in Legal and Constitutional History* (London, 1962).

[65] N. Neilson, *Economic Conditions on the Manors of Ramsey Abbey* (Philadelphia, 1899); M. Hastings and E. G. Kimball, 'Two distinguished medievalists: Nellie Neilson and Bertha Putnam', *Journal of British Studies* 18 (1979), 142–159.

reduced to basic motivations such as greed and control over others, and that only concrete forces such as economics matter.[66] Instead, he identified voluntary association as a hallmark of English national development – the group life exemplified in churches, sodalities, clubs, trade unions, and even hospital and asylum boards contributing to social cohesion as much as did individualism or the state. Associations mixed public and private, showing, for Maitland, the instinct for cooperation in a pluralistic model of English political development. He called it 'corporateness' – that is, the permanent existence of a constituted group whose members changed, creating 'a living organism and a real person, with body and members and a will of its own'.[67] These associations had no formal legal status, but enjoyed rights inherent in their role in communities, through a trust that 'embodies a contract about how property is to be deployed'.[68] There was a strong 'drive to association', especially, but not exclusively, in the north and west of the United Kingdom.[69]

Maitland – and others among those whom Anthony Black calls English 'guild socialists' – admired nineteenth-century German jurist Otto von Gierke's vision of 'the identity of state and people' – 'the constitutional state' – and his hope to maintain the autonomy of 'the lesser communities of public law', such as the town and guild, in an era of territorial sovereignty, rampant nationalism and burgeoning central power.[70] A Liberal and legal reformer, Maitland may not have been overtly

[66] For reactions against this approach among recent scholars, see, e.g., K. Wrightson, *Ralph Tailor's Summer: A Scrivener, His City and the Plague* (New Haven, 2011); L. A. Pollock, 'The practice of kindness in early modern elite society', *Past and Present* 211 (2011), 121–158.

[67] F. W. Maitland, 'The corporation sole', *Law Quarterly Review* 16 (1900), 335–354; Otto von Gierke, *Political Theories of the Middle Ages*, trans. with an introduction by F. W. Maitland (Cambridge, 1900), p. xxvi; S. J. Stoljar, 'The corporate theories of F. W. Maitland', in L. C. Webb (ed.), *Legal Personality and Political Pluralism* (Melbourne, 1958), pp. 20–44.

[68] J. H. Langbein, 'The contractarian basis of the law of trusts', *Yale Law Journal* 105 (1995), 625–675, p. 671.

[69] S. Reynolds, *Kingdoms and Communities in Western Europe, 900–1300* (Oxford, 1997 [1984]), pp. 77, 138; R. Davies, 'Kinsmen, neighbours, and communities in Wales and the Western British Isles, 1100–1400', in P. Stafford, J. L. Nelson and J. Martindale (eds), *Law, Laity, and Solidarities: Essays in Honour of Susan Reynolds* (Manchester, 2001), pp. 172–187. Association is discussed more fully later in the chapter.

[70] A. Black, *Guilds and Civil Society in European Political Thought from the Twelfth Century to the Present* (London, 1984), p. 216. Other labels for those with similar, if not identical, interests include Christian or Fabian socialists: M. Grimley, *Citizenship, Community, and the Church of England: Liberal Anglican Theories of the State between the Wars* (Oxford, 2004), pp. 65–69.

expressive about politics, narrowly construed, but his edition of Gierke made a subtle political statement about the role of active citizenship in English constitutionalism and English life.[71] At once descriptive and didactic, he took sides, just as those in his writings fought their corners.[72]

Yet there was a tension here, because the history of the rise of the common law taught by Maitland was one of unusual centralization, the source of law being a central one (the king and his legal entourage). Elton's approach to centralization also privileged the state, but because of his background as a central European émigré and a liberal British conservative. And he wrote in a British context in which the rule of law had been largely subordinated to policy created by legislatures and enforced by bureaucracies and constabulary.[73] For Maitland, the Crown was important to the origin of certain liberties, such as trial by jury, *habeas corpus*, the king's law (common to all) and even Parliament. Local government was, however, just as important as high politics, the manor as significant in its own way as the King's Council in making England 'a much governed nation' ruled with the consent of citizens who had positive, as well as negative, duties.[74] Neither syndicalist nor doctrinaire utilitarian, Maitland's views reflected Victorian debates on the place of individual, community and state, including revisiting Tudor concerns about the relationship between locality and the emergence of both state and nation.[75]

[71] Elton, *Maitland*, pp. 15–16; J. Stapleton, 'English pluralism as cultural definition: the social and political thought of George Unwin', *Journal of the History of Ideas* 52 (1991), 665–684. There is a curiously scornful analysis of Maitland's attitudes to politics and religion in M. Cowling, *Religion and Public Doctrine in Modern England, Vol. 3: Accommodations* (Cambridge, 2001), pp. 469–477.

[72] ODNB.

[73] J. H. Baker, *An Introduction to English Legal History* (2nd edn, London, 1979), p. 131. We might also note Garthine Walker's identification of Elton's unwitting espousal of modernization theory: G. Walker, 'Modernization', in *Writing Early Modern History* (London, 2005), pp. 33–35; M. Bentley, *Modernizing England's Past: English Historiography in the Age of Modernism, 1870–1970* (Cambridge, 2005). Elton did not 'do' locality and his work largely lacks a sense of place: P. Collinson, 'Geoffrey Rudolph Elton, 1921–1994', *Proceedings of the British Academy* 94 (1997), 429–455, p. 436.

[74] F. W. Maitland, *The Constitutional History of England* (Cambridge, 1908), pp. 501, 505; Maitland, 'The shallows and silences of real life', in *Collected Papers*, vol. I, pp. 467–479.

[75] C. Dewey, 'Images of the village community: a study in Anglo-Indian ideology', *Modern Asian Studies* 6 (1972), 323–327; S. Webb and B. Webb, *English Local Government from the Revolution to the Municipal Corporations Act*, eleven vols (London, 1906–1929). With an acute eye for paradoxes, Maitland noted that 'village communists' like Stubbs and Maine were 'men of the most conservative type', whereas a defender of individual property rights like Frederic Seebohm was a 'thorough liberal': H. A. L. Fisher,

Recent interpretations of early modern political change more closely follow Maitland than Elton, emphasizing the participation of England's people in the standardization of government, and especially the role of unpaid officials and local associations in filling the spaces of civil society between 'Man and state'.[76] As Maitland observed, '[a]lmost every well-to-do-man was a trustee' – an amateur 'statesman' participating in these intermediate unions.[77] Political development for Maitland and for those who follow him, such as Michael Braddick, Steve Hindle and Phil Withington, was a story of reciprocal, if increasingly unequal, relationships in negotiating change.[78]

Part of this greater concern with local government has been a revival of interest in the manor on the part of early modernists, who had once followed Maitland and written it off as moribund by the sixteenth century.[79] The parish too has become a focus for scholars.[80] This

*Frederick William Maitland, Downing Professor of the Laws of England: A Biographical Sketch* (Cambridge, 1910), p. 49; C. H. S. Fifoot, *Law and History in the Nineteenth Century* (London, 1956), pp. 8, 12–16, believed that contemporary concerns with ethics, evolution and educating society weakened the scholarship of Maitland and others.

76 Maitland, 'Moral personality and legal personality', in *Collected Papers*, vol. III, 311; Pollock and Maitland, *History of English Law*, vol. I, p. 688.

77 F. W. Maitland, 'Trust and corporation', in H. D. Hazeltine, G. Lapsley and P. H. Winfield (eds), *Maitland: Selected Essays* (Cambridge, 1936), pp. 141–222, at p. 175; cf. M. Goldie, 'The unacknowledged republic: officeholding in early modern England', in T. Harris (ed.), *The Politics of the Excluded, c.1500–1850* (Basingstoke, 2001), pp. 153–194.

78 M. Braddick, *State Formation in Early Modern England, c.1550–1700* (Cambridge, 2000); S. Hindle, *The State and Social Change in Early Modern England, 1550–1640* (Basingstoke, 2000); P. Withington, *The Politics of Commonwealth: Citizens and Freemen in Early Modern England* (Cambridge, 2005).

79 F. W. Maitland, 'Leet and Tourne', in H. M. Cam (ed.), *Selected Historical Essays of F. W. Maitland* (Cambridge, 1957), pp. 41–51, at p. 41; M. Griffiths, 'Kirtlington Manor Court, 1500–1650', *Oxoniensia* 45 (1980), 260–283; M. McIntosh, *A Community Transformed: The Manor and Liberty of Havering, 1500–1620* (Cambridge, 1991); C. Harrison, 'Manor courts and the governance of Tudor England', in C. W. Brooks and M. Lobban (eds), *Communities and Courts in Britain, 1150–1900* (London, 1997), pp. 43–60. Brooks, *Law, Politics and Society*, contains extensive discussion of manor (and church) courts. See also P. Holdsworth, 'Manorial administration in Westmorland, 1589-1693', *Transactions of the Cumberland & Westmorland Antiquarian & Archaeological Society*, 3rd ser. 5 (2005), 137–164; B. Waddell, 'Governing England through the manor courts, 1550–1850', *Historical Journal* 55 (2012), 279–315. This development is an interesting example in which Maitland still influences early modern history, even when apparently wrong.

80 S. Hindle, 'A sense of place? Becoming and belonging in the rural parish, 1550–1650', in Alexandra Shepard and Phil Withington (eds), *Communities in Early Modern England* (Manchester, 2000), pp. 96–114, at p. 100; B. A. Kümin, *The Shaping of a Community: The Rise and Reformation of the English Parish, c. 1400–1560* (Aldershot, 1996); A. J. L. Winchester, 'Dividing Lines in a moorland landscape: territorial boundaries in

historiographical trend – a sort of institutional 'history from below' – originated in the 1860s with the work of Gierke, whom Maitland later introduced to English scholarship. Particularly important were Gierke's ideas about the progressive dialectic between the horizontal principle of *Genossenschaft* (association or fellowship) and the hierarchical one of *Herrschaft* (lordship or sovereignty).[81] Walter Ullmann later conceptualized these as 'ascending' and 'descending' ideas of authority, seeing a shift from the former to the latter in the late Middle Ages and beyond.[82] Yet participation, dialogue and selective appropriation long remained important to political culture at the level of villages and towns, even within a theory and practice of governance in which external authority and its agencies (such as select vestries and parish constables as local administrators for justices of the peace) were increasingly intrusive and demanding.[83]

Maitland was, however, sceptical of Victorian aspirations for a 'science of the body politic', seeking instead quietly to scale down sociology to something more human.[84] Because of the way in which it developed, law almost displaced sociology. As Ullmann observed: 'By viewing law as a social phenomenon, medieval jurisprudence was forced to elucidate some basic principles about society, and was thus led to consider topics which, under modern conditions, would be dealt with, not by the lawyer, but by the sociologist.'[85] Maitland also remarked, more forthrightly: 'My own belief is that by and by anthropology will have the choice between being history and being nothing.'[86] His concern was with

upland England', *Landscapes* 1 (2000), 16–34; K. L. French, *The People of the Parish: Community Life in a Late Medieval English Diocese* (Philadelphia, 2001); N. J. G. Pounds, *A History of the English Parish: The Culture of Religion from Augustine to Victoria* (Cambridge, 2000); K. D. M. Snell, *Parish and Belonging: Community, Identity and Welfare in England and Wales, 1700–1950* (Cambridge, 2006).

81 Black, *Guilds and Civil Society*, p. 28, translates *Genossenschaft* as 'comradeship'.

82 O. von Gierke, *Community in Historical Perspective*, ed. A. Black (Cambridge, 1990), pp. 9–10; W. Ullmann, *Principles of Government and Politics in the Middle Ages* (2nd edn, New York, 1966), p. 19.

83 A. B. White, *Self-Government at the King's Command: A Study in the Beginnings of English Democracy* (London, 1933).

84 F. W. Maitland, 'The body politic', in H. D. Hazeltine, G. Lapsley and P. H. Winfield (eds), *Maitland: Selected Essays* (Cambridge, 1936), pp. 240–256.

85 W. Ullmann, *The Medieval Idea of Law as Represented by Lucas de Penna* (London, 1946), p. 163.

86 Hazeltine et al., *Maitland: Selected Essays*, p. 249. The rehistoricization of social anthropology is now very evident, for example in E. Gellner, *Nations and Nationalism* (Oxford, 1988), and J. Goody, *The European Family* (Oxford, 2000). See also D. M. Varisco, '*Pars pro toto* observation: historical anthropology in the textual field of Rasulid Yemen',

simplified, speculative, unilinear models of human evolution current in the late nineteenth century, but we may wonder if his thought lay behind Thompson's acerbic review of *The Family Life of Ralph Josselin* – notably, his condemnation of Macfarlane's 'lumpish and unsubtle' sociological categories.[87] After all, the founding editors of *Past and Present* had already described sociology as dangerous for history.[88] Thompson also chafed against the sharp edges of structural Marxism, preferring (as did Maitland) to stick with the agency of real people, using law.[89]

Thompson sought to distance himself further from another important current in post-war history, the *Annales*. He dismissed this school's rejection of immediate legal (and political) dimensions of historical experience in favour of the determining role of long-term demographic and other material formations.[90] The *Annales* movement arose from late-nineteenth-century continental currents within geography, economics, sociology and anthropology, as well as history, which also touched British shores.[91] Bloch, for his part, had plainly read some of Maitland – remarking on his wish to write history that would make the reader hungry to learn and using the 'retrogressive method' of *Domesday Book* – but found that his approach had less to offer medieval French social history, because England was so different.[92] Bloch's agenda was also different and, for all

*History and Anthropology* 26 (2015), 92–109. W. I. Miller, 'Review of John Bossy, ed., *Disputes and Settlements: Law and Human Relations in the West* (1983)', *American Journal of Legal History* 30 (1986), 266–268, neatly turns Maitland round to show what social history, and social and legal anthropology, have done for legal history since the 1970s.

87 E. P. Thompson, 'Anthropology and the discipline of historical context', *Midland History* 1 (1972), 41–55, p. 54. Thompson also attacked the use of dichotomies, which have been embedded in disciplines such as sociology since the days of Henry Maine, Ferdinand Tönnies and Emile Durkheim, and 'which as polarities are linked by processes of irreversible, sequential change': ibid.

88 The Editors, 'Introduction', *Past and Present* 1 (1952), i–iv, p. ii; R. Samuel and G. Stedman Jones, 'Sociology and history', *History Workshop Journal* 1 (1976), 6–8; M. Braddick, 'The early modern English state and the question of differentiation, from 1550 to 1700', *Comparative Studies in Society & History* 38 (1996), 92–111.

89 Thompson, 'The poverty of theory'.

90 Thompson, *Whigs and Hunters*, p. 268; Merrill, 'Interview with E. P. Thompson', p. 9.

91 Other early twentieth-century British scholars also influenced the *Annales*. For example, Tawney was a sponsor of the new journal in 1929: Kelley, *Fortunes of History*, p. 321; L. Goldman, *The Life of R. H. Tawney: Socialism and History* (London, 2013).

92 M. Bloch, 'Mémoire collective', *Revue de Synthèse Historique* 40 (1925), 73–83, p. 81; Bloch, 'Review of *Collected Papers*', pp. 138–139; M. Bloch, *Feudal Society*, trans. L. A. Manyon (London, 1961), pp. xx–xxi, 429–431. Bloch approved of Maitland's comparative method and regretted, in the 1920s, that he was not more widely read in France. D. R. Kelley, *Frontiers of History: Historical Inquiry in the Twentieth Century*

his interest in continuities and coherences, Maitland set the tone for later English social history more clearly than did the *immobilisme* and *determinisme* of the *Annalistes*, including an enduring and distinctive interest in 'politics, power, conflict, change', which they largely ignored.[93] Because he 'thought orthodox history a contradiction in terms', Maitland was able to offer his own lasting alternative: a different version of 'total history' over the 'long term'.[94]

Maitland's method has also lingered longer when understanding the mental world of English people – what he called 'their common thoughts about common things' and later historians generally term 'popular attitudes'.[95] Cam, paraphrasing Trevelyan, said that Maitland 'uses law as a tool to open the mind of medieval man'.[96] Maitland accepted the rationality of what were very different modes of thought, and he studied them 'seriously and systematically'.[97] This distinguished him from near-contemporaries such as Dutch historian Johann Huizinga, who offered a phenomenological analysis of pre-Renaissance structures of consciousness as they focused on ritual, assuming medieval mentalities to be imperfect in emotion, imagination and reason.[98] More modern French

(New Haven, 2006), pp. 116, 138, thinks that Bloch owed much to Maitland (and Pirenne), while G. Lefebvre, 'Review of Cam, *Selected Historical Essays*', *Annales* 16 (1961), 175–177, agreed with her that Maitland had been better appreciated on the continent than in United Kingdom, in the half-century since his death: G. Le Bras, 'Le sens de la vie dans l'histoire du droit: l'oeuvre de F. W. Maitland', *Annales d'Histoire Economique et Sociale* 7 (1930), 279–301.

93 J. Obelkevich, 'New developments in history in the 1950s and 1960s', *Contemporary British History* 14 (2000), 125–142, p. 135; G. Bouchard, *Le village immobile, Sennely-en-Sologne au XVIIIe siècle* (Paris, 1972); P. Burke and E. J. Hobsbawm, 'Reflections on the historical revolution in France: the Annales school and British social history', *Review (Fernand Braudel Center)* 1 (1978), 147–164. Maitland also recognized the oligarchic nature of the government of the manor, parish and borough – something that the German historical school had played down:. Maitland, *Domesday Book*, pp. 406–415. K. Wrightson and D. Levine, *Poverty and Piety in an English Village: Terling, 1525–1700* (London, 1979), is the most noteworthy realization of this insight among early modernists. It is interesting that Wrightson's pupils have been leaders in reintroducing law into social history: see, e.g., P. Griffiths, A. Fox and S. Hindle (eds), *The Experience of Authority in Early Modern England* (Basingstoke, 1996).

94 ODNB; *Collected Papers*, vol. I, pp. 485, 491–492.

95 Maitland, *Domesday Book*, p. 520; K. Thomas, *The Ends of Life: Roads to Fulfilment in Early Modern England* (Oxford, 2009), p. 1, speaks for countless early modernists when he prefaces his study with Maitland's aspiration that 'the thoughts of our forefathers . . . will become thinkable once more'.

96 Cam, 'Introduction', p. xii.

97 Southern, 'Review essay', 108.

98 J. Huizinga, *The Waning of the Middle Ages: A Study of the Forms of Life, Thought and Art in France and the Netherlands in the Fourteenth and Fifteenth Centuries* (London, 1924,

historians of early modern 'popular culture' largely continued along this line, treating the ideas and practices they observed as inherently absurd.[99] Maitland's approach was more relativist, reading the documents closely for what they actually said about underlying mindsets.

Maitland was not at ease with religious history, although some of those influenced by him made good use of his methods to illuminate faith and its context.[100] The best recent scholars of practical religion before and after the Reformation, such as Ronald Hutton and Eamon Duffy, employ the same kinds of legal sources as Maitland – notably, churchwardens' accounts[101] – and they share with Maitland an ability to appreciate the importance of religious belief in a very different material and intellectual context, without necessarily possessing faith themselves.[102] Mary Bateson wrote on religion, even if her work on boroughs was far more important.[103] Maitland's influence is clearer in this last field, and he and Charles Gross were the 'true founders' of modern urban history – especially its institutional side.[104]

One might conclude by pondering what Maitland would have made of postmodern influences on the writing of early modern history –

[1919]); J. Huizinga, *Homo Ludens: A Study of the Play-element in Culture*, trans. R. F. C. Hull (London, 1944 [1938]). The founding editors of *Past and Present* may have had this approach in mind when dismissing 'psychological maladjustments' as an explanation of *anything* historical, let alone change: The Editors, 'Introduction', p. ii.

99 S. Clark, 'French historians and early modern popular culture', *Past and Present* 100 (1983), 62–99. See, e.g., J. Delumeau, *Sin and Fear: The Emergence of a Western Guilt Culture, 13th–18th Centuries*, trans. E. Nicholson (New York, 1991[1983]).

100 ODNB.

101 E. Duffy, *The Stripping of the Altars: Traditional Religion in England c.1400–c.1580* (London, 1992); R. Hutton, *The Rise and Fall of Merry England: The Ritual Year, 1400–1700* (Oxford, 1994); R. Hutton, *The Stations of the Sun: A History of the Ritual Year in Britain* (Oxford, 1996).

102 Fifoot, *Maitland*, pp. 179–181, 219–226; F. W. Maitland, *Roman Canon Law in the Church of England: Six Essays* (London, 1898), p. vi; *Letters*, vol. I, no. 418; *Letters*, vol. II, no. 12. Where Maitland was playfully agnostic and anti-clerical, Duffy wears his Catholic faith openly and Hutton does not seem to wear anything religious at all. Maitland nevertheless recognized the importance of the church in bringing about important changes, such as the gradual demise of slavery and the ending of trial by combat and ordeal: Maitland, *Domesday Book*, pp. 23–36.

103 M. Bateson (ed.), *Records of the Borough of Leicester*, seven vols (Cambridge, 1899–1905); M. Bateson (ed.), *Borough Customs*, two vols (London, 1904–1906); Brundage and Cosgrove, *Great Tradition*, pp. 191–192.

104 D. M. Palliser, 'Introduction', in D. M. Palliser (ed.), *The Cambridge Urban History of Britain, Vol. 1, c. 600–c. 1540* (Cambridge, 2000), p. 8. This follows H. J. Dyos, 'Agenda for urban historians', in H. J. Dyos (ed.), *The Study of Urban History* (London, 1968), pp. 1–46, at p. 29, and P. Clark and P. Slack, *English Towns in Transition, 1500–1700* (London, 1976), p. 2.

especially arguments over canons of proof. He thought that historical method was scientific, but only 'in the sense in which the method of a Sherlock Holmes would be scientific. The end of it all is a story, a causally connected story tested and proved at every point.'[105] As Eric Hobsbawm notes, Maitland was 'unaware of the requirements of post-modernism, but perfectly conscious that the past is another country where things are done differently, that we must understand it even though the best interpreters still remain biased strangers'.[106] Elton put it slightly differently, to deal with postmodernist scepticism as much as the longer-running attempt to make history into a science: 'The post-Newtonian view of the physical world, denying the absolute, allowing for the unpredictably contingent, and accepting the effect of the observer upon the matter observed, might not be a bad analogy for good history.'[107] As Elton knew, Maitland still has much to teach current English (and British) social (and political) historians, who have 'inherited much of the intellectual project of the old legal tradition', which included Montesquieu, Adam Smith, Marx, Weber and Durkheim – that this approach is an integral part of history as a whole, vital to recreating a reliable picture of past societies.[108]

[105] *Maitland: Selected Essays*, p. 241; Milsom, 'Maitland', pp. 274–275.

[106] E. J. Hobsbawm, *On History* (London, 1998), pp. 263–264.

[107] G. R. Elton, *Return to Essentials: Some Reflections on the Present State of Historical Study* (Cambridge, 1991), p. 51. The founding editors of *Past and Present* had also grappled with this issue: The Editors, 'Introduction', pp. i–iii.

[108] Kelley, *Human Measure*, p. 13. Brooks, *Law, Politics and Society*, p. 1, argues for a broader reintegration of 'the history of law, legal institutions and the legal professions with the general political and social history' of early modern England.

5

# Fountains of Justice

## James I, Charles I and Equity

R. W. HOYLE*

Could an English king sit as a judge in his own courts? The answer, it might be supposed is 'no' – and yet, under James I and Charles I (and even later), the suggestion that they could was occasionally advanced and de facto sometimes they did. The capacity of the monarch to act judicially is therefore worthy of our attention. It is a story (in part) of what did not happen, of unrealised fears of what might have been possible. It focuses attention on the place of Chancery as the King's own court, the forum in which his conscience might be exercised, presided over by a judge whose connection to the king was qualitatively different from that of the judges presiding over the common law jurisdictions of King's Bench and Common Pleas.

### I

We should not forget that James I was a foreign king, brought up in a different system of law. What he found, on his accession to the English throne, was a complicated and differentiated system of courts within which the individual courts jostled for position. The common law was administered by a professional cadre that had a strong intellectual and social solidarity based on a single system of education at the Inns of Court. Common law ideas were also pervasive amongst the gentry, many of whom had at least some experience of education at the Inns even if they had never had any intention of practising. Judges, whilst chosen by

* This chapter continues my work on petitions and offers the opportunity to present some of the research on the Ellesmere papers undertaken in a month I spent at the Huntington Library in 2000 on a British Academy fellowship, for which I remain grateful. For some of the most telling examples, however, I am indebted to Dr Simon Healy.

the king, were drawn from the senior members of the legal profession who formed the order of sergeants: the judges needed to have the respect of, and to be the intellectual equal to, the counsel who appeared before them. James Morice had said, in his reading on the prerogative given in 1578, that: 'If the king do make a patent unto one who never studied the laws of the realm . . . authorising him thereby to be a justice of one bench . . . this man is no sufficient judge lawfully ordained by the king's prerogative.'[1] The pool of qualified individuals was therefore limited. The increasing practice of extracting a fee from a judge for his appointment to the office did not greatly change this.[2]

The common law was not the only system of law in England, but the common lawyers had a low regard for ecclesiastical law and the church courts, and claimed supremacy over them. The practice of issuing prohibitions, used most notably to remove tithe cases from the church courts to be tried in a common law jurisdiction, created a running sore in relations between church and state.

It is possible to see the various jurisdictional disputes of the early seventeenth century as being either about the pursuit of business and fees or the clash of big and angular personalities, but the fact that these disputes took place reflects the uncertainties of an untidy system in which jurisdictions overlapped, thus allowing litigants to advance their causes through multiple suits in different courts and to adopt strategies of trying to move litigation between courts or having one court prevent litigation in another. Moreover, there were principles involved and not merely fees.[3]

In some ways, James I's accession may have come as a shock to the legal profession. The king saw himself as the intellectual equal of the

[1] See BL, Egerton MS 3376, f. 30v. I am grateful to Robert Weatherley for drawing this to my attention.

[2] There appears to be no readily available discussion of the appointment of judges in the early seventeenth century. For earlier practice, see Sir John Baker, *The Oxford History of the Laws of England, Vol. VI, 1483–1558* (Oxford, 2003), p. 423; for later practice, W. R. Prest, *The Rise of the Barristers. A Social History of the English Bar, 1590–1640* (Oxford, 1986), pp. 135–145.

[3] Sir John Baker's classic account of the events leading to 1616 seems to come down to personalities. He quotes Sir Francis Bacon with approval – 'When the men were gone, the matter was gone' – but when he said this, he may have meant that the dismissal of Coke was a decisive blow to the opinions he held: Sir John Baker, 'The common lawyers and the Chancery: 1616', in Allen D. Boyer (ed.), *Law, Liberty and Parliament: Selected Essays on the Writings of Sir Edward Coke* (Indianapolis, 2004 [1969]), pp. 254–281. His most recent account places more weight on the questions of law involved: Sir John Baker, *The Reinvention of Magna Carta, 1216–1616* (Cambridge, 2017), ch. 10.

lawyers; indeed, from his actions, it might seem that he was a lawyer manqué.[4] Unlike the late Queen, James wished to be involved in the adjudication of the most important disputes, which tended to be concerned with questions of jurisdiction. He displayed a taste for having legal questions argued out before him. But it seems plain enough that James was not overly impressed by the learning of the common law lawyers (or what he may have regarded as their professional obscurantism), their capacity to argue over jurisdiction and their willingness to intrude on the royal prerogative. It was not merely that James hankered after a simpler system of law (he spoke wistfully of having seen trials without lawyers take place in Denmark),[5] but also that his view of the relationship of the king with the law sat uncomfortably with that of the common lawyers. There was inevitably a great deal of friction between the lawyers and James over this, and so this is the question we shall explore first.

The fullest statement of James's understanding of the law comes from his speech in Star Chamber in 1616, in which he laid down rules about the jurisdiction of his courts.[6] This was a final statement that came at the end of a succession of disputes, the most important of which arose out of the use of prohibitions against the ecclesiastical courts in tithe cases.

## II

Prohibitions were not a new problem at the time of James's accession, nor were they a readily solvable one. Indeed, there was a question as to where any solution might come from. In the articles exhibited by Archbishop Bancroft in 1605 (the *articuli clerici*), it was argued that the king had the power to reform abuses in prohibitions, but the judges maintained that if there were an abuse, it would be for Parliament to resolve.[7] It was unlikely that Parliament would legislate on the question in a way that the church found acceptable and, for this reason, if for no other, a line of argument was developed that the king could not only control the use of

[4] See here Christopher W. Brooks's assessment that 'James was arguably the most intellectually qualified monarch to sit on the English throne since the Conquest': C. W. Brooks, *Law, Politics and Society in Early Modern England* (Cambridge, 2008), p. 153.

[5] 'A speach in the Starr-Chamber, the XX of June Anno 1616', in C. H. McIlwain (ed.), *The Political Works of James I* (Cambridge, MA, 1918), p. 332.

[6] Ibid. pp. 326–345.

[7] Printed in T. B. Howell (ed.), *State Trials* (London, 1816), vol. II, cols 131–158. The reference to Parliament is at col. 134. For prohibitions, see Brooks, *Law, Politics and Society*, pp. 109–118.

prohibitions, but also sit judicially to decide suits. This was the position pressed on the king in a further stage of the controversy in 1607, which brought the famous standoff between the king and Sir Edward Coke. Archbishop Bancroft had made a further complaint to the king about the restraints being placed on the powers of the church courts by prohibitions. The judiciary were assembled to advise the king, and Coke describes himself as speaking on their behalf and with their agreement. The evidence for what happened there is a memorandum prepared by Coke and published posthumously.[8] Bancroft argued that where there were no statutes defining aspects of ecclesiastical jurisdiction, the king might decide it himself, for 'that the judges are but delegates of the king and that the king may take what causes he shall please to determine from the determination of the judges, and may determine them himself. And the Archbishop said this was clear in divinity, that such authority belongs to the king by word of God in scripture.'[9] Bancroft may well have been basing his arguments on a paper attributed to John Cowell, Professor of Civil Law at Cambridge, which demonstrated that the king had all the powers that Bancroft claimed for him.[10] Cowell articulated much the same sort of views in *The Interpreter* (1607), which came under sustained criticism in the 1610 Parliament.[11]

Coke answered that 'the king in his own person cannot adjudge any case, either criminal, as treason, felony etc. or betwixt party and party, concerning his inheritance, chattels or goods etc., but this ought to be determined and adjudged in some court of justice, according to the law and custom of England'.[12] Coke conceded to the king the right to sit in

[8] *Prohibitions del Roy* 12 Co. Rep. 63 (77 *English Reports* 1342). There are aspects of this that need to treated with caution, and, long ago, Usher suggested that the memorandum was actually the conflation of several meetings written up by Coke to place him in the centre foreground and to advance his views. For his reconstruction of the meeting, see R. G. Usher, 'James I and Sir Edward Coke', *English Historical Review* 18 (1903), 664–675, and R. G. Usher, *The Reconstruction of the English Church*, two vols (New York, 1910), vol. II, pp. 213–216.

[9] *Prohibitions del Roy* 12 Co. Rep. 63 (77 *English Reports* 1342).

[10] BL, Lansdowne MS 211, ff. 141r–227v. The first section is headed 'that the king hath power in his person to hear and determine all kind of causes when it shall please His Majesty' (f. 141r), the second, 'that the king hath authority to ratify both his jurisdictions and to reform the abuses of prohibitions' (f. 145r). A further text that appears to contain much of the same material is Lambeth Palace Library MS 2026: E. G. W. Bill, *A Catalogue of Manuscripts in Lambeth Palace Library, MSS 1907–2340* (Oxford, 1976), pp. 73–75.

[11] J. P. Sommerville, *Politics and Ideology in England, 1603–1640* (London, 1986), pp. 121–127, gives a useful account. Cowell's *The Interpreter* (1607) was dedicated to Bancroft.

[12] *Prohibitions del Roy* 12 Co. Rep. 63 (77 *English Reports* 1342).

the House of Lords. *Together*, they formed the supreme judge over all other judges. They had the power to hear appeals from King's Bench. The king might sit in Star Chamber, but this was to consult with the judges on questions posed to them and not *in judicio*. He might sit in King's Bench where it was held that the king was always present in the court in the judgment of law, but it was the court that gave judgment and not the king. The court's justices were sworn to execute justice according to law and custom.

Coke cited a statute of 2 Edward III which expressly forbade the king to take a cause out of one of his courts and decide it himself: 'The judges informed the King that no king after the conquest assumed to himself the right to give any judgment in any cause whatsoever which concerned the administration of justice within this realm, but these were solely determined in the courts of justice.'[13] Nor did the king have the power to arrest any man, for the party arrested could not have remedy against the king: '[S]o if the king give any judgment, what remedy can the party have[?] . . . And it was greatly marvelled that the archbishop durst inform the king that such absolute power and authority, as is aforesaid, belong to the king by the word of God.'[14]

James was not having it:

> [T]hen the King said that he thought the law was founded upon reason and that he and others had reason as well as the judges, to which was answered by me [Coke], that true it was that the God had endowed His Majesty with excellent science and great endowments of nature: but His Majesty was not learned in the law of his realm of England, and causes which concern the life or inheritance or goods or fortunes of his subjects, are not to be decided by natural reason but by the artificial reason and judgment of law, which law is an act which requires long study and experience before that a man can attain to the cognizance of it: that the law was the golden met-wand and measure to try the causes of the subjects; and which protected His Majesty in safety and peace; with which the king was greatly offended and said that he should be under the law, which was treason to affirm, as he said, to which I said that Bracton saith, '*quod Rex non debet esse sub homine, sed sub Deo et lege*'.[15]

Coke's account ends with Bracton; he does not say that James was furious and conducted a rant from the throne, or that Coke had to fall to the floor to assuage royal anger and be rescued by the intervention of Robert Cecil.

[13] *Prohibitions del Roy* 12 Co. Rep. 64 (77 *English Reports* 1342).

[14] Ibid.

[15] *Prohibitions del Roy* 12 Co. Rep. 64–65 (77 *English Reports* 1343).

Even if the account should not be read absolutely literally, there is much in this exchange to ponder: the advice the king received from the clerical estate that he had discretion of a sort that the common lawyers simply would not accept; his view that he was above the law; the lawyers' view that the law could be exercised only by a professional cadre with the appropriate learning and training. Were all common lawyers accepting of the view articulated by Coke? There is a question about the opinions held by James's Lord Chancellor, Sir Thomas Egerton, Lord Ellesmere, created Viscount Brackley shortly before his death in 1617. Coke was plainly alarmed by the opinions of his renegade colleague, and kept a list of 'dangerous points and absurd opinions' held and articulated by Ellesmere, which finally amounted to seventeen numbered points and a concluding (eighteenth) critique of Ellesmere's conduct in the trial of the earl of Somerset.[16] The absurd opinions can be divided into a number of categories: what Ellesmere told the king he could do (for example determine *Calvin's case* himself); Ellesmere's cynical, politic opinions ('He said openly he would favour any man the king favoured and no longer than the king favoured him'[17]); and his understanding of the Lord Chancellor's role. It would appear that he deliberately distanced himself from the judges, 'being often moved to stand with the judges when they were complained of to the king, he answered he would not lie in the gap for any man'.[18] His detachment from the judiciary as a whole was also shown by his advice that the king should deal with the judges separately and make more use of the law officers.[19] Coke accused Ellesmere of placing less emphasis on precedent and said that, by doing so, 'he subverts the certainty of law'.[20] As Chancellor, Ellesmere held that he stood above the other judges and was responsible to the king alone ('that the chancellor ought not to be judged by any judge of the [common] law, but by the king alone'[21]). Coke believed that Ellesmere had told the king 'that he as chancellor was the keeper of the king's conscience and therefore whatsoever the king decreed he would decree accordingly'.[22]

16 The autograph source for this, cited twice by J. H. Baker, 'Egerton, Thomas, first Viscount Brackley (1540–1617)', *Oxford Dictionary of National Biography* (ODNB), is Cambridge University Library MS Ii.5.21, f. 47r–v. A copy is in University College London, Special Collections, MS Ogden 29, ff. 568–569: see Brooks, *Law, Politics and Society*, pp. 149–150.

17 Ms Ogden 29, f. 569v.

18 Ibid., f. 569r.

19 For examples, see Baker, *Reinvention*, p. 425.

20 Ms Ogden 29, f. 568v.

21 Ibid.

22 Ibid., f. 569v.

There is obviously a great deal here that discomforted the remainder of the judiciary and the profession as a whole. One lawyer, Thomas Tourner or Turner, went so far as to record his fears for the future of tyranny exercised through the Lord Chancellor and the end of parliaments.[23] There is nothing in the list of errors, though, which amounts to a general declaration that James could decide all or any case in person without consulting the judges. If, however, Ellesmere really did tell the king that he could decide *Calvin's case*, then there was little that he could not decide, but Coke does not claim that either Ellesmere or James held that the king had a general power to decide all cases. The statement that the Chancellor was the king's conscience was a commonplace one, although not one of great antiquity,[24] and Ellesmere's statement that he would be bound to decree as the king desired is no more than a statement of *realpolitik*.

Ellesmere did write and speak about the prerogative on a number of occasions and it is not clear from this body of material that he subscribed to the views that – following Coke – have been attributed to him. Ellesmere's opinions rested on his position as Lord Chancellor; they were also based on his understanding of the position of a judge. It might be argued that they were exactly the position that a former law officer of the Crown might take (although plainly Coke had not absorbed them). As eludicated by Knafla, Ellesmere's ideas rested on the idea of *merum imperium* (full power and sovereignty). For Ellesmere (and Cowell), aspects of *merum imperium* could be delegated to judges (or other officeholders) who acted as a substitute for the king. As a delegated power, it could be revoked, so, in effect, an officeholder of whatever sort held the power only during the king's pleasure and to do his will. Because the office was only lent to the judge or officeholder, there was always the possibility of appeal from him to the king for the redress of wrongs committed in the king's name; the right of access to the king from his subjects was something in which the king profoundly believed. As Ellesmere argued, the alternative was that an officeholder 'might well esteem himself to be above the king's laws [and] will administer justice contrary to the justice of the land'.[25] In fact, Ellesmere stopped well short of a fully absolutist position; rather, he held that the monarch

23 BL, Add. MS 35957, f. 55v, cited by ODNB, 'Egerton, Thomas', and Baker, *Reinvention*, p. 421.

24 Baker, *Reinvention*, p. 411.

25 L. A. Knafla, *Law and Politics in Jacobean England: The Tracts of Lord Chancellor Ellesmere* (Cambridge, 1977), p. 198.

was bound by the laws that he and his predecessors had created. He told the House of Lords on 1614 that 'the king hath no prerogative but that which is warranted by law and the law hath given him'.[26]

In Ellesmere's analysis, the position of the judge was insecure: the judge was the king's servant and certainly his dependent. It was perhaps this perspective on the judge's position that made Ellesmere's advocacy of Coke's dismissal thinkable. But Ellesmere was Lord Chancellor and doubtless acutely aware of the insecurities inherent in his position. Wolsey had been dismissed in 1529. The Lord Chancellor was only partly a judge: he was first the head of one of the great departments of state and only second a judge in his own court. Whilst the majority of Lord Chancellors were common lawyers, not all were, and it is here that monarchs could appoint people from outside the circle of career lawyers. The most obvious example of this, of course, would be Wolsey himself, but a more recent example would be Sir Christopher Hatton. James I appointed Sir Julius Caesar, a civilian and not a common lawyer, as Master of the Rolls in 1614 (but with assistant judges to assist him). A career common lawyer, Sir Francis Bacon, followed Ellesmere in 1617, but it has been shown that the other candidates considered that year were clergy, including George Abbott, Archbishop of Canterbury.[27] In 1621, the king's selection fell on the Dean of Westminster, John Williams. Williams knew more law than has sometimes been acknowledged, but he was certainly not a practising lawyer.[28] The appointment of the Lord Chancellor offered the monarch more freedom than he had in the appointment of judges elsewhere in the judiciary. Where a justice was one of the leaders of the legal profession, the Lord Chancellor was in a direct relationship with the king. This was recognised: on entering office, Williams was reminded that 'the power of judicature according to equity and conscience' that he had accepted was 'the king's conscience committed to the chancellor: and if the chancellor shall of his own private conscience be of another opinion than he is persuaded the king his master would be, he is to judge according to the king's conscience and not his own'.[29] When Ellesmere said (if indeed he said it) that 'whatever the king decreed in any case he would decree accordingly', he seems to have been stating the hard reality of the Lord Chancellor's position and

[26] Ibid. p. 76.

[27] G. W. Thomas, 'James I, equity and Lord Keeper John Williams', *English Historical Review* 91 (1976), 506–528, pp. 518–519.

[28] Ibid., pp. 524–525.

[29] Ibid., pp. 514–515.

not making any statement about his preference for royal absolutism. He was not in a position in which he could refuse a direct royal instruction.

It should not be thought, though, that Ellesmere was simply a passive figure; he was tenacious in his defence of the Lord Chancellor's powers. Both Baker and Knafla have shown how he used his standing with the king to reverse the judges' ruling in *Finch* v. *Throgmorton* (1598), in which it was decided (in Egerton's absence) that the Lord Chancellor could not subpoena a party for a cause that had already been determined at common law. In 1615–1616, he won the argument over the right of Chancery to consider a common law verdict on appeal, as it were; conversely, he stopped King's Bench from using writs of praemunire to prevent him from doing so. His manoeuvrings led to the King's speech of 20 June 1616, which announced the king's resolution of the dispute.[30]

## III

The question of whether the standing of common law judges came from their status as senior members of the profession or their royal appointment is one of the major themes of the first section of the King's speech.[31] James explained why he had not rushed to make a public statement on the law: he had patiently served a double-length apprenticeship in the law since his accession.[32] Mature consideration, though, had led him to conclusions that the common lawyers would surely find barely acceptable. In the first part of speech, he said repeatedly that judicial authority derived from the king and king alone. The judges stood in the same relationship to the king as the king stood to God. The judges were not to make law, but to declare it: 'It is the king's office to protect and settle the true interpretation of the law of God within his dominions and it is the judge's office to interpret the law of the King whereunto themselves are also subject.'[33] Their interpretations were to be subject to common sense. The lawyers' learning was ever-so-gently ridiculed: 'For though the Common law be a mystery and skill best known unto yourselves, yet if your interpretation be such as other which have logic and common sense understand not the reason, I will never trust such an interpretation.'[34] And so the lawyers were cut down to size: they were not to encroach on

[30] Baker, 'The common lawyers and the Chancery: 1616'; Knafla, *Law and Politics*, ch. 7.
[31] 'A speach in the Starr-Chamber', pp. 326–345.
[32] Ibid., pp. 328–329.
[33] Ibid., p. 327.
[34] Ibid., p. 332.

the prerogative. If a question concerned the prerogative, they were to consult the king or his counsel.[35] They were to keep within their own benches and were not to invade the jurisdiction of other courts. James made particularly sharp comments against those who had moved a writ of praemunire against Chancery and forbade it to happen again. They were to act in harmony. The lawyers were warned against introducing novelties: '[T]hey were to maintain the ancient law pure and undefiled, as it was before.'[36] The king therefore took it upon himself to regulate the relations between the courts, laying out their spheres of competence. The judges, it would be recalled, had argued that this should be done by statute. There was a bill introduced to regulate the relationship between Chancery and the common law courts in 1614, and a whole suite of bills introduced in 1621.[37] But James had already annexed the power to determine jurisdiction to the prerogative. Here, we can see the influence of Cowell, as articulated by Bancroft.

There was much here that was to the discomfort of the legal profession, this being very much a layperson's perspective on the law and its working. What is perhaps most important is what it does *not* say. As in James's treatment of Cowell, there is perhaps a hesitancy, a reluctance to be inflammatory, which stopped the king short of saying in public what he may well have believed in private. It is never explicitly claimed in the speech that the king was above, rather than under, the common law, although it is surely implied. There is no claim that the king could sit as a judge and decide cases. In this respect, the speech marks a retreat from the high churchman's view. Nor is there any claim that the king could instruct the Lord Chancellor, although he acknowledged that Chancery was the dispenser of the king's conscience.

## IV

Having seen what the king came to believe, we now turn to what he did – that is, from theory to practice. James did interfere with the courts in a small way and, on occasion, he did issue quasi-judicial orders. Let us treat them in turn.

Given James's willingness to receive petitions and the importance he attributed to them, it was almost certainly inevitable that he would

35 Ibid., pp. 332–333.
36 Ibid., p. 336.
37 Thomas, 'James I, equity and Lord Keeper John Williams', pp. 521–522.

receive some petitions asking for favour in the courts, if only for the early hearings of suits.[38] James acknowledged in 1616 that, as king of Scotland, he received petitions both to hasten and to delay suits. He held that it was wrong for a king to delay justice.[39] A review of the register of petitions maintained by Sir Roger Wilbraham as one of the Masters of Requests suggests that petitions asking the king to intervene in judicial processes were never numerous and raised no great questions of principle. There were petitions requesting that hearings should be accelerated or seeking to bring suits to an end. One, from a petitioner who had plainly run out of money (he was in prison for debt), asked for his case to be referred to the Lord Chancellor and some of the judges for a final resolution.[40] A few asked for commissions to be issued and suits at common law stayed.[41] Others sought the presence of the Lord Chancellor at their hearings.[42] One litigant asked for a final decree to be made, which the king also sought so that he could stop being pestered by the petitioner.[43]

A further circumstance in which the king might receive petitions was where litigants in Chancery felt hard done by. As the king himself acknowledged, there was no appeal from Chancery. It was possible to proceed by a bill of review, but with the precondition that the litigant had to have accepted, and implemented, a previous decree of the court. There was the option of securing a private Act of Parliament to reverse a Chancery decree – surely out of reach for most disgruntled litigants – and there was the option of appealing direct to the king.[44] An example of the latter comes from the travails of one Timothy Pinkeny in a suit against Sir John Kennedy for debt. The suit had been heard by Bacon, who referred it to arbitrators, who agreed that Kennedy owed Pinkeny £700. The case then lapsed on Bacon's dismissal. It was decreed by Williams, but he reversed the referees' findings, and Pinkeny petitioned

[38] R. W. Hoyle, 'The Masters of Requests and the small change of Jacobean patronage', *English Historical Review* 126 (2011), 544–581.

[39] 'A speach in the Starr-Chamber', p. 330.

[40] R. W. Hoyle and D. Tankard (eds), *Heard before the King: Registers of Petitions to James I, 1603–1616* (List and Index Society Supp. Ser., 38–39, 2006), nos 2003, 2169, 2384, 2514, 2558. Henry E. Huntington Library, San Marino, Ellesmere (hereafter HEHL, EL) MSS 5952, 5975–5978 are petitions and associated documents asking that Star Chamber cases should be heard.

[41] Hoyle and Tankard (eds), *Heard before the King*, nos 1717, 2521.

[42] Ibid., nos 1687, 1837, 2928, in which it was asked that additional judge be appointed to assist the (non-lawyer) Chamberlain of Chester.

[43] Ibid., nos 1854, 2288.

[44] 'A speach in the Starr-Chamber', p. 334. For bills of review, see W. J. Jones, *The Elizabethan Court of Chancery* (Oxford, 1967), p. 293.

the king. His petition was referred to two members of the Privy Council, who ordered that Williams should rehear the case, which he did, but Williams still refused to admit Pinkeny as a creditor. In 1624, Pinkeny appealed to the House of Lords and, because Williams failed to implement the Lords' order, Pinkeny appealed again in 1626.[45]

There is little sign that the king was involved in any of these petitions in any meaningful sense; instead, he referred them to the appropriate officer for action, information or a recommendation as to how to proceed. The problem arose when the king was seen to be taking an interest in a petitioner's complaint and started to behave in ways that might have been read as being partial. In a few cases in which the king had a degree of personal interest in the petitioner or he felt that the complainant had suffered a gross miscarriage, one the Masters of Requests or secretaries of state might write to the appropriate officer, sending on the petition. This was the case with a petition submitted to the king by a minor household servant, John Lepton, in 1616. Some years before, Lepton had contracted debts with Sir Edwin Sandys, for which Sir James Perrott had stood surety with Lepton, and Lepton had given Perrott a bond in £1600 to save him harmless. To cut through a tangled story, this was now the subject of an action in Chancery, but Sandys had secured a judgment on the bond at the previous Kent assizes, leaving Lepton liable for the bond of £800 to Sandys and the bond of £1600 to Perrott (and all for an initial debt of £240). He looked for the king's 'special favour and assistance', asking that the king should order the Lord Chancellor to call Sandys, Perrott and Lepton before him to take such order as should be agreeable to 'equity and conscience' or, at the least, to award an injunction to stay the judgment given at Kent assizes until the cause had received a final hearing in Chancery. It fell to Sir Roger Wilbraham to write to Ellesmere, enclosing the petition, expressing the king's sympathy with Lepton's predicament and asking – as Lepton had requested – that Ellesmere call the parties before him and settle the dispute 'without prolix suits in law as that Mr Lepton be not oppressed to his utter ruin for a debt of so small a sum'.[46]

A similar matter is the King's involvement in the Chancery suit *Skillicorne* v. *Wolverston*.[47] John Skillicorne was a Lancashire gentleman

[45] James S. Hart, *Justice upon Petition: The House of Lords and the Reformation of Justice, 1621–1675* (London, 1991), p. 48.

[46] HEHL, EL MSS 385, 5974.

[47] For Wolverston, see Andrew Thrush and John P. Ferris (eds), *The History of Parliament, The House of Commons, 1604–1629*, six vols (London, 2010), vol. vi, pp. 837–838. What

with a manor in the Fylde; Wolverston was a gentleman pensioner from 1603 or 1604, and so almost certainly a man known to the king and able to gain his ear. Wolverston sat as the member for Cardigan boroughs in the Parliament of 1614 and seems to have been of some assistance to the Crown's interest. James thought that he deserved a favour in return and Wolverston seems to have been only too eager to exploit the king's willingness to help him. In fact, Wolverston was engaged in litigation in Chancery over an interest in the manor of Preese in Lancashire before the Parliament and it may be that his election to the Commons was itself a delaying tactic. The background to the suit was that Skillicorne came to London in March 1609 and, needing to borrow money, was introduced by his brother-in-law, one Walter Gower, to Wolverston, who lent him £220 and the price of a gelding on a statute for £400. Some weeks later, Skillicorne borrowed a further £250 from Wolverston, and agreed to mortgage his estate to him for £500 and £50 interest. The following February, Gower and Wolverston plotted to acquire Skillicorne's interest. Their proposal was that Skillicorne should be paid a further £1000 (making £1500 in total), and that Wolverston should pay an annuity of £200 per year to Skillicorne and his wife for their lives. The conveyancing was done by Wolverston's brother, a Gray's Inn lawyer. The account of the case in Ellesmere's papers shows how, at every stage, the arrangements proposed by Wolverston and Gower were disadvantageous to Skillicorne. The result was that Skillicorne lost lands worth £400 per annum. He received for his title only £1000, £500 of which remained unpaid. Nor was he able to receive his annuity, for after Wolverston had acquired the manor, it had been extended for the payment of his (Wolverston's) debts. Wolverston had known all along that the land could not pay an annuity to Skillicorne; because he had denied this on oath, Ellesmere also held that Skillicorne had perjured himself.

Skillicorne commenced suit against the Wolverston brothers and Gower in Chancery, which brought the affair to Ellesmere's attention. He heard the case on 14 June 1613 and quickly concluded that the transactions between Skillicorne and Wolverston were essentially fraudulent. The Wolverston brothers had exploited Skillicorne's 'weakness and simplicity' and his trust in his wife's brother. But Ellesmere trod carefully, because one Wolverston brother was a royal servant and the other, a lawyer, and hence Ellesmere proposed an arbitration, with the

follows is largely based on HEHL, EL MS 5964 (a breviate of the suit dated 17 November 1614).

aim of untangling the conveyance so that Skillicorne had his land back and Wolverston, his money. Wolverston cooperated with neither these arbitrators nor a subsequent arbitration that Ellesmere tried to arrange in the autumn. In December, Ellesmere made an order in Chancery that Skillicorne should have the land and Wolverston, his money reimbursed. Skillicorne was to supply accounts of what he had disbursed and received. Only partial accounts were received, and then the Addled Parliament intervened and no more could be done for a time.

In July, Skillicorne offered to pay £2000 to Wolverston to purchase any interest he might have in the land and to unravel the previous conveyances. In July, Ellesmere ordered that, unless Wolverston showed cause, £2000 was to be paid to him on St Bartholomew's Day (24 August) at the Rolls Chapel. This order prompted the first appeal to the king. Wolverston claimed that he was being pressed in a case in Chancery out of term to which he was unable to attend. This was barely true, but, on 18 August, James sent a signet letter to Ellesmere, telling him not to allow any hearing until the new law term began.[48] Perhaps fortified by the king's letter, no one appeared to receive the consideration or sign the conveyance to Skillicorne. On 10 October, counsel for Skillicorne asked for an absolute decree to be made, but Ellesmere, aware of the king's interest, issued a subpoena giving a fortnight's notice for Wolverston and his counsel to attend the court on 27 October.

On 25 October, Sir Thomas Lake wrote to Ellesmere, saying that Wolverston had petitioned the king a second time, complaining that no one would act as his counsel. The king, Lake said, had never heard of such a thing and did not know what to make of it. Ellesmere was to defer the hearing until the king returned to London.[49] Now, whether this letter failed to reach Ellesmere in time or whether he ignored it cannot be determined, but, at the hearing on 27 October, Wolverston sent in a letter saying that no one would take instruction from him. This was not true: his counsel was in court and complained that Wolverston had never given him any instruction. Yet Wolverston was given another hearing on 8 November; his counsel appeared on 12 November and again on 17 November. On the last occasion, counsel said that they had met with Wolverston several times and, because he would not take their advice, they had washed their hands of him. Wolverston was then allowed to address the court and produced a list of eighteen exceptions

[48] HEHL, EL MS 5962.
[49] HEHL, EL MS 5963.

against Ellesmere's orders, after which Ellesmere proceeded to decree the case against him. A day was fixed for the reimbursement of Wolverston's consideration; again, no one appeared to receive it.

This was not the end of it. On 25 December, Ralph Winwood told Ellesmere that Wolverston had preferred a further petition against him and asked Ellesmere to let him know the state of the case. The petition, or a copy of it, survives in Ellesmere's papers, together with Ellesmere's report.[50] This is keyed to the petition using letters A–L; there is also a much abbreviated version. What Wolverston sought was a commission to review the Chancellor's decree and, until that time, an order staying the execution of the decree, so that he would not be forced to part with what he called 'his inheritance'. How the petition and Ellesmere's response to it were received is unknown, for the archive ends at this point. However, the suit in Chancery continued into 1615, with Ellesmere attempting to discover what compensation was due to Wolverston for the improvements he had made to the Lancashire estate. It then peters out. Wolverston did not give up, however: he petitioned Parliament in 1624 for a private Act of Parliament to overturn the Chancery decrees, and to settle the estate on him and his heirs in accordance with the conveyances made a decade earlier. Ultimately, the Wolverston family secured possession of the estate.[51]

It seems unarguable that the original dealings between Skillicorne and Wolverston were deeply to Skillicorne's disadvantage, that there were also elements of fraud in the conveyances and that Ellesmere – particularly after the king's interest became known – bent over backwards to appease a vexatious litigant. But Wolverston had got his teeth into Skillicorne's estate: he claimed to have been improving it, although he could produce no accounts for his expenditure; and he maintained that Skillicorne was unable to find the money to buy it back from him (although the money appears to have been tendered). It is probably not to the credit of the king that he allowed himself to get embroiled in a junior courtier's litigation, but, other than write letters, it could not be said, from what we know, that he did anything very material to advance Wolverston's suit other than to prolong it. On the other hand, the fact that one party had attracted the king's interest and had commendatory letters that allowed them to queue-jump in Chancery, or to have their

50 HEHL, EL MS 5967–5969.

51 TNA, C 33/127, pp. 788–9, 1060v; Parliamentary Archives, HL/PO/JO/1011/23; VCH *Lancs.* VII, p. 178; Lancashire Archives, DX 692.

grievances settled extracurially by specially convened tribunals, placed that party at an advantage over the other, so whilst the king did not directly interfere, he may well have advantaged his servants by the very expression of his concern for their problems. We have seen how wary Ellesmere was in dealing with Wolverston; the terms on which the parties appeared in court or before the justices might well have been subtly different.

A third instance of the king attempting to aid a courtier and becoming too deeply involved in his affairs concerns George Marshall, an equerry in the royal stables who rose to being a gentleman of the Privy Chamber.[52] Marshall, who claimed to have been the first Englishman to have brought news of the old Queen's death to James, received for his reward the nomination of two Knights of the Bath at James's coronation. One of these, he sold on for 1,000 marks to his brother-in-law, William Pope. Fifteen years later, he attempted to collect this money with a suit in Chancery. The court was disinclined to believe Marshall, but he secured a letter from James himself vouching for his role in arranging knighthoods. Chancery therefore made a decree against Pope in 1620. The whole shabby episode was then criticised in the Parliament of 1621; the king rescinded his letter and asked for the decree to be cancelled. In the end, the decree was merely suspended, the cancellation of a decree by royal fiat perhaps being more than Lord Chancellor Verulam could stomach because it plainly led into deep waters.

## V

If dealing with petitions was generally a system of triage, sending petitions on to the appropriate person in law or government, James also edged into a more overtly judicial role on a number of occasions. He is known to have sat in Star Chamber on at least one occasion, even though Coke had denied his right to do so. James also took a more overtly judicial role on at least two occasions on which he attempted to resolve inheritance disputes within the aristocracy. There is then a third occasion on which he may have intended to make an award and a fourth on which it was suggested that he should intervene.

52 Thrush and Ferris, *History of Commons, 1603–1629*, vol. v, pp. 260–261.

The Star Chamber suit in question was brought by Lady Exeter against Anne, Lady Ros or Roos, and her mother, Lady Lake, daughter and wife of Sir Thomas Lake, then Secretary of State, in 1618.[53] Lake secured a marriage for his daughter with William Cecil, Lord Ros (1590–1618) in early 1617, about the time he was promoted to the secretaryship. Ros was a Catholic and, shortly after his marriage, was appointed Ambassador Extraordinary to Spain. There then followed an unseemly squabble within the family over Ros's property, in which Sir Thomas applied pressure on him to make conveyances to the benefit of his daughter in return for financing his ambassadorial costs. The marriage was, in any case, unsatisfactory, with allegations being made of Ros's impotence, and the threat was made by Lady Ros and Lady Lake that his sexual inadequacies would be exposed and an annulment sought. Ultimately, Ros fled abroad to escape his in-laws and died in Naples in the summer of 1618.[54]

Ros's grandfather, the earl of Exeter, with his young wife Frances, sought to protect Ros from the predatory Lakes. Towards the end of 1617, Lady Ros and her mother circulated the claim that the countess of Exeter was in a sexual relationship with her step-grandson and that she had tried to poison Lady Ros. This was backed up by incriminating (but forged) letters. As John Chamberlain commented in a letter to Sir Dudley Carleton, Lady Exeter wished to clear herself from 'foul scandals of precontracts, adultery, incest, murder, poison and such like peccadillos'. The two chief justices were asked to investigate in January 1618. The following month, Lady Ros was examined by the full Council and committed to the custody of the Bishop of London for refusing to answer their questions. Chamberlain reported that the earl of Exeter had spoken to the king, asking him to take charge of the case 'as a judge and a just judge and not as an arbitrator'. The Lakes, meanwhile, sought a trial at law and in the Star Chamber, options which Exeter rejected as being too protracted.

Exeter did not get an immediate trial. Evidence was gathered over 1618 and, by November of that year, Chamberlain could claim that it extended to 9,000 pages. But Exeter did get the king in Star Chamber. In December,

[53] There seems to be no definitive account of this suit. The following is based on Roger Lockyer, 'Lake, Sir Thomas (bap. 1561, d. 1630)', Alastair Bellany, 'Cecil, Anne, Lady Ros (1599x1601–30)' and Alastair Bellany, 'Cecil, William, sixteenth Baron Ros (1590–1618)', all in ODNB; Norman Egbert McClure (ed.), *The Letters of John Chamberlain*, two vols (Philadelphia, 1939), vol. II, pp. 132, 144, 183, 192, 207, 211, 213–214, 215–216.

[54] *CSPD 1611–18*, pp. 542–543 (Lord Ros to the king, explaining his flight).

Chamberlain had heard that the case would be heard after Candlemas and that the 'king means to sit there himself, if he can have the patience to hear it out'. In the event, the king sat for five days (really, long mornings) in Star Chamber in early February. The court's verdict was decisively for Lady Exeter: all of the Lakes were fined, and Lady Ros was fined and imprisoned.

James seems to have become involved at the personal request of the earl of Exeter. It was a charge on his time, but he perhaps felt he had to do it because the trial touched on courtiers and other persons close to him, and, in the end, on the reputation of his court. He acknowledged that some would doubt his partiality, but the king justified his role by the peculiarity of the suit. The trial, though, also fits a larger pattern of the king becoming embroiled in aristocratic disputes over inheritance in the mid-1610s, after, one notes, the fall of Coke.

The first occasion on which it was suggested that the king should become involved in an inheritance dispute comes from the challenge made to the will of Thomas Sutton, the founder of Charterhouse.[55] Sutton, it will be recalled, was fantastically rich. A widower, he had only an illegitimate son, for whom he made no provision, and a nephew, one Simon Baxter. By the mid-1590s, Sutton was contemplating using his considerable fortune to found a hospital. He secured a statutory basis for this in 1610, but then shifted its location from Essex to his recently acquired property of the Charterhouse in London. After Sutton died at the end of 1611, Baxter tried to challenge his uncle's will and to take possession of the Charterhouse; in January 1612, he was called before the Council and bound in £100,000 to accept the king's award and arbitration. Sir Francis Bacon took the opportunity that Baxter's challenge presented to articulate his own doubts about Sutton's project and set out his own suggestions about how his endowment should be used. He was conditional, though, about the king's right to intervene: if the project were good in law, then he would not advise any intervention; if the defects in Sutton's scheme were such that a court of equity could rectify them, then a court should 'remedy and cure' – 'But if there be a right and birth-right planted in the heir and not remediable by courts of equity, and that right be submitted to your Majesty, whereby it is both in your power and grace what to do.' In short, Bacon laid out the

[55] For the following, see James Spedding, *The Letters and the Life of Francis Bacon* (London, 1868), vol. iv, pp. 248–250; *The Case of Sutton's Hospital* (1612) 10 Co Rep. 1 (77 *English Reports* 937); Robert Smythe, *Historical Account of the Charter-House* (London, 1808), pt 2, ch. 2.

circumstances in which the king could take Sutton's foundation into his own hands and reshape it, and, because this option was plainly Bacon's preference, he wrote at length about how the Charterhouse might be diverted from its founder's intention into objectives of which Bacon approved.

How far the king considered using Baxter's challenge to overturn Sutton's plans is unknown, but Baxter was allowed to bring an action of trespass in King's Bench in Michaelmas Term 1612, which was argued by heavyweight counsel, with Bacon as solicitor-general, amongst others, appearing for the plaintiff and Hobart as attorney-general for the defendants. The case was then referred to the Exchequer Chamber, where it was argued the following year before all the judges and a verdict given against the plaintiff. The king, overtly at least, played no further role in the pleadings, although he did accept a gratuity from Sutton's executors of £10,000 to be employed in the repair of Berwick bridge, and Baxter received a manor in Lancashire, doubtless for his acquiescence in the judges' decision.

A second proposal that the king should intervene in an inheritance dispute comes from the Talbot earls of Shrewsbury. Gilbert, seventh earl, died in May 1616 without a son living, but with three married daughters. Much earlier in life, he had set about to disinherit his brother Edward, who succeeded him as eighth earl. The fortunes of the eighth earl in the short period in which he held the earldom have yet to be investigated, but, on the one hand, he had a grievance that his brother had disinherited him of lands worth £20,000 'at least' entailed to him by his father in 1573 and, on the other, Chamberlain commented, on the eighth earl's death in February 1618, that he had recovered a great deal of the Talbot estates from his sister-in-law, the seventh earl's widow, his nieces and their husbands. A letter to the earl discussing his legal strategy of September 1617 shows the king's involvement in the disputes and intention to arbitrate. Given that the earl died only months later, this perhaps came to nothing.[56]

The two cases in which the king did intervene were superficially similar to the Talbot case in that the old earl had died without a male heir of his body. If the title were entailed on the male heir and the lands on the heirs general, then the title would pass to a brother or other male relation who would be left, as the eighth earl of Shrewsbury put it, without the means

[56] J. P. Cooper (ed.), *Wentworth Papers, 1597–1628* (Camden fourth ser., 12, 1973), pp. 96–99; *Letters of Chamberlain*, vol. II, p. 139.

'reasonable and necessary [for] a nobleman of my rank', whilst the estates passed out of the family by the marriage of the female heir.[57] In the Talbot case, the male heir was disinherited in favour of Talbot's nieces; in the two cases that concern us here, the female heir was disinherited to protect the bearer of the title and, understandably, the women objected to their treatment.

In the first case, the only child of the third earl of Cumberland's living at the time of his death was Lady Anne Clifford (two sons having predeceased him); his male heir, to whom the title descended, was therefore his brother Francis, subsequently fourth earl. Faced with the dilemma of disinheriting his daughter or his brother, the third earl chose to disinherit his daughter, offering her instead a portion of £15,000, to be paid on condition that Anne did not challenge his will. She married Richard Sackville, earl of Dorset, in 1609 as either a young woman with an opulent portion or, if she could recover what she regarded as her inheritance from her uncle, as the heiress to extensive estates in Westmorland and Yorkshire. Initially, Dorset was more interested in the cash than the ancestral Clifford estates.[58]

The third earl died on 30 October 1605. A little over a year later, Lady Anne lodged a petition laying claim to her father's estates. This was passed to the Earl Marshal, but to what end is unclear. Litigation, initially in the Court of Wards, was then more or less continuous until the king made his award in 1618. Three points might be made. The first is that the third earl's estates were a composite, acquired at different times and held by different tenures. There was no single solution to Anne Clifford's claims. It was, however, held in 1609 that her maximum claim was to the estates in Westmorland and the Honour of Skipton in Yorkshire, which were the first-acquired core estates of the family, and that she had no right to the former monastic lands acquired by her grandfather and great-grandfather. The second is that the earl's lawyers, when they recognised the need to resettle the estates in the early 1590s, had made a series of errors that Lady Anne's lawyers were able to uncover and exploit. The third is Anne's unshakable conviction in her rights and the tenacity with which she pursued her cause; hence there were a succession of hearings, initially in the Court of Wards and then in 1615 in Common

57 For a discussion of the general issue, see B. Coward, 'Disputed inheritances: some difficulties of the nobility in the late sixteenth and early seventeenth centuries', *Bulletin of the Institute of Historical Research* 44 (1971), 194–215.

58 The following account is based on R. T. Spence, *Lady Anne Clifford* (Stroud, 1997), esp. ch. 3, where much additional detail will be found.

Pleas. Ellesmere had ruled that Anne could have the lands, or the portion, but not some of the lands and all of the portion. Not unreasonably, her uncle insisted that he would not pay the portion until Lady Anne released all further claims in the estates to him. The result of the Common Pleas trial was an award by Sir Henry Hobart and the other judges of Common Pleas whereby the earl would buy out his niece's interest in the estates to which she had an entitlement for £17,000 (or £20,000, if she agreed), but the earl's interests would be limited to his heirs male. However, because the judges' ruling was in the nature of an arbitration, they insisted that all of the parties consent to it, and whilst Cumberland and Dorset were agreeable, Lady Anne was not. After Lady Anne's mother died on 24 May 1616, Dorset too backed away from the settlement, warming to the idea that he might acquire the estates.

It was in these circumstances that Dorset and Cumberland, having threatened to resolve their differences by joust, approached the king, asking him to make a final determination of the cause. On 8 January 1617, Dorset and his wife were summoned into the royal presence and asked to place the whole matter in the king's hands. Lady Anne stated her reservations. Nonetheless, two days later, the king heard the case in the presence of the parties and their lawyers. He pronounced his award on 14 March 1617. Dorset and Cumberland immediately signed it; Lady Anne did not. The award was essentially the judges' award of 1615. It gave the earl the lands and Lady Anne, £20,000 in compensation. Like the earlier award, it also entailed the core Clifford estates on the fourth earl's male heirs, and, for this reason, they eventually reverted to Lady Anne and her descendants. All that the earl secured from the award was a very expensive interest for his life and that of his son.

There was then the question of compliance. Lady Anne never consented to the making of the award nor to the award itself. In this, she had the support of friends, including Anne of Denmark, who thought her hard done by. It was matter of pride to her that she resisted every inducement – every threat – to sign it. She even took the unsigned settlement with her to Westmorland and left it there. Dorset assigned manors worth £25,000 to Cumberland as a form of conditional bond to be forfeited and sold if Lady Anne should commence suit again. The arrangements for the future tenure of the Westmorland estates – whose tenants were largely to fund the award – were to be confirmed by private Act, but this never happened, although a bill was introduced into the 1621 Parliament. The king's award was implemented as if all the parties had signed it and, ultimately, it served Lady Anne's purposes very well, but it also shows the limits of royal power and authority.

Whether the king was well advised to have become involved may be questioned. It might be argued that legal process had run as far as it could and only the king could hope to declare a definitive settlement. The issues were ones not merely of inheritance, but also of government: the Cliffords remained important figures in the North and on the Borders, and the disputes over the Westmorland estate following the death of the countess of Cumberland caused local disturbances. Any argument that the fourth earl needed to be favoured over his niece for the maintenance of good government has to be weighed against James's more or less simultaneous treatment of the earl of Ormond, in which he did the opposite. Because this episode is largely unknown to English historians, it is worth recounting it at length.[59]

Thomas, tenth earl of Ormond, was head of the pre-eminent Old English family in Ireland. His surviving issue was a daughter, Elizabeth. He elected to make a nephew, Theobald Butler, subsequently Viscount Tulleophelim (or Lord Tully), his heir and Theobald married his daughter. This was all negotiated with the queen's sanction in the last years of her life. However, Ormond seems to have held Tully in low esteem. He gave the couple an inadequate allowance and they ran into severe financial difficulties. Personal relations were poor. Moreover, the marriage produced no children (which may be the underlying reason for Ormond's evident scorn for his son-in-law) and, at the end of 1613, Tully died. The old earl lived on for most of a year, before dying in November 1614. Given that the estate was entailed on the heir male, the title and estates passed to Sir Walter Butler of Kilcash. Elizabeth was faced with a succession of problems. Like Lady Anne, she was deprived of the family estates, but she also had her husband's debts to carry, for which her father was reluctant to accept responsibility. It seems likely that she travelled to England with a grievance and in the hope that James would take an interest in her predicament, which he did.

James saw the opportunity to broker a marriage between Elizabeth and a second rank figure around the English court, Richard Preston, Lord

[59] I was introduced to this episode by David Edwards, *The Ormond Lordship in County Kilkenny, 1515–1642: The Rise and Fall of Butler Feudal Power* (Dublin, 2003), pp. 108–125. The present account follows Edwards, but adds details from a reading of the manuscript sources in the National Library of Ireland (hereafter NLI), MS 11,044 and 11,046.

Dingwall.[60] Preston had joined the Scottish court in the early 1590s and was amongst the Scots who transferred to England. In 1610, he served as the king's envoy to Venice and was raised to the peerage as Lord Dingwall. The marriage may well have been a reward for Preston, the means to give him the solvency that he lacked, as well as a lifeline for Elizabeth Butler. Elizabeth's father was told by letter not to interfere or object and the marriage took place in October or November 1614.[61] Elizabeth was quickly pregnant, her daughter being born on 25 July 1615. The king, having made the marriage, now threw his weight behind efforts to dispossess the new earl of Ormond of his estates.

Sir Walter Butler, the new earl, had little credit at court. It seems likely that he had visited England only once and, as a traditional Roman Catholic, he probably found the county uncongenial. He had alienated both James and the Dublin administration by joining the attempt to reject James's choice of speaker for the Irish Parliament of 1613. For these reasons, he could count on no favours and had few connections on whom to call. Whatever his rights at law (and it seems that his title to the estates was generally recognised in Ireland), he had a weak hand to play. There were questions about the debts of the late Viscount Tully, the share of the possessions of the late earl due to his daughter and the new earl, and the entitlement of another Butler, Sir Thomas, to parts of the estates.[62]

On 14 March 1615, James wrote to Ormond, calling on him to submit the points of difference between him and Lord and Lady Dingwall to the arbitration of friends.[63] James seems not to have envisaged being the arbitrator himself, but acting as a higher mediator, 'to interpose as there shalbe cause, our persuasion and mediation between you, in case you differ upon any points by the stiffness of either of your friends to whom you shall submit yourselves'. Ormond was to nominate friends. For the king's convenience, the arbitration would take place in London, and Ormond was told to travel there at the end of the next session of the Irish Parliament, bringing his evidences with him. Whilst James stressed his impartiality, there was surely a sting in his letter when he said that Dingwall had already consented to the king's commandment. Ormond had little option but to submit himself. He arrived at the court at Newmarket in November, but was still trying to see the Lord

[60] Dingwall now has a biography: T. V. Wilks, *Of Neighing Coursers and of Trumpets Shrill: A Life of Richard, first Lord Dingwall and Earl of Desmond (c. 1570–1628)* (London, 2012).

[61] Wilks speculates that Dingwall carried the king's letter to Ormond: ibid., pp. 43–44.

[62] *Calendar of State Papers Ireland* (hereafter *CSPI*) *1615–25*, p. 18.

[63] HMC *Ormonde* I, pp. 6–7; see also *CSPI 1615–25*, p. 19.

Chancellor in February 1616.[64] It may be noted that any veneer of impartiality on James's part progressively disappeared. So, writing to an unknown recipient (probably Ellesmere) on 8 December, James said that Lady Dingwall acknowledged 'the king as her father under God', adding that she had no jointure 'except the king's favour', and that it was for this that she had married Dingwall.[65] Dingwall may also have had the support of George Villiers, Duke of Buckingham.[66]

The parties went to arbitration on the goods of the late earl in December 1615. The Dingwalls had the Master of the Rolls in Ireland and the King's solicitor; Ormond was plainly outgunned. The Lord Deputy, the Irish Lord Chancellor and the Lord Chief Justice were to serve as umpires.[67] This may have been revoked, for, on 1 April, Ormond entered into a bond to accept the terms of an arbitration over for the money, plate and jewels of the late earl. A commission to examine the causes between Ormond and Dingwall was issued a few days later.[68] If an arbitration was ever made covering these areas of dispute, it does not survive. At some point, attention shifted from the late earl's possessions to his estates. An opinion was sought from Sir Henry Montagu (successor to Coke as chief justice of the King's Bench), Sir Henry Hobart (attorney-general) and Sir John Doddridge (a judge in King's Bench). This panel appears to have split in favour of the earl.[69] Negotiations may have continued through 1616 and early 1617, and whilst it is possible – although unevidenced – that there was a failed arbitration, on 14 April Ormond and Dingwall entered further mutual bonds in £100,000 to conform to the king's award.[70]

The sequence of events is revealed by the preamble to the king's award.[71] The king maintained that he was solely motivated by the desire to establish peace between 'parties so near in blood', and to avoid the multiplicity of suits and wasting of their estates that might ensue.

64 *CSPI 1615–21*, pp. 34, 61, 97, 118.

65 Ibid., p. 100.

66 Wilks, *Of Neighing Coursers and of Trumpets Shrill*, pp. 47–49.

67 NLI, MS 11,046 (15).

68 'Calendar of Ormond deeds', VIII (ts in the searchroom of the NLI), no. 3586; *CSPD 1611–18*, p. 361.

69 NLI, MS 11046 (9).

70 NLI, MS 11046 (34).

71 For convenience, I have used the text in *Calendar of Carew Manuscripts Preserved at Lambeth Palace Library*, six vols (1867–1873), vol. vi, pp. 371–374. The full text was enrolled on the Irish Patent Rolls: *Calendar of Patent Rolls Ireland, James I* (fasc. 1966), pp. 455–459.

(We may take this with a pinch of salt.) First, he had referred the questions to his learned counsel to establish whether they depended on clear or doubtful points in law. Counsel reported in writing that there were difficulties in law arising from the earl's settlements, which left it uncertain how much of his inheritance he wished the Lady Elizabeth and Walter, earl of Ormond, to possess. (This has to be questioned: the earl's preference in the matter is clear.) The king then referred the matter to three judges, who were to hear both parties and their counsel. They reported that the issues were incapable of clear resolution and that they could not tell how the issue would be resolved if all of the judges were to look at the matter. (This may be the opinion mentioned earlier.) For this reason, they declared that it was appropriate for the questions to be settled by the king himself – 'that it was proper for us to give a decree therein by way of equity *as if we were sitting in our person in our court of Chancery*' [emphasis added]. It may be suggested that the judges saw the problems as being not legal, but political – that is, how to satisfy the king's desire to make the Lady Elizabeth her father's heir against her father's clearly expressed intention. At a later date, James claimed that Sir John Everard and Robert Rothe, the old earl's lawyers, had confessed that the ancient entails of the house of Ormond had been barred and that the earl's title was vulnerable to being overthrown by the Lady Elizabeth; hence the king had been implored by both parties to rescue the situation.[72] This seems unlikely.

James was certainly willing to boast about the time the arbitration had taken: '[A]t length, after many days and much time spent in hearing both the said parties, their counsel and allegations on both sides, we have by the assistance of our chancellor and the most principal of our judges and by the advice and opinion of our learned counsel, made and published the our final order and award . . ..'[73] It was then the king's award, but not solely made by him, for he was guided by the judges. That said, the award, when it came, on 3 October 1618, rested less on the earl and countesses' respective titles than on the equity of the latter's claims.

The king's award began by considering the settlements made with the queen's sanction in 1602. Here, the late earl had agreed to settle on his daughter after her death an income of £800, of which only £400 had been actually settled on her and Viscount Tully in her lifetime. The king determined to raise the endowment up the £800 promised, and this

[72] HMC *Ormonde* I, p. 81.
[73] Ibid.

allowed him to divert a large part of the estates to Dingwall and his wife, including many of the largest and most improvable manors, as well as the ancestral castle and estate of Kilkenny. The earl was left with a rump of scattered estates.

Next, the award recited articles of agreement dated 4 January 1616 and a bond dated the 18 January, following which the earl accepted responsibility for the payment of the debts of the late Viscount Tully (although, as he objected later, he was neither heir nor executor to the Viscount).[74] He was to do this within three years and satisfy the earl's sureties within a further six months. Then, it ordered the estate's deeds to be delivered into the Dublin Chancery, where they would be accessible to both parties. Finally, the parties were to seek to secure a statutory confirmation in the next (Irish) Parliament, but the award was also to be sent down 'in our realm of Ireland as an act of state before our Deputy and Council'.

The award was therefore based not on the settlements made earlier, but on the undertaking to assign a specific value in lands to the Lady Elizabeth Butler. The king seems to have ignored the fact that, until the award, Lady Elizabeth had been receiving her £800 in a mixture of rent and cash paid by the earl. The reason why the lands allocated to Lady Butler fell short was that a proportion of them were held by beneficial lease and that, as the leases fell in, their value would far exceed £800.

The earl and Lord and Lady Dingwall were called before the Privy Council on 11 November, where they were asked whether they would perform the king's award. Ormond complained that he had received 'hard measure' both because of error and misinformation given to the king concerning the value and nature of the lands in the award. He asked to be relieved from its terms. The Council rebutted his complaint, stressing the king's 'great wisdom, moderation and justice'. If there were any errors, then they were on both sides and so cancelling. The Council therefore urged Ormond to cease complaining about the award and to make his submission. It instructed him not to take his complaints to the king, either by petition or other means. Ormond stopped well short of saying that he would accept the award, whilst the Dingwalls, perhaps realising their good fortune, said that they were ready to sign any assurance.[75] It seems that Ormond did petition the king, repeating his claim that James had been ill-informed and offering a list of five points

[74] The date given in the printed text in the *Carew Manuscripts*, vol. VI, p. 373, is in error. For his objection, see NLI, MS 11,046 (45), m. 3.

[75] *Acts of the Privy Council, 1618–19*, pp. 301–302.

that he wished the king to consider. He acknowledged that he counted for little in the king's estimation.[76] There is no sign that the king was willing to revisit the award. In February 1619, it was sent to the Lord Deputy in Ireland, who was instructed to put the parties in possession of the lands allocated to them.[77] The award was then allowed to remain unsigned until Ormond was called before the Privy Council in June, where, one assumes after again refusing to sign the award, he was committed to the Fleet[78] – and then, in a further striking demonstration of the king's partiality to Dingwall, they assigned the earl's bond to fulfil the terms of the award to the king himself, so that it could be collected as a Crown debt. In July, James ordered that the debt was to be levied.[79] The same month, Dingwall was made earl of Desmond – an Irish title then in abeyance, but another of the great houses of late medieval Ireland – and this cannot have been anything other than a further slight aimed at Ormond.[80]

With the passage of time, it became increasingly clear that the award was, in some respects, a dead letter. In July 1619, the earl's son, Viscount Thurles, was censored by James for collecting the rents of lands assigned to the Dingwalls/Desmonds and the Lord Deputy was ordered to imprison Thurles for contempt unless he desisted – but contempt of what? Thurles may well have been summoned to England to explain himself, for he was drowned in a shipwreck whilst crossing the Irish Sea in December 1619.[81] The previous month, Ormond had been presented with the settlement deed in the Fleet, but had refused to sign it. He remained determined to reject the award and adopted a strategy of remaining in the Fleet to outlive the king, perhaps calculating that Desmond's standing would not be so great under James's successor.[82] Ormond also had two opinions from counsel that the award had not been properly prepared and was void. The bond Ormond entered was for the king to issue an award under the signet, but the award had been made under the broad seal. It seems that the signet was affixed to the Desmond copy of the award, but only after Ormond raised questions about its

76 NLI, MS 11,046 (29).
77 HMC *Ormonde* I, p. 79.
78 *CSPI James I*, p. 248; *Acts of the Privy Council 1618–19*, p. 461.
79 NLI, MS 11,046 (34); HMC *Ormonde* I, pp. 80–81.
80 Wilks, *Of Neighing Coursers and of Trumpets Shrill*, p. 107.
81 Edwards, *Ormond*, p. 119.
82 'Calendar of Ormond deeds', VIII (ts in the searchroom of the NLI), D 3636, *CSPI*, no. 656.

validity, by which time he had sent his copy to Ireland to prove that it was not sealed with the signet. Out of reach, it was never sealed with the signet.[83] The first and shorter opinion held that the failure to make the award under the signet invalidated the whole process.[84] The second and much longer opinion argued again that the award had not been properly made and was invalid – nor could the retrospective addition of the signet to Desmond's copy redeem the situation. Moreover, this opinion argued that the award had been made by the king as a private person. This was implied both by the nature of the bond and by the fact that the award was to be issued under the king's private seal. To counter arguments that the award had been made under the prerogative and so the king could behave as he wished, the opinion laid out how:

> [T]he king hath two powers, one absolute, another limited, one merely as king, another as a common person. The power that the king hath in this case is merely by the election of the parties whereby he sitteth in the seat of a particular judge and arbitrator, therefore the king hath no more prerogative than any other common person should have had.

The award made under the great seal was void at law, and hence the king had no power to award the possession of the lands to the earl and countess of Desmond. Counsel therefore recommended that Ormond should proceed by action of trespass to recover the land – probably not a practical proposition.[85]

In June 1620, James, perhaps realising the fundamental problem of enforcement and the questions that were being raised about the validity of the award, instructed the Chancellor of Ireland to decree the award in Chancery on a bill to be moved by the earl and countess of Desmond and see that it was performed. The decree was made: the following year, two of the earl's lawyers were arrested for their non-compliance with the decree and called to London for punishment.[86]

At some time, Ormond submitted a second petition. This began by referring back to the earlier one. The king had evidently held that it was Ormond's choice whether he be restrained or at liberty and that, when he submitted, he should be released. Ormond therefore began by submitting himself to the king 'as the fountain of justice' and asked the king to take

[83] NLI, MS 11,046 (36) (letter of 16 November 1619). The original of the award at D3619 is without the signet.

[84] NLI, MS 11,046 (37).

[85] NLI, MS 11,046 (28).

[86] HMC *Ormonde* I, pp. 81–82.

a charitable view of his refusal to execute the settlement tendered unto him by the Desmonds. His refusal was not out of any 'wilful humour', but out of 'conscience, honour and law'. Ormond then noted that Desmond had assigned his bond to the king:

> ... suggesting that he had forfeited the same, intending by the power of your majesty prerogative to sell all your petitioner's leases and personal estate and to extend all his lands in His Majesty's lands upon that pretence, whereby your majesty being a judge and arbitrator shall be made a party in that business ... which your petitioner humbly submits to your princely consideration.

Ormond went on to ask the king to recall the arguments that he had previously made in his defence, 'which liberty and freedom the meanest subject in his majesty's dominions claimeth to be his birthright'. Ormond then made the argument that the award was void because it had not been sealed with the signet, and advanced the view that the king was at liberty to think again and make a new award. We have no evidence as to how this was received, but it is hard to think that it was anything but badly.[87]

It seems likely that there was some direct negotiation in the early 1620s between Ormond and the Desmonds in which the countess agreed to release to Ormond a number of manors. There were also discussions to heal the breach by the marriage of the Desmond's young daughter to Ormond's grandson, but these fell through in 1621 and, for a time, the Desmonds looked to marry their daughter into the Villiers clan.[88] The collapse of these negotiations prompted a third petition, which was referred to the Lord Keeper, John Williams, the Lord Chief Justice, Henry Montagu, then Viscount Mandeville and the retired Lord Deputy of Ireland, Oliver St John, Viscount Grandison, and whilst they recommended that the king offered some leeway on matters of 'no great moment' on the award, they saw Ormond's submission to it as the necessary prerequisite for negotiation. They also advised on the negotiations of the marriage of Ormond's heir to the daughter of Lord and Lady Desmond, whose failure they blamed on Ormond.[89]

In about March 1624, Ormond prepared another long petition, arguing the details of the award and the multiple injuries it did to him (and others), and asking for it to be reconsidered. But whilst he seemed to have dug in for the long haul, he also volunteered to execute the deed of

[87] NLI, MS 11046 (28, 29).
[88] Wilks, *Of Neighing Coursers and of Trumpets Shrill*, pp. 109–112.
[89] The petition is probably *CSPI 1615–25*, no. 806; NLI, MS 11044 (61).

settlement later in the year. He may have recognised that his hand had been strengthened when it was discovered that Desmond had been plotting to bring forward an imposter as earl of Ormond.[90] Even so, it was March 1627 before he gained his liberty – but, in the end, Ormond outlived them all. The countess of Desmond died whilst travelling to Ireland in October 1628 and her husband drowned later that month whilst crossing the Irish Sea on the way to her funeral; Ormond survived to 1633. The estates were finally reunited by the marriage in 1629 of Elizabeth Preston, daughter of the earl and countess of Desmond, with Ormond's grandson, James, in time twelfth earl of Ormond.

## VI

It is possible, perhaps even likely, that the abortive Talbot award, and the Clifford and Ormond awards, like the King's engagement with the Star Chamber case between the countess of Exeter and Lady Lake and Lady Ros, all arose out of personal appeals to the king for his intervention. The timing here might be significant, coinciding with the dismissal of Coke and the ascendency of Sir Francis Bacon in 1616. One assumes that Bacon and the law officers advised James that this was something he could do, and that much of the preparatory work fell on them.

Ormond's case was, if nothing else, an evil precedent for the future. The king had made an award to which Ormond had given his consent in advance, having had little option but to do so and perhaps trusting that the award would be a more impartial adjudication than it turned out to be. Ormond was then imprisoned for refusing to put his name to the award; his appeals were ignored, and his bond was forfeited and prosecuted. The award was read into the records of the Irish Chancery even though Ormond had not given his consent to it and it had not been completed in accordance with the initial agreement between the parties. For those who noticed, Ormond's experience had frightening implications for the future: a subject could be coerced into a penal bond to observe the king's award against which he had no appeal. If he refused to accept it, he could be imprisoned and financially ruined.

The problem that both the Clifford and Ormond awards threw up was one of enforcement. Neither Ormond nor Lady Anne ever signed their awards, although they were implemented without their consent. What,

[90] NLI, MS 11044 (45); HMC *Cowper* I, pp. 169–170.

however, would have happened if a party to a royal award were to petition Chancery for its enforcement, as had been done in the Ormond case?

## VII

A number of instances have come to light of Charles I intervening in the affairs of aristocratic families and making awards, apparently to protect the interests of women, but these are of less interest than Charles' novel use of awards and the dangers that these posed.[91]

One of the difficulties the king faced was how to bring about meaningful reform without parliamentary sanction. A statute was deemed to have been made with the consent of the nation. Moreover, statutes were equipped with penalties for non-compliance. A royal award arbitrating between parties concerned only a small number of people whose compliance could be achieved by personal bonds. A decree that had a larger social purpose could bear on hundreds, if not thousands, of people and, as with taxation, if issued under the prerogative alone, was likely to be opposed by at least some of those affected. The problems posed by reform without a parliament were therefore considerable, but they did not deter Charles.

In May 1634, the Privy Council received a petition from clergy in London, stressing their poverty.[92] It described how the sources of income available for the support of the clergy had declined since the Reformation and outlined a long series of grievances that prevented them from receiving what they considered to be their due. The clergy wished to have a Chancery decree of 1546 revived, which would give them a tithe on rental value at 2*s.* 9*d.* in the pound.

[91] The instances discovered so far are between: John Lord Roberts and his son-in-law, Charles Lord Lambert (1629), TNA, SO 1/1, f. 208v, *CSPD 1629–31*, p. 192, and Richard Cust, *Charles I and the Aristocracy, 1625–1642* (Cambridge, 2013), p. 87 (although Simon Healy suggests to me that no award was made); between the earls of Arundel and Pembroke (1632), BL, Add. MS 33596, ff. 1, 5; for Lady Mary Herbert (1636), Bodleian Library, Bankes MSS 48/23, enrolled TNA, C66/2739, no. 25; and for Lady Elizabeth Stanley (1635) *CSPD 1634–35*, p. 567, 1635, pp. 36–37, Lancashire Archives, DDK 11/17, 11/19 (which recites the award).

[92] For the following, see Christopher Hill, *Economic Problems of the Church, from Archbishop Whitgift to the Long Parliament* (Oxford, 1956), pp. 280–283; T. C. Dale, 'Introduction', in T. C. Dale (ed.), *The Inhabitants of London in 1638* (London 1931), pp. iv–xii; comments in Kevin Sharpe, *The Personal Rule of Charles I* (New Haven, 1992), p. 315.

The clergy's petition was argued before the king in the Privy Council on 5 November, in the presence of the Recorder of London and some of the City's aldermen. They were asked to agree to the king acting as arbitrator between the City and its clergy. The City was reluctant to accept this, but finally submitted to the king in December. However, there then seems to have been a lull for four years. In May 1638, the Council returned to the issue, and the City and the clergy were told to produce certificates of the value of every house in every parish within the City's boundaries. This was done during the summer of 1638 (largely by the clergy alone), although some returns were still outstanding in October of the year. The king then deferred any further consideration of the proposal in January 1639, as relations with Scotland deteriorated, and so the moment was lost.

Nothing came of the campaign of the London clergy, although, as with Ormond, the City was in a weak position once it had been forced to submit to the king's arbitration. Nonetheless, the clergy's case seems to have caught the king's attention. The London petition engendered a copycat petition from Norwich, making much the same points about the poverty of the clergy and their reliance on voluntary donations. A petition from the Norwich clergy was considered at the Council board on 21 January 1637 before the king himself. He sought further information, requiring the clergy and citizens to set down in writing how much each minister of each parish had in income from his benefice and how much from the voluntary contribution of his parishioners. They were also to present certificates of the number of houses with their rents, together with the number of inhabitants of each parish. The clergy's representatives declared their willingness to submit to the king's order and to secure the consent of the clergy not present. The representatives from the City argued that they had no authority to proceed in this way. The king considered the matter again in Council on 1 April, when the certificates and submissions were received and considered.[93] The king expressed dissatisfaction with aspects of what had been placed before him, but proceeded to issue his award.[94] This, he said, was to provide 'some competence of livelihood and maintenance' to the clergy and to prevent further disputes. The award began by considering the practices in other towns, including London, then ordered that the clergy should be

[93] *Privy Council Registers in Facsimile*, II, pp. 524–525, III, pp. 61–62; *CSPD 1637–38*, p. 167.

[94] The award was enrolled on the patent rolls, C66/2804, no. 14. It is printed in Humphrey Prideaux, *An Award of King Charles the First, under His Broad-Seal . . . with a Treatise Vindicating the Legality and Justice of that Award* (London, 1707).

paid a tithe (in effect, a rate) of 2*s*. in the pound on the value of all houses, shops and other property within their parishes. Payments were to be made quarterly. Disputes were to be settled in either Chancery or in the consistory court of the Bishop of Norwich. The award was to be issued under the Great Seal (which was done in August), and entered in the records of both Chancery and the consistory court.

This may have been a notable victory for the clergy. It may also have been met with resistance in Norwich itself. In 1639, one Samuel Booty, vicar of St Stephens, brought bills against two parishioners, Judith Peckover and Rose Heath, both widows.[95] Whether Booty was bringing a case on his own behalf or launching a test case on the behalf of the Norwich clergy as a whole is unknown. In short, he sought the performance of the king's award. Peckover had refused to cooperate with him by refusing to tell him what her property was worth. In response, Peckover merely submitted a demurrer, saying that she was advised by her counsel that no tithes were liable on houses or other property. She maintained that the submission of the mayor and corporation to the king's award did not bind the inhabitants of the city. Moreover, the appropriate place for any trial was in King's Bench. Whilst the king's right to make the award was not challenged, these lines of argument, either independently or taken together, served to nullify it.

Chancery recognised the gravity of the challenge. The demurrer was heard and utterly dismissed on 10 February 1640 by Sir John Finch, newly appointed Lord Keeper. The formal record is worth quoting in full:

> His lordship declared that His Majesty was the royal fountain from whence all streams of justice are properly derived and all the courts of justice are but His Majesty's instruments for distributing of justice amongst his people, and therefore his lordship held that said plea and demurrer to be no less frivolous and unfit to be allowed by this court then bold and saucy towards His Majesty and much derogating from His Majesty's justice.

Exemplary costs were awarded against Peckover and she was instructed to answer the plaintiff's bill fully. Heath's demurrer was dismissed in the same words.[96] But the drift of events was against Booty and it seems unlikely that any answer was submitted – none can be found – because

[95] Only one bill (and demurrer) appears to survive, TNA, C 2/ChasI/B107/17.

[96] TNA, C 33/177, ff. 234r, 404r. The order of 10 February was noticed by a Chancery reporter. Either he or his editor found the order so odd that they added *Quaere. Booth* v. *Peckover* (1639–40) 1 Chan. Rep. 138 (21 *English Reports* 530).

the next law term coincided with the Short Parliament. The award was then the subject of complaint to the Long Parliament and 'quashed' before it was ever put into effect.[97] By the end of the seventeenth century, its very existence had been forgotten.[98]

It is fascinating – if frightening – to speculate how this might have turned out. It hardly seems likely that Finch would have tolerated doubts about the legality of the king's award or its enforcement through Chancery. The way was therefore open for the king, with a pliable Lord Chancellor or Lord Keeper, to register his decrees in Chancery (or for one of the parties to them to do so) and then to use the court to achieve their enforcement. A mechanism for rule without parliaments had been established – perhaps unintentionally, but the possibility had been plain for quarter of a century – with all the dangers that that implied.

## VIII

As we noticed, Turner's concern was that if Chancery were to secure a recognised right to act as a court of appeal from the common law jurisdictions, then business would flow to it. Verdicts at the common law made before a jury might be overturned by a single judge. Moreover, if the Lord Chancellor were to act politically, on instructions received from the monarch or Privy Council, verdicts at the common law that the Crown disliked, or thought undesirable precedents, might also be overturned. Hence the common law would be placed in jeopardy in two ways, by litigants not knowing if a common law judgment really ended their litigation and by common law precedents being negated by the Chancellor. In this chapter, we have identified a third fear: that Chancery could be the instrument by which the Crown could issue and enforce edicts, whether awards made between the parties in which the king played the role of arbitrator, or social reforms in which the king's decision could be decreed by Chancery and then enforced by it. In this respect, the case of the earl of Ormond formed a dangerous precedent for the future, albeit that the King's disputed award was registered in the Irish, rather than English, Chancery. It showed all too plainly why the king should never get involved in litigation between parties. There was confusion between the king as an individual and the office that he held. It laid him open to accusations of partiality and favouritism. There was

97 Sharpe, *Personal Rule*, p. 315.
98 Prideaux, *Award*, pp. 9–10.

no appeal, not even on points of error. There were problems of enforcement. Nonetheless, Charles continued to make arbitrations from time to time, although the mechanisms he used are unknown.

The award that Charles made to establish a new funding regime for the Norwich clergy was very different in character. The aim was to establish a new system of taxation in the city. It was surely inevitable that it would encounter resistance and so the question of enforcement was bound to arise. Whether Booty was a stooge, bringing a test case on behalf of the Norwich clergy as a whole, or a maverick pursuing his own agenda, he was certainly raising a question that someone, sometime, would have been bound to ask. There can be no doubt that, in different circumstances, it would have been decreed by Chancery. There was no legal reason why it should not have been, for it was an expression of the King's will – neither Ellesmere, in one generation, nor Finch in the next could resist that – and so the enforcement of the decree would have fallen on Chancery, a task that it was surely ill-equipped to fulfil.

Of course, none of this came to pass. Chancery barely features in the complaints about the law and judges in the Short Parliament and in the early weeks of the Long Parliament. Members of Parliament had more immediate concerns to debate. And so we can conclude that Charles's habit of making awards drew little comment, except in Norwich, where the king's award must have become a dead letter as circumstances altered over the course of 1640.

It might be held that this chapter is an exploration of 'what might have been', but we can conclude that the danger that Chancery could be used as Bacon's 'court of absolute power',[99] which could undermine the common law, remained a real one through to the civil war. As late as the eve of the Restoration, the Duke of Newcastle, in his advice to Charles II, could maintain that the king had every right to sit judicially and that, whilst he did not think the king should do it often, Newcastle urged the king to sit as a judge if only 'to examine the apparent corruption of some judges and put them out, which act will gain your majesty much love'.[100] The road not taken was never lacking in advocates.

[99] Baker, 'Common lawyers and the Chancery: 1616', p. 268.

[100] Thomas P. Slaughter (ed.), *Ideology and Politics on the Eve of the Restoration: Newcastle's Advice to Charles II* (Philadelphia, 1984), p. 31.

# 6

# The Inns of Court, Renaissance and the Language of Modernity

PHIL WITHINGTON

William Prynne's *Histrio-mastix, the player's scourge* (1633) is one of the most notorious treatises of the early Stuart era.[1] A long and exhaustive attack on all aspects of contemporary theatrical culture – and the sinful manners that playwrights, players, plays, playing, playhouses, play-going and theatrical patronage inculcated – it resulted in Prynne's trial in Star Chamber and his infamous punishment: the public burning of all copies of his book and the cropping of his left ear (a punishment that was reprised, more savagely, three years later).[2] Prynne's exegesis and his trial have accordingly received a good deal of attention from historians of censorship, puritanism, and the political and ideological tensions that characterized England in the 1620s and 1630s.[3] Characterizations of this prolific polemicist range from the 'moderate' victim of Carolinian state intolerance and Laudian interference to the seditious and puritanical misanthrope who was lucky to lose only an earlobe.[4] What may be less clear, perhaps, is why a chapter on the relationship between English law and Renaissance should begin with the author of one of the iconic texts of seventeenth-century confessional politics.

[1] *Histrio-mastix the players scourge, or, actors tragaedie, divided into two parts … By William Prynne, an utter-barrester of Lincolnes Inne* (1633).

[2] For the most recent treatment, see Mark Kishlansky, 'A whipper whipped: the sedition of William Prynne', *Historical Journal* 56 (2013), 603–627.

[3] Annabel Patterson, *Censorship and Interpretation* (Madison, 1984), p. 115; Anthony Milton, 'Licensing, censorship and religious orthodoxy in Stuart England', *Historical Journal* 41 (1998), 625–651, p. 629; Arnold Hunt, 'Licensing and religious censorship in early modern England', in Andrew Hadfield (ed.), *Literature and Censorship in Renaissance England* (New York, 2001), pp. 127–146, pp. 143–144.

[4] William Lamont, *Marginal Prynne, 1600–1669* (London, 1963), especially pp. 28–48; Kishlansky, 'A whipper whipped'.

There are two reasons. The first is obvious enough. When Prynne researched, wrote and published *Histrio-mastix* in the later 1620s and early 1630s, he did so as a young and respected barrister based physically, as well as socially and emotionally, at Lincoln's Inn in London. Prynne defined his authorial identity at the time by his membership of the Inn, describing himself on the numerous frontispieces of his early moral and religious tracts as either 'an utter-barrister of Lincoln's Inn' or 'Gent. Hospitii Lincolniensis'.[5] He also dedicated *Histrio-mastix*, his *magnum opus*, directly to the Inns – and he did so not once, but twice: in the first dedicatory epistle, 'To His Much Honoured Friends, the Right Worshipful Masters of the Bench of the Honourable Flourishing Law-Society of Lincolnes-Inn'; in the second, 'To the Right Christian Generous Young Gentlemen-Students of the 4 Famous Inns of Court, and especially those of Lincolnes Inn'.[6] Thereafter, the lawyers charged with acting in Prynne's defence in the court of Star Chamber were mostly from Lincoln's Inn, as were a number of his prosecutors.[7] This may have been a public controversy of national and, indeed, international significance, but its key protagonists were all men who had been intellectually shaped by – and who continued to live and work in – the small legal precincts and societies of early modern London.

The second reason for starting the chapter with *Histrio-mastix* is much less obvious than Prynne's legal antecedents and networks, but quite as telling in terms of the argument that follows. It is based on the fact that, in the hundred or so years before Prynne published his rant against theatrical culture, the word 'modern' was first introduced into vernacular English printed discourse as a translation of the Latin *modernus* and, in particular, the French *moderne*.[8] As I have argued elsewhere, the domestication of 'modern' was part and parcel of a more general process of

[5] *The perpetuitie of a regenerate man's estate ... By William Prynne Gent: Lincolniensis* (1626); *The vnlouelinesse, of loue-lockes ... By William Prynne, Gent. Hospitij Lincolniensis* (1628); *Healthes: sicknesse ... By William Prynne Gent. Hospitii Lincolniensis* (1628); *A briefe suruay and censure of Mr Cozens his couzening deuotions ... By William Prynne Gent. Hospitij Lincolniensis* (1628); *The Church of Englands old antithesis to new Arminianisme ... By William Prynne Gent. Hospitij Lincolniensis* (1629); *God, no impostor nor deluder ... By William Prynne, and utter barrester of Lincolnes Inne* (1629); *Anti-Arminianisme. Or The Church of Englands old antithesis to new Arminianisme ... by William Prynne, an utter-barrester of Lincolnes Inne* (1630); *Lame Giles his haultings ... By William Prynne, an vtter-barrester of Lincolnes Inne* (1630).

[6] Prynne, *Histrio-mastix*, *r; ibid, *5.

[7] Kishlansky, 'A whipper whipped', pp. 613–614.

[8] Phil Withington, *Society in Early Modern England: The Vernacular Origins of Some Powerful Ideas* (Cambridge, 2010), pp. 73–101.

linguistic vernacularization.[9] This was an extraordinarily complicated process of linguistic and cultural change whereby, among other things, foreign words such as 'democracy' were domesticated into English ('Englished') and English words such as 'happiness' underwent significant semantic change to translate foreign and ancient terms and concepts.[10] 'Modern' is a nice example of the former kind of semantic change: a foreign word entering the English lexicon. And what is especially striking about its use in English is that, as in its usage in European and classical culture, 'modern' did not look forward, as we might assume today, towards a progressive future; rather, it looked backwards, establishing a self-consciously dialectical relationship with *previous* epochs and ages – in particular, the classical culture of 'the ancients'.[11] Or, to put that slightly differently, in sixteenth- and early seventeenth-century England, the use of the term 'modern' became one of the more reliable indicators of a quintessential feature of 'Renaissance' thinking: the habit of looking backwards – to the knowledge and culture of 'ancient' epochs – to evaluate, compare and reform the 'modern' present.[12]

What is interesting about Prynne is that between the 1530s, when 'modern' first appeared in printed English, and the 1630s, when it had become a relative commonplace in vernacular print, *Histrio-mastix* contained more uses of 'modern' than any other vernacular printed text.[13] Indeed, no other text came close. 'Modern' or variants of it appear 135 times in *Histrio-mastix*, followed by Edward Grimstone's translation of Pedro Mexia's *The Treasury of Ancient and Modern Times* (1613), in which it appears 100 times, and by Thomas Jackson's *The Eternal Truth of Scriptures* (1613), in which 'modern' is used 69 times.[14] *Histrio-mastix*

9 Withington, *Society*, pp. 10–13.

10 Phil Withington, 'An Aristotelian moment: democracy in early modern England', in Michael Braddick and Phil Withington (eds), *Popular Culture and Political Agency in Early Modern England* (Woodbridge, 2017), pp. 203–223; Phil Withington, 'The invention of happiness', in Joanna Innes and Michael Braddick (eds), *Happiness and Suffering in Early Modern England* (Oxford, 2017), pp. 23–45.

11 Hans Ulrich Gumbrecht, 'Modern, Modernitat, Moderne', in Otto Brunnet, Werner Conze and Reinhart Koselleck (eds), *Geschichteliche Grundebegriffe. Historisches Lexikon zur Politisch-Sozialen Sprache in Deutschland, Band 4 Mi-Pre* (Stuttgart, 1978), p. 12.

12 Withington, *Society*, pp. 73–101.

13 The claim is based on searches of Early English Books Online–Text Creation Partnership (EEBO–TCP) between 9 November 2017 and 13 January 2018.

14 Pedro Mexia, *The treasurie of auncient and moderne times – Containing the learned collections, iudicious readings, and memorable obseruations: not onely diuine, morrall and phylosophicall. But also poeticall, martiall, politicall, historicall, astrologicall, &c,*

is a long book and Prynne a verbose writer; nor does the quantity of words necessarily illuminate the ways and contexts in which the term is used (although, in Prynne's case, his sense of modernity was most definitely constructed through dialogue with the ancient past). But even if we take only the numbers as an index, it is clear that, in his attack on theatricality, Prynne's engagement with the language of modern was intense.

Prynne, then, was a lawyer embroiled in some of the main cultural and political debates of the period and a writer who, in his modernism, epitomized a certain Renaissance way of thinking – of looking backwards, to the ancients, to make sense of and influence both the present and the future. As such, he nicely introduces the main themes of this chapter, which reconsiders the relationship between English law and Renaissance through the prism of early modern languages of modern. The nature of this relationship – and whether, indeed, there is even a relationship to speak of – has been a perennial historiographical concern since F. W. Maitland's famous lecture on 'English law and the Renaissance' in 1901.[15] Certainly, it is a question that Christopher W. Brooks wrestled with throughout his career – from an early essay on 'History, English law and the Renaissance', co-written with Kevin Sharpe in 1976, to his reconstruction of the Elizabethan 'common law mind' in 2008, to the posthumous chapter on 'law, literature and history in Restoration England'.[16] Viewing these contributions in the round, Brooks clearly felt that the relationship was strong and important – that 'the Renaissance' left an indelible mark on how English lawyers thought and went about their business, with significant ramifications for society and culture more generally. But Brooks developed this view in the face of powerful and influential arguments to the contrary. These interpretations held that it was the imperviousness of English law to the

trans. Edward Grimstone (London, 1613); Thomas Jackson, *The eternall truth of scriptures, and Christian beleefe, thereon vvholly depending, manifested by it owne light* (London, 1613).

15 Frederic William Maitland, *The English Law and the Renaissance (The Rede Lecture for 1901)* (Cambridge, 1901).

16 Christopher W. Brooks and Kevin Sharpe, 'History, English law, and the Renaissance', *Past and Present* 72 (1976), 133–146; Christopher W. Brooks, *Law, Politics and Society in Early Modern England* (Cambridge, 2008), pp. 66–87; Christopher W. Brooks, 'Paradise lost? Law, literature and history in Restoration England', in Lorna Hutson (ed.), *The Oxford Handbook of English Law and Literature, 1500–1700* (Oxford, 2017), pp. 198–218.

Renaissance that was, in many respects, its defining feature, and that this imperviousness made for a peculiarly insular and comparatively unlearned legal fraternity and legal culture.[17]

This chapter contributes to the debate by examining the engagement of Innsmen with the language of 'modern' as it became a feature of English vernacular print over the course of the sixteenth and early seventeenth centuries. Its argument is simple. On the one hand, insofar as the imprint of 'modern' in printed texts is anything to go by, English common law remained remarkably resistant to Renaissance influences: well into the seventeenth century, England's printed legal lexicon was notable for the almost complete absence of 'modern'. On the other hand, by the same measure, men of the Inns of Court were increasingly energetic as protagonists of the English assimilation of 'modern' – and the modern–ancient dialectic – into other fields of vernacular knowledge. Common law as an esoteric and technocratic language may well have been protected as immutable and 'insular'.[18] But its erstwhile students and practitioners – and the societies that gave them their professional and social identities – were nevertheless utterly implicated in the broader process of English Renaissance.

To make this argument, the chapter divides into three sections. The first outlines the century-long debate over the relationship between English law and Renaissance. The chapter then turns to the English assimilation of the term 'modern' into printed discourse. It discusses in more detail how 'modern' signified a dialectical conception with the past and, utilizing digital technology, considers which authors were most responsible for adopting it, and into which areas of learning and knowledge they did so. It is especially concerned with the role of the Inns of Court and Innsmen in this process of vernacularization. The final section then considers the extent to which legal discourse was inflected by the dialectic between ancient and modern.

[17] Donald R. Kelley, 'English law and the Renaissance', *Past and Present* 65 (1974), 24–51; J. G. A. Pocock, *The Ancient Constitution and the Feudal Law: A Study of English Historical Thought in the Seventeenth Century* (Cambridge, 1987), especially chs 2 and 3. Brooks explicitly directs his arguments against Pocock in Brooks, *Law, Politics and Society*, p. 82.

[18] Sebastian Sobecki, *Unwritten Verities: The Making of England's Vernacular Legal Culture, 1463–1549* (Notre Dame, 2015), p. 29.

## 'Little Renaissances' and 'Hidden Treasures'

When Chris Brooks and Kevin Sharpe published 'History, English Law and the Renaissance' in 1976, they were only the latest to join a long-standing debate that can be traced at least to F. W. Maitland's Rede Lecture of 1901. Maitland noted that English common law is 'not a place in which we look for humanism or the spirit of the Renaissance: rather we look there for an amazingly continuous persistence and development of medieval doctrine'.[19] He argued that, nevertheless, between the 1520s and 1550s, conditions were in place for 'the continuity of English legal history' to be 'seriously threatened'. These included: a Tudor despot intent on exerting his will in church and state, and flirting with Roman – civil – law to do so; a burgeoning culture of legal humanism on the Continent and in Scotland that encouraged the widespread appropriation of Roman law, or what Maitland styled the 'Reception'; and a somewhat depleted mid-century common law profession compared with England's effervescent and influential civilians, who were trained at the universities, rather than the Inns, and were held in professional distrust by common lawyers.[20] Maitland concluded by suggesting the main reason why English common law not only bucked the continental trend towards 'Reception', but also went on to enjoy 'a little Renaissance' or 'Gothic revival' of its own – namely, that 'medieval England had schools of national law'. It was the institutionalization of legal education within the Inns of Court – of 'academic teaching' by societies of legal practitioners – that ultimately ensured medieval 'persistence' in an era of humanism and change.[21]

Maitland's short lecture anticipates most fronds of the argument over English law and Renaissance as they unfurled thereafter. One is the jurisdictional disputes between common and civil law, and whether the hegemony of the former was ever really 'seriously threatened' in the Henrician and Marian eras. For the likes of Geoffrey Elton and S. E. Throne, Maitland overstated the danger.[22] But, as Dafydd Jenkins has observed, the point of Maitland's question was not so much the scale of the 'threat' as it was the apparently unique capacity for English law to

[19] Maitland, *The English Law and the Renaissance*, p. 3.

[20] Ibid., pp. 17, 20, 15.

[21] Ibid., pp. 29, 25.

[22] S. E. Thorne, 'English law and the Renaissance', in *La Storia del Diritto Nel Quadro Delle Scienze Storiche* (Florence, 1966), pp. 437–445; G. R. Elton, *Studies in Tudor and Stuart Politics and Government* (Cambridge, 1974), vol. I, p. 339, n. 1; Brian P. Levack, *The Civil Lawyers in England, 1603–1641* (Oxford, 1973), pp. 124–125, 132–133.

reproduce itself without explicit recourse to Roman law: the less 'threatened' it was, the greater that capacity must have been.[23] A second is the insularity of English common law and the relative absence, or not, of Renaissance humanist influences on legal and historical scholarship when compared with the rest of Europe. In the influential arguments of J. G. A. Pocock and Donald R. Kelley, English legal thinking was increasingly and deliberately enclosed against continental trends in humanist scholarship and reform: not for them any 'little Renaissance'.[24] Brooks and Sharpe contested this perspective. As they saw it, Tudor lawyers were much more receptive to legal humanism, and also much less confident in the operations of their own system, than the historiographical orthodoxy suggested. They argued that Sir Edward Coke, the Jacobean doyen of Pocock's 'common law mind', did not so much inherit a medieval doctrine rooted in immemorial custom and artificial reason as invent it. And they suggested that the widespread acceptance of 'the common law myth of Coke' by the 1620s was the result of political tensions, and the need for 'certainty' and legitimacy on constitutional matters: 'As the political conflict intensified, the stand on precedent and the "old constitution" became established.'[25]

Brooks's early concern for English law's 'little Renaissance' recurs repeatedly in his own work thereafter – most convincingly in his reconstruction of early modern legal learning and the Elizabethan 'common law mind'.[26] This described a much more classically informed and intellectually variegated mentalité than Pocock's circumscribed and monocultural sketch – one that accommodates the wide learning and range of reference of Elizabethan lawyers. Its emphases complement the third feature of Maitland's argument, although perhaps not quite in the ways Maitland envisaged: the cultural significance of England's 'school of laws'. Most important in this respect has been the work of Brooks's contemporary, Wilfrid Prest, who corrected the traditional assumption that London's legal Inns underwent no transitions between the medieval and modern eras, and also established an analytical framework for thinking about their early modern members – alumni, benchers (governors), barristers, Innsmen (students), residents, stewards,

[23] Dafydd Jenkins, 'English law and the Renaissance eighty years on', *Journal of Legal History* 2 (1981), 107–142, p. 108.

[24] Kelley, 'English law', p. 25; Pocock, *The Ancient Constitution*, pp. 56–57.

[25] Brooks and Sharpe, 'History, English law and the Renaissance', pp. 134, 141–142.

[26] Brooks, *Law, Politics and Society*, pp. 23–29, 66–67, 82–84.

servants – as 'cultural brokers' in larger social and cultural worlds.[27] The two points are interconnected: the 'transformation of the Inns from small, inward-looking professional fraternities to large, complex, quasi-collegiate public institutions' meant that members and alumni were not merely lawyers, but also translators, authors, playwrights; politicians, governors, patrons; readers, correspondents, audiences; urbane consumers and landed gentry.[28] The Inns may well have protected English common law as a living and hegemonic discourse by institutionalizing its jargon and procedures, and effectively controlling access into legal practice. But, as contemporaries well knew, the Elizabethan expansion of the Inns into England's 'third university' also meant that they contributed to the social mobility and broader intellectual formation of England's moneyed and genteel classes.[29]

Within legal historiography, then, it is in terms of both the construction and reproduction of law as a field of knowledge *and* the institutions and practitioners of law in their broader social and cultural contexts that the debate over the relationship between law and Renaissance has developed. This trajectory has encouraged interventions from at least two other disciplines. Most straightforwardly, literary and intellectual historians have focused on Innsmen as producers and consumers of literary and political culture, emphasizing their classical reach and referents.[30] They have identified the widespread use and circulation of legal tropes and language in ostensibly 'literary' texts, not least in Renaissance drama.[31] And they have suggested the assimilation of more general classical skills and techniques – most notably, styles of rhetoric – into

[27] Wilfrid R. Prest, *The Inns of Court under Elizabeth I and the Early Stuarts, 1590–1640* (London, 1972), pp. 1–20; Wilfrid R. Prest, *The Rise of the Barristers. A Social History of the English Bar 1590–1640* (Oxford, 1986), p. 324.

[28] Prest, *Inns of Court*, pp. 4, 137–173; Prest, *Rise of the Barristers,* chs 6 and 8; J. H. Baker, 'The Third University, 1450 1550: law school or finishing school?', in Jayne Elizabeth Archer, Elizabeth Goldring and Sarah Knight (eds), *The Intellectual and Cultural World of the Early Modern Inns of Court* (Manchester, 2011), pp. 8–21.

[29] Thomas Smith, *De republica Anglorum. The maner of governement or policie of the realme of England* (London, 1583), E1r; Keith Wrightson, *English Society, 1580–1680* (London, 1982), pp. 192–193.

[30] See, e.g., Michelle O'Callaghan, *The English Wits: Literature and Sociability in Early Modern England* (Cambridge, 2009); Jessica Winston, *Lawyers at Play: Literature, Law and Politics at the Early Modern Inns of Court, 1558–1581* (Oxford, 2016).

[31] Lorna Hutson, *The Invention of Suspicion: Law and Mimesis in Shakespeare and Renaissance Drama* (Oxford, 2007); Quentin Skinner, *Forensic Shakespeare* (Oxford, 2014).

the professional armoury of the successful common lawyer.[32] In all respects, the connections between law and Renaissance are palpable. Somewhat differently, social historians have demonstrated the importance of law in arbitrating social conflicts and structuring social and economic relationships. In this analytical tradition, Renaissance has not figured especially highly as an interpretative consideration – although Brooks, in advocating the more general societal influence of law, as well as the complicated cultural formation of lawyers, is an exception to this rule. But what social historians have done is point towards the potential means by which litigation and legal process disseminated values and norms more widely. Law was very much a resource that could be appropriated by individuals, classes and parties to suit purposes and needs.[33] But, as Brooks argues, by resorting to law, individuals and communities could not help but act, at some level, according to the precepts of those who 'did' law – that is, the legal profession, broadly defined.[34] And, if that is the case, then debates over the provenance and content of law, including the broader intellectual formation of its practitioners, clearly had ramifications far beyond the benches and quills of the Inns and courtrooms themselves.

But this debate not only interrogates the nature of law in early modern England. It also begs the question of what is meant by 'Renaissance' – a category of analysis that has undergone a fair amount of critique over the last few decades, even within Italian historiography.[35] Clearly, what Maitland had in mind when he used the concept was not the kind of cultural production or aesthetic systems studied by historians of art and familiar to the popular historical imagination. Neither does the label refer to the esoteric classicism of aristocratic scholars or somehow grandiosely encapsulate, in the

[32] Lorna Hutson, 'Rhetoric and early modern law', in Michael MacDonald (ed.), *The Oxford Handbook of Rhetorical Studies* (Oxford, 2017), pp. 397–407; James McBain, '"Attentive minds and serious wits": legal training and early drama', in Lorna Hutson (ed.), *The Oxford Handbook of English Law and Literature, 1500–1700* (Oxford, 2017), pp. 80–96.

[33] Andy Wood, *The Politics of Social Conflict: The Peak Country, 1520–1770* (Cambridge, 1999); Steve Hindle, *The State and Social Change in Early Modern England, 1550–1640* (Basingstoke, 2000).

[34] Brooks, 'Paradise lost?', pp. 199–201; Craig Muldrew, *The Economy of Obligation: The Culture of Credit and Social Relations in Early Modern England* (Basingstoke, 1998).

[35] Edward Muir, 'The Italian Renaissance in America', *American Historical Review* 100 (1995), 1113–1118.

fashion of Burckhardt, an entire epoch: the 'birth of individualism', for example, or 'intellectual freedom'.[36] But, noting what Maitland did *not* mean by the term is easier than establishing what he *did* mean by it, because he never offers a full definition. This elusiveness characterizes the debate thereafter. On the one hand, Renaissance is a proxy for civil and Roman law and the linguistic and historical skills required to study them. On the other hand, it is implicated in literary and cultural activity more generally, and invoked by the classical learning and skills of lawyers. Either way, it is rarely named or discussed explicitly.

Thus, although this debate has proved extremely important for thinking about the nature of English law, it remains unclear what English law can tell us about Renaissance. The short answer is 'quite a lot'. Maitland's discussion was, after all, a direct response to Mandell Creighton's discussion of the 'The Early Renaissance in England'.[37] For Creighton, 'Renaissance' was a European-wide 'movement' intent on 'regaining its forgotten treasures': the 'civilization' of ancient Rome and especially Greece, with 'civilization' denoting entire ways of thinking and behaving.[38] This 'movement' started first in Italy, 'the most ancient nation', and came to England belatedly in the fifteenth century. That it did so was not because of any stylistic appeal, because 'Englishmen were little moved by aesthetic perceptions' and 'England was exceptionally callous to the attractions of culture, as such'.[39] Nor was it due to court patronage or the influence of foreign scholars. Rather, for ancient culture to have any lasting appeal in England, it needed to be 'proved to be useful, or true'. The 'New Learning, if it was to take root in England, must come into definite connexion with English life and temper'. Most importantly, it required 'practical utility': to provide skills that could be used to do and say things in the present.[40] And, for this to happen, Creighton insisted, it had to become institutionalized within the existing system of university education.[41] It was with the generation of Thomas Linacre, Thomas Latimer and William Grocyn that Oxford and Cambridge became 'the organs of national life for the purpose of promoting learning', subsequent

36 Jason Scott Warren, *Early Modern English Literature* (Cambridge, 2005).
37 Mandell Creighton, *The Early Renaissance in England* (Cambridge, 1885); Maitland, *English Law*, p. 1.
38 Creighton, *Early Renaissance*, p. 8.
39 Ibid., p. 31.
40 Ibid., pp. 31–32.
41 Ibid., p. 34.

investment and curriculum reform making them sites where Europe's 'forgotten treasures' were 'fitted for home consumption'.[42]

Renaissance for Creighton, then, was more than simply the reclamation and appropriation of ancient culture; it was also an educational agenda, or even ideology, that depended on a number of factors to take root in early modern England. It required influential institutions to sponsor and teach it; for knowledge practitioners – in medicine, for example, or religion – to be receptive to it; and for society, more broadly, to recognize its practical utility. Creighton sketched, in short, a convergence of principles, practices and skills that together amounted to a cultural process whereby 'foreign treasures' were domesticated for 'home consumption' and impressed 'upon the imagination of the multitude'.[43]

Maitland implicitly acknowledged this story to argue that, in the particular case of law, legal institutions served to limit, rather than to encourage, Roman influences on its theory and practice. But the work of Brooks and Prest suggests, in turn, that the Inns of Court were nevertheless integral to institutionalizing Renaissance in other ways. Most obviously, they were part of a more general expansion in educational institutions that privileged the humanist curriculum.[44] Innsmen brought classical skills and knowledge with them, from grammar schools and university, and more general reading, to enhance their legal learning and practice; in the Inns, they engaged with the ancients as self-defined 'societies' though poesy or religion or translation, as part of their broader liberal education and career advancement.[45] Sociologically, law was one of the quintessential early modern 'professions' that enabled the middling sorts, broadly defined, to discover 'foreign treasures' and to adopt the classically informed masculine habitus that was supposed to characterize the professions by the end of the sixteenth century.[46] Practically, the prominence of both lawyers and law in a whole range of settings and relationships indicates the social and political utility of this particular field of knowledge. That thirty-one of the fifty-nine commissioners who

[42] Ibid., p. 43.

[43] Ibid., p. 9.

[44] Wrightson, *English Society*, pp. 184–185.

[45] Winston, *Lawyers at Play*, pp. 1–12.

[46] Wilfrid Prest, 'Lawyers', in Wilfrid Prest (ed.), *The Professions in Early Modern England* (New York, 1987), pp. 64–89; O'Callaghan, *English Wits*, pp. 16–17; Jessica Winston, 'Legal satire and the legal profession in the 1590s: John Davies' Epigrammes and professional decorum', in Lorna Hutson (ed.), *The Oxford Handbook of English Law and Literature, 1500–1700* (Oxford, 2017), pp. 121–141.

signed Charles I's death warrant attended the Inns of Court is a startling reminder of the role of lawyers in the political life of the nation.[47] But, as Brooks notes, law was also 'a key to understanding economic relationships in both a rural and an urban setting (including customary tenures and obligations) as well as those between individual and local communities'.[48] This 'key' may have been an arcane and self-referential set of procedures and codes, jealously guarded by those trained to use it. But how and why it was used – and to serve which principles – were not reducible to that discourse itself: just as individuals and groups turned to law for their particular needs and interests, so too the broader intellectual formation and concerns of Innsmen clearly mattered.[49] Indeed, as *Histrio-mastix* nicely demonstrates, their concerns could become more pressing than the law itself.

There are sound reasons, then, for arguing a symbiotic relationship between law and Renaissance in early modern England – certainly when Renaissance is conceptualized as a cultural process, rather than simply as an aesthetic or an epoch. Of course, many factors contributed to early modern education, social mobility, professionalization, masculinity, litigation, state formation, constitutional politics and the printed public sphere. But the domestication of ancient culture – institutionalized, in this instance, at the Inns of Court – was deeply implicated in all of these developments by the time of Prynne's trial in the 1630s. His travails were due, in turn, to a text that vividly illuminates another dimension of this process of cultural domestication – namely, the translation of classical and neo-classical words and concepts into vernacular English, and their appropriation and popularization thereafter.[50] The next section accordingly turns to Prynne's influential embrace, along with many other Innsmen, of the language of 'modern'.

## The Language of Modern

One feature of early modern vernacularization was the translation of classical and continental words and concepts into national languages: part of that process recently described by Neil Rhodes whereby 'pure' and

47 The proportion of regicidal Innsmen is calculated from the *Oxford Dictionary of National Biography* (ODNB) and may be an underestimate.

48 Brooks, 'Paradise lost?', pp. 199–200.

49 Brooks, *Politics, Law and Society*, p. 29.

50 See Jose Murgatroyd Cree, 'Protestant evangelicals and "addiction" in early modern England', *Renaissance Studies* 32 (2017), 446–462; Withington, *Society*, pp. 10–13.

primitive knowledge – of Greece and Rome, for example, or the Christian fathers – was made 'common' for a wider reading public.[51] The Reformation, which looked to democratize the true word of God, was one cultural consequence of this imperative. But, when viewed in these terms, vernacularization was also a crucial dynamic of Creighton's concept of Renaissance, because it created the language through which 'hidden treasures' of antiquity became available for 'domestic consumption' and the 'imagination of the multitude'. More to the point, as a relational word that usually invoked comparison with previous epochs, either explicitly or implicitly, 'modern' was more than just another of the thousands of 'hard words' to enter into and transform the English language at this time; rather, it was a signifier of the ancient–modern dialectic itself. Indeed, in early modern England, there was probably no better signifier of an active and meaningful engagement with the ancients than the use of the word 'modern'.

As with many words, therefore, the semantics of modern in the sixteenth and seventeenth centuries are different from those of the twenty-first century. Indeed, as Hans Ulrich Gumbrecht argued long ago, the idea that modernity marked a liberation from history – marking the current moment as 'the past of the future present' – was a fairly unusual and often pejorative meaning of 'modern' before the nineteenth century.[52] Much more common were two relational and backward-looking senses of the term. The first of these was the idea that to be modern was simply to be the most recent instance of a recurring phenomenon. Just as the modern pontificate was also the current pontificate – he held office in relation to those who had previously held office and who would do so subsequently – so modern warfare was the most recent manifestation of a recurring and perennial human practice. The second meaning was the idea of new as opposed to old. This was usually articulated in terms of epochs – that is, modern times were defined in relation to older epochs from the past, with the relationship between periods usually involving comparison and emulation. And what is striking about early moderns was the particularly intense dialectic that they envisaged between the contemporary and the classical worlds. Indeed, it was precisely this conceit of a modern 'now' separated from the classical 'then' by a post-Roman 'dark age' that gave rise to the

[51] Neil Rhodes, *Common: The Development of Literary Culture in Sixteenth-Century England* (Oxford, 2018), pp. 10–11.
[52] Gumbrecht, 'Modern', p. 12.

concept of the 'Middle Ages' (which was first coined in Italy as *media tempestas* in 1496, *media aetas* in 1518 and *medium aevum* in 1604).[53]

Early English uses of modern have not, by and large, received the same serious historical attention as Gumbrecht's survey of European sources. What treatments there are have tended to assume that 'modern' was an early Enlightenment term that was either popularized by the infamous 'ancients versus moderns' quarrel at the end of the seventeenth century or, in the more fanciful argument of Alan Houston and Steve Pincus, which signalled a self-conscious and definitive break with the past circa 1660.[54] As a result, its more complex semantics and longer genealogy have been obscured – so much so that the most compelling semantic history of modern jumps from Renaissance Italy to Enlightenment France.[55]

Digital technology can help us to recover this genealogy. For example, the appearance of a word on printed title pages catalogued in Early English Books Online (EEBO) and the English Short Title Catalogue (ESTC) is a suggestive indicator of its visibility and comprehensibility in the early modern period.[56] A survey of uses of 'modern' on printed title pages reveals that it was first used in the title of a vernacular printed text in 1579, for Leonard Digges' *An Arithmetical Military Treatise Named Stratioticos*.[57] Published after Leonard's death by his son, Thomas, *Stratioticos* supplemented the practical use of the ancient knowledge of mathematics for military purposes with a section on 'Modern Military Discipline, Offices, Laws, and Duties in every well governed Camp and Army to be observed'.[58] In so doing, Leonard and Thomas Digges deployed modern in a complicated, but also typical, way. On the one hand, it referred to 'Gothic' (post-Roman) military culture, which compared unfavourably with that of the ancients. On the other hand, it

[53] Ibid., pp. 10–12, 22. Oxford English Dictionary (OED) entries for 'modern' are organized along similar lines.

[54] Joseph M. Levine, *The Battle of the Books: History and Literature in the Augustan Age* (Ithaca, 1991); Alan Houston and Steve Pincus, 'Modernity and later seventeenth-century England', in Alan Houston and Steve Pincus (eds), *A Nation Transformed: England after the Restoration* (Cambridge, 2001), pp. 1–19, p. 10.

[55] Matei Calinescu, *Five Faces of Modernity* (Durham, 2007), pp. 19–35.

[56] The methodology is explained in Withington, *Society*, pp. 6–9.

[57] Leonard Digges, *An arithmeticall militare treatise, named Stratioticos compendiously teaching the science of nu[m]bers, as well in fractions as integers, and so much of the rules and aequations algebraicall and arte of numbers cossicall, as are requisite for the profession of a soldiour* (London, 1579).

[58] Ibid., frontispiece.

referred to recent improvements in European militarism resulting from the rediscovery of classical theory and its combination, by innovative generals, with the best of contemporary experience and practices.[59] After the second edition of *Stratioticos* was published in 1590, 'modern' gradually began to appear on increasing numbers of title pages, becoming a signifier of the ancient–modern dialectic within a range of subject areas. It appeared on 10 first-edition title pages and 16 all-editions in the 1590s, with books on militarism and geography the main discursive fields to claim the label. This figure had risen to 61 first-edition and 122 all-edition title pages by the 1650s, with religion and politics the most common subject areas. By the 1690s, modern appeared on 125 first-edition and 299 all-edition title pages, with almost 60 per cent of titles now coming from the fields of art, music and literature.[60]

The increasing use of 'modern' on title pages from 1579 suggests that the word carried resonance and meaning for at least sections of the vernacular reading public. But is it the whole story? What patterns emerge, for example, if we move beyond the number of title-page appearances of 'modern' to look for when and how 'modern' was used in EEBO–TCP content – that is, in the 40 per cent of digitized English printed text that is now reliably searchable between 1473 and 1700? Figure 6.1 points towards a longer English genealogy in print dating back to at least 1532, when 'modern' was used six times in *The Glass of Truth* (1532), an anonymous religious polemic sometimes attributed to Henry VIII. This usage, however, went largely unheralded, 'modern' thereafter appearing in only one or two texts per decade until the 1570s, when eleven authors or their translators used it. If this suggests a context for Digges placing the word on the title page of *Stratioticos*, then the real and permanent upsurge in modernity came in the 1590s, when the number of texts using the word rose from twenty-one to eighty-nine.

As importantly for the current discussion, Figure 6.2 shows the number of texts using 'modern' by legally educated writers – that is, Innsmen or, in a small number of instances, civilians (of which there are one in the 1580s and five in the 1590s). These start to appear in the 1570s. Indeed, Leonard Digges, the first author to use 'modern' on a title page, was a member of Lincoln's Inn.

Authors who could make some claim to a legal education, or who at least were members of an Inn, were responsible for around a third of all

[59] Withington, *Society*, pp. 76–77.
[60] Ibid., pp. 81, 85.

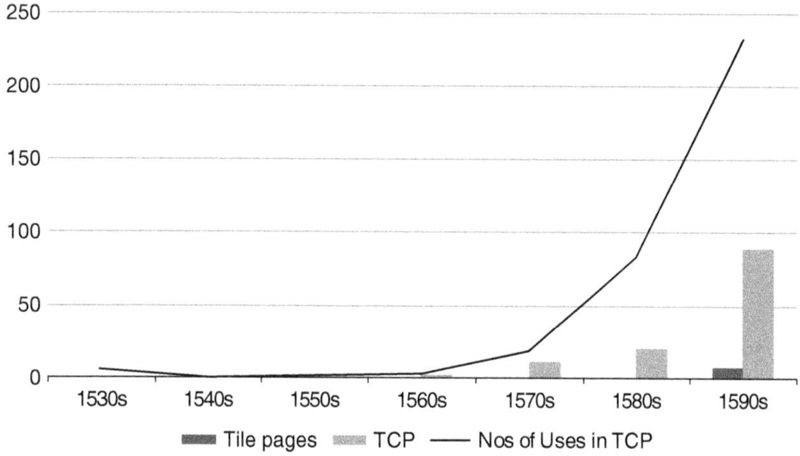


**Figure 6.1** 'Modern' on English title pages, EEBO–TCP texts and EEBO–TCP content to 1599.
Data drawn from www.textcreationpartnership.org/

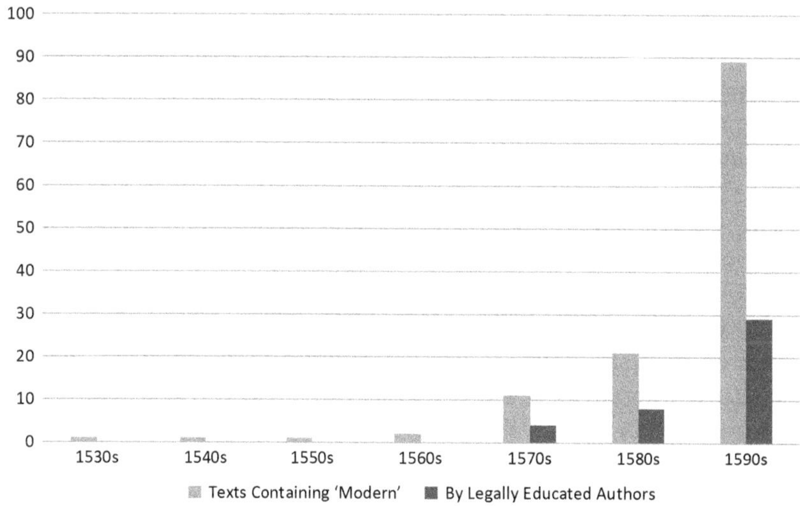


**Figure 6.2** Number of English vernacular printed texts on EEBO–TCP containing 'modern' and by legally educated authors, 1530–1590s.
Data drawn from www.textcreationpartnership.org/

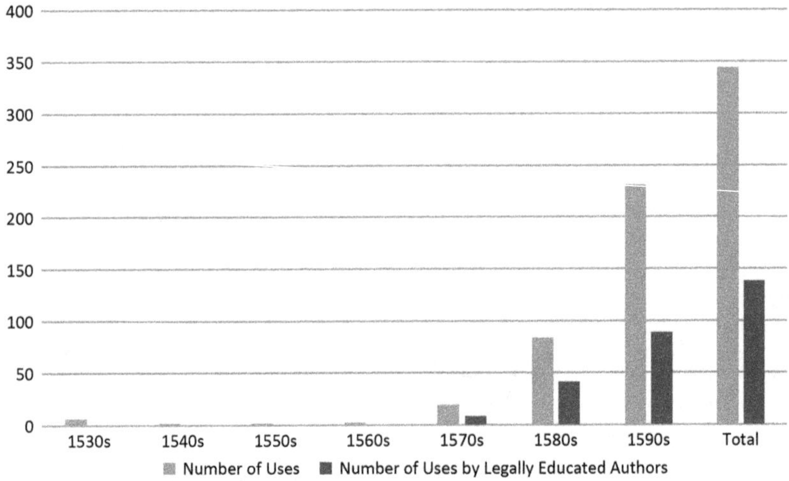


**Figure 6.3** Appearances of 'modern' in English vernacular printed texts in EEBO–TCP and in texts by legally educated authors, 1530s–1590s.
Data drawn from www.textcreationpartnership.org/

'modern' texts in the 1570s, 1580s and 1590s. Figure 6.3 confirms the intersection between English law and 'modern' that this suggests. It shows that appearances of 'modern' in English vernacular printed texts per decade rose from 2 in the 1560s to 19 in the 1570s, 84 in the 1580s and 231 in the 1590s. The proportion of these uses that can be attributed to legally educated authors was 42 per cent in the 1570s, 49 per cent in the 1580s and 39 per cent in the 1590s. Viewed in these terms, English modernity was clearly a *fin-de-siècle* phenomenon, with the decade of moment the 1590s, rather than the 1690s. And Innsmen were very much among its midwives.

The EEBO–TCP data reveals two further aspects of the vernacularization process and the role – or not – of legally trained writers. The first is the relative importance of direct translations of contemporary continental works – in particular, French and Italian texts – into English. Aside from *The Glass of Truth*, the trickle of texts to use 'modern' before the 1570s were all translations (three French and one Italian). The second aspect of the vernacularization of 'modern' worth noting is the range of discourses with which it was associated by the end of the sixteenth century. Title pages somewhat misleadingly suggest that militarism was

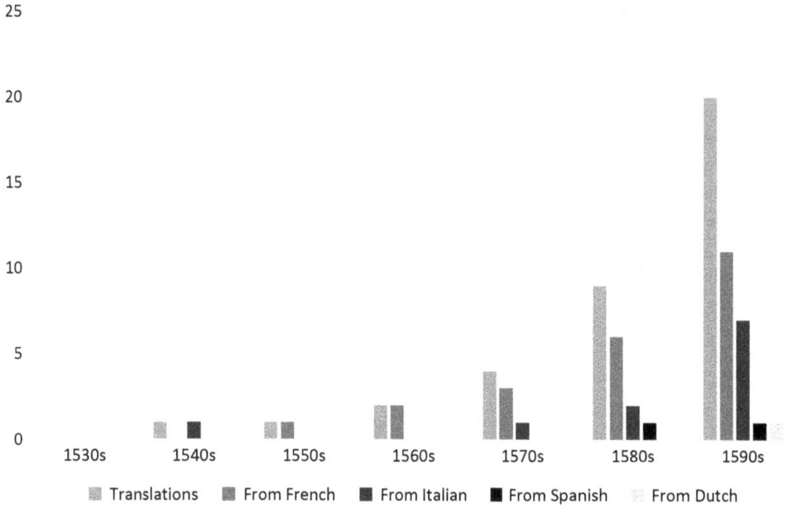


**Figure 6.4** Number of English vernacular printed texts containing 'modern' from translations and by country, 1530s–1590s.
Data drawn from www.textcreationpartnership.org/

the key field of knowledge within which the term was introduced into English. However, surveying textual content more generally reveals a much more variegated story. 'Modern' was used in works of religion, rhetoric, philosophy and geography up to the 1560s. Political writings predominated in the 1570s, albeit the numbers remained small. Thereafter, there was an expansion in subject areas, with literary and geographical writings prominent in the 1580s, and literary, religious, military, political and historical writings preponderant by the 1590s. Importantly, law in itself was *not* a discipline to adopt 'modern' as a referent in printed vernacular texts before 1600. But authors with connections to the Inns of Court were very active in using the term in other fields of knowledge.

Figure 6.5 is more specific. It represents the proportion of texts using 'modern' with Innsmen as authors, divided by subject matter between the 1530s and 1590s.

The columns at 100 per cent reflect the small number of texts produced – that is, that the only educational or logic treatises to use the language of 'modern' were written by an Innsman: *Elementarie* (1582) by Richard

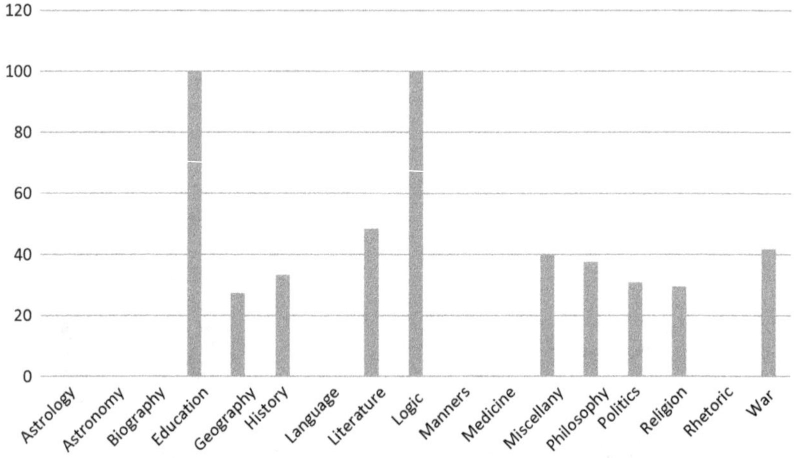


**Figure 6.5** Percentages of texts with 'modern' by legally educated authors, 1530s–1590s.
Data drawn from www.textcreationpartnership.org/

Mulcaster (Lincoln's Inn) and *The Art of Logic Plainly Taught in the English Tongue* (1599) by Thomas Blundeville (Gray's Inn).[61] These solitary contributions were important in establishing the term in English. But more significant statistically is that, by the 1590s, the crucial decade in the semantic history of 'modern', Innsmen wrote twelve of the twenty-two literary texts, four of the nine historical works, four of the eleven military texts and four of the fourteen religious treatises that employed the language of 'modern'. Law itself may not have absorbed the language of 'modern' by the end of the sixteenth century, but Innsmen most certainly had.

## English Law and Modernity

The ambivalent relationship between English law and modernity was presaged as early as 1532, in the first vernacular text to use 'modern'. *The Glass of Truth* was a dialogue between 'The Divine' and 'The Lawyer' about the status of Henry VIII's marriage to Catherine of Aragon from

[61] Richard Mulcaster, *The first part of the elementarie vvhich entreateth chefelie of the right writing of our English tung* (London, 1582), pp. 100, 102; Thomas Blundeville, *The art of logike Plainely taught in the English tongue, by M. Blundeuile of Newton Flotman in Norfolke, aswell according to the doctrine of Aristotle, as of all other moderne and best accounted authors thereof* (London, 1599).

the perspective of the church and the law. As a pro-Henrician tract, the interlocutors agreed that the marriage was illegitimate because, according to the Old Testament, no man could marry his brother's widow. They also concluded that the Pope did not have the power to dispense with 'the law divine'.[62] It was over the question of papal dispensation that 'the Divine' distinguished between 'ancients' and 'moderns', offering to 'shewe you whatte the olde auncient doctours do saye, or what the modernes, whiche somewhat flattereth the popes authoritie, sayeth'. He observed that, 'for some of the modernes make to moche of your lawe, in wrestyng of scripture for auauncement of dignite: whiche the olde fathers do clene forbydde and contempne: and lykewise also dyuers other modernes. Wherby you may well perceiue that there is some alteration emonge them.'[63]

From this specific example, the Divine extrapolated a more general conception of ecclesiastical authority that privileged the ancient fathers over moderns:

> For the Churche of god hath his foundation sette vppon a firme and stedfaste stone of truth and faythe: and not vpon the mutable and wylfull pleasure of Peters successours. But your lawe doth so moche attribute to man (as moderne glossers dothe expoune) that it wolde make man, whiche is but frayle [ . . . the . . . ] directour, gouernour and as superiour to the very worde of god.[64]

However, when 'the Lawyer' was given the opportunity to conceptualize legal authority, he refrained from either using the noun 'moderns' or simply deferring to the wisdom of the ancients. Acknowledging 'that the lawe in his due course exercised, ought to be directed by truthe onely', the Lawyer outlined a process whereby truth was established in various stages. 'Deeds' that 'do appere evidently' were 'greatly to be consydered and weyed'. If the truth was not obvious, then 'it is to be referred to that which the ancient fathers approved in law, or the assent of counsels generall do saye, and affirme to be true and lawe'. If still 'the truth cannot be fully gathered or made plainly to appere, then judgementes and opinions of doctors, sounding to reson so farre as man's witte can comprehende, and not discrepant from goddess lawe: be to be ensued & folowed'.[65] It was likely, as the Divine noted, that this dependence on

62 Anon., *Glasse of Truth* (London, 1532), p. G5r.
63 Ibid., p. G5v.
64 Ibid., p. E2v.
65 Ibid., p. E3v.

human wit 'may sometime fortune an errour', but the Lawyer insisted that it was precisely because of the unreliability of individuals that a stable and agreed repository of 'truth' – and so 'justice' – was required: 'what the lawe calle the truthe, is to be taken for a truthe: untylle the contrary may evidently appere'.[66]

The reluctance of the Lawyer to refer to current legal practitioners as 'moderns', as opposed to the precocious (and pejorative) use of the term by the Divine to describe contemporary churchmen, anticipates both the absence of the dialectic from subsequent treatises on law and the manner in which the term was eventually introduced into printed English legal discourse in the early 1600s. Because while Innsmen were industrious in drawing out England's *fin-de-siècle* modernity in literature, religion and other fields of knowledge, it was their rivals, the university-trained civilians, who eventually brought the terminology to bear on English law. Notable in this respect was John Cowell's 1607 *The Interpreter*.[67] Cowell was a practising civilian who, as Regius Professor at Cambridge between 1594 and 1611, worked for 'the reinvigoration of the civil law in order to restore it to the importance it had held in ancient Rome and medieval Europe'.[68] His text was presented as a response to advances in European legal scholarship and a contribution to a trans-national legal community. As Cowell put it, '[t]he Civilians of other nations have by their mutuall industries raised this kinde of worke in their profession, to an unexpected excellencie'.[69] The result was a law dictionary that gave definitions of both common and civil law terms, Cowell explaining that, 'wherein my intent is, by collating the cases of both lawes, to shewe, that they both be raised of one foundation and differ more in language and terms than substance, and therefore were they reduced to one method (as they easily might) to be attained (in a maner) with all one paines'.[70]

No matter these scholarly ambitions, *The Interpreter* was attacked in the House of Commons in 1610, for defining a king as having 'absolute' power above the law, and by common lawyers, for its jurisdictional and conceptual temerity.[71] Suspicions were high because Cowell's previous

[66] Ibid., p. E4.
[67] John Cowell, *The Interpreter: or Booke containing the signification of words* (London, 1607).
[68] Levack, *Civil Lawyers*, p. 52.
[69] Cowell, *Interpreter*, p. *3r.
[70] Ibid., p. *3v.
[71] Levack, *Civil Lawyers*, pp. 4, 81, 103.

publication, *Institutiones juris Anglicani* (1605), had placed common law within the broader framework of civil law with an eye on merging English and Scots law after the Union of the Crowns in 1603. Cowell's application of the language of 'modern' in 1607 was another stage in this cosmopolitan and integrative agenda. He used the word six times. In five instances, it described a modern language (French, German and English three times) by connecting current words with their Latin or ancient origins, for example '*Forsechoke,* seemeth to signifie originally as much as *forsaken* in our moderne language, or *(derelictum)* with the Romaines'.[72] On the other occasion, it positioned contemporary civilians in relation to their ancient predecessors: 'Banishment ... is also of our moderne Civilians called *(bannimentum)* which was auncientl tearmed *(deportatio)* if it were perpetuall, or *(relegatio in insulam,)* if for a time.'[73] This use of 'modern' laid English law open to geographical and temporal influences that common lawyer professionals, it seemed, could hardly countenance.

It was in the midst of this controversy that 'modern' was first used in vernacular print to characterize English common law. The culprit was none other than Sir Edward Coke – opponent of Cowell (whom Coke called 'Dr. Cowheel'), the personification of Pocock's 'common law mind', and leading lawyer of the Jacobean and Caroline eras.[74] In contrast to Cowell, in his *A Book of Entries* (1614) Coke used 'modern' purely in the sense of the most current manifestation of a perennial phenomenon – 'the practise of the law' – with all epochal or geographical dialectics thoroughly elided.[75] He did so not for 'the common good and benefit' of a trans-national republic of legal letters nor even his country, but rather for 'all the studious and learned professors of the laws of England'. And instead of signifying ancient genealogies of shared legal 'substance' – in Latin, French and German – 'modern', for Coke, pointed towards an intimidating array of technical procedures and processes, developed indigenously over the last few centuries, by which English law worked. Indeed, Coke assured his readers that the 'precedents' he chose to publish 'are of greater authoritie and use, and fitter for the moderne practice of the law, for that they be for the most part of later

[72] Cowell, *Interpreter*, pp. Dd5v, Gg5v, Ppp2r, Zzz4r.

[73] Ibid., p. I1r.

[74] ODNB, Cowell, John (1554–1611), by Brian Levack; Pocock, *Ancient Constitution*, pp. 31–32; Allen D. Boyer, *Sir Edward Coke and the Elizabethan Age* (Stanford, 2003).

[75] Edward Coke, *A booke of entries . . . for the moderne practise of the law* (London, 1614).

times' – that is, of the reigns of Elizabeth and James. These amounted to the:

> . . . perfect and approved presidents of counts, declarations, informations, pleints, inditements, barres, replications, reioynders, pleadings, processes, continuances, essoines, issues, defaults, departure in despite of the court, demurrers, trialls, iudgements, executions, and all other matters and proceedings (in effect) concerning the practique part of the laws of England, in actions reall, personall, and mixt, and in appeales.[76]

Like 'the Lawyer' in *The Glass of Truth*, that is, Coke took the authority of English law to lie in the technicalities of current practice rather than the recovery and interpretation of Roman and post-Roman precepts.

But this nationalistic, presentist and technocratic use of 'modern', and the refutation of civil law that it facilitated, should not imply that Coke was somehow unaffected by or ignorant of Renaissance humanism. As the product of Norwich Grammar School, Trinity College, Cambridge, Clifford's Inn and Inner Temple, Coke's intellectual formation was as archetypically humanistic as his subsequent commitment to public life as a statesman and parliamentarian.[77] And there are other, more specific, influences evident in the text. Generically, *A Book of Entries* was very much in the tradition of the Renaissance advice or 'how to' book, which aimed to popularize esoteric skills through print, and its basic conceit of focusing on practice and experience rather than 'universalities' and 'theoricke' was typical of the genre. That Coke chose to justify this focus with Hippocrates' dictum '*Ars longa, vita brevis, studium difficile, occasion praeceps, experimentum periculosum*' suggests an accentuated desire to display his own learning and that of his profession. As he translates it: 'A learned man of the laws of this realm is long in making, the student thereof, having *sedentarium vitam*, is not commonly long lived, the study abstruse and difficult, the occasion sodaine, the practise dangerous.'[78] Indeed, Coke wore his classical learning fairly flagrantly and archetypally. Extensive Latin quotes from Cicero, a kind of honorary patron saint of the early modern Inns, dominate the title page; the text is littered with Latin adages thereafter.[79] Moreover, from the outset, Coke presents these modern legal practices as a kind of rhetoric – or what he and lawyers termed 'pleadings': the technical

76 Ibid., frontispiece.

77 Boyer, *Sir Edward Coke*, pp. 1–27.

78 Coke, *A booke*, 'Preface'.

79 Brooks, *Law, Politics and Society*, pp. 62–63.

expertise he espouses is a prerequisite of professional aptitude, but it also links to other, more general capacities of judgement and rhetorical skill acquired through humanist education.[80] Coke displayed, in short, plenty of the habits of England's Renaissance even as he knowingly protected the source of his own social and political power – the common law – from the Romanizing threat posed by civilians. Effacing the dialectical qualities of 'the moderne practice of the law' was one tactic to hand.

## Conclusion

That Prynne's *Histrio-mastix* used the language of 'modern' more often than any other printed text before 1640 was no accident. Innsmen were intimately acquainted with the vocabulary and, from the 1610s, even began to apply it to their sphere of expertise, albeit in a non-dialectical manner that helped to protect their authority and business from the more cosmopolitan and epochal modernity of civilians. But, in the meantime, they had also been crucial to importing the term into other fields of learning. Indeed, the two discourses with most printed texts with 'modern' in them by 1600 were literature (twenty-nine texts) and religion (seventeen texts), with Innsmen writing fourteen (44 per cent) and five (29 per cent) of each.

It was precisely these two intellectual fields that Prynne engaged with in *Histrio-mastix*. On the one hand, modern English theatrical culture was not only the most recent manifestation of a perennial human activity, but also directly and unusually emulative 'of such Playes, or Enterludes, as were usuall among the Greekes, and Romans'.[81] Prynne noted, for example, that he did not need 'to record those seuerall prophane, and grosse *Obscenities, those Amorous streines, Lasciuious passages*, and unsauourie Jests, which are scattered in *Aristophanes, Terrence, Plautus, Catullus, Tibullus, Propertius, Ouid*, and other ancient *Comedians*, and wanton Poets'; rather he would 'confine my selfe unto the Comedies, and popular Enterludes of our present Age, *which farre exceede them in all these.* Alas, what are the Maior part of all our Moderne Stage-Playes, but so many Lectures of Ribaldry; so many Abstracts, Compendiums, or Miscellaines of sublimated, Elegant, Wittie, or more Accurate, and choyce Obscenities?'[82]

80 Brooks, *Law, Politics and Society*, p. 19; Sobecki, *Unwritten Virtues*, pp. 31–32.
81 Prynne, *Histrio-mastix*, p. 7.
82 Ibid., p. 70.

On the other hand, the authority for his moral criticism emanated from an equally powerful dialectic between modern and ancient culture. Prynne was relentlessly cautious in positioning his own critique within a threefold reformatory tradition: of the ancients (or pagans), the patristics (or fathers), and the moderns. As he put it:

> ... wee haue the expresse authorities, not onely of *Plutarch* ... *of Dionysius Hallicarnasseus* ... *of Valerius Maximus* ... *Of Thucidides* ... *Of Liuie* ... *Of Demosthenes* ... *Of Horace* ... *Of Athenaeus* ... [Of] *Diodorus Siculus* with sundry other Pagan Authors: but likewise of *Tatianus* ... *Of Theophilus Antiochen* ... *Of Clemens Alexandrinus* ... *Of Tertullian* ... *Of Cyprian* ... with other Fathers: *Of Iohn Mariana, Master Northbrooke: Doctor Reinolds, and Master Gosson, in their Bookes against Stage-Playes* ... *Of Master Godwins Roman Antiquities* ... with many other Moderne writers.[83]

For Prynne, then, both theatre and its criticism were expressly and intensely modern – not in the current and presentist sense adopted by Coke, but in the full genealogical and dialectical meaning of the term. For a writer as inured to the rhetorical device of *copia* as Prynne, this helps to explain the proliferation of 'modern' over the course of an extremely long treatise. But there was more to his amplification than mere rhetoric. For Prynne, modernity intimated authority: his polemic contained '*nought else but resolved, universally received ancient (though now forgotten) truthes: so farre from any suspicion of* factious Novalty, *or* puritanicall singularity, *that they that have the concurrent testimonies, the unanimous resolutions of* sundry sacred texts of Scripture, of the whole primitive Church and Saints of God'.[84] When Prynne was tried for sedition he accordingly petitioned to have his notes of 'Canons of 55 ... Synods and Counsels', 'the works of 71 Fathers and ancient Christian writers ... 150 Christian Authors of all sorts ... 40 Heathen philosophers', plus the edicts of sundry Christian yea Pagan Nations' used as legal evidence. He was not 'novel' or 'singular' in his opinions; he was a 'modern'.[85]

That the judicial commission ruled Prynne's evidence inadmissible is unsurprising: his modernity carried little authority with 'modern' legal practice and was viewed as a stalling tactic designed to subvert the trial.[86] However, following Prynne's punishment, the four Inns of Court were nevertheless able to apologize to Charles I and Henrietta Maria for their

83 Ibid., p. 29.
84 Ibid., p. **r.
85 Ibid.
86 Kishlanksy, 'A whipper whipped', pp. 615–616.

brethren's mistakes by tasking another Innsman, an inhabitant and member of Gray's Inn, to write an apology. The Innsman in question was playwright and satirist James Shirley and the result was a court masque, *The Triumph of Peace*, which dramatically restated the order, beauty and harmony derived from wise monarchical rule.[87] It was a resounding, if expensive, success. And although clearly different from *Histrio-mastix* in many respects, *The Triumph* likewise had the Renaissance dialectic embedded within it: the sixteen 'Masquers' – 'the sonnes of Peace, Law and Justice' – sitting together with their 'habits . . . mixt, between the ancient and moderne'.[88] The Inns of Court may indeed have protected the autonomy of common law as a professional and powerful sphere of practice – but they were also integral to the organization of Renaissance as a pervasive cultural process: of making England modern.

[87] James Shirley, *The triumph of peace: A masque, presented by the foure honourable houses, or Innes of Court. Before the King and Queenes Majesties, in the Banquetting-house at White Hall, February the third, 1633* (London, 1633).

[88] Ibid., p. 17.

7

# The Micro-Spatial Dynamics of Litigation

## The Chilvers Coton Tithe Dispute, *Barrows* vs. *Archer* (1657)

STEVE HINDLE*

On 10 October 1654, agricultural labourers in the Warwickshire village of Chilvers Coton took in the corn harvest in a 20-acre field near Temple House at the western end of the parish. Together, they cut eighteen loads of rye, four loads of wheat and ten loads of maslin, and they set them upright in 'cockes and shockes'. Before the grain could be carted away, however, there was one other task to be accomplished: they were required to separate out the tenth part of the crop as tithe. Their failure to do so opened an archival window through which, at a distance of over 350 years, the historian can discern a social, economic and cultural landscape, the contours of which would otherwise be invisible. That window swung open in 1657 because the lord of the manor not only claimed the rights to the tithe on all that grain, but also resolved to mobilize those rights *at law*.

For historians familiar with the work of Christopher W. Brooks, it should come as no surprise that this harvest scene is documented in the record of a lawsuit: in this case, the exemplification of a verdict at common law in Richard Newdigate of Arbury Hall *versus* Richard Chamberlain of Astley Castle concerning the right to rectorial (or 'great') tithes on those

* Neither the conception nor the completion of this chapter would have been possible without the help of Drs Heather Falvey (who provided invaluable research assistance at an earlier stage of the project) and Angela Nicholls (who provided digital photos of a significant number of auxiliary documents from the Warwick County Record Office at very short notice). I am also grateful to Heather, and to Catherine Wehrey-Miller and Natalie Serrano, for their forensic and critical reading of the text. Chris Whittick and Stephen Taylor offered significant advice about the interpretation of material in the archive of Newdigate estate deeds and about John Barrows' fate after 1663, respectively. The closure of the Lichfield Joint Record Office has led to the relocation of all of the diocesan records to the Staffordshire Record Office, Stafford: hence all LJRO references are to documents now held in Stafford.

20 acres of land in Chilvers Coton.[1] This is exactly the kind of formal legal text of which Brooks enjoyed such authoritative command. But Brooks was emphatically not 'merely' a *legal historian* interested in the genealogy of formal actions; he was also a *historian of the law-in-society*, recognizing the astonishing potential of the records of the law courts to disclose a broad range of social and economic activities and the networks that supported them. Whether read along or against the grain, Brooks was well aware that bills, answers, affidavits, interrogatories and depositions might reveal far more than the issues formally at stake in a lawsuit. Precisely because this was a culture in which so many economic activities were, as he so artfully put it, 'engrossed on parchment and sealed in wax', Brooks recognized that both the witness testimony recorded in depositions and the allegations implied by pleadings constituted an invaluable source for the study not only of the pathology, but also of the health, of social relations.[2]

Brooks accordingly developed a formidable reputation as one of the pre-eminent practitioners of a new legal history, inflecting his forensic analysis of patterns of litigation both with significant expertise in the lineage of legal forms and jurisdictions, and with a vivid sociological imagination of the kind that is envied among practitioners of the social history of the law. His most obvious scholarly achievement was to document, on the basis of remarkable archival heroism, the astonishing scale of the increase in litigation in English society in the late sixteenth and early seventeenth centuries.[3] But he supplemented those startling metrics with an astute reading of the causes (although, tellingly, only to a lesser extent of the consequences) of the growing use of the law as a mechanism of dispute settlement.[4] These traditions came together best in his work in the wonderful chapter on 'Law and "community"' in his magisterial *Law, Politics and Society in Early Modern England*. Echoing both his deep-rooted scepticism of the 'pathological' interpretation of the increased use of the law courts as 'hyper-lexis' (the belief that there is excessive litigation in any particular context) and his well-known characterization of vexatious suits as but 'a species of flotsam and jetsam which floated in on

[1] Warwick County Record Office, Warwick (hereinafter WCRO), CR136/C895 (Exemplification of verdict in *Newdigate* vs. *Chamberlain*, 1657).
[2] Christopher W. Brooks, 'A law-abiding and litigious society', in John Morrill (ed.), *The Oxford Illustrated History of Tudor and Stuart Britain* (Oxford, 1996), p. 143.
[3] Christopher W. Brooks, *Pettyfoggers and Vipers of the Commonwealth: The 'Lower Branch' of the Legal Profession in Early Modern England* (Cambridge, 1986), pp. 58–74.
[4] Brooks, *Pettyfoggers*, pp. 75–111.

the flood-tide of litigation', that chapter offered a broadly positive reading of the cultural significance of litigation in seventeenth-century society.[5] As critics have pointed out, however, Brooks arguably underestimates the degree to which litigiousness, by definition, challenged the long-standing societal preference, deeply rooted in Christian ethics of mercy, charity and forgiveness, for extra-legal modes of conflict resolution. If the ideals of peacemaking and reconciliation so painstakingly reconstructed by Craig Muldrew and others, and the informal disputing process (involving forgiveness, composition, mediation and arbitration) that they had traditionally informed, enjoyed so much cultural purchase, what does the rise in litigation tell us about changing discourses of charity and neighbourliness?[6] If, to use Michael Clanchy's resonant idiom, 'law' was increasingly trumping 'love', what did all of this litigation actually mean to those to those who participated in it and to the communities in which they lived?[7]

This chapter seeks to reopen the debate about the social meaning of litigation in early modern England by asking searching questions about the *experiential* aspect of going to law. While Brooks proved beyond all reasonable doubt that the rate of litigation increased dramatically in the late sixteenth and early seventeenth centuries, there is overwhelming contemporary evidence that defendants did not enjoy being sued and that plaintiffs did not enjoy having to sue them. By placing litigation in its most intimate context (at the heart – the church, churchyard and vicarage – of a specific local community), this chapter reconstructs the legal, social and spatial dynamics of a tithe dispute that came to a head in the Warwickshire parish of Chilvers Coton, near Nuneaton, in a suit brought

[5] Christopher W. Brooks, *Law, Politics and Society in Early Modern England* (Cambridge, 2018), pp. 241–277; cf. Christopher W. Brooks, *Lawyers, Litigation and English Society since 1450* (London, 1998), pp. 3, n. 10, 13–14, 22–25, 86–87 ('hyperlexis'); Brooks, *Pettyfoggers*, p. 111 ('flotsam and jetsam').

[6] Craig Muldrew, 'The culture of reconciliation: community and the settlement of economic disputes in early modern England', *Historical Journal* 39 (1996), 915–942; Steve Hindle, 'The keeping of the public peace', in Paul Griffiths, Adam Fox and Steve Hindle (eds), *The Experience of Authority in Early Modern England* (London and New York, 1996), pp. 213–248; Steve Hindle, *The State and Social Change in Early Modern England, c. 1550–1640* (London and New York, 2000), pp. 89–90, p. 93; Keith Wrightson, 'Mutualities and obligations: changing social relationships in early modern England', *Proceedings of the British Academy* 139 (2006), 157–194; Keith Wrightson, 'The "decline of neighbourliness" revisited', in Norman L. Jones and Daniel Woolf (eds), *Local Identities in Late Medieval and Early Modern England* (Basingstoke, 2007), pp. 19–49.

[7] Michael Clanchy, 'Law and love in the Middle Ages', in John Bossy (ed.), *Disputes and Settlements: Law and Human Relations in the West* (Cambridge, 1983), pp. 47–68.

before the Court of Exchequer.[8] The following discussion opens out the archive of that litigation (from its precedents, through its parties and its pleadings, and ultimately into its depositions) to reveal the multiple layers of social and economic interaction divulged or insinuated by the documentary record. Through reconstruction of the agricultural context in which tithe obligations were required and honoured, and cross-reference of the witness testimony with the extraordinarily detailed seventeenth-century archive of the parish, it is possible to locate the protagonists not only in their broad cultural context, but also in highly specific social-structural and spatial hierarchies. In so doing, it puts *neighbourliness* in its micro-spatial sense – who lived next door to whom; who grazed their flocks with whom; who sheared their sheep; which neighbours gave evidence for or against whom – back onto the agenda of the social history of litigation.

## I. Precedents

Tithe disputes were, of course, far from uncommon in early modern England. Relative to the plentitude of historiographical attention that has been paid to other types of litigation (that concerning credit and debt,[9]

[8] This chapter derives from a larger project, entitled 'The Social Topography of a Rural Community', which seeks to reconstruct the pattern of social, economic and spatial relations in the parish of Chilvers Coton. See Steve Hindle, 'Fiscal seigneurialism in late-seventeenth-century Warwickshire: Sir Richard Newdigate and the "Great Survey" of Chilvers Coton', in Christopher Dyer and Catherine Richardson (eds), *William Dugdale, Historian, 1605–86: His Life, His Writings and His County* (Woodbridge, 2009), pp. 164–186; Steve Hindle, 'Below stairs at Arbury Hall: Sir Richard Newdigate and his household staff, c. 1670–1710', *Historical Research* 85 (2012), 71–88; Steve Hindle, 'Work, reward and labour discipline in late seventeenth-century England', in Steve Hindle, Alexandra Shepard and John Walter (eds), *Remaking English Society: Social Relations and Social Change in Early Modern England* (Woodbridge, 2013), pp. 255–280; Steve Hindle, 'Self-image and public image in the career of a Jacobean magistrate: Sir John Newdigate in the court of Star Chamber', in Michael Braddick and Philip Withington (eds), *Popular Culture and Political Agency in Early Modern England and Ireland: Essays in Honour of John Walter* (Woodbridge, 2017), pp. 123–144; Steve Hindle, 'The sad fortunes of the Reverend John Perkins: scenes of clerical life in late seventeenth-century England', in Trevor Dean, Glyn Parry and Edward Vallance (eds), *Faith, Place and People in Early Modern England: Essays in Honor of Margaret Spufford* (Woodbridge, 2018), pp. 70–92.

[9] See, e.g., Craig Muldrew, 'Credit and the courts: debt litigation in a seventeenth-century urban community', *Economic History Review*, 2nd ser., 46 (1993), 23–38; Craig Muldrew, '"A mutual assent of her mind"? Women, debt litigation and contract in early modern England', *History Workshop Journal* 55 (2003), 47–71.

for instance, or alleging defamation of character[10]), tithe disputes are relatively underrepresented in the literature on seventeenth-century litigation.[11] What little scholarship there is suggests that the intensity with which tithe was contested might be an index of the scale of anti-clericalism,[12] or, in a more nuanced position, that tithe resistance may best be interpreted as a means by which congregations held their clergy to account as they demanded higher standards of pastoral care.[13] The situation in the mid-seventeenth century was particularly complicated, not least because the jurisdiction that had traditionally been the forum for the adjudication of tithe disputes – the church courts – had collapsed by the mid-1640s,[14] and because the 1650s saw the emergence of specific dissenting and radical groups for whom resistance to tithe was a special badge of honour.[15] Neither of these factors should be overstated: as Spaeth has shown, the jurisdiction over contested tithe shifted from that of ecclesiastical justice to the courts of equity – specifically, the Exchequer[16] – and although the emergence of the Quakers in particular might once have encouraged the belief that 'the whole history of the

[10] See, e.g., James A. Sharpe, 'Defamation and Sexual Slander in Early Modern England: The Church Courts at York', University of York Borthwick Paper no. 58 (1980); Laura Gowing, 'Gender and the language of insult in early modern London', *History Workshop Journal* 35 (1993), 1–21; Laura Gowing, 'Language, power and the law: women's slander litigation in early modern London', in Jenny Kermode and Garthine Walker (eds), *Women, Crime and the Courts in Early Modern England* (London, 1994), pp. 26–48; Fay Bound, '"An angry and malicious mind"? Narratives of slander at the church courts at York, c. 1660–c. 1760', *History Workshop Journal* 56 (2003), 59–77.

[11] F. G. Emmison, 'Tithes, perambulations and Sabbath-breach in Elizabethan Essex', in Frederick Emmison and Roy Stephens (eds), *Tribute to an Antiquary: Essays Presented to Marc Fitch by Some of His Friends* (London, 1976), pp. 177–215; W. J. Sheils, '"The right of the church": the clergy, tithe, and the courts at York, 1540–1640', in W. J. Sheils and Diana Wood (eds), *The Church and Wealth* (Oxford, 1987), pp. 231–255; Peter Marshall, 'Discord, stability and ministry in a Yorkshire parish: John Otes and Carnaby, 1563–1600', *Yorkshire Archaeological Journal* 71 (1999), 185–199; Donald Spaeth, *The Church in an Age of Danger: Parsons and Parishioners, 1660–1740* (Cambridge, 2000), pp. 133–154; Paula Simpson, 'The continuum of resistance to tithe, c.1400–1600', in Robert Lutton and Elizabeth Salter (eds), *Pieties in Transition: Religious Practices and Experiences, c. 1400–1640* (Aldershot, 2007), pp. 93–108; R. B. Outhwaite, *The Rise and Fall of the English Ecclesiastical Courts, 1500–1860* (Cambridge, 2006), pp. 23–32.

[12] E. J. Evans, 'Some reasons for the growth of rural anti-clericalism, c. 1750–c. 1830', *Past and Present* 66 (1975), 84–109.

[13] Spaeth, *The Church in an Age of Danger*, pp. 152–154.

[14] Outhwaite, *Rise and Fall of the English Ecclesiastical Courts*, pp. 78–82.

[15] Barry Reay, 'Quaker opposition to tithes', *Past and Present* 86 (1980), 98–120; Adrian Davies, *The Quakers in English Society, 1655–1725* (Oxford, 2000), pp. 30–34.

[16] Spaeth, *The Church in an Age of Danger*, pp. 74–78.

1650s can be told in terms of tithes', it is clear that hostility to tithe was by no means confined to those who might be stigmatized as sectaries.[17] There were, in short, numerous reasons why tithe might be resisted, not the least significant among which was the ambiguous position of the clergyman himself, who was forced by his (often precarious) economic circumstances to reconcile the role of pastor with that of taxman. Precisely because tithes were an inescapable fact of life for rural people, their annual payment was almost certainly perceived as just one more financial commitment to be avoided, denied or deferred – in this sense, no different from rent, or the poor rate, or indeed any other form of tax.

This theme is entirely characteristic of the dispute over small tithes between John Barrows, vicar of Chilvers Coton from 1638 until 1663, and his parishioner, labourer William Archer, which is first inscribed into the historical record in the spring of 1657. Barrows was, however, by no means the first vicar of Chilvers Coton to sue one or more of his parishioners for tithe. Contention had previously erupted in 1602 in a consistory court action, during the course of which the Reverend Richard Taylor claimed that one Edward Lane had defrauded him of tithes payable on his flocks – specifically, on twelve sheep, nine of which had lambed before he sold them, and on another nineteen ewes that he had subsequently purchased and sheared. Given that there was a custom 'inviolably observed and kept' within the parish 'for 10, 20, 30, 40, 50, 60, 70 yeares last past' and 'from tyme whereof the memory of man is not to the contrarie' that the vicar was due a farthing for every sheep grazed between Candlemas and Lady Day, a halfpenny for every sheep sold thereafter and a further halfpenny for every fleece in lieu of tithe wool, and that this was a sheep-farming community in which flocks could be very extensive, the sums at stake were not, cumulatively, insignificant.[18]

It was not until the incumbency of John Malin (vicar from 1621 until 1638), however, that tithe contention developed into tithe antagonism. Malin alleged, in 1632, that he was owed tithe by one William Lucas on almost eighty loads of spring wood that Lucas had in the three preceding years felled in the New Park and the Lady Grove, each of which Malin believed to be worth between 20*d*. and 2*s*., to a total value of £8, the tithe

[17] Martin Ingram, *Church Courts, Sex and Marriage in England, 1570–1640* (Oxford, 1987), p. 109; Spaeth, *The Church in an Age of Danger*, pp. 141–145; cf. Christopher Hill, *The World Turned Upside Down* (London, 1972), p. 187.

[18] Lichfield Joint Record Office, Lichfield (hereinafter LJRO), B/C/5/1602 (Chilvers Coton: *Taylor* vs. *Lane*); cf. Andy Wood, *The Memory of the People: Custom and Popular Senses of the Past in Early Modern England* (Cambridge, 2013), pp. 94–96.

on which amounted to 16*s*. The evidence generated by the suit is revealing not only about tithing customs and about the local demand for firewood, but also about the cost of litigation and the potential of tithe disputes to generate both retaliatory ('cross') and supplementary ('shoring') actions. While Malin himself noted that this prosecution alone had cost him well over £5 in legal fees, witnesses laconically recalled that Lucas was not the only parishioner to have been sued by Malin in recent years.[19] By the late 1630s, the litigation had spiralled out of the consistory at Lichfield and into the Court of Arches at Westminster, and had extended beyond the cottages of Malin's more humble parishioners as far as the gentry seats of the Chamberlains (at Temple House) and the Newdigates (at Arbury Hall). In 1637, Lord of Arbury John Newdigate III complained to Archbishop Laud that Malin had sued him over small tithes for which he was not liable. Although Newdigate conceded that the living was poor and that the vicar required further support, he declined to make any financial commitment until Malin, who was by then terminally ill, had gone to a better place.[20] Richard Chamberlain was no less antagonistic: despite impending Chancery litigation with Newdigate, he agreed with his opponent about Malin's lack of gratitude either for tithes paid or for charity dispensed, expressing his frustration with 'the unjust clamours of our unworldly and intemperate vicar, a man unworthy of the title of that worthy calling'.[21]

By the time that John Barrows succeeded Malin in 1638, therefore, relations between the vicar and his parishioners in Chilvers Coton were toxic, and the payment of tithe had become corrosive of ideals of Christian charity and obligation. Faggots of firewood and fleeces of wool were not merely valuable assets in the makeshift economies of the husbandmen and labourers; they were invaluable currency in the sporadic income of the vicarage, and had accordingly come to symbolize a struggle over scant resources between an impoverished clergyman and his recalcitrant congregation.[22]

[19] LJRO B/C/5/1632 (Chilvers Coton: *Malin* vs. *Lucas*); WCRO CR136/C1128 (Draft of church court case, *Malin* vs. *Lucas*); C1099g (Statement by William Lucas in case concerning John Malin, c. 1632).

[20] WCRO CR136/B627, ff.2v, 3v, 8v, 9v (charges in the Court of Arches, 29 February to 21 October 1637); C1040 (John Newdigate III to Archbishop William Laud, c. 1637–1638).

[21] WCRO CR136/C1129 (Richard Chamberlain to Bishop Robert Wright, 6 April 1635).

[22] Steve Hindle, *On the Parish? The Micro-Politics of Poor Relief in Rural England, c. 1550–1750* (Oxford, 2004), pp. 27–48.

## II. Parties

The Reverend John Barrows was probably born around 1612, describing himself as aged 47 when he gave evidence in Nuneaton before a Chancery commission in March 1659.[23] He was instituted as vicar of Chilvers Coton at the age of 26, having been ordained in 1630 and previously served as the curate at Over Whitacre (some 6 miles distant). He moved into the vicarage on the south side of Bridge Street, a few yards from the adjacent parish church of All Saints, in November 1638.[24] By 1645, he had not only married, but had married well, his bride being Ann, granddaughter of Henry Mountford of Park Farm, one of the wealthiest and most reputable of Barrows' parishioners.[25] The vicarage in which John and Ann Barrows started their family was already well appointed, having ten rooms, including an entry, a hall, an inner parlour, a parlour, a clay chamber, a buttery, a kitchen, a kitchen chamber, a cheese chamber and a study.[26] The living was, nonetheless, poor. John Newdigate III thought that 'the vicarage was of small value, not worth £40 a year' and needed at least another £10 annually.[27] In this assessment, Newdigate was far too optimistic. Even when ultimately supplemented with the kind of gift that the landlord had in mind, the economic resources available to late seventeenth-century vicars were meagre: Chilvers Coton was far from a prize living, being formally valued at as little as £17, with associated rights in respect of its small glebe (worth a further £8) and of its small tithes (worth about £12).[28] Barrows' predecessors had little alternative, therefore, but to exploit the agricultural resources of the parish: at his death in 1621, for instance, Arthur Oldham owned seventeen cattle and two pigs, and had significant store of wool, hay, corn, hemp and manure.[29] Seventeenth-century vicars of Chilvers Coton were, perforce,

[23] The National Archives, Kew (hereinafter TNA), C22/994/24 (Interrogatories and Depositions in *Newdigate* vs. *Chamberlain*), m.2 (depositions taken at Nuneaton, 31 March 1659, at the house of William Dudley, gent: John Barrows of Chilvers Coton, clerk, aged 47, sworn for both the plaintiff and the defendant).

[24] Clergy of the Church of England Database (http://theclergydatabase.org.uk/) (hereinafter CCEd): Location ID 2462 (Chilvers Coton); Person ID 24713 (John Barrows of Chilvers Coton, vicar).

[25] TNA, PROB 11/194, will of Henry Mountford of Chilvers Coton, gentleman (proved 3 November 1645).

[26] LJRO Inv Arthur Oldam, vicar of Chilvers Coton (31 July 1621).

[27] WCRO CR136/C1040 (Newdigate to Laud, c. 1637–1638).

[28] Hindle, 'Scenes of clerical life', pp. 75, 77.

[29] LJRO Inv Arthur Oldam (1621).

active farmers in the fields and on the commons, as well as conscientious shepherds of their flock as it gathered in the pews of All Saints.

Barrows' precarious economic plight aroused sympathy quite quickly. As early as November 1641, when he had been resident less than three years, Barrows was the beneficiary of the largesse of one of Chilvers Coton's more prosperous inhabitants. The gift did not, however, originate with the Newdigate lords of the manor. Indeed, it was one of the Newdigate family's rivals, the Woods, who declared their intention to bequeath property in support of the new vicar and his successors: in making his will in Barrows' presence, William Wood stipulated that Barrows should, from the point when the ground next lay fallow, enjoy the rights and profits of six fields and their associated common rights lying together at the top of the hill in Coton Outwoods on the Nuneaton parish boundary. And when Wood's estate was settled as a result of his passing early in 1642, Wood's 'loving friend' John Barrows was appointed his executor.[30] This was by no means a coincidence, for Barrows' involvement in the testamentary proceedings of his wealthy parishioners was significant and enduring. He was executor not only to Wood himself in 1642, and to his widow Anne in 1654 and his daughter-in-law Lucy in 1661; but also to his new bride's grandfather, the gentleman Henry Mountford in 1645.[31] These were, by any definition, the chief inhabitants of the parish: the Wood estate remained in the family until the mid-1680s, by which time it was the third largest in Chilvers Coton; and Mountford had been central to the politics of the parish from his involvement as head constable in the Coton Croft enclosure riots during the Midland Rising of 1607 through to the billeting of parliamentary troops during the early years of the civil war.[32] In addition to settling the estates of some of the most prosperous of his parishioners, however, Barrows was also very active in the politics of probate in the less affluent households of the community, orbiting the deathbeds of the sick as they cast up

[30] TNA, PROB 11/188, will of William Wood of Chilvers Coton, gentleman (proved 16 February 1642).

[31] TNA, PROB 11/241, will of Anne Wood of Chilvers Coton, widow (proved 4 October 1654); PROB 11/194, will of Henry Mountford of Chilvers Coton, gentleman (proved 3 November 1645).

[32] WCRO CR136/V101 (Survey of Griff and Coton, vol. I), p. 109 ([later addendum] on the distribution of land); Hindle, 'Sir John Newdigate in the court of Star Chamber', pp. 134–136 (cf. Steve Hindle, 'Imagining insurrection in seventeenth-century England: representations of the Midland rising of 1607', *History Workshop Journal* 66 (2008), 21–61); TNA, SP28/128 (Commonwealth Exchequer Papers), parish accounts for Chilvers Coton, Warwickshire (1643–1647).

their accounts and ultimately witnessing their wills. About one in four extant wills surviving from seventeenth-century Chilvers Coton were subscribed by the parish clergymen, but Barrows significantly exceeded that mean, personally witnessing almost one in three of the wills proved during his incumbency.[33] And the social and economic distribution of those whom he counselled as they lay dying suggests that he had won the confidence of a significant cross-section of his parishioners: between 1641 and 1662, he witnessed the wills of three yeomen, two husbandmen, two labourers, a blacksmith, a nailmaker and a widow.[34] Among the most prosperous of these, the yeoman Edward Atkins left material goods worth almost £64; among the least affluent, the nailmaker Thomas Smith, less than £10. In both cases, moreover, Barrows himself was among the men trusted to appraise the testator's inventory.[35] He was evidently in these parishioners' households right up until the moment of their passing: on 18 April 1653, Barrows heard the labourer Richard Johnson whisper his last wishes only two or three days before he died.[36] But he was also there in the immediate aftermath as their estates were settled, and as their material goods were listed and valued.

Although the earliest extant will witnessed by Barrows dates from 1641, he appears to have built himself into the social and economic networks of the parish even more quickly. He recalled in 1659 that he had, at the earliest opportunity, attended the courts baron of the manor of Griff and Coton, which had been held for three consecutive years at Park Farm in The Woodland of the parish. As minister, he knew it was his obligation to become acquainted with the manorial court proceedings, and he remembered specific orders and fines that had been issued there between 1639 and 1641.[37] Like his successors, he doubtless fulfilled his obligation, in the immediate aftermath of the annual Michaelmas

[33] Hindle, 'Scenes of clerical life', especially pp. 88–90.

[34] LJRO, wills of David Rowley, labourer (1641); Edward Atkins, yeoman (1648), Samuel Brown, blacksmith (1662), Thomas Smith, nailmaker (1662); TNA, PROB 11/239, will of Richard Johnson of Chilvers Coton, labourer (proved 7 March 1654); 11/244, will of Sarah Johnson of Chilvers Coton, widow of Richard (proved 17 July 1655); 11/256, will of Francis Fairfax of Griff, yeoman (proved 14 June 1656); 11/267, will of John Inceley of Chilvers Coton, husbandman (proved 15 September 1657); 11/267, will of Thomas Clarke of Chilvers Coton, husbandman (proved 20 October 1657); 11/284, will of George Walker of Chilvers Coton, yeoman (proved 7 December 1658).

[35] LJRO inventories of Edward Atkins, yeoman (1648); Thomas Smith, nailmaker (1662).

[36] TNA, PROB 11/239, nuncupative will of Richard Johnson of Chilvers Coton, labourer (proved 7 March 1654).

[37] TNA, C22/994/24, m.2.

meeting of the manorial court, to read from the pulpit after the Sunday morning service the text of the manorial regulations through which the jurors governed and ordered the local agrarian community. If the pulpit was the principal medium of political communication in communities like Chilvers Coton, vicars like Barrows were the jurors' mouthpiece.[38] By 1644, only five years after his arrival, he was sufficiently respected to be appointed trustee to a complex marriage settlement between the Baker and Clarke families, responsible for implementing not only the usual provisions of jointure and dower to the bride, but also the less orthodox stipulation of cash sums to be paid to the groom's siblings on their own wedding days.[39]

Barrows was also a central node in the charitable networks of the parish: under the terms of the will of William Baker of 1604, 4*s.* were to be given to the poor of Chilvers Coton at the discretion of the vicar annually every Whitsuntide.[40] Over the following decades, the dole migrated from Whitsuntide to Christmas and morphed from a cash payment into a gift-in-kind, with the bread being distributed not by the vicar, but by the tenant of the land with which the endowment was financed. In December 1650, Barrows wrested back control of Baker's dole from the landlord William Rason, apparently sued him for arrears of rent, and, together with his own wife Ann, certified the names of the recipients and the longevity of their status as almspeople. Although there were doubtless others who had been regular beneficiaries, 'some of whom were absent and others dead', Barrows named eleven parishioners, nine of them women (four of these, as might be expected, widows) and two men who had come to rely upon this seasonal dole: nine of them had been given the bread dole for between ten and twenty years; the other two – a young widow and her daughter – for less than five.[41] In light of this initiative, it is not difficult to imagine that the poor of the parish regarded Barrows and his wife as the guardians of their interests. One of them made that debt of gratitude explicit: when Thomas Edson died suddenly as a childless bachelor early in 1664, he had a minimal estate, valued at

38 Hindle, 'Scenes of clerical life', p. 85; cf. Hindle, 'Sir Richard Newdigate and the "Great Survey" of Chilvers Coton', especially pp. 177–178.

39 WCRO CR136/C883–84 (marriage settlement between William, son of Roger Baker, and Anne Clarke, widow, 1644).

40 LJRO inventory of William Baker, yeoman (probate 4 August 1604); WCRO CR136/V12 (Survey of Griff and Coton, vol. III), p. 58 (17th article, 'Charitable Uses').

41 WCRO CR136/C889 ([John Barrows'] evidence of payments of bequest to poor of Chilvers Coton, 24 December 1650).

only £3-10*s*. (and even that small sum consisted of debts owed to him), but he bequeathed it all verbally on his deathbed to Barrows' wife Ann, because she had 'maynetayned' him in his need.[42]

In all of these respects, therefore, John Barrows could reasonably claim that he was successfully shepherding his entire flock, from nailmakers to yeomen farmers, from single mothers to war widows, from the meek and humble to the rich and powerful. When, as we shall see, this reputation was sorely tested in the late 1650s, his first instinct was to summon a wide cross-section of his congregation in his defence, asking them directly to testify whether or not he had fulfilled 'the office of a minister in teaching of the word and administering the sacraments' and had 'conscionably discharged his pastoral office as vicar' of Chilvers Coton.[43]

Barrows' antagonist, the labourer William Archer, lived on Jeph's Croft, three-quarters of a mile to the west of All Saints church on Paradise Lane, the western boundary of the most southerly of the three great common fields in the parish. By 1657, Archer was married, with five surviving children, the eldest of whom, Nicholas, was aged 20 and the youngest, Thomas, 7, so it is probable that Archer was in his late forties when he ran afoul of John Barrows.[44] He was a tenant of the Wood estate, paying an annual rent of £3 for a house, two closes, an orchard and 16 acres of strips in the common fields. One of his neighbours described him as 'a householder with a wife, a backside and garden place'. The holding was described in more detail in 1685 as a tenement 'with buildings orchards gardens & backside' and 'all that close thereunto adjoining containing approximately four acres and half a yardland' in Windmill Field.[45] Despite the adjacency of this tenancy to the common field system, the occupant had no right of pasture there. To have on his doorstep almost 500 acres of pasture, sufficient to graze well more than 600 sheep, to which he was denied legal access must have been a source of both frustration and temptation for Archer.[46]

Whether access to common right was a source of contention, Archer's neighbours had certainly heard him lose his temper long before he fell

42 LJRO nuncupative will of Thomas Edson of Chilvers Coton (probate 26 August 1664).

43 TNA, E134/1657/Trin3, m2 (First interrogatory on behalf of Barrows, May 1657).

44 The household demography can be retrospectively reconstructed from the names and ages recorded in the occupational 'census-type listing' of December 1684: WCRO CR136/v112, pp. 64–73, nos 20 (Thomas Archer, butcher, aged 34), 65 (Nicholas Archer, labourer, aged 47) and 84 (Richard Archer, labourer, aged 38).

45 LJRO will of William Wood of Pedimore, gent. (23 July 1685).

46 WCRO CR136/V109 (Survey of Griff and Coton, vol. II), pp. 73–77 (Third article, pts 9 and 10, 'Pasturage in the Common Fields').

out with the vicar. One or more of them evidently reported Archer's verbal violence first to the parish, and eventually to the county, authorities: 'several articles exhibited' against him and subsequently 'proved by oath in open court' in 1652 alleged that Archer was a 'fearful swearer and blasphemer of the holy name of God', who had sworn at least twenty-one profane oaths in the space of four days. The magistracy found the accusations sufficiently credible to bind him to his good behaviour for three years and, although he was not required to pay legal costs, £3-10*s*. of his goods were distrained to the use of the poor.[47] Perhaps Archer's profanity was alcohol-fuelled: one of his neighbours, John Perry, was almost simultaneously fined for keeping 'a house of great disorder [and] gaming' and for 'entertaining people drinking and beswilling on the Lord's day'.[48]

The forfeiture of goods worth over £3 was not insignificant to Archer: that sum actually exceeded his annual rent. He was not, however, a very poor man – or at least not in the bureaucratic sense of being dependent on parish charity or relief. In 1656, he was listed as one of the eighty-four separate individuals charged with paying poor rates. His levy was a mere sixpence, calculated at the rate of tuppence per £1 rental value of his tenancy. As such he was one of the lesser ratepayers, but not quite in the category of the most humble: forty-two ratepayers were assessed at far less than Archer's sixpence, and twenty of those at only tuppence, implying that they were cottagers paying annual rents of only £1. Although Archer was, therefore, almost exactly at the median point of the ratepaying hierarchy, it would be misguided to describe him as middling, still less as prosperous: his contribution to the poor rate was almost infinitesimal, constituting only one quarter of 1 per cent of the total levy. William Archer was therefore one of those numerous labouring men who occupied that interstitial position in the seventeenth-century social order: he was poor, but not on relief.[49] Discriminated against and disregarded by a supercilious clergyman, Archer characterized himself (with the special pleading so common among defendants) simply as 'a poore man'.[50] However Archer might have described himself,

[47] S. C. Ratcliff, H. C. Johnson and N. J. Williams (eds), *Warwick County Records*, nine vols (Warwick, 1835–1864) (hereinafter *WCR*), vol. III, p. 88 (Epiphany 1652); cf. Bernard Capp, *England's Culture Wars: Puritan Reformation and Its Enemies in the Interregnum, 1649–1660* (Oxford, 2012), pp. 92–100.

[48] *WCR* III, p. 120 (Trinity 1652).

[49] Hindle, *On the Parish?*, pp. 227–299.

[50] TNA, E134/1657/Mich10 (seventh interrogatory on behalf of Archer, August 1657).

he was the only parishioner John Barrows ever sued for tithe, and even then it was almost twenty years after the vicar had first come to Chilvers Coton.

## III. Pleadings

Although neither of the two extant sets of pleadings in *Barrows* vs. *Archer*, filed in the Exchequer in the spring and autumn of 1657, includes a bill of complaint, each nonetheless contains one or more sets of interrogatories (perhaps best described as 'leading questions'), drawn up in the first case both for the plaintiff and for the defendant, but in the second for the plaintiff only. The vast analytical potential of interrogatories as a genre of legal documentation has only recently been recognized.[51] When read carefully, they permit the reconstruction of the allegations that Barrows made about Archer and vice versa. The first series, administered to witnesses deposed on behalf of Barrows at Nuneaton on 26 May 1657, consisted of thirteen questions.[52] The implications of the assumptions underlying these questions were that Barrows had long been renowned throughout the parish as a conscientious clergyman; that everybody knew what tithes were customarily paid to him and to his predecessors; that Archer regularly pastured and sheared sheep in the parish; that the two of them had previously come to an agreement over money to be paid by Archer in composition for tithes payable on his flock; that Archer had breached the terms of that agreement; that Archer had subsequently boasted that he would never pay tithe and that his own recalcitrance would inspire others to withhold it; that he had deviously offered to pay tithe to the vicar of neighbouring Nuneaton on the grounds that his sheep had crossed the parish boundary; that Archer also generated income from selling acorns and other mast he gathered in the parish; that he was, by nature, a litigious and idle man, who prospered even despite his indolence; and that the whole dispute had, in any case, already been arbitrated in Barrows' favour by two local gentlemen.

Archer's counter-narrative can be reconstructed from the interrogatories administered to witnesses who deposed on his behalf some three

51 Heather Falvey, 'Relating early modern depositions', in Carl J. Griffin and Briony McDonagh (eds), *Remembering Protest in Britain since 1500: Memory, Materiality and the Landscape* (Basingstoke, 2018), pp. 81–106, especially pp. 86–89.

52 TNA, E134/1657/Trin3, m.2. The interrogatories were drawn up as a result of a commission issued to William Perkins Sr and three other local gentlemen on 11 May 1657: TNA, E134/1657/Mich10, m.3.

months later on 25 August 1657.[53] The nine questions implied that Archer was not only a sheep farmer, but also harvested fruit from his orchard, and kept both cattle and poultry; that whatever sheep he did graze were pastured on Nuneaton common across the parish boundary and that he paid tithe to the vicar there on those flocks; that whatever acorns he collected were subject not to tithe, but to nominal common of herbage, which Archer regularly paid; that there had, in fact, been an agreement over tithe composition and that Archer had enthusiastically given security to obey its terms; that Barrows was not only delinquent as a clergyman, but dismissive and disdainful of poor men; that although Barrows had accepted Archer's invitation to visit his home, he had refused to baptize his newborn child on the grounds that the family were poor; that he had no such qualms about the domestic baptisms of the children of other wealthier families; that Barrows regularly brought frivolous and vexatious suits against Archer and other parishioners; and that Barrows preached only occasionally, that he was disloyal to the republican government, that he disobeyed its laws and ordinances, and that his personal conduct was disrespectable.

It is an indication of the attritional nature of seventeenth-century litigation that Barrows' second set of interrogatories, administered to witnesses only three months after their first iteration, were almost entirely derivative of the first.[54] Thirteen questions were consolidated into twelve and more detail was requested on the mechanism of tithe collection; on the size of Archer's flocks; on the precise terms in which Archer had boasted of his resistance to Barrows' demands; on the relationship between arrangements for tithe and common of pasture in Nuneaton and Chilvers Coton, and specifically whether there were any reciprocal agreements between the two parishes; and on the circumstances in which Barrows had demanded that Archer should pay tithe on his acorns. Barrows had, it seems, readily identified the pressure points in his adversary's case and calmly kept jabbing away at them.

So much, then, for the conflicted, contradictory and convoluted legal narratives offered on behalf of the protagonists. The range of witnesses called on either side to validate or undermine them is in itself, moreover, indicative of the social and economic alliances in the village. Archer could produce only five witnesses to support his case and two of them were gentlemen not even resident in Chilvers Coton. Both gave evidence

[53] TNA, E134/1657/Mich10, m.5.
[54] TNA, E134/1657/Mich10, m.3.

specifically about the arbitration brokered some two years previously: Richard Clements of Nuneaton had himself been one of the arbitrators, while Richard Pierce of Coleshill, some 10 miles distant, had apparently witnessed and subscribed the bond of agreement. Only Pierce added anything material in Archer's favour, swearing that, in 1654, Barrows had maliciously and unsuccessfully sued Archer twice in the common law courts, with costs awarded against him. The three Chilvers Coton witnesses who gave evidence on Archer's behalf were scarcely more forthcoming: although the gentleman Thomas Spratt conceded that he had, in fact, given Archer leave to gather mast in the grounds of his property, he was unaware that Barrows had demanded tithe on that crop. The weaver James Holmes, however, believed that Barrows had, in fact, claimed acorn tithe and that this demand was unprecedented. Archer received most vocal support from the 80-year-old tanner Edward Lee, who also claimed to be aware of previous tithe litigation by Barrows and believed it to be frivolous. Even in giving evidence *against* Barrows, however, Lee was forced to admit that the vicar was 'an honest man for ought he knoweth or heard' who preached twice every Sunday and was 'well affected to the present government'.[55] That the vicar's reputation should be described so explicitly in the idiom of loyalty and allegiance to the republican regime tantalizingly implies a political or theological dissociation between Barrows and Archer that is otherwise obscure in the historical record. Archer's dubious reputation as a swearer and curser may just hint that the Chilvers Coton tithe dispute was one more skirmish in the cultural war between the godly and the profane.[56]

This modest show of support for Archer seems all the more lukewarm in comparison to the chorus of approval for Barrows, who succeeded in rallying no fewer than twenty-two men to give evidence on his behalf and even in securing testimony from sixteen of them on two separate occasions: once in May; then again in August. It is significant that this chorus was exclusively male, since the witnesses were all heads of household, responsible as patriarchs for meeting their families' obligations to the

[55] TNA, E134/1657/Mich10, m.4 (depositions on behalf of Archer, 25 August 1657).

[56] Compare Capp, *England's Culture Wars*, pp. 98–100. The widespread use of the term 'well-affected' to describe those 'honest radicals' who were loyal to the parliamentary and republican regimes of the 1640s and 1650s is a recurrent theme in John Walter, *Covenanting Citizens: The Protestation Oath and Popular Political Culture in the English Revolution* (Oxford, 2017), and David R. Como, *Radical Parliamentarians and the English Civil War* (Oxford, 2018).

vicar.[57] Whether their wives were similarly enthusiastic may be open to question, not least since women (by no means all of them Quakers) were so prominent in the 1659 petitioning campaign against tithes.[58] Eighteen of Barrows' twenty-two witnesses, including a gentleman, ten husbandmen, two nailmakers, a silk-weaver, a yeoman, a girdler, a stapler and a shoemaker, were residents of Chilvers Coton. They ranged in age from 20 to 70 and many of them claimed to have known Barrows for a decade or more: at least one, Richard Paul, had been familiar with him for twenty years; while several others were confident that Barrows had been a conscientious clergyman for between thirteen and sixteen years.[59]

## IV. Testimony

The twenty-seven depositions in *Barrows* vs. *Archer* disclose various layers of social and economic interaction between the protagonists. At the most formal level, they allow us to piece together the entangled pre-history of litigation in which the Exchequer suit was itself enmeshed. It becomes clear that Barrows had unsuccessfully sued Archer at common law in the courts of Hemlingford hundred in 1654; that the original agreement over composition payments for the tithe payable on Archer's sheep had been reached in 1655; that the terms of that agreement were 10*s*. a year for the following three years and that several parishioners, including yeomen and husbandmen across the parish of Chilvers Coton, were made aware of it; that, when Archer breached the terms of that agreement, Barrows asked one of Archer's neighbours, the 23-year-old gentleman Thomas Spratt of Paradise End, to broker a mediation to ensure payment of the outstanding sum and the legal costs he had incurred by bringing an action to receive it; that Spratt's mediation floundered in the face of Archer's scorn and derision; that Archer had visited Richard Pyke, the newly appointed vicar of Nuneaton, and, in the presence of credible witnesses, had offered him money for tithes in respect of the sheep he claimed to have grazed in the parish; that he

[57] Wood, *The Memory of the People*, pp. 305–309; Alexandra Shephard, *Meanings of Manhood in Early Modern England* (Oxford, 2003), pp. 186–192.

[58] Naomi Pullin, *Female Friends and the Making of Transatlantic Quakerism, 1650–1750* (Cambridge, 2018), pp. 225–226.

[59] TNA, E134/1657/Trin3, m.3 (depositions on behalf of Barrows, 26 May 1657); E134/1657/Mich10, m.2 (depositions on behalf of Barrows, 25 August 1657). Six of those who deposed in May were not called again in August, but the other sixteen were joined by a seventeenth witness who had previously been sworn on behalf of the defendant.

had subsequently persuaded other Chilvers Coton sheep farmers to pay tithe to Pyke, but that Nuneaton parishioners had talked them out of it; that the two gentlemen who had been tasked to arbitrate the dispute were Richard Newdigate of Arbury Hall and Thomas Clements of Nuneaton, and that their 'reference' or 'settlement' was witnessed and subscribed by Francis Friswell, a 45-year-old silk-weaver from Chilvers Coton, and by Richard Pierce, a 38-year-old gentleman from Coleshill; and that they required Archer to pay Barrows £6 in several instalments, and to sign and seal several bonds of agreement to do so, and did not require Barrows to release Archer of any other legal obligations.

Several features of this narrative are entirely typical of what has become known as the 'disputing process', originally conceptualized by legal anthropologists and more recently adopted by social historians of the law.[60] That a difference of opinion over rights and obligations resulted in the first instance not in litigation, but in an informal agreement, and ultimately in a semi-formally arbitrated attempt at settlement is entirely typical of the pattern of conflict resolution, as students of seventeenth-century society are coming to understand it. But there are nuances here that are worthy of attention: the disputing process was not necessarily *linear*, progressing inevitably and smoothly from composition to mediation to arbitration. On the contrary, it had switchbacks and reversals, with attempted mediation in this particular case taking place only *after* aspirations for an arbitrated settlement had been frustrated and with open contempt for the moral authority of those who attempted to negotiate a peaceful outcome. There was evidently a spectrum of outcomes to dispute in early modern society and historians of the law might usefully develop a more sophisticated typology of the range of possibilities.

At a secondary level, the testimony discloses in extraordinary detail the actual issues at stake in the litigation – specifically, the tithing customs of the parish. The most comprehensive statement came from the 36-year-old husbandman Peter Holmes. Holmes was familiar with the custom that the vicar was due tithe on 'wooll lambes piggs geese and calves' from all of the inhabitants. At Easter, he was entitled to the oblations traditionally recorded in his 'Easter book', together with 'eggs and all other vicar's dues'. He received tithes on lambs at May Day; on calves when

[60] Simon Roberts, 'The study of dispute: anthropological perspectives', in Bossy (ed.), *Disputes and Settlements*, pp. 1–24; Hindle, *The State and Social Change*, pp. 94–95.

they were a fortnight old or when they were fit for the butcher; on pigs at the age of three weeks; and on geese at about Lammastide. Parishioners, Holmes insisted, had always paid the vicar at those times, and Holmes believed that Archer had, until recently at least, been among them. Holmes also specified the Easter dues: tuppence for every married person, tuppence for every servant, tuppence for every recipient of communion and fourpence for every tradesman or aleseller. He was asked specifically about the tithe on wool and on acorns, and noted that the 'usual rate' payable to the minister was 'one half-penny for every sheepskin'; that mast was not usually subject to tithe; and that it was surprising that Barrows had demanded it.[61] Almost all of the witnesses maintained an eloquent silence on arable crops, punctuated only by an isolated aside that the vicar was not entitled to payments on corn or hay, for these were the much more valuable rectorial tithes at issue between the landlord and his tenants.[62]

At a tertiary level, the depositions offer a perspective on related rights and obligations that, although not central to the issues at stake, informed contemporary understandings of the appropriate allocation of resources. These tangential rights and obligations in play in the dispute were most obviously those concerning common of pasture, and specifically whether there were any inter-commoning arrangements between the parishes of Chilvers Coton and Nuneaton, especially at the boundary between Coton Outwoods and Nuneaton Common.[63] Witnesses on behalf of Barrows were vehement in their insistence that there was no reciprocal right of pasture between the two parishes and that, because pasturage on Nuneaton Common was a prerogative exercised exclusively by Nuneaton townsmen, Archer had never been legally entitled to graze his sheep there. It therefore followed that if Archer's sheep had been depastured in Nuneaton, it was part of Archer's deliberate strategy to defraud Barrows of tithe.

[61] TNA, E134/1657/Trin3, m.3 (deposition of Peter Holmes of Chilvers Coton, husbandman, on behalf of John Barrows, complainant, taken at Nuneaton, 26 May 1657); cf. S. J. Wright, 'Easter books and parish rate books: a new source for the urban historian', *Urban History Yearbook* (1985), 30–45.

[62] TNA, E134/1657/Trin3m, m.3 (deposition of John Perry Sr of Chilvers Coton, husbandman); cf. fn. 1 above.

[63] Leigh Shaw-Taylor, 'The management of common land in the lowlands of southern England circa 1500 to 1850', in Martina de Moor, Paul Warde and Leigh Shaw-Taylor (eds), *The Management of Common Land in North-West Europe, c. 1500–1850* (Turnhout, 2002), pp. 59–85.

At a fourth level, the depositions disclose the practices of a sheep-farming economy. Witness testimony reveals that there was widespread local knowledge about who was pasturing their sheep on particular plots of ground and whether they were entitled to do so. Sheep farmers, wool merchants and others knew that Archer's flock grazed in Coton Outwoods, the 60-acre common in north of the parish, rather than across the boundary on Nuneaton common; Archer's sheep were distinctively branded and therefore easily recognized. The nature, frequency and significance of the piecemeal exchanges that cumulatively constituted the textile economy are also imbricated in the testimony: it is evident that Archer did not invariably shear his sheep himself, but had, on occasion, paid two local husbandmen 1*s.*, with food and drink between them, for doing so on his behalf; that the going rate for shearing was a halfpenny per fleece; and that the stapler John Jeffrey, who lived on Wash Lane on the parish boundary with Nuneaton, bought over £3 worth of wool from Archer in each of the years 1655 and 1656. Then there were the contested perceptions of the scale of Archer's sheep-farming activities: while one witness believed that, in 1656 alone, Archer had shorn at least six sheep and reared at least fifteen lambs, others thought that his flock was much more extensive, numbering between sixty and eighty.

It is only by reading the evidence for its incidental detail that the multiple folds of village antagonism become clear, and, in some cases, the recorded testimony catches only the faintest echo of what must have been intense vitriol and recrimination. Those witnesses who recalled Archer's boast that he would 'tame' John Barrows, just as he had tamed William Rason, would immediately have recognized the reference to a seven-year-old dispute over the right to distribute William Baker's ancient bread dole – but only a historian familiar with the deepest, darkest recesses of the Newdigate estate papers would have sufficient local knowledge to make that connection. Running through all of the testimony is the recurrent theme of the assessment of credit, worth and reputation. Who was credible? Who behaved according to conscience? Who enjoyed the trust of his neighbours? In part, these were judgements based on familiarity and the longevity of 'social memory'.[64] Thus Barrows' witnesses rehearsed the view that he was 'a peaceable quiet man amongst his neighbours'; that he had used the law only very

[64] Wood, *The Memory of the People*, pp. 22–29.

reluctantly, suing only Archer over tithes in almost twenty years in the vicarage; and that he was an honest man who preached twice to his congregation every Sunday and was loyal to the republican regime. Archer, by contrast, was represented as 'a very litigious man, much given to lawsuits'.

The jewels in the crown of the testimony are arguably those nuggets of reported speech that bring the voices of the illiterate (and therefore otherwise inaudible) into the historical record. With the shards of oral culture scattered throughout the depositions, it is difficult for the historian to obey the self-denying ordinance against making personality judgements about the character and conduct of the protagonists. Archer claimed that, in resisting tithe payments, he had set the parishioners 'such an example that they would be bound to pray for him'; that he had boasted that 'his name was sturdy'; that he had threatened that 'ere he was done with [Barrows] he would make him so tame that anyone might deal with him'; that he had bragged that he had 'conquered' that 'contentious fellow' William Rason and would make Barrows 'just as tame'; and that he had gloated that any one of his neighbours would be thought 'a foole' if he paid his tithe: in 'hearing' all of this, the historian might be tempted to agree with another of the witnesses that Archer was nothing but a 'brangling scourvy fellow'.[65] That temptation is all the greater when the subject matter of reported speech extends beyond the issues at stake into more general commentary on local social and economic arrangements: thus Archer is said to have scorned Thomas Spratt's mediation with the comment that 'he owed [Barrows] not the tenth part of a farthing for he had paid him too much already' and to have claimed, when criticized for his antagonism to the vicar, that 'the more [money] he spent in lawsuits the more he had, for [so much money] would come upon him that he could not keep it off'. When the Nuneaton gentleman Nicholas Beck told Archer that he suspected that his offer of tithe payment to Richard Pyke rather than to Barrows was made 'more out of malice than conscience', he was making an assessment of Archer's moral compass that inevitably colours any historian's reading of the testimony. These excerpts of 'quoted' speech are, however, mere reportage and it is well to remember that all of this testimony about the idiom in which perceptions were expressed is partial, in both senses of that adjective. When the nailmaker Thomas

[65] TNA: E134/1657/Mich10, m.2 (deposition of William Smith of Chilvers Coton, husbandman, aged about 24, 25 August 1657).

Knight concludes his account of Archer's threats and recriminations, his evidence trails off with the frustrating summary that Archer had uttered 'many similar words', reminding us of the incomplete nature of the historical record. That record, moreover, was generated in the context of an adversarial legal culture in which the undermining of one's opponent's character was not only instinctive, but also reflexive. Defendants and their witnesses almost invariably argued that plaintiffs' allegations were frivolous, as did the 80-year-old tanner Edward Lee, while plaintiffs and their deponents frequently implied that recalcitrant defendants were litigious, determined only to have their day in court, as did the 24-year-old husbandman William Smith.

## V. Silence

The 'many other words' to which the nailmaker Thomas Knight referred in giving evidence on behalf of John Barrows ultimately trail off into silence. There are no extant further proceedings in *Barrows* vs. *Archer* and it therefore remains uncertain whether the suit itself came to judgment or whether it sparked further litigation in other jurisdictions. In this respect, the case is entirely characteristic of the hundreds of thousands of lawsuits that were filed in seventeenth-century England. It is a paradox of the archive of litigation that the millions of words of pleadings and testimony engrossed across acres of parchment generated so very few entries in bound volumes of verdicts and decrees. Indeed, so common was it for a suit to be settled out of court rather than forced to judgment that both contemporaries and historians have come to recognize that this outcome may have been precisely what plaintiffs were, in fact, seeking. The primary motive for initiating litigation may not been to secure a favourable verdict, but to encourage, persuade or coerce an opponent to come to a negotiated settlement. From this perspective, in theoretical terms at least, there was no tension between an adversarial legal system, on the one hand, and the culture of reconciliation, on the other: the issuing of a writ was just a way of explaining to, or reminding, one's opponent that grievances should be taken seriously and settled. Such a positive reading of the social meaning of litigation is, however, predicated on the assumption that most disputes arose, and that most litigation was fought, between parties who were relative social equals. Seventeenth-century English society was, however, ridden with inequality, and it is almost certain that some defendants in lawsuits felt either obliged to settle with wealthier and more powerful opponents or were browbeaten and intimidated into doing so.[66] Not for nothing did poor men very often claim that they could not get justice precisely *because* their opponents were 'well-friended' both within and beyond the courtroom. The sheer weight of testimony that John Barrows was able to mobilize in support of his claim to tithe, and the significant social capital shared by those who gave evidence on his behalf, is a salutary reminder of the inequalities of wealth and power that underlay many seventeenth-century lawsuits.

The outcome of *Barrows* vs. *Archer* therefore remains uncertain. A little more, however, can be said about the subsequent fate of the protagonists. William Archer died in his late fifties or early sixties and was buried in Chilvers Coton in 1671. His family remained in the parish, however, and by 1684 two of his children, the then 38-year-old labourer Richard and the then 34-year-old butcher Thomas, were householders with families of their own. Richard Archer seems to have inherited the tenancy of the cottage in which his father had lived. Like his father, however, Richard enjoyed a dubious reputation among his neighbours. He lived in Paradise Lane with his common-law wife Mary, a liaison thought to be all the more scandalous since she was twelve years older than him, and the two of them were presented and excommunicated in the late 1670s for having 'married' clandestinely. In 1689, he was indicted for an assault on Mary White, the wife of one of his neighbours, and was presented in 1694 (in an echo of the concerns about his foul-mouthed father) as a profane swearer and curser.[67]

John Barrows himself disappears from the historical record even more quickly. In the years following the 1657 dispute, he witnessed several more wills in Chilvers Coton; in the early 1660s, he was assessed on five chimneys for the hearth tax on the vicarage and he subscribed to the Act of Uniformity on 11 August 1662.[68] More poignantly, he experienced a personal tragedy of his own in December 1662, when he and his wife

[66] Keith Wrightson, 'The politics of the parish in early modern England', in Paul Griffiths, Adam Fox and Steve Hindle (eds), *The Experience of Authority in Early Modern England* (London and New York, 1996), p. 20.

[67] LJRO B/V/1/82 (Visitation Book of the Archdeaconry of Coventry, 1679–1680), ff. 22v (7 October 1679), 32v (12 December 1679) 37v (17 March 1680), 47 (20 May 1680); *WCR* III, p. 257 (Michaelmas 1689): *WCR* IX, p. 32 (Easter 1691); *WCR* IX, p. 100 (Michaelmas 1694).

[68] Margaret Walker (ed.), *Warwick County Records, Hearth Tax Returns, Volume I: Hemlingford Hundred, Tamworth and Atherstone Divisions* (Warwick, 1957), p. 202; CCEd, Person ID 24713 (John Barrows of Chilvers Coton, vicar).

Ann buried one of their children, John.[69] In October 1663, Barrows ceded the living, and whether or not he and Anne and their surviving children were still resident, she was remembered as the beneficiary of one parishioner's will in January 1664.[70] Barrows may well have moved on to the living in the Leicestershire parish of Hinckley, possibly remaining there until a 'John Barrows' was succeeded by a new vicar in July 1683.[71] There is, however, no record of Barrows' own burial and no extant probate material. His pastoral achievement nonetheless seems to have been impressive: to have calmed the antagonism over tithe that had been endemic in Chilvers Coton at the time of his institution in 1638 was no mean feat. It is remarkable that further litigation over tithe payments was deferred for almost twenty years and that, when it did finally erupt, Barrows was able to mobilize significant support from his congregation. This enviable record is thrown into greater relief by the miserable experience of one of his successors. By the time the Reverend John Perkins died in 1691 after eleven years' residence in All Saints vicarage, he had not been asked to witness the wills of any of his parishioners and was owed tithes to the value of £10 – over 80 per cent of the dues due to him annually.[72] It is a fair assumption that Richard Archer was, like his father before him, among those delinquent parishioners who was behind on his payment of tithe to the vicar of Chilvers Coton. Wherever he was ultimately laid to rest, by contrast, the Reverend John Barrows was doubtless fondly remembered by his parishioners.

[69] WCRO DR62/1 (Register of baptisms, marriages and burials, 1654–1699), burial of Jon Barrows, son of John Barrows, clerk, 9 December 1662.

[70] LJRO (nuncupative), will of Thomas Edson (1664).

[71] CCEd, Person ID 86112 (John Barrows of Hinckley, vicar); Location ID 7675 (Hinckley).

[72] Hindle, 'Scenes of clerical life', especially p. 87.

# 8

# 'Law-Mindedness'

## Crowds, Courts and Popular Knowledge of the Law in Early Modern England

JOHN WALTER

One of the hard-won truths that we owe to Christopher W. Brooks's herculean labours in the thickets of English early modern court records is the centrality of 'law-mindedness' to that society. Brooks suggested that law-mindedness ran deep in the society of early modern England. Without putting a precise social boundary to this, he showed that it was to be found in the ranks of the middling sort about whose role in that society he also made important arguments.[1] Focusing on popular knowledge of the law demonstrated in early modern crowd actions, this chapter seeks to extend the social contours to law-mindedness. It explores the sources of this popular knowledge in wider societal access to the law and in the experience of authority in the spaces between government and local self-governance. An examination of the evidence of popular 'law-mindedness' to be found in early modern crowd actions reveals the sometimes surprising social depth to popular knowledge of the law. Crowds appealed to the law to justify and legitimise their actions, and popular knowledge of the law often shaped the form their protests took. The knowledge they displayed could be highly technical. But it could also reflect the ambiguous interface between the law and popular understanding of it. The crowd's ability, perhaps knowingly and certainly sometimes playfully, to 'misunderstand' the law could also *license* protest. Exploring the evidence to be found in legal contests thrown up by disputes over access to grain and land in the politics of subsistence, this

[1] Christopher W. Brooks, 'Professions, ideology and the middling sort in the late sixteenth and early seventeenth centuries', in Jonathan Barry and Christopher Brooks (eds), *The Middling Sort of People: Culture, Society and Politics in England, 1550–1800* (Basingstoke, 1994), pp. 113–140.

chapter questions how far popular knowledge of, and access to, the law helped not only to shape, but perhaps also to constrain, the pattern of early modern crowd actions.

## I

Key to Brooks's argument for law-mindedness was the centrality of laws, lawyers and litigation to the framing and regulation of economic, social and political relationships and the important role played by contemporary thinking about the law to conceptualisations of state and society. Early modern England was bound together by the law. Law played a central role in the ordering of people's material and affective lives. It was the discourse of law that informed their understanding of the nature of political authority, of the liberties and rights they enjoyed under law within the early modern polity, and even their identity as a 'freeborn' people living under the rule of law.

Beyond this central argument, a range of other (related) factors helped to explain the purchase that law had on people's lives and thinking. Given the law's central role in mediating a wide range of relationships, Brooks famously showed that a period that registered considerable demographic and economic growth witnessed a significant increase in litigation, in both the Crown's equity and common law courts: the period 1560–1640, he argued, was 'one of the most litigious periods in English history'.[2] Allied to this (and prompting the familiar chicken-and-egg question favoured by critics of the legal profession), he demonstrated that the period also witnessed a significant increase in the number of lawyers. Attorneys, multiplying faster than the population, were increasingly active in both the capital's courts and in the provinces.[3] Brooks was able to demonstrate that this growing presence of lawyers gave greater access to legal advice, further confirmation of which we shall see in disputes examined here. In characteristically painstaking work, he was also able to argue that the cost of litigation made it possible for those beyond county and local elites to access even the Crown's equity courts: 'going to law in the late sixteenth and early seventeenth centuries', he argued, 'was both easy and relatively inexpensive'.[4]

[2] Christopher W. Brooks, *Pettyfoggers and the Vipers of the Commonwealth: The 'Lower Branch' of the Legal Profession in Early Modern England* (Cambridge, 1986), p. 79.

[3] Ibid., pp. 112–113.

[4] Ibid., p. 106.

Given Brooks's argument about the increasing volume of cases in the Crown's courts, popular experience of litigation itself promoted knowledge of the law. In addition to this bottom-up growth, driven by social and economic change, the nature of the early modern English state also increasingly exposed far more men and women to the law. Rule in the provinces was largely conducted through courts of law. As Brooks observed, 'no institutions were more ubiquitous in early modern England than courts of law'.[5] Popular knowledge of the law therefore also reflected the experience of the law in courts in which members of the local community served as local officials and jurors or attended as suspect, victim, witness or spectator. Going to law made attendance at court a regular point of contact between the people and the law.

Given that much government was self-government at the king's command, the government deliberately sought to promote knowledge of its laws. Royal proclamations, read from the market cross or another public site, directly communicated the government's laws and administrative measures. Statutes too might be required to be publicly read. As William Lambarde's handbook for justices of the peace informed them, they were 'bounde to informe the people . . . and therof it is, that many statutes doe expres[s]ly command, that they shall be openly read (or declared) at the Sessions'.[6] Meetings of provincial courts were meant to include at their opening a reading of all of the statutes then in force; in Lancashire, a lengthy parchment roll was specially kept for this purpose.[7] A Star Chamber bill could then refer to those 'who in the eyes of theire Contrye are & would be accompted of good & Cyvyll conversacon & usually resorting to gen[e]rall assises & quarter sessyons . . . where they might heare the good Lawes & statut[e]s of this Realme of England'.[8]

The twice-annual meeting of the assizes presided over by royal judges sent on circuit in the provinces offered an important opportunity for the government to publicise its policies and laws. As the Lord Keeper noted in his address to the judges about to go on circuit in the summer of 1635, 'twise a-year at the least Justice followeth the Subjects home to their own Doors . . . it giveth the People a better knowledge of Justice, and the end

[5] Ibid., p. 33.

[6] William Lambarde, *Eirenarcha or the Office of the Justices of Peace* (London, 1619 [1581]), pp. 404–405.

[7] Christopher W. Brooks, *Law, Politics and Society in Early Modern England* (Cambridge, 2008), p. 298.

[8] TNA: STAC 8/71/6.

of it'.[9] The Lord Keeper's address formed the basis of the charge publicly delivered at assizes by the judges, often in buildings themselves decorated with painted scripts extolling the virtues of the law.[10] An address to the court that included a list of the government's current concerns and the legislation that it wanted enforced in particular, charges were also delivered at the quarterly meeting at the court of quarter sessions in the counties; at the most local level, meetings of the manor court might also open with a charge.[11] Charges had, in Brooks's phrase, 'a self-educative purpose'. Often a competitive exercise offering an opportunity for members of the county's rulers to parade their legal knowledge and exercise their rhetorical skills, the charge to local courts mixed listings of the statutes in force and their rationale with more philosophical musings on the role of the law in state and society.[12] Lambarde's detailed charges at quarter sessions in Kent suggest that he took seriously his own advice in *Eirenarcha* 'to informe the people'.[13] In addition, judges who shared popular fears about the consequences of enclosure or profiteering in the grain trade might amplify the government's message in their charge. Articles against Sir Edward Coke in the Parliament of 1621, for example, included the accusation that 'to get peoples love he made Tenants and copy-holders, having right of common, to stand against inclosures'.[14]

Performing the law offered further opportunity for learning about the laws in force. Exemplary prosecutions, for example, of enclosers or middlemen in the grain trade required offenders to acknowledge their crime publicly, 'for the better manifestation of the offence to the

[9] J. S. Cockburn, *A History of the English Assizes 1558–1714* (Cambridge, 1972), p. 181; John Rushworth, *Historical Collections Private Passages of State, Vol. 2, 1629–38* (London, 1721), p. 294.

[10] See, e.g., Edward Jacob, *The History of Faversham* (Sheerness, 1974 [1774]), pp. 214–217.

[11] Brooks, *Law, Politics and Society*, pp. 426, 255.

[12] For a discussion of charges, see Brooks, *Law, Politics and Society*, pp. 298–305; Brooks, 'Professions, ideology and the middling sort', pp. 117–118; Cockburn, *History of the English Assizes*, pp. 58–59, 181–182; Steve Hindle, *The State and Social Change in Early Modern England, c. 1550–1640* (Basingstoke, 2000), p. 6; Anthony Fletcher, *Reform in the Provinces: The Government of Stuart England* (New Haven, 1986), pp. 166–175. For examples of charges, see V. M. Larminie, *The Godly Magistrate: The Private Philosophy and Public Life of Sir John Newdigate 1571–1610* (Oxford, 1982); for examples of charges itemising laws in force, see *Wiltshire Archaeological and Natural History Magazine* (Devizes, 1874), vol. xiv, p. 215 (1580); Hertfordshire Record Office, VIII.B.153 (1638); BL, Harleian MS 160, ff. 170–176v (n.d.).

[13] Conyers Read (ed.), *William Lambarde and Local Government: His 'Ephemeris' and Twenty-Nine Charges to Juries and Commissions* (Ithaca, 1962), pp. 65–189.

[14] Wallace Notestein, Frances Helen Relf and Hartley Simpson (eds), *Commons Debates, 1621*, seven vols (New Haven, 1935), vol. ii, p. 472.

Countrey'. After widespread attacks by crowds on depopulating enclosures in the Midlands Rising of 1607, the government told the county authorities, 'we think it not unfit that by such meanes as yow shall hold most convenient to be divulged in the Countrey that the persons noted to be guilty of these oppressions are sent for by his Ma[jes]t[ie]s commaundem[en]t to receive the censure of the laws for their offences'. Placards at the place of punishment informed audiences of the nature of the crime to be punished, while in what remained a predominantly oral culture the manipulation of symbols at the pillory visualised the offence punished, and sermons at the scaffold (or assizes) both detailed the crime and philosophised about the law.

For those able to read, print too had an increasingly important role to play. Proclamations were posted and statutes printed. Contemporary references to the farmer reading *Coke on Littleton* at the plough might have romanticised reality, but yeomen can be shown to have had copies of legal treatises, including Littleton on tenure, among their possessions.[15] The multiplication of printed law reports and handbooks for justices of the peace or constables provided access to the law for those able to purchase and read them or living in parishes where churchwardens' accounts record the purchase of these and printed collections of statutes.[16] The numerous ballads and cautionary tales of early modern cheap print, in which crime, cozening and oppression loomed large, also extended the purchase of the law on popular culture.[17]

Last, and by no means least in explaining the frequently detailed knowledge of the law that early modern crowds displayed, was the increasing availability of legal advice from lawyers whose growing presence in early modern society Brooks's work did much to establish.[18] Occasionally, commoners involved in disputes with enclosers numbered a lawyer active among their ranks, as in the dispute at Hillmorton in Warwickshire over the attempt by the lord of the manor to enclose the open fields.[19] But the more frequent involvement of attorneys or their clerks as advisers to those protesting reflects one consequence of the

[15] Mildred Campbell, *The English Yeoman under Elizabeth and the Early Stuarts* (London 1960 [1942]), p. 267.

[16] E. C. R. Brinkworth (ed.), *South Newington Churchwardens' Accounts, 1553–1684* (Banbury, 1964), p. xviii.

[17] James Sharpe, 'The people and the law', in Barry Reay (ed.), *Popular Culture in Seventeenth-Century England* (Beckenham, 1985), pp. 256–259.

[18] Brooks, *Pettyfoggers and Vipers*.

[19] TNA: STAC 8/40/2; /6/4; see also TNA: STAC 8/303/6.

explosion in the number of attorneys that Brooks identified. The law-rich environment of the early modern town in particular offered multiple opportunities to access to legal advice. For example, in the dispute at Thimbleby and Horncastle in Lincolnshire, it was alleged that it was the High Steward, an attorney at law, who advised those challenging enclosure by a neighbouring lord of the manor.[20] That enclosure disputes might include gentlemen for whom some period of education in the Inns of Court was a necessary consequence of their landed wealth also served to circulate knowledge of the law among protesters. Cases between feuding gentry involving disputes between lords of the manor (especially over rights to inter-commoning) or with external agents of enclosure could see gentlemen active with advice and assistance to provide crowds with legal counsel.[21] This was especially the case in the large-scale enclosure projects in the fens and royal forests where enclosure by Crown, courtiers and city financiers threatened the interests of local elites. Although we need to exercise care when confronted by Star Chamber stories told to the court by plaintiffs anxious to implicate gentry rivals, there are plenty of examples of gentlemen to whom crowds turned for advice directing them to the services of a local attorney. In a Jacobean dispute at Great Wolford in Warwickshire, the gentleman named by the new lord of the manor as instigator of the destruction of his enclosures claimed only that 'for Comforte and Advise unto ... friendlie and honest ... neighbours [he] directed them to such Councell as he knewe to be fitte for them'. This legal advice doubtless helps to explain how these commoners came to commence a Chancery suit against the lord of the manor and why, to his annoyance, they were able to subvert his attempt to have his enclosures protected by swearing the peace out against those whom he had set to guard them.[22]

The collection of common purses allowed communities of commoners themselves to seek legal advice and to initiate legal actions in their causes. Commoners, as at Grace-Dieu in Leicestershire, met together 'in Lawfull & neighbourlie sorte' and agreed to take counsel.[23] The twin poles of

[20] TNA: STAC 8/145/20.

[21] For examples, see R. B. Manning, 'Antiquarianism and the seigneurial reaction: Sir Robert and Sir Thomas Cotton and their tenants', *Historical Research* 3 (1990), 277–288; Steve Hindle, 'Persuasion and protest in the Caddington common enclosure dispute 1635–1639', *Past and Present* 158 (1998), 37–78; John Hawarde, *Les Reportes del Cases in Camera Stellata, 1593–1609*, ed. W. P. Baildon (London, 1894), pp. 49–52.

[22] TNA: STAC 8/55/13; TNA: STAC 8/78/13; Warwickshire Record Office, MI 167/644–5, 649.

[23] TNA: STAC 8/71/6.

village life – the church and the alehouse – served as sites for the agreement, assessment and collection of a common purse.[24] Sometimes, it was the place of enclosure itself. In the dispute between the earl of Derby and his tenants at Bassenthwaite in Cumberland over his enclosure out of the wastes, the tenants were said to have met on the waste at a place aptly named 'freedome'. There they had agreed to assess themselves at a half-year's rent to support legal action against the earl, to fine anyone not participating in their protest the sum of 12*d.* (and, so it was alleged, all to give three blows to anyone trying to erect the enclosure so it could not be known who was guilty of their assault or murder).[25] In the dispute at Hillmorton, the commoners had agreed to assemble at the ringing of a bell and, assessing themselves after the rate of 2*s.* 6*d.* for every quarter yardland and cottage, had raised a common purse of some £13. 6*s.* 8*d.* Common purses were frequently to be found, and might be considerable, in the north-west in defence of the local custom of tenant right or in the actions against Charles I's large-scale enclosures in western forests and eastern fens.[26]

## II

A sympathetic member of Parliament, in a debate over a bill to regulate enclosure in the harvest failures of the 1590s, cautioned, 'it be not fit Mr Speaker to be published among the ruder sort, who if they were privy to their own strength and liberty allowed them by the law would be as unbridled and [*sic*] untamed beasts'.[27] Knowledge of legislation formed part of the news that early modern men and women eagerly devoured, and it might be cited (or creatively misread) to legitimise acts of protest. Following the destruction of an enclosure at York in 1536, a local cooper claimed that he had been told by one of the City's members of Parliament, information he later reattributed to the women of the town, that 'it was enactyd by the Parlyament that ther[e] shuld be no common be dyked nor enclosed'. At Norwich, in Edward VI's reign, an

[24] For some examples, see TNA: STAC 8/84/19, 227/12, 251/22, 275/7, 278/5, 216/12 and 156/32.

[25] TNA: STAC 8/256/17 and 16.

[26] R. W. Hoyle, 'Lords, tenants and tenant right in the sixteenth century: four studies', *Northern History* 20 (1984), 38–63; TNA: STAC 8/34/4; TNA: STAC 8/6/4; TNA: PCR 2/51, 354–355; SP 16/132/63, /230/51, 450/80, 18/37/11 and /39/92.

[27] Historical Manuscripts Commission, *Calendar of the Manuscripts of the Most Hon. Marquis of Salisbury* (London, 1883–) vol. VII, pp. 541–543, quotation at p. 542.

alehouse conversation between a cook and a blacksmith about the 'Godly acts that were coming down' led the blacksmith to claim that the king had sent down Acts that all freehold and copyhold enclosures were to be pulled down; if the enclosures within the town's lands were not removed, he and a hundred or more would pull them down. This appears to have been a widespread belief. A year or two later, a Hereford mason sought to drum up support for pulling down local enclosures by 'affirming that it was the kyngs comaundement by his p(ro)clamacons that they should brake upp all inclosures'.[28]

Popular knowledge of the law also helped to shape protest. Protesters employed tactics, derived from knowledge of the law, to assert the legitimacy of their protest and to evade the potentially draconian punishments that prosecution of riot as felony or treasonable assembly (rather than misdemeanour) might threaten. In what was the most common form of protest in this period, crowd actions against enclosure, the very form that the protest took often mimicked the moves needed to be taken to initiate a lawsuit over disputed land claims. In pulling down a hedge to assert rights of common over land – the defining action of most crowd actions against enclosure – protesters could claim legal precedent, as the speaker in the Elizabethan Parliament acknowledged, for the right to remove an illegal encroachment. Thus, those accused of pulling down a wall at Little Houghton in Northamptonshire in 1608 and of threatening to 'turne their plowes into pastures & make all common for corne' claimed in their defence that, as feoffees of the town lands, they had leased the disputed land to one of their number to try the title and had peacefully broken down the mud wall to seal the lease, with others merely present there in their capacity as witnesses to the lease.[29] In a dispute at Bishops Wilton in Yorkshire, those accused of pulling down a gentleman's enclosure claimed to be acting by virtue of their office as bylawmen, and to have made gaps only of sufficient size to allow access for the commoners' cattle and sheep onto what they claimed was Lammas land.[30] Access to legal advice at Great Wolford doubtless helps to explain

[28] Angelo Raine (ed.), *York Civic Records* (Yorkshire Archaeological Soc. Rec. Ser., CVIII, 1945), vol. IV, p. 2; W. Rye (ed.), *Depositions Taken before the Mayor and Aldermen of Norwich, 1549–1567* (Norwich, 1905), pp. 52–53; Hereford Archives and Records Centre, *Hereford City Records*, transc. F. C. Morgan, vol. I, f. 293. I am grateful to Keith Thomas for this reference.

[29] TNA: STAC, 8/295/22; A. W. B. Simpson, *An Introduction to the History of the Land Law* (Oxford, 1961), p. 136.

[30] TNA: STAC 8/36/20.

the careful claims of the commoners at court to have had only a small gap made by two men to allow access for their sheep and cattle to land over which they too claimed common rights after the harvest.[31]

Citing the precedent of earlier legislation, the sympathetic Elizabethan member of Parliament had gone on to observe 'that where the wrong and mischief spreads to an universality, there the people may be their own justices'.[32] Making a gap in a hedge and/or depasturing enclosures with commoners' cattle might deliberately reference actions at law to bring an action of trespass or *novel disseisin* or, in the case of impounded livestock, of *replevin* to try the title to the land.[33] At Coventry, where there were long-running disputes over the enclosure of the City's commons, it was the Corporation itself, faced with illegal enclosure, which ordered two men to make a gap in the hedge and to put in cattle. At Spondon and Borrowash in Derbyshire, in a case in defence of customary common rights over the common fields and moorland that the cottagers claimed to have enjoyed time out of mind, two men went and pulled down only part of a dead hedge and put in their cattle, while other persons deliberately 'stood a farr of[f] and looked on'.[34] The strength of this popular belief in the legitimacy of the act of 'possessioning', a peaceable action to try right, and not therefore riot, as commoners brought before court claimed, persisted into the eighteenth century – even in the face of increasing judicial hostility.[35]

In cases of crowd actions over enclosure brought into Star Chamber, the court that heard most such cases, it was common enough for the destruction of the hedges and ditches to be assigned to only two commoners.[36] For example, copyholders of inheritance at Tydderington in Cheshire who were alleged to have pulled down a new enclosure and kept it open by force claimed to have had a gap made by a pair of servants only to put in their cattle – a numerical tactic repeated by those accused of riotous destruction of the drainage works in the Lincolnshire fens in 1642.[37] Such cases reveal another aspect of the law

31 TNA: STAC 8/55/13 and 78/13; SP 12/251/123.

32 Historical Manuscripts Commission, *Calendar of the Manuscripts of the Most Hon. Marquis of Salisbury*, vol. VII, pp. 541–543, quotation at p. 542.

33 Eric Kerridge, *Agrarian Problems in the Sixteenth Century and After* (London, 1969), p. 82; Simpson, *Land Law*, p. 42; Brooks, *Pettyfoggers and Vipers*, p. 66.

34 TNA: STAC 8/260/15.

35 E. P. Thompson, *Customs in Common* (London, 1991), pp. 117–118 and n. 3, 119–120.

36 For examples of this, see TNA: STAC 8/42/11, /54/6, 8/187/13 and 8/251/27.

37 TNA: STAC 8/299/21; Historical Manuscripts Commission, *Fifth Report of the Roayl Commission on Historical Manuscripts* (London, 1876), p. 25.

that might be turned to popular advantage: 'For the number,' said the author of *The Countrey Justice*, a popular justices' *vade-mecum*, 'there must necessarily be three persons at the least, so gathered together, or els it can be no Riot, Rout, or unlawful assembly within the meaning of these statutes.'[38] It took three to make a riot, 'three or more in one companie (which the Law properly calleth a multitude)', advised William Lambarde.[39] As a report of proceedings in Star Chamber noted, ruling in a 1602 case, 'there was no proof of riot, because there were but two rioters'.[40] Thus, in a dispute in Somerset in 1612 in which the commoners were said by the plaintiff to have operated in 'riotous warlike and trooping manner', they countered that they had agreed to put in their cattle to try the title and that there were never more than two of them present.[41] At Poynton in Cheshire, commoners who were alleged to have assembled in a crowd more than a hundred strong and pulled down an enclosure with 'verye manye greate and terrible showts and outcries' claimed to have done so only by twos to let in their cattle.[42] Similarly, in a dispute at Chilvers Coton in Warwickshire over the attempt to coppice and keep enclosed commonable land, the commoners had agreed that if the lord of the manor were to attempt to re-erect the enclosure, they should throw it down again to try the title – but that only two of them should do it.[43]

Popular knowledge and legal advice determined the restriction of numbers. Those accused in Star Chamber of riotously pulling down enclosures, like the Leicestershire commoners who had collected a common purse at Grace-Dieu, cited the legal advice they had received to restrict their numbers.[44] In the long-running dispute at Grewelthope in Yorkshire in 1606 over the enclosure and mining of moorland by Sir Stephen Proctor, Proctor complained that the wives of the commoners,:

> ... fearing they mighte be troubled for coming in such multitudes, and fynding by some Councell and advyse that their goeing in soe great a number would make notorious Ryotts and should receave great punyshment ... in deceipt and p[re]vencon of justice did thereupon by the advyse and direccon of their said husbands, plot ... to single themselves, and to goe but two at once.

38 Michael Dalton, *The Countrey Justice, Containing the Practise of the Justices of the Peace out of Their Sessions* (London, 1622 [1618]), p. 201.
39 Lambarde, *Eirenarcha*, p. 125.
40 Hawarde, *Reportes del Cases*, p. 157.
41 TNA: STAC 8/155/10.
42 TNA: STAC 8/292/12.
43 TNA: STAC 8/157/18; see also TNA: STAC 8/152/20.
44 TNA: STAC 8/71/6, 8/215/16 and 219/9; Hawarde, *Reports del Cases*, pp. 49–52.

Again, in the famous dispute in the 1650s over the drained lands at Epworth in Lincolnshire, in which Leveller leader John Lilburne acted for the commoners, it was local attorney Daniel Noddel who had advised them to act two by two and who then delighted in telling those sent by the sheriff to remove the commoners' cattle, 'looke you here is noe force'.[45]

Commoners might then make creative use of popular knowledge of the law, playing with contemporary conventions of time and space to evade the restrictions on numbers 'in one companie'. In a dispute at Stixwould in the Lincolnshire wolds, those who threw down enclosures there insisted that they had done so 'by twoe and twoe only togeather about a bowe shoot one from the other', while at Grewelthorpe moor, the wives had attacked the enclosure, 'first by two of them and therafter a small distance of tyme interposed, by two other and soe by two and twoe until they all had overgone their sev[er]all turnes'.[46] But while the legal form might structure the shape the protest took, where this involved force of numbers and a considerable level of destruction (as here), it may be suggested that appeals to legitimation by law were often merely tactical.

The activities of the Grewelthorpe wives under their leader Captain Dorothy point towards another common tactic informed by popular understanding of the law. The frequency with which it was women who pulled down enclosures and the claim of those active in the destruction of disputed enclosures that they were 'lawlesse, and that there was noe law for women' again suggests widespread knowledge of the law and use of its ambiguity to mobilise protest.[47] Despite attempts by the courts to prevent women from 'hiding behind their sex', the legal position of women before the law remained ambiguous in early modern England.[48] As the justices' handbooks informed their readers, 'if a number of women (or children under the age of discretion) do flocke together for their own cause, this is

[45] Keith Lindley, *Fenland Riots and the English Revolution* (London, 1982), pp. 188–222; TNA: SP 18/37/1; Joy Lloyd, 'The communities of the manor of Epworth in the seventeenth century', PhD thesis, University of Sheffield (1999); C. Holmes, 'Drainers and fenmen: the problem of popular political consciousness in the seventeenth century', in Anthony Fletcher and John Stevenson (eds), *Order and Disorder in Early Modern England* (Cambridge, 1985), pp. 166–195.

[46] TNA: STAC 8/113/11 (see also /129/13 and /17/23), and /227/3.

[47] TNA: STAC 8/295/11. For other examples, see STAC 8/12/7 and /198/31, /17/11, /160/18, 247/10, /293/12 and 295/11.

[48] John Walter, 'Faces in the crowd: dender and age in the early modern English crowd', in Helen Berry and Elizabeth Foyster (eds), *The Family in Early Modern England* (Cambridge, 2007), pp. 96–124, pp. 113–114.

none assembly punishable . . . unlesse a man of discretion moved them to assemble for the doing of some unlawfull act'.[49] Thus, in the case at Chilvers Coton, in which the men had sought the protection of agreeing that only two should act, it had been the wives of the community who had pulled down the enclosure; in their depositions, the women were careful to state that, on learning of the enclosure, they had called to one another 'on a sudden', and that they had acted in their husbands' absence and without their knowledge or procurement.[50] At Nether Wyresdale in Lancashire, the women of the community had pulled down the disputed enclosure after having been told that 'that woeman [*sic*] were lawless and that they might boldly w$^{th}$out anie ffeare of punishment pull down the hedges and ditches'. Despite a 1605 Star Chamber ruling that 'the husband is answerable notwithstanding the action was without his privity', communities of commoners continued to use this defence, with, on occasion, cross-dressing men again managing both to reference and ridicule the law.[51] As one Star Chamber plaintiff and victim of female enclosure rioters complained, they had acted 'upon the[i]re phantasticall ymaginac[i]ons conceaved amongst themselves, that women were lawlesse, and not subiect to the lawes of the realme as men are but might in such cases offend without drede or punishment of law'.[52]

Exploitation of the interregnum between the death of the old and succession of the new monarch to time protests offers another example of popular understandings of, and of protesters' ability to exploit ambiguity within, the law. The popular belief that the authority of those appointed by the monarch ended with their death was a real enough problem to occasion debate among the royal judges and to warrant the immediate issuing of proclamations on the monarch's death to continue in office all those holding royal appointment.[53] In what came to be known as 'busy' or 'ill week', belief in an interregnum saw an outbreak of cross-border raiding between Scots and English at the death of Elizabeth I.[54] At a popular level, any ambiguity might be elided in the claim that the law died with the monarch. At Thriplow in Cambridgeshire in the 1603 interregnum, an

49 Lambarde, *Eirenarcha*, p. 180.

50 TNA: STAC 8/157/18.

51 Hawarde, *Reportes del Cases*, pp. 103–104, 247; TNA: STAC 8/197/18 and /286/25.

52 TNA: STAC 8/223/7.

53 James F. Larkin and Paul L. Hughes (eds), *Stuart Royal Proclamations 1603–1625* (Oxford, 1973), pp. 4–6; James F. Larkin (ed.), *Stuart Royal Proclamations 1625–1646* (Oxford, 1983), pp. 4–6.

54 Catherine M. F. Ferguson, 'Law and order on the Anglo-Scottish borders, 1603–1707', PhD thesis, University of St Andrews (1981), f. 100.

enclosure out of the open field was pulled down by those who, their victim complained, 'nowe (thoughe falselie) p[er]swade themselves of a kind of interim or intermission of go[vern]m[en]t, and in respect thereof hope to escape the punishment due'. Similarly, in the destruction of enclosures by the women at Nether Wyresdale in April 1603, it had been reported that, following the death of the queen, 'they might then doe the same wthout daunger of lawe for that there was now no lawe in fforce'. That, in this case, Shrove Tuesday was the day chosen by the women to pull down the enclosures was perhaps deliberate: this was a day long associated in popular culture with the belief that laws were suspended for that day. Again in the 1625 interregnum, a crowd of some sixty cutting wood on Thirsk moor in north Yorkshire were reported to have justified their actions 'by giving forth in speeches that his late Matie was dead, and that there was no law in force, or any person that durst molest or have authoritie to punish them'.[55]

An interregnum might popularly be held to last not only to the proclamation, but to the coronation, of a new monarch: 'he is no kinge tell [till] he be Crowned' declared an Essex butcher of James I, a belief voiced elsewhere in the county in 1603.[56] Thus those attacking the drainage works in the Lincolnshire fens in 1603 were reported to have claimed 'that there was noe danger ... for until yor Matie was crowned there was noe lawe wherefore they might doe what they would', adding for good measure, 'that the p[ar] liament would cleare all'.[57] A variant of this belief that the death of the monarch created an interregnum was to be found in the actions of a crowd of women who, in a recurring dispute at Enfield, stopped the felling and taking away of wood from the forest there, claiming that the patent by which wood had been felled was ended by the queen's death.[58]

Popular knowledge of the law was also much in evidence in crowd actions over food.[59] A government acutely aware of the threat that episodes of dearth and hunger posed to the social order was again

[55] TNA: STAC 8/153/2 and /203/30; J. C. Atkinson (ed.), *Quarter Sessions Records, Vol. III, 1620–1633* (York, 1885), pp. 233–234.

[56] J. S. Cockburn (ed.), *Calendar of Assize Records: Essex Indictments James I* (London, 1982), pp. 3–4; Wiltshire and Swindon History Centre (hereinafter WSHC), QS Gt Roll Mich. 1642, not no.

[57] TNA: STAC 8/7/3.

[58] TNA: SP 14/1/25; William Page (ed.), *Victoria County History of England: Middlesex*, twelve vols (London, 1911), vol. 2, p. 91.

[59] John Walter, 'Grain riots and popular attitudes to the law: Maldon and the crisis of 1629', in John Brewer and John Styles (eds), *An Ungovernable People: The English and Their Law in the Seventeenth and Eighteenth Centuries* (London, 1980), pp. 47–84.

careful to publicise the laws regulating the grain trade and, from the later sixteenth century, the bundle of measures issued under royal authority as books of orders specifically introduced to police the grain market. These books of orders were put into print, as were London's 'Lawes of the Market' in the capital.[60] Royal proclamations and charges to the special juries, whose role it was to conduct censuses of grain held in store and to present offences against laws regulating the forestalling of markets and hoarding of grain, actively sought to publicise policy and to recruit the people in its enforcement.[61] Thus, as in Somerset in the dearth of 1649, magistrates directed that the dearth orders be published at the time of the 'full market' in every market town and in every parish church.[62]

Here, too, crowd actions over food were often structured by popular knowledge of the law. Crowds, occasionally accompanied by local officials, mimicked the actions meant to be taken by the authorities, whose orders they sometimes cited.[63] As a crowd of women in Oxfordshire in the dearth of 1693 described their actions, 'they were resolved *to put the law in execution* since the magistrates neglected it'.[64] Crowds seized illegally exported grain or simply removed the sails of the ship;[65] they stopped grain bought in the local market by middlemen being moved out of the locality and returned it to the local authorities;[66] they sold it at a 'just price', which, in the London disturbances of 1595, turned out to be

60 Paul Slack, 'Books of Orders: the making of English social policy, 1577–1631', *Transactions of the Royal Historical Society* 30 (1980), 1–22; Anon., *The Lawes of the Market* (London, 1595).

61 James F. Larkin and Paul L. Hughes (eds), *Tudor Royal Proclamations*, three vols (Oxford, 1964–1969); James F. Larkin and Paul L. Hughes (eds), *Stuart Royal Proclamations 1603–1625* (Oxford, 1973); James F. Larkin (ed.), *Stuart Royal Proclamations 1625–1646* (Oxford, 1983). For charges to the special juries, see Read, *William Lambarde*, pp. 161–168.

62 Somerset Heritage Centre (hereinafter SHC), QSOB 1646–1656, ff.137r–v; Raine, *York Civic Records*, vol. v, p. 44; Leicester & Leicestershire RO, Leicester Borough Records, IV, 3/68.

63 WSHC, Q/S Gt Roll Trin 1614/108; Bristol Archives, JX/1/6 (unfol., info. of David Morris, 27 February 1673/4); M. D. G. Wanklyn, 'The Bridgnorth food riots of 1693/4', *Transactions of the Shropshire Archaeological and History Society* 68 (1993), 92–102, p. 100.

64 Anthony à Wood, *The Life and Times of Anthony Wood, Antiquary of Oxford, 1632–1695, Described by Himself*, ed. Andrew Clark, four vols (Oxford, 1895), vol. iii, p. 434 (emphasis added).

65 TNA: SP 16/187/12–13 and /497/6.

66 SHC, Q/SR 63.3/51.

the price set by the Lord Mayor;[67] or they confiscated the grain, claiming the reward offered in royal proclamations of half the seized grain.[68] As protesters in Sheffield insisted, they acted because the practices to which they objected were 'not according to ye law'.[69]

## III

The powerful sense of rights that lay at the core of protests within the politics of subsistence meant that their defence might also include going to law. In protests over food, recourse to law took the form of petitioning magistrates to take action against offences that the law condemned as illegal. But protests over enclosure could employ both physical force as a direct expression of communal disapproval and going to law. Enclosure 'riots' might then be either an adjunct or alternative to litigation.

Common rights were grounded in local law – in the *lex loci* of custom. Custom granted common rights and, traditionally, these might be defended in court by oral testimony of the long and uncontested usage ('beyond the memory of man') from which rights were held to originate. Custom was, however, more mutable than this suggests. It was, in effect, a shifting index of changes in the balance of power between lords and tenants – a process in which litigation registered both change and resistance.[70] Much of the micro-politics of settling custom within the manor is now lost to us, although, where these disputes surfaced in the royal courts, they can be revealing about the politics that this occasioned.[71] Disputes between lords and tenants about enclosure increasingly involved recourse to the royal courts for their resolution.

[67] W. Hudson and J. C. Tingey (eds), *The Records of the City of Norwich*, two vols (Norwich, 1906), vol. ii, pp. 163–165; TNA: SP 16/133/19 and 19.i; London Metropolitan Archives, COL/RMD/PA/01/002, f. 20; BL, microfilm M485: Hatfield House MS 32/106; Harleian MS 2143, f. 57$^{v}$.

[68] TNA: SP 16/191/4; SP 14.73/174–6; Hughes and Larkin, *Tudor Royal Proclamations*, vol. iii, p. 171.

[69] Sharpe, 'People and the law', p. 261.

[70] Andy Wood, 'The place of custom in plebeian political culture', *Social History* 22 (1997), 46–60; Andy Wood, *The Memory of the People: Custom and Popular Senses of the Past in Early Modern England* (Cambridge, 2013); E. P. Thompson, 'Custom, law and common right', in *Customs in Common* (London, 1991), pp. 97–184; Rab Houston, 'Custom and context: medieval and early modern Scotland and England' *Past and Present* 211 (2011), 35–76.

[71] R. W. Hoyle, 'Introduction: custom, improvement and anti-improvement', in R. W. Hoyle (ed.), *Custom, Improvement and Anti-Improvement* (Abingdon, 2011), pp. 1–12.

From the late sixteenth century onwards, access to the law for manorial tenants in actions against their lord was facilitated by decisions in the common law that worked to give certain classes of customary tenant an estate in their holding and the right to seek protection for their property in the royal courts.[72] However, a distinction in popular involvement with the courts needs to be made here. The protection offered under the common law was to property and the tenures by which it was held. Those with secure and defensible tenures, such as copyhold of inheritance, by means of which they might claim an estate in the land, might expect protection at common law.[73] Others on less secure tenures, or those squatting in forest and fen, could not.

Detailed work on the local context of legal cases over enclosure might suggest significant differences between legal actions that were, in reality, designed to renegotiate the terms of enclosure between encloser and substantial farmers in an 'enclosure agreement' and those that involved poorer commoners whose use rights in commons and to compensation were less secure or non-existent in the eyes of the law. Some cases in court alleging riot were, in reality, fictitious collusive actions between middling-sort farmers and lords of the manor to clarify and confirm rights by securing a favourable legal ruling. This was certainly the case with many Chancery decrees.[74] Since majority agreement was secured by acreage, not numbers, so-called agreements could generate hostility among those now without legal claim to common right. If not deliberate, it was certainly unfortunate that Eric Kerridge, in support of his claim that enclosures proceeded legally and without oppression, should choose to reprint the late sixteenth-century enclosure agreement for Haselbeech in Northamptonshire.[75] As Kerridge does not tell us, eight years later the enclosures there were at the centre of the Midlands Rising and attracted large, angry crowds.[76]

72 Christopher W. Brooks, 'The agrarian problem in "revolutionary" England 1640–1689', in Jane Whittle (ed.), *Landlords and Tenants in Britain 1440–1640: Tawney's Agrarian Problems Revisited* (Woodbridge, 2013), pp. 183–199; Brooks, *Pettyfoggers and Vipers*, p. 134.

73 Kerridge, *Agrarian Problems*, pp. 32–93.

74 E. C. K. Gonner, *Common Land and Inclosure* (London, 1912), p. 168; R. W. Hoyle and Mark Marston (eds), *Calendar of Chancery Decree Rolls (C78/86–130)* (List & Index Soc., 254, 1994).

75 Kerridge, *Agrarian Problems*, pp. 176–179.

76 John Martin, *From Feudalism to Capitalism: Peasant and Landlord in English Agrarian Development* (Basingstoke, 1986 [1983]), p. 184.

Although change was gradual and legal opinions remained divided, over time common law courts sought confirmation of customary rights appendant to tenures not in praxis or popular memory of long and undisputed usage, but in the written word.[77] Commoners at Takeley on the borders of Hatfield forest, for example, claimed their right of common by the annual presentation of what the 1639 Commission for the Disafforestation of the Forest reported as 'a strange substance of old iron which they termed a share'. This was, in fact, a reference to the medieval settlement between the commoners and the lords of Hatfield manor, commuted to money in 1328, by which they were granted rights of common in return for an annual rent that included five ploughshares.[78] But behind the dismissive words of the enclosure commissioners' report can be sensed the clash between oral and literate culture.

Going to law had other disadvantages. Court cases were, in effect, a continuation of conflict by other means. Litigation allowed propertied plaintiffs to deliberately paint poorer opponents as, in the words of one early seventeenth-century case before Star Chamber, 'turbulent p[er]sons being people of the basest and meanest sort readyest to unlawfull & riotous assemblyes, having no meanes or estates whereby to be punished if they should incur the dangers of you Ma[ts] laws'.[79] Riotous and *dis*-orderly, their actions challenged those concepts of order, property and authority whose upholding lay at the core of the paeans of praise heaped upon the law. The law might be relatively affordable and accessible, as Brooks has argued, and common purses might allow communities of commoners to initiate suits against their lords and enclosers. Certainly, in the pastoral economies of forest and fen, where disafforestation and drainage threatened the right to graze livestock on extensive wastes that were valuable to both subsistence commoners and capitalist farmers, a coalition of otherwise contradictory interests helps to explain the persistence there of opposition to enclosure with its combination of common purses and court cases with physical force into the eighteenth century and beyond. But elsewhere, acceptance of *negotiated* enclosure by capitalist farmers undermined the coalition of commoners that had sustained protest and funded litigation.

[77] See the helpful discussion in Adam Fox, *Oral and Literate Culture in England 1500–1700* (Oxford, 2000), ch. 5.

[78] Derek Shorrocks, 'Hatfield Forest 1547–1857, a story of conflict', *Essex Review* 64 (1955), 58–59.

[79] TNA: STAC 8/216/29.

As this coalition fragmented, the weight of 'power and purses' counted against poorer tenants, cottagers and day labourers, who were now more likely to appear as petitioners to authority or as the accused in the criminal courts. It was perhaps this group, among whom the popular distrust of law and lawyers that also characterised popular law-mindedness was more strongly held, who were most likely to resort to physical force and the outright rejection of enclosure from which they could not legally expect to profit. Although plaintiffs before Star Chamber had good cause to exaggerate this, appeals to 'club law' countered enclosers' use of the common law and equity courts. For example, poorer commoners at Kirby Malzeard declared that, since they were not able to wage law with Sir Stephen Proctor, he being a great man, they would get their common by club or Halifax law, while the women led there by Captain Dorothy were reported to have said, 'that Lawe or no Lawe, come what will, Lyfe or death', they would destroy the enclosure. Almost ten years later, the commoners at Kirby Malzeard were still said to be threatening 'that if according to the lawe of the lande the said C [100] acres should be there after inclosed yet they . . . would laie open the same by or w$^{th}$ Clubbe lawe'.[80] Over time, these changes meant that poorer commoners were more likely to resort to 'riot', rather than the law. But the threat of victimisation brought by loss of land and growing dependence on their 'betters' for work and poor relief helps to explain a shift in emphasis from direct action to the 'crime of anonymity'.[81]

## IV

In a polity in which authority put an emphasis on the link between law, order and obedience, popular knowledge of the law offered legitimation for protests within the politics of subsistence, as well as in other areas of disputed popular rights not discussed here.[82] It could also, as we have seen, help to shape the forms that protests over both land and food took. The defence of common rights by collecting common purses, consulting

[80] TNA: SP STAC 8/227/49, /227/3 and /20/23.

[81] On which see, E. P. Thompson, 'The crime of anonymity', in Douglas Hay, Peter Lindebaugh, John G. Rule, E. P. Thompson and Cal Winslow (eds), *Albion's Fatal Tree: Crime and Society in Eighteenth-Century England* (London, 1975), pp. 255–344.

[82] See, e.g., Andy Wood, 'Custom, identity and resistance: English free miners and their law c. 1550–1800', in Paul Griffiths, Adam Fox and Steve Hindle (eds), *The Experience of Authority in Early Modern England* (Basingstoke, 1996), pp. 249–285; Andy Wood, *The Politics of Social Conflict: The Peak Country 1520–1770* (Cambridge, 1999).

attorneys and initiating suits in the courts was not an alternative to physical force, but often ran in parallel with the destruction of enclosures. In going to law, commoners too, if well resourced, might employ the tactic of vexatious prosecution by initiating multiple suits across courts.[83] This could lead to long-running guerrilla campaigns being waged in the courts and periodically punctuated by the renewed destruction of enclosure on the disputed land.[84] Where lawyers were available, there might be a more rigid adherence to the legal procedures necessary to defend a claim to common rights. But popular law-mindedness also allowed protesters to play with the law to allow the forceful expression of community disapproval that was key to the successful defeat of enclosure: exploiting the ambiguities around (married) women's legal status; stretching the period of interregnum at the death of a monarch; taunting their victims in their loose employment of the spatial and temporal boundaries to pairing off; pulling down whole enclosures and depasturing whole herds where only a small gap and single animal were necessary to initiate a legal action. Jacobean tenants at Langley who refused to pay their rents also played with the idea of the monarch as the fount of justice. They were reported to have claimed, that 'the kings Matie by his Proclamation for disolvinge the Parliament hath made their former Customs good, in that his Matie in the last p[ar]te of his Proclamacon is graciously pleased to declare (that his highness will Governe his subiects in the same maner as the king and Queens of the best government have heretofore governed'.[85] Such misunderstanding were more wilful than a reflection of popular ignorance, although those charged with riot could be quick to petition for clemency on the grounds of their ignorance of the law.

It is also worth speculating as to whether popular knowledge of the law constrained, as well as condoned, forms of crowd action. A Lincolnshire blacksmith, for example, told fellow commoners that he could go with them to pull down an enclosure, but in daytime, not at night, 'least if any house were broken or any man robbed, they should have bene all hanged for it'.[86] A man who had been one of a crowd who, in 1596, had stopped

[83] According to an encloser in Ullesthorpe, now in Leicestershire, his yeoman opponents agreed to lay their purses together to 'maintayne multitude[s] of actions' against him and the more to vex him divided these between a number of courts: TNA: STAC 8/87/7.

[84] S. Hipkin, '"Sitting on his penny rent": conflict and right of common in Faversham Blean, 1595–1610', *Rural History* 11 (2000), 1–35.

[85] TNA: SP 14/128/48.

[86] TNA: STAC 8/219/20.

grain being transported through Canterbury for export to France had previously gone to a local attorney's clerk 'to aske counsel by the reste of the Compaines aduise'. Having been advised that, 'lawfully', 'they might staye it, but not touch the Corne', 'soe they tooke noe weapon in hande nor did take anye of it awaye', this they had done – 'in her Ma$^{ts}$ behalf'.[87] Similarly, at Norwich in the severe dearth of 1527, it was said 'that the Commons of the City were ready to rise upon the rich men'. However, one of a crowd of women who had stopped grain being moved out of the city's market to the wharfs and had sold it to other women at a price they themselves determined, told afterwards of their attempt to return the proceeds of their sale to the City's officials or owners of the grain, because, as she said, 'she thought iff she had put it in her purse it shold have ben stolen'.[88] If crowd actions over food challenged the government's stereotype of the 'grain riot' as collective theft with violence, and did not spill over into the attacks on the social and political order threatened in sedition, this was perhaps at least in part because knowledge of the law brought with it an awareness of the savage retaliation that that the law of property threatened. Thus popular law-mindedness might explain why, despite the government's frequent endorsement of the popular belief in hoarding as a major cause of dearth, crowds in this period did not break into barns and granaries nor plunder grain in the marketplace, but restricted themselves to seizing grain in transit, deliberately copying the actions the laws and authority prescribed.

Crowd actions within the politics of subsistence, as in other areas such as taxation and religion not discussed here,[89] were informed by a discourse of rights. Only very occasionally did protesters in the politics of subsistence claim to be free-born men (although such claims became more common in agrarian and other protests during the English Revolution).[90] But since they sought to enforce what their knowledge of the law told them were lawful rights, protesters could claim that they 'were good members of a Common wealth for that they endeavoured and

[87] Kent History and Library Centre, QM/SB 82.

[88] Goddard Johnson, 'Chronological memoranda touching the City of Norwich', *Norfolk Archaeology* 1 (1847), 140–166, p. 144; Hudson and Tingey (eds), *Records of the City of Norwich*, vol. ii, pp. 163–164.

[89] For taxation, see Clive Holmes, 'Parliament, liberty, taxation and property', in J. H. Hexter (ed.), *Parliament and Liberty from the Reign of Elizabeth to the English Civil War* (Stanford, 1992), pp. 124–152; for religion, see, e.g., the closely argued remonstrance by a Colchester churchwarden against Laudian altar policy: TNA: PRO, SP16/314/130.

[90] For an example from the Lincolnshire fens in 1616, see TNA: STAC 8/306/26.

sought to keepe Lands from being enclosed' and that they acted 'for the good of the Country'.[91] An underlying belief in *lawful* rights meant that law-mindedness could also sponsor a critical attitude to the exercise of authority by monarch, magistrate or manorial lord. As Brooks rightly speculated, going to law might then promote 'a high degree of political consciousness that was', as he suggested, diffused more widely than we might expect.[92]

[91] TNA: STAC 8/284/31; SHC, Q/SR 72.1/25.

[92] Christopher W. Brooks, 'Litigation, participation and agency in seventeenth- and eighteenth-century England', in David Lemmings (ed.), *The British and Their Laws in the Eighteenth Century* (Woodbridge, 2005), pp. 155–181, p. 158.

9

# Local Laws, Local Principles

## The Paradoxes of Local Legal Processes in Early Modern England

PETER RUSHTON

The paradox of the early modern state was that, to become stronger and more effective, it needed the local authorities to take on more responsibilities. It was the integration of centre and periphery that made government, from tax collecting to welfare policies and law enforcement, so successful. The same was true of law. In the 'parish state' and in the counties, local officers adopted national practices and put into place national patterns of administration and law.[1] Yet the way in which these were carried through remains in some ways obscure. It is the purpose of this chapter to explore some of the character of local legal practices and to uncover the influences on local decisions, to raise questions about this process. It is easy to posit a centralising, reformist and coercive process in 'absolute' states elsewhere in Europe, but it is hard to perceive how this could have been possible in England. More likely is the willing adoption of a nationwide legal culture and principles, under a process that ended with both consent to national policies and adoption of their directives among local officials. In the absence of national bureaucracies or systems of inspection – beyond, perhaps, the customs and excise service – this was more than just engineering the consent of the local; rather, it necessitated the local community eagerly adopting the values and principles of law and policy – truly the 'hegemony of the law' – and yet adapting them to local needs in response to the cases and problems brought to courts and officials such as magistrates.[2]

[1] Steve Hindle, *On the Parish? The Micro-Politics of Poor Relief in Rural England, c. 1550–1750* (Oxford, 2004).

[2] G. Morgan, *The Hegemony of the Law: Richmond County, Virginia, 1692–1776* (New York, 1989).

In exploring the key question of whether there was any such thing as local law, or local legal cultures, in particular places or 'communities', which contrasted with, or even deviated from, the intentions of central law and government injunctions, much may depend on the perspective taken. For instance, local legal cultures might be detected in distinctive patterns of prosecution and punishment, or in ways of dealing with disputes and finding their resolutions, rather than in the promulgation of novel interpretations of existing laws. Similarly, while a degree of uniformity is implied in the fact that every parish and county possessed the same array of officials and formal processes, from parish constables and overseers of the poor, to sheriffs and magistrates and quarter sessions, this should not be taken to imply that policies and practices were identical. In many aspects of law and regulation, such as anxieties about vagrancy, illegal alehouses or the priorities of the Poor Law authorities, the social relations of locality, from parish to county level, had a great influence.[3]

A comment is needed on the concentration in this chapter on the early modern period, because most of the institutions discussed, including court leets, church courts, quarter sessions and other major courts were of long-standing, mediaeval origin. If the roots of these institutions ran deep, most historians have long regarded the seventeenth and eighteenth centuries as involving a major transformation in the English state and its engagement with the lives of ordinary people. As Sharpe has noted, the century from the middle of the sixteenth century is generally regarded by historians 'as the key period in which new relationships within the local community, and new relationships between local communities and central authority, were formed'.[4] It is worth noting that there were parallels in a number of western European states at the same time, as Michael P. Breen has pointed out.[5] Early modern states increasingly saw systematisation and uniformity of practice as an ideal to be imposed, but it proved never entirely achievable, given the diverse interests of local elites; hence the relationships between centre and periphery (for want of

[3] See J. Sharpe, 'Law enforcement and the local community', in Lorna Hutson (ed.), *The Oxford Handbook of Law and Literature* (Oxford, 2017), pp. 221–238; David Hitchcock, *Vagrancy in English Culture and Society, 1650–1750* (London, 2016); Jonathan Healey, *The First Century of Welfare: Poverty and Poor Relief in Lancashire, 1620–1730* (Woodbridge, 2014).

[4] Sharpe, 'Law enforcement', p. 235.

[5] Michael P. Breen, 'Law, society, and the state in early modern France', *Journal of Modern History* 83 (2011), 346–386.

another phrase) were never clearly formalised at this period. England was no exception, and it is difficult to understand how these different levels interacted and whether they moved together or in conflict. As David Lemmings has observed, 'a veritable patchwork of courts survived from medieval times' and there were no systematic deliberate efforts at integration or coordination.[6] While few of these institutions had purely judicial functions, the local manor or borough courts, as well as the church courts, had procedures and rules that made them far from the informal and extra-judicial processes that Lenman and Parker called 'community law', which was, in their view, aimed at social peacemaking rather than regulation or discipline.[7] On the contrary, as Christopher W. Brooks has argued, in England there had grown up a common culture of legal recording and procedure in the localities away from the central courts dominated by the elite:

> If we move beyond the royal courts in London to the localities . . ., where most legal business in fact took place, there were many hundred, manorial and borough courts of various sizes and shapes. Such tribunals were usually limited in their jurisdiction either by the geographical range of their competence or by a ceiling on the value of the goods or money at issue about which they could make decisions (usually but not invariably 40s) . . . Their procedures, and very often the form of their records, were similar.[8]

If there was change at the local level, it was not from the informal to the formal, the extra-judicial to official courts, but from institutions whose regulations and practices were largely decided autonomously, to ones on which new elements were imposed from above by parliamentary statutes. This was intervention in, rather than a takeover and replacement of, these local forums, because many local customs and regulations were left largely intact. Older ways of settling disputes, even if they took the form of complaints about crimes and misdemeanours, survived and flourished, as we shall see. Yet new legislation and the imposition of duties and regulations by central laws proliferated from the Tudor period onward.

[6] David Lemmings, *Law and Government in England during the Long Eighteenth Century: From Consent to Command* (Basingstoke, 2011), p. 18.

[7] B. Lenman and G. Parker, 'State, community and criminal law in early modern Europe', in V. A. C. Gatrell, B. Lenman and G. Parker (eds), *Crime and the Law: The Social History of Crime in Western Europe since 1500* (London, 1980), pp. 11–48, p. 23.

[8] Christopher W. Brooks, *Law, Politics and Society in Early Modern England* (Cambridge, 2008), p. 12.

Parliamentary legislation across many areas of regulation was a feature of the late sixteenth century, culminating in the Poor Law of 1601, and new duties were imposed on magistrates. This has been viewed as the absorption of the *local* state into national frameworks, as part of national state formation. As Braddick comments, '[s]ocial historians of early modern England have been impressed by the increasing range of administrative measures undertaken by local governors in order to preserve social order'. This was in some ways, he suggests, a 'patriarchal state' – one might almost add 'paternalistic' too – driven to intervene not only in local processes, but also in the personal lives of many members of the society, particularly of the poor. It was one of many 'manifestations of an increasing use of state power in the localities'.[9] Yet there was pressure from below, for example in local demands for national legislation implementing the lessons of welfare experiments in the late sixteenth century that influenced the 1601 Poor Law, which allowed varied forms of local fundraising. This interplay between the local and the national, and mutual coordination, also lay behind the fiscal–military mobilisation of early modern England, the general production of conformity to the 'confessional state' and acceptance of dynastic change.[10]

It should be noted that there were different forms of imposition from the centre, not all of them involving Parliament. One was the Elizabethan reorganisation of the church – in effect, its first organisation as a Protestant church within a confessional state – and the development of a cadre of appropriately educated clergy. This meant that moral discipline, although using courts and forms that went back into the high Middle Ages, penetrated into the most remote areas such as the Pennines, the Borders and Northumberland by 1600. The apparently vigorous presentment of offenders may be the outcome of this revived organisation, as Margaret Spufford suggested, rather than a reflection of growing puritanism or moralism. A renewed organisation produced, and invited, more business.[11] In all of these forms of courts, personal engagement with the law was widespread in the sixteenth and seventeenth

[9] Michael J. Braddick, *State Formation in Early Modern England, c. 1550–1700* (Cambridge, 2000), p. 103.

[10] Ibid., p. 104; M. K. McIntosh, 'Poverty, charity, and coercion in Elizabethan England', *Journal of Interdisciplinary History* 35 (2005), 457–479; for the variations in rate of adoption and means of implementation of the Poor Law in the north east, see Peter Rushton, 'The Poor Law, the parish and the community in north east England, 1600–1800', *Northern History* 25 (1989), 135–152.

[11] M. Spufford, 'Puritanism and social control', in A. Fletcher and J. Stevenson (eds), *Order and Disorder in Early Modern England* (Cambridge, 1985), pp. 41–57.

centuries, and, in criminal law and civil processes alike, 'the English system depended for its operation on the initiative of individuals with a grievance who set the procedures in motion', resulting in the involvement of laypersons from a fairly broad social spectrum who acted as local officials and jurors.[12] In the English system, with few new courts, litigants – and defendants – increased hugely in the period before the established judicial forums. Some crucial changes probably contributing to this trend concerned women's access to courts, particularly at the local levels, where ease of access and cheapness invited greater participation.[13]

This does not indicate slavish adherence to the letter of the law, though. Early in the 'crime wave' of scholarly interest in crime, historians suggested that the conceptual gulf between the letter of the law and popular ideas about deviance was so wide that the records of crimes coming to court in the period were useless for the purposes of establishing a 'real' crime rate: '[T]he people of early modern Europe were almost without exception reluctant prosecutors.' This was because of the existence, as Keith Wrightson put it, of 'two concepts of order': the letter of the law contrasted in many areas with popular notions of deviance, which often reflected local cultures and relationships – in some places, crimes such as smuggling, most famously, were scarcely thought of as 'crime' at all.[14] Similarly, many crimes of assault or even of seizing property were not seen as offences: in Rothbury (Northumberland), in the early eighteenth century, it was reported, two men of the village who had sexually assaulted a woman were surprised to hear that it was a hanging offence. With regard to assault, both public attitudes and official policies seemingly changed towards the end of the eighteenth century, as Peter King has shown, although which was the leader in the process is not entirely clear.[15] Thus standardisation of the law was partly a matter of a changing

[12] Brooks, *Law, Politics and Society*, pp. 14–15.

[13] Tim Stretton, *Women Waging Law in Elizabethan England* (Cambridge, 2009); Gwenda Morgan and Peter Rushton 'The magistrate, the community and the maintenance of an orderly society in eighteenth-century England', *Historical Research* 76 (2003), 54–77; see also the discussion of summary justice later in the chapter.

[14] Lenmań and Parker, 'State, community', p. 15; Keith Wrightson, 'Two concepts of order: justices, constables and jurymen in seventeenth-century England', in J. Brewer and J. Styles (eds), *An Ungovernable People: The English and Their Law in the Seventeenth and Eighteenth Centuries* (London, 1980), pp. 21–46.

[15] John Thomlinson, 'Diary of John Thomlinson', in J. C. Hodgson (ed.), *Six North Country Diaries* (Durham, 1910), pp. 64–167, pp. 79, 99; Peter King, 'Punishing assault: the transformation of attitudes in the English courts', *Journal of Interdisciplinary History* 27 (1996), 43–74.

climate of opinion and education in how it should be implemented, as much as demand that it should be enforced. Nevertheless, discretion and variation were fundamental at every level, from the accuser to the jury to the judge and the Secretary of State. Discretion was greatest at the start, at the lowest level of the victim making a complaint and the magistrate framing the indictment. Subsequently, an action could be redefined as a crime by the jury as they convicted on a lesser charge, or by an appeal to London that resulted in a lesser punishment than, in theory and law, the crime deserved. There was discretion and, as Peter King has proposed, substantial scope for innovative local practices of punishment. Local decisions, although taken within the scope of parliamentary statutes, were therefore not determined in an automatic or mechanical way.[16] It is not unrealistic to suggest that there were local *cultures* of punishment, because the evidence indicates that, for example, in the quarter sessions sentences for petty larceny, neighbouring counties adopted contrasting policies towards the mixed menu of punishments, of whipping, imprisonment or transportation. Before 1750, some counties, such as Durham, ignored the provisions of the 1718 Transportation Act, while its neighbours adopted it from the first. There was more uniformity across the north east after the middle of the eighteenth century, but even then some jurisdictions such as Newcastle upon Tyne, where half or more of those accused of theft at the quarter sessions were women, were significantly more likely to use imprisonment than other counties. It seems that the judicial independence of county magistrates could result in very different outcomes for those convicted of the same offences and contrasting rates of execution.[17]

Laws could also be created at local levels, or, at least, bye-laws, which were vital in regulating community relations and often essential to preventing nuisances and neighbourly disputes. Some involved the maintenance of common properties, or health and hygiene.[18] In manorial and borough courts, town councils and mining courts, there was much

[16] Peter King, *Crime and Law in England, 1750–1840: Remaking Justice from the Margins* (Cambridge, 2009).

[17] Gwenda Morgan and Peter Rushton, *Rogues, Thieves and the Rule of Law: The Problem of Law Enforcement in North-East England, 1718–1800* (London, 1998); Gwenda Morgan and Peter Rushton, *Eighteenth-Century Criminal Transportation: The Formation of the Criminal Atlantic* (Basingstoke, 2004); Peter King and Richard Ward, 'Rethinking the Bloody Code in eighteenth-century Britain: capital punishment at the centre and the periphery', *Past and Present* 228 (2015), 159–205. On the cultural approach to punishment, see Philip Smith, *Punishment and Culture* (Chicago, 2008).

[18] Leona Skelton, *Sanitation in Urban Britain, 1560–1700* (London, 2015).

rule-making, and control of these forums by local elites ensured that there were often conflicts over their regulations or restrictions. Ancient forms of local law such as manorial courts remained in place – often the only workable form of local government. Rights were frequently claimed and enforced through these courts, or denied.[19] Yet community rights as a whole, defended against other claims by rival communities, could also be protected.

How should we interpret centre–periphery or state–locality legal relations in this period, therefore, and the legal cultures, or, more properly, legalistic policies developed at the local level? There are ambitious grand narratives in the recent historiography of state formation involving the integration of the local into national frameworks, first recognised in terms of English tax-raising, the development of Poor Law systems and the enforcement of settlement laws, and the training of local magistrates and their parish officers into a national system.[20] For example, at the start of the seventeenth century, William Lambarde complained of the 'stacks of statutes' from the centre falling on local justices of the peace.[21] There were some substantial changes in the framework of laws, particularly in the area of criminal penalties, and in the administrative duties legally imposed on magistrates in terms of taxation, the regulation of businesses such as alehouses and markets, and the Poor Law. With regard to church law, too, the movement of clergy and legal officials around the country and the system first, of High Commissions and, after the interregnum, of diocesan discipline, produced a considerable level of consistency, although it has been argued that procedures could vary flexibly from diocese to diocese.[22] In the assizes, the judges travelling from London addressed grand juries with regard to national problems and perhaps saw part of their role as educating localities in the recent national thinking. By the mid-eighteenth century, there were many advice books for magistrates, particularly by Richard Burn, which offered systematic advice and

[19] Brodie Waddell, 'Governing England through the manor courts, 1550–1850', *Historical Journal* 55 (2012), 275–315.

[20] John Brewer, *Sinews of Power: War, Money and the English State, 1688–1783* (London, 1989); Braddick, *State Formation.*

[21] Quoted in John H. Langbein, 'The origins of public prosecution at common law', *American Journal of Legal History* 17 (1973), 313–335, p. 334; Neil Younger, 'William Lambarde on the politics of enforcement in Elizabethan England', *Historical Research* 83 (2010), 69–82.

[22] See S.M. Waddams, *Sexual Slander in Nineteenth-Century England: Defamation in the Ecclesiastical Courts, 1815–1855* (Toronto, 2000), p. 68.

legal knowledge: his manual for magistrates and parish officers had grown to four volumes and was in its tenth edition by 1766. It might not have taken the rise of a forceful state to ensure some level of national uniformity, therefore.[23] Indeed, suggests Lemmings, historians have drawn two contrasting views of the relationship between the central state and the localities. One is a picture of a top-down process driven by centralised authority, harnessing 'civil society to the juggernaut of the state', largely for financial reasons to provide the funds for fighting wars. Through this kind of structure, and the use of troops in times of disorder, Lemmings argues that there was a danger of developing an 'increasing separation between government and public' and the corrosion of the more participatory 'culture of law that had been the very essence of the early modern state'. The contrasting model suggests a much looser relationship with the centre, with the concept of the state as a 'reservoir of authority' for ensuring peace – a resource to be drawn on, but not deployed at all times. This allows relative autonomy at the local level, rather than complete subordination, and the role of the centre in supporting the periphery.[24]

There are therefore different narratives in the historiography of the relationship between centre and locality with regard to law in the early modern period. One emphasises the rise of the statutory laws and the imposition of administration and regulation on local authorities. The concomitant of that is the decline both of local autonomy and local custom. The integration of the local also took the form of greater enforcement of religious conformity and social order, the latter backed up by the rapid deployment of military force used, at least in north-east England in the eighteenth century, as a first, rather than a last, resort in the face of riots.[25] Yet, as Sharpe has observed, the reach of Westminster into local society was only partial and complete uniformity of effect could not be assured by legislation alone.[26] There was, as Craig Muldrew has put it, a 'culture of reconciliation', concerned, as anthropologists have discovered among many non-industrial and non-state societies, with the restoration of social relationships, rather than their disintegration through uncompromising accusation. The key feature of this process in

[23] Lenman and Parker, 'State, community'; Richard Burn, *The Justice of the Peace and the Parish Officer*, four vols (10th edn, London, 1766).

[24] Lemmings, *Law and Government*, pp. 7, 8, 14.

[25] Morgan and Rushton, *Rogues*.

[26] Sharpe, 'Law enforcement', p. 223.

early modern England is that legal forums were central.[27] The resulting process of negotiation, involving a locality that was required to obey Parliament in areas it disliked and yet which, at the same time, also *needed* Parliament to pass laws enabling the locality (for example) to improve roads and harbours, suggests a mixture of collaboration and bargaining that was not all one-way. Steve Hindle's 'parish state' or Mike Braddick's concept of 'state formation' both point to the way in which centre and periphery were engaged in continually negotiating power and legitimacy. The 'state' was not a rigid institution, but a *process*, with no completely fixed or predictable outcomes. In what follows, a (necessarily) brief analysis will be offered of the complex interactions between the national and the local in the field of law, taking church courts and the magistrates in and out of quarter sessions as the key areas in which this can be examined.

## Church Courts

In the church courts, a national system met local cultures and customs – sometimes, in confrontation; in other instances, in collaboration. This is not the place to revisit the historiography of its popularity, but the system of courts, inherited from the medieval church, was left intact by the Church of England in the sixteenth century. It had its own procedures, which were disliked by both common law theorists and puritans alike – particularly the oath-taking process whereby a person could be forced to speak in their own prosecution known as 'presentment' (too like the Star Chamber for comfort in the early seventeenth century). Yet some accommodation with local customs was forced upon it, to persuade or force ordinary people to conform to its practices. The scope of the church courts was wide, controlling or trying to influence many areas of private life and personal belief: vital areas such as proving a will, moral and religious regulation of misbehaviour (particularly sexual – and hence the popular name the 'bawdy courts'), defamation or slander disputes, and areas such as tithes, which were deeply unpopular. The church court system may not have offered quite as much scope for discretion as the local processes of the town or manor, or the processes before justices of the peace, for the visiting archdeacons and chancellors may have seen

[27] Craig Muldrew, 'The culture of reconciliation: community and the settlement of economic disputes in early modern England', *Historical Journal* 39 (1996), 915–942; Simon Roberts, *Order and Dispute: An Introduction to Legal Anthropology* (Harmondsworth, 1979).

their role as securing enforcement from above, with little scope for negotiation. At the same time, they were dependent, as was all local law enforcement, on parish officers such as churchwardens, and they received the cases presented to them by the local clergy and parish officials. Ingram makes the point that the church courts' effectiveness grew where their values fitted with the notions of respectability of those who dominated the parishes. The discretion may therefore have centred on pre-court social relations in which a person's 'deviance' was defined as a problem that needed to be officially addressed. Local memories may have not helped: in 1620, in Northumberland, one woman before the visiting archdeacon was known by the parish to have stood excommunicated, after being presented for fornication, for either sixteen or twenty years (no one could be sure which). Significantly, she was still regarded as a problem for the parish.[28] The potential for conflicting values, and the awkward position of officials such as churchwardens between the community and the law, emerge from communities that somehow did not produce sinners for the church visitations. One churchwarden in Northumberland was accused in an archdeacon's court of 'concealing dyvers offences albeit he is a churchwarden, contrary to his oath'; he reported that 'he knew of divers offences but would not reveal anie of them till he were called in question'.[29] There were also instances in which communities complained to the visiting archdeacons about their local clergy, turning the church against itself: three people in Earsdon (Northumberland) claimed to have learnt their 'witchcraft or sorcerie' from the former curate in the parish.[30] Nor was the authority of the church universally accepted. There were also rival clergy, nearly all Catholic – 'seminary priests' – marrying couples, baptising children and 'churching' their mothers. Sometimes, couples left Durham to go to a seminary priest in Northumberland (one young woman in 1624 insisted on that form of baptism for her child and 'churching' of herself). Puritans did not accept the restrictions such as burial in 'consecrated ground': one man of Houghton-le-Spring, in 1618, 'tooke up the body of his mother after she was buried and laid it another place'.[31] There was even some outright scepticism: one man, in 1635, was hauled before the

[28] Martin Ingram, *Church Courts, Sex and Marriage in England, 1570–1640* (Cambridge, 1987), pp. 323–324; Durham University Library (hereinafter DUL) DDR/A/ACN/1/2, ff. 18v and 55v.

[29] (DUL) Special Collections, DDR/A/ACN/1/2, f. 92.

[30] Ibid., f. 53a.

[31] (DUL) Special Collections DDR/EV/VIS/2/2, ff. 145 and 157v; DDR/A/ACD/1, f. 346.

High Commission for saying that 'if anie would show him a devil he would believe there was a god' (another thought his horse was as likely to go to heaven as himself).[32] Yet, despite profound religious divisions, the essential focus of enforcement in terms of marriage in church and the importance of public religious ritual seems to have been successful. In the eighteenth century, disciplinary presentments declined substantially, perhaps because of this success in winning most of the population to moral conformity, but also because issues such as pregnancy outside marriage and other family problems were also being handled by Poor Law officials and local magistrates, often acting in concert. A combination of secular and religious authorities gradually produced compliance.[33]

As these examples indicate, moral conformity may not have involved complete acceptance of Anglican hegemony, but the control of crucial resources in the Poor Law and in parish record-keeping such as births and marriages gave the church great force. In other areas, the church had to work with the grain of local custom; indeed, custom determined the official practice. Establishing the local rule necessitated a process of investigating communal memory. In Wolsingham (County Durham), a dispute over the collection of tithes involved asking an elder of the community how it had traditionally been done. The question was about tithing – that is, taking a tenth – of products that did not come in tens. A senior member of the parish testified to the 'traditional' method he had known throughout his lifetime: if a person had five beehives, they were allowed keep back their best one, while the parish priest or deputy took one of the others and sold it, keeping half the sale price; lots were then cast for the value of the other half, giving the church a 50:50 chance of getting 20 per cent. If a person had ten beehives, they were allowed to keep back two of their best.[34] This is an example of a court being asked to accept local custom as rightful practice – in effect, endorsing the way in which the community had come to an arrangement with the church to ensure balance and fairness. The role of custom has long been a focus of

[32] (DUL) Special Collections HUNTER MSS 16, f. 127v.

[33] See Ingram, *Church Courts*; Rebecca Probert, *Marriage Law and Practice in the Long Eighteenth Century: A Reassessment* (Cambridge, 2009); W. Gibson and J. Begiato, *Sex and the Church in the Long Eighteenth Century: Religion, Enlightenment and the Sexual Revolution* (London, 2017); Martin Ingram, 'The reform of popular culture? Sex and marriage in early modern England', in Barry Reay (ed.), *Popular Culture in Seventeenth-Century England* (London, 1985), pp. 129–165.

[34] DUL Special Collections DDR/EJ/CCD/1/10, ff. 121–123.

radical historians such as E. P. Thompson and the social historians influenced by him, and it has been observed that 'custom has recently returned to its rightful place at the centre of historical understandings of the plebeian culture of early modern England'; moreover, 'it was in its legal form that custom held its greatest force within plebeian political culture. In law, local custom applied only to specific jurisdictions, typically manors, parishes or boroughs.'[35] Custom did not create the law of tithes, but it did affect the way in which it was implemented in local communities.[36] It was often in legal contexts that the conflict between law and custom was fought out, and not always to the detriment of custom. Custom, in these close communities, defined forms of decent behaviour, as well as the relationships of power: it set limits to power and established key areas of rights to treatment that acknowledged the interests of the less powerful. Historians have noted that the 'force of the past was present in plebeian resistance'; some of these conflicts were collective and violent, but others took the form of legal dispute and settlement.[37]

The church courts also dealt with bad behaviour in other ways. Slander suits alleging defamation of character remained a major part of the church's judicial business into the eighteenth century and are found right up to the final removal of their powers to adjudicate in this area in the mid-nineteenth century. They reflect widespread popular usage of the courts. Unchristian actions attacking personal reputation were subject to church law and people could be presented by church officials for them. Most cases, though, derived from personal suits for slander alleging something that undermined a person's moral character; many were pursued at the diocesan consistory court, where evidence was often collected in the form of lengthy depositions. The importance of reputation to early modern society was not simply a matter of honour or personal dignity. Words were dangerous things, and a damaged reputation could destroy both the victim's economic security and their safety from more serious, criminal accusations. This was most obvious in cases alleging witchcraft or sexual misdemeanours. Defamation cases could

[35] Andy Wood, 'The place of custom in plebeian political culture: England, 1550–1800', *Social History* 22 (1997), 46–60, pp. 46 and 47; E.P. Thompson, *Customs in Common* (London, 1993).

[36] For a longer discussion of the problem of the recognition of custom as law, see Neil Duxbury, 'Custom as law in English law', *Cambridge Law Journal* 76 (2017), 337–359; E. Coke, 'Case de modo decimando', in *The Reports of Sir Edward Coke* (Dublin, 1796), vol. 7, pt 13, pp. 37–47.

[37] Wood, 'The place of custom', p. 52.

make up to a fifth of the business of consistory courts in some exceptional periods and went on being important to some people, as late as the early nineteenth century.[38] Women brought 79 per cent of defamation cases in the Durham courts in the period before 1640: Bishop Barnes of Durham always thought that northerners resorted too easily to 'slanders, false reports and shameless lyes'. Sexual slanders dominated: women were allegedly whores, while men were whoremongers. A handful of more serious offences – witchcraft and theft – were also alleged. In the 1630s, the civil courts seem to have tried to limit themselves to cases alleging serious crimes, taking that business away from the church courts, but the latter also heard this type of case, even though they were not in theory supposed to. Witchcraft; illegal practices of magic; infanticide; theft: 'Thy eld mother was a wych, canst not the young theef learn from the olde?' The allegation suggests that witchcraft could be hereditary or, at least, run in families, which made the slander case particularly important for more than just the insulted individual person.[39] The court's role in these cases was part punishment, if a clear act of deviance could be established, or, perhaps better, reconciliation and the restoration of good neighbourly relations. Like the institutionalised methods of peace-making in Malinowki's studies of the Trobriand Island culture, although without the 'black magic', the church courts aimed to prevent 'the use of violence' and to restore 'equilibrium'.[40] As in other cases in early modern law, such as those for assault, where apparent forms of complaint seem to be close to personal prosecution, the outcome – perhaps the major aim of the complainants – was not formal punishment so much as an admittance of fault and apology.[41]

In theory, after the rise of common law remedies for slander and libel, the church courts should have experienced a decline: the civil courts offered money by way of damages, while the church could impose only a public penance – the offender barefoot in a white sheet before the congregation, admitting their sin of being un-Christian. Other forms of redress were also available, through lone magistrates and forms of summary justice. Yet, despite declining business, the church maintained

[38] See Waddams, *Sexual Slander*.

[39] James Raine (ed.), *Depositions and Ecclesiastical Proceedings from the Courts of Durham* (London, 1845), p. 318; Barnes, quoted in C. I. A. Ritchie, *The Ecclesiastical Courts of York* (Arbroath, 1956), pp. 225–226.

[40] B. Malinowski, *Crime and Custom in Savage Society* (London, 1926), p. 86.

[41] Norma Landau, 'Indictment for fun and profit: a prosecutor's reward at eighteenth-century quarter sessions', *Law and History Review* 17 (1999), 507–536.

important courts, at least in some people's personal lives, as a means of protecting their personal reputation and honour. It was not until the mid-nineteenth century that defamation was removed from their jurisdiction, although by that time victorious plaintiffs received an apology – a recantation – in the church vestry. A mechanism for dealing with insults was clearly needed, in London and elsewhere, and some still went to the church courts. Throughout the period, the nature of the insults remained remarkably standard (as Waddams's research shows clearly).[42] The 1853 case from Merthyr Tydfil that provoked the 1855 abolition concerned Charlotte Jones allegedly saying to Louisa Roberts, 'You are a whore, and a damned whore too'. Because she had refused to appear or pay the fee, Jones had been imprisoned for a year or more. The problem of defamation in the church courts therefore ended as it had begun. At this time, the majority of defendants were men and 90 per cent of the plaintiffs, women.[43]

## Justices of the Peace

A less standardised, but still national, system, also with medieval origins, was that of the justices of the peace and their varied processes, which included the formal county quarter sessions. Together, they provided the nearest thing to a county government available before the late nineteenth century: as Norma Landau has observed, 'the eighteenth-century English state worked through the courts. The working of the courts was therefore central to the state.' In many ways, the magistrates and their processes were unique in Europe, because they had both judicial and administrative functions, and an enormous amount of government was placed on their shoulders.[44] Their responsibilities were therefore extraordinarily wide, ranging from hearing criminal and civil cases, through regulating alehouses and setting bread prices and wages, as well as dealing with vagrancy and the Poor Law, to managing key institutions such as houses of correction. Rather belatedly, historians have come to recognise that a great many decisions were made by individual justices, working alone

[42] See Anna Clarke, *The Struggle for the Breeches: Gender and the Making of the British Working Class* (Berkeley, 1995), pp. 48, 53, 56; Waddams, *Sexual Slander*.

[43] See Waddams, *Sexual Slander*, pp. xi, 4, 6, 7, 10; Clarke, *The Struggle for the Breeches*, pp. 52–56; Tim Meldrum, 'A women's court in London: the Bishop of London's consistory court', *The London Journal* 19 (1994), 1–20.

[44] Norma Landau, 'Introduction', in Norma Landau (ed.), *Law, Crime and English Society, 1660–1830* (Cambridge, 2004), pp. 1–16, p. 10.

or together, with little by way of official record of court proceedings. The scant supply of surviving personal diaries and notebooks has been essential to the analysis of this process over the last twenty years of scholarship. Unlike the archdeacons and ecclesiastical chancellors of the church court system, the justices (magistrates) were very much part of the society in which they acted in judicial or quasi-judicial ways: in effect, they had legal control of the local society in which they were embedded. As Fletcher and Stevenson put it:

> They sought, through the exercise of office, to heighten and enhance their reputation and prestige, to offer a local leadership that would mark them out in the eyes of the community of the neighbourhood. This objective did not dictate a formal, directive approach to government, but rather suggested that [justices of the peace] should be prepared to meet the populace at least half way.[45]

Justices increasingly acquired appellate jurisdiction over the decisions of individual or pairs of justices. In matters of Poor Law administration, for example, the quarter sessions were practically the last court of appeal, often having to decide issues of responsibility in disputes between parishes. This required a delicate juggling of cooperation with, and yet regulation of, fellow magistrates.[46]

Locality almost certainly made a difference to how justices conducted themselves and the kinds of compromises they were willing to make: the processes of summary justice in London lacked the sense of personal knowledge that the 'justicing' notebooks of relatively isolated rural magistrates reveal. The single justice was close to his village neighbours and more likely to be engaged with them on several fronts. In the rural areas, justices were chosen from people of higher status than in the large towns, suggests Peter King, and that may have enabled them to draw on non-judicial reserves of deference; they developed what Norma Landau has called 'varieties of paternalism', as appropriate.[47] Again, Keith Wrightson's notion that there were 'two concepts of order' provides a vital insight into both diversity among justices and their likely conflicts with their communities. Yet all studies indicate that there were also

[45] Fletcher and Stevenson, *Order and Disorder*, p. 16. For the work of a lone magistrate, see Morgan and Rushton, 'The magistrate', pp. 54–77.

[46] Norma Landau, *The Justices of the Peace, 1679–1760* (Berkeley, 1984), pp. 42–43.

[47] Peter King, 'The summary courts and social relations in eighteenth-century England', *Past and Present* 183 (2004), 125–172, p. 166; Landau, *Justices of the Peace*, p. 173; see also Robert Shoemaker, *Prosecution and Punishment: Petty Crime and the Law in London and Rural Middlesex, c. 1660–1725* (Cambridge, 1991).

matters in relation to which the justices provided an instrument of popular will, reflecting local opinion about problems. As Drew Gray explains: 'Justices were mediators within their communities, figures of authority within a paternalistic society, who supposedly administered justice by dint of that authority without the need for legal justification.'[48] Those who came to them often sought resolution for their personal disputes, rather than an application of the strict letter of the law. At the same time, from the early eighteenth century, there is evidence that much of the business at quarter sessions – particularly in settlement and rate cases – was handled by lawyers, and in County Durham, even apprentices and servants could be represented in court by counsel. In these cases and at that level, it is likely that a more legalistic tone entered the proceedings, although the outcomes were still often aimed at reconciliation.[49]

Variations in practice between magistrates were therefore probably widespread and, from the surviving evidence, reflected both external factors such as the local economy and its social relations, the demands by individual complainants and the way in which they framed their pleas, and the relationship of the magistrate to the community in terms of social standing and economic power. Professional status could reinforce judicial authority. In 1756, the Reverend Edmund Tew, rector of Boldon, was challenged by a local man, John Bell, who called him a 'fool' and sneered that he would go to the King's Bench. Tew had Bell arrested and locked up in Durham jail; after his release (procured by two local men), Bell was forced to beg forgiveness of Tew and the constable on his knees in front of the whole congregation (and to pay a guinea to the poor of three parishes) – a procedure more reminiscent of the penalties of the church courts. Similarly, John Bridon was jailed in Durham after claiming that he had not received justice from Tew in a civil case, but was released upon 'falling on his knees and paying 10 shillings to the constable for horse hire etc'.[50] These unusual examples show the lengths to which some justices were prepared to go when personal feelings ran high in

48 Drew D. Gray, 'Making law in mid-eighteenth-century England: legal statutes and their application in the justicing notebook of Phillip Ward of Stoke Doyle', *Journal of Legal History* 34 (2013), 211–233, p. 232.

49 See also Drew D. Gray, *Crime, Prosecution and Social Relations: The Summary Courts of the City of London in the Late Eighteenth Century* (Basingstoke, 2009); Gwenda Morgan and Peter Rushton (eds), *The Justicing Notebook (1750–64) of Edmund Tew, Rector of Boldon* (Woodbridge, 2000); Morgan and Rushton 'The magistrate'; P. Rushton, '"The Matter in variance": adolescents and domestic conflict in northeast England, 1600-1800', *Journal of Social History* 25 (1991), 89–107, p. 94 (on lawyers).

50 Morgan and Rushton, *Justicing Notebook*, pp. 72, 63.

local communities. It is notable that such behaviour was very rarely challenged in the higher courts, although Douglas Hay has found one instance (in 1811) in which an employer, a justice, who prosecuted his own employee – and sentenced him to flogging – was subsequently taken to the King's Bench (where the case failed).[51]

The picture we have is of thousands of problems being settled locally by a single magistrate or, at best, being taken to the quarter sessions for resolution. The locality, or the county, could therefore develop a distinctive, if not entirely unique, culture of justice in this area, dependent on its economic foundation. One aspect of magistrates' mediation or intervention lay in their responsibilities under the 1563 Statute of Artificers. As noted already, by the eighteenth century, some of the contesting parties consulted lawyers, suggesting that legalistic caution was intruding into the proceedings at quarter sessions. In the more private setting of the lone magistrate, though, more local factors may have dominated. The nature of the local economy and its forms of servanthood or apprenticeship, the internal structure and working relationships of households, and the gender balance of those employed all showed great variation across the country. This is one area in which contractual employment and training relationships, involving servants and apprentices, were severed as a response and solution to abuse and violence. Although the economy depended on these relationships, the lone magistrate seemed to have acted in ways that offered some protection against extreme abuse.[52]

Another area of intervention was the problem of often serious cases of domestic violence towards wives or female servants: as in other areas of personal violence towards women, it is likely that these too came to a magistrate acting alone, who may have provided a practical solution that may have had little to do with formal 'law'. For example, Dorothy Weddal made a complaint before Edmund Tew against her husband James, a boatman of South Shields in 1763, for beating her with a rope,

[51] Douglas Hay, 'Patronage, paternalism, and welfare: masters, workers, and magistrates in eighteenth-century England', *International Labor and Working-Class History* 53 (1998), 27–48.

[52] See Rushton, 'The matter in variance', pp. 89–107, for north-east cases at quarter sessions; Bridget Hill, *Servants: English Domestics in the Eighteenth Century* (Oxford, 1996); Carolyn Steedman, *Master and Servant Love and Labour in the English Industrial Age* (Cambridge, 2007), finds few employment disputes before the justices, although they interrogated servants about their pregnancies or their settlements; Jeanne Clegg, 'Good to think with: domestic servants, England 1660–1750', *Journal of Early Modern Studies* 4 (2015), 43–66.

following her with a knife and denying her maintenance. The matter was 'agreed' between them. Five months later, she again complained to Tew about her husband, this time for 'beating and chaining [her] down to a log for more than two hours . . . when naked, and threatening her life'. His solution was to induce James, although we are not told how, to enter the 'King's service' – presumably, the Navy.[53] Although this was a practical, if not a legal, separation, it was clearly preferable to any attempt to maintain the existing relationship. Justices also faced problems of husbands deserting their families or threatening to eject their wives. Here, the problem was in part of the likely burden on the Poor Law funds, as well as marital breakdown: in another case, Tew heard accusations of a husband turning his wife out of doors and refusing her maintenance, as well as threatening her life. Where possible, a marriage might need preservation by ensuring protection from malicious rumour and the slanderer became the object of Tew's actions: one man was summoned because he called a married woman a 'whore and thereby breaking the peace betwixt her and husband'.[54] As Amussen has pointed out, the authorities were willing to set limits to male power where husbands' extreme behaviour had, in effect, betrayed men's patriarchal responsibilities and threatened the peace of the community – yet violence was almost fundamental to many social relationships, between young and old, and within the household itself. Setting an appropriate limit to the level of violence, drawing a line between discipline and abuse, was one problem that was not covered by law or legal advice to magistrates.[55] With regard to violence towards servants and apprentices – particularly if the case involved sexual violence – magistrates such as Tew were happy to terminate the contract and order compensation to the victim (as were some quarter sessions).[56] Household structures in this aspect were not regarded as sacred, but in serious cases had been transformed through personal complaints from being considered a private wrong to being accepted as a public problem.

53 Morgan and Rushton, *Justicing Notebook*, pp. 168, 183 (6 May and 29 October 1763).

54 Ibid., pp. 146 and 177; see also ibid., pp. 114, 123, 191 for other cases of marital strife.

55 Susan Dwyer Amussen, *An Ordered Society: Gender and Class in Early Modern England* (Oxford, 1988), pp. 101–102; Susan Dwyer Amussen, 'Punishment, discipline, and power: the social meanings of violence in early modern England', *Journal of British Studies* 34 (1995), 1–34. See also Joanne Bailey and Loreen Giese, 'Marital cruelty: reconsidering lay attitudes in England, c. 1580 to 1850', *The History of the Family* 18 (2013), 289–305.

56 Rushton, 'The matter in variance'.

The lone justice was therefore the linchpin of the judicial system. One might quibble at the use of 'courts' to describe the personal process of individual complaint to a lone magistrate, but the overview here is sound:

> The role of the summary courts was highly paradoxical. On the hand they were a vital resource for the propertied. They resolved inter-parish disputes. They protected property. They provided a means of disciplining troublesome members of the labouring poor. On the other hand, the summary courts could be described as 'the people's courts' . . . A very wide variety of men and women brought assault cases, poor-law appeals, master-servant disputes and huge range of other issues to these tribunals. Moreover, in many cases they were successful in obtaining judgments which curbed, to some extent at least, the powers of the local employers and vestry.[57]

These scarce sources show a different picture from the court records on which all criminal historians had relied traditionally. The magistrate as revealed in the notebooks is a mixture of mediator, arbitrator, peace-keeper and peace-enforcer (to use the distinction used by the modern British Army), and decisive judge.

The extent and nature of discretion that the magistrates exercised are equally revealed in the way in which the letter of the law was applied in cases sent to court. In the seventeenth century particularly, a frequent charge heard at the quarter sessions was defamation, which could be personal or political – that is, slander or sedition. This was a vague area and the scope of quarter sessions did not obviously include defamation unless it formed part of a wider disorder or threatened it. Nevertheless, insults that were indistinguishable in substance from those heard by the church courts were found at quarter sessions among the indictments and summonses, and tended to be brought by men. Recognisances and summons to appear to answer the accusations were issued, as in many misdemeanours such as assault (and, in many cases, the defamation allegation was accompanied by one of 'riot and assault' against the victim). The choice of charge, moreover, seems to have borne little relationship to the language used or the victim making the complaint. Responses to the insults, as revealed in the indictments, seem highly variable. In the North Riding of Yorkshire, there was at least one personal defamation allegation of witchcraft treated not as personal defamation, but as sedition against the state, and another allegation was similarly

[57] Peter King, 'The summary courts and social relations in eighteenth-century England', *Past and Present* 183 (2004), 125–172, p. 169.

labelled seditious when a man (also, not a magistrate) was called a 'branded rogue'.[58] By contrast, some insults to magistrates were seen as personal, while others were treated as seditious attacks on government (strictly, against the monarch and their appointed officials). It seems as though, when deciding how to indict personal insults, magistrates were at times willing to brush off insults rather than to treat them as a threat to the state itself. Opposition to the current monarch or government policies, on the other hand, and Jacobite sentiments in particular, might be seen as seditious and prosecuted accordingly.[59] Precise reasons for these apparent inconsistencies cannot be inferred from what are brief accounts of cases and court decisions, and there may indeed may not have been a 'strategy' as such, but more of a local culture of legal response that stemmed from the sense of security of the magistrates and their relationships with their communities.

## Conclusion

The picture here will be no surprise to scholars who have delved into the law's place in local social relations, but the relation of these processes to national shifts in law in the period is still difficult to establish with confidence. Local courts and legal processes offered a wide choice for legal action to many kinds of people, particularly if the manorial courts are included in the view: many were traditional, rural, courts concentrating on policing the grazing and other rights, including the management of remaining commons, but some, such as Manchester, Salford and Preston, adapted to dealing with the problems of urban growth and commercial activities. Regulating markets, ensuring fair weights and measures, prosecuting fraudulent dealers and bawdy housekeepers, as well as enforcing apprenticeships in activities such as shop-keeping, were all the business of what was increasingly Manchester and Preston's only form of urban government before the nineteenth century.[60] The idea of law as a 'multi-user right' has some validity in these local forums,

58 North Yorkshire County Record Office, Riding MF100, f. 106, October 1670 (theft), and January 1672–1673 (burnt in the shoulder), MF101, April 1575, f. 120 (witchcraft) and f. 205 (thief).

59 Peter Rushton, 'The rise and fall of seditious words, 1650–1759', *Northern History* 52 (2015), 68–84.

60 Waddell, 'Governing England', p. 280; for eighteenth-century semi-urban actions, see *The Court Leet Records of Manchester* (Manchester, 1888–1889), vols 7 and 9, especially vol. 9, pp. 2, 247 (claims of duties of the courts); A. Hewitson (ed.), *Preston Court Leet Records: Extracts and Notes* (Preston, 1905), pp. 140–141, 164, 169, 193.

although the respectable and the more affluent may have had more regular access. The appearance of so many women before a lone magistrate such as Edmund Tew of County Durham almost certainly reflected his ready availability within walking distance and the absence of charges for his service.[61] Wherever people turned, they had faith to some degree that there would be some kind of legal resolution to their personal problem, and the authorities felt obliged both to solve that problem and to pay attention to resolving the wider social and community issues that lay behind them. The letter of the law may not have been, at all times, the predominant factor. The nature of justice in this period has been suggestively called 'legalism without law': interpretations of statute or common law offences, as well as regulations, could vary considerably according to local cultures and social relations.[62] Yet the courts' resolution of cases created a public record of the decisions – vital if claims were made or rights asserted. In this way, local *legal cultures* could be developed that retained the formal framework of statute law, while adopting solutions such as penalties to local conditions. With regard to all of the courts discussed in this chapter, a number of conclusions might be drawn about the values, if not the actual letter, of the law-making carried out in the localities. Values such as good neighbourliness lay behind many cases and a sense of proper order – including mutualities of duty and obligation – also shaped decisions, even where relationships were acknowledged to be unequal (such as between masters and their servants or apprentices). Society needed to go on and continuity mattered, so what anthropologists have called 'the restoration of social relations' was a central concern. These values rarely underpinned acceptance of individual freedoms, but worked within accepted hierarchies of gender and economic and social status. Discretion was as key an element here as in the criminal law, but the dimensions of discretion have not been very well rooted by historians in distinctive localities and communities. All law in this period, however standardised, had to be adapted to local relations and priorities. Moreover, the unwritten had a great importance in many

[61] J. Brewer and J. Styles (eds), *An Ungovernable People: The English and Their Law in the Seventeenth and Eighteenth Centuries* (London, 1980), p. 20; see also Douglas C. Hay, 'Master and servant in England: using the law in the eighteenth and nineteenth centuries', in Willibald Steinmetz (ed.), *Private Law and Social Inequality* (Oxford, 2000), pp. 227–264; Morgan and Rushton, 'The magistrate'.

[62] James McComish, 'Defining boundaries: law, justice and community in sixteenth-century England', in Fernanda Pirie and Judith Scheele (eds), *Legalism, Community and Justice* (Oxford, 2014), pp. 125–150, quotation at pp. 133, 142.

communities: memory was both a resource and an assertion of right in the teeth of the statutory law. For the whole early modern period, as Peter King has suggested, 'an understanding of the nature of these courts and of the heavy, if deeply constrained, use the poor made of them, is therefore vitally important if historians are to explore fully the shape and texture – the multi-dimensional tensions and compromises – that lay at the heart of . . . social relations'.[63]

[63] King, 'Summary courts', p. 169. See also Richard J. Ross, 'The memorial culture of early modern English lawyers: memory as keyword, shelter, and identity, 1560–1640', *Yale Journal of Law and the Humanities* 10 (1998), 229–326.

# 10

## 'So Now You Are Wed Enough'

### Clandestine Unions in the North-West of England in the First Half of the Eighteenth Century

JOANNE BEGIATO*

### Introduction

In 2008, in his *Law, Politics and Society in Early Modern England*, Christopher W. Brooks remarked on the difficulties of measuring 'how far religious ideas, most often expressed in sermons, corresponded to life as lived in real families. Much the same can be said of legal practices and ideas . . . it is no easier to prove the take up of legal ideas by the population at large than it is religious ones.'[1] Although pinning down specific ideas and their origins is always challenging, social historians would nevertheless argue that church court cause papers offer one means of tracing the circulation of religious and legal ideas and practices within families, especially where marriage breakdown is concerned. Spouses deployed scripture, morals conventions, and concepts of contractual rights and patriarchal privileges in their marital litigation, for example, as well as using the services of religious and legal personnel to resolve their conflict.[2] The making of marriage offers a further way of assessing

* Quotation from Borthwick Institute of Archives (hereinafter BIA) Trans. CP. 1764/1, William Cowper 833–842. In writing this chapter, I am grateful to Daniel Reed, for carrying out research into the clerical background of Christopher Bulcock, as well as searching out leads and filling gaps in my understanding of clerical ordination. William Gibson and Rebecca Probert were kind enough to read an earlier iteration, and I hope that the final version has addressed their suggestions satisfactorily. Michael Brown has assisted by discussing the case with me, reading this formulation and taking on other tasks to free me to finish it. I also want to thank Michael Lobban and Adrian Green for their helpful comments in situating the study within the wider volume.

1 Christopher W. Brooks, *Law, Politics and Society in Early Modern England* (Cambridge, 2008), p. 383.

2 See, e.g., Joanne Bailey, *Unquiet Lives: Marriage and Marriage Breakdown in England, 1660–1800* (Cambridge, 2003).

people's response to religious and legal ideas within the family. This chapter therefore explores a lengthy 'Jactitation of Marriage' action from the mid-eighteenth century to consider how far couples conformed to marital law in the period prior to Hardwicke's Marriage Act 1753. It suggests that people engaged with religious and legal practices when establishing families, but did so in ways that sought to prioritise their own needs and were shaped by local conditions. Three findings emerge. First, marital behaviour could be diverse outside of the hotspots for clandestine marriage in London, as a result of local religious and economic circumstances and customs. Second, not all couples sought a ceremony that conformed entirely to religious and legal forms, although they were prepared to adapt their behaviour if the authorities required them to do so. In more remote areas, even this might be somewhat ambiguous. In the case examined, there seems to have been some confusion over whether the celebrant's ordination was sufficient to make a union valid or whether he had to be mentally capable of discharging the functions of a clergyman. Third, the chapter proposes that it is possible to evaluate the extent of marital conformity over time by attending to the continuities underlying irregular marriages of the early modern period, eighteenth-century clandestine unions and the 'imprudent' marriage of the turn of the eighteenth century, which are usually examined as discrete phenomena.

## Marital Law and Conformity

To be deemed regular, the making of marriage had to comply with a number of requirements in canon law: it was to be preceded by either the calling of banns in the church of the parish in which the couple lived, or the purchase of a marriage licence; and be celebrated by a clergyman in church, before two witnesses, at specified hours and days of the year.[3] A union that was carried out by an ordained clergyman, but which occurred without public notification of intent and which was performed outside the neighbourhood of residence of bride and groom was deemed 'clandestine'.[4] This union provided the same legal rights to a couple who had married regularly, but as, Rebecca Probert observes, was problematic

[3] Rebecca Probert, *Marriage Law and Practice in the Long Eighteenth Century: A Reassessment* (Cambridge, 2009), p. 6.

[4] Gill Newton, 'Clandestine marriage in early modern London: when, where and why?' *Continuity and Change* 29 (2014), 151–180, p. 151; Probert, *Marriage Law and Practice*, pp. 7–8, 166. This differs from Eleanor Gordon's definition, in which it a marriage

because it was difficult to prove that the union had occurred. Moreover, it opened the couple and the celebrant up to ecclesiastical censure.[5] The extent to which clandestine marriage was considered deviant behaviour has been the subject of debate for some time. Initially, historians of marriage viewed Hardwicke's Marriage Act 1753 as a break in marriage practices, ending a long period during which couples could wed simply by exchanging consensual vows. Rebecca Probert's close examination of law reports, local censuses and parish registers revised this account of the making of marriage. She argued that the Act was not a rupture that introduced a more prescriptive model, since there never had been a 'pluralistic system, in which multiple forms of marriage were accepted'.[6] Actually, such irregular unions were simply the exchange of promises: contracts to wed. In Probert's view, nearly everyone was wed in a church by a clerical celebrant. In fact, even couples who married clandestinely were not particularly deviant in their behaviour.[7] If some couples sought clandestine unions for purposes of secrecy, hiding a ceremony from a minor's parents or shielding a pregnant bride, the majority of clandestine marriers were wed in a church by a Church of England clergyman and fell into the category of 'clandestine' simply because they married in a non-home parish. This conformity was most marked outside London, which had the largest numbers of clandestine marriages before the Act; in the provinces, 'it was relatively rare for such marriages to take place outside a church'.[8]

This picture of widespread compliance with marital law in the long eighteenth century is supported by the broader scholarship on marriage, which sees it as an institution that underpinned social order. The union of two individuals was the business of the community and, at many times, the nation, owing to its economic and procreative functions. Early modernists, for example, used court records to show that state and society were in broad agreement about the stabilising effect of matrimony.[9] Historical demographers identified nuptiality as the driving force of population size, producing a picture of shared marital values and

performed by an unauthorised celebrant: Eleanor Gordon, 'Irregular marriage: myth and reality', *Journal of Social History* 47 (2013), 507–525, p. 513.

5 Probert, *Marriage Law and Practice*, p. 178.

6 Ibid., pp. 2–3.

7 Ibid., pp. 110–130.

8 For consistent use of a clergyman to perform clandestine marriages, see ibid., pp. 193, 197–198.

9 For example, Martin Ingram, *Church Courts, Sex and Marriage in England, 1570–1640* (Cambridge, 1987); Keith Wrightson, *English Society 1580–1680* (London, 1982).

strategies across the nation and over several centuries in which couples postponed marriage until they could afford to set up an independent household.[10] According to this 'big picture' of entering marriage, for perhaps three centuries most couples married prudently, planned their union well in advance, secured the appropriate financial resources and were joined together by an Anglican clergyman in church.

This picture of long-term and universal marital conformity is nuanced at the macro and micro levels. As early as 1999, Steve King questioned the Cambridge Group for the History of Population and Social Structure's conceptualisation of English marital patterns, primarily in relation to its assumptions that couples married only when they could achieve economic independence. As he observed, the 'mean of family reconstitution still conceals wide dispersal of marriage ages (and presumably marriage motivations) within and between communities'.[11] The claim that everyone married prudently in the long eighteenth century has been skilfully questioned by Emma Griffin's work on courtship and illegitimacy, which uses working-class autobiographies to nuance generalisations offered by quantitative research.[12] She contends that we should 'reconsider widely held assumptions that marriage customs remained stable over the long eighteenth century'.[13] While some individuals espoused prudent values about entering stable, economically viable unions, in practice, she argues, there was often little in the way of financial planning. In fact, apparently prudent marriers often united without savings, but in the hope of future resources; prospects were equated with fitness to marry. By the later eighteenth century, she finds that even future potential earnings were not considered by those whom we might categorise as imprudent marriers, such as young partners who made hasty weddings, often after the woman was pregnant or delivered of her child and without any familial support. For Griffin, the shift towards younger age at marriage in some subsets of the population was less the result of improved economic opportunities allowing people to marry younger and more the result of industrialisation, which meant that families, communities and

[10] E. A. Wrigley and R. Schofield, *The Population History of England, 1541–1871: A Reconstruction* (Cambridge, 1981).

[11] Steven King, 'Chance encounters? Paths to household formation in early modern England', *International Review of Social History* 44 (1999), 23–46, p. 26.

[12] Emma Griffin, 'A conundrum resolved? Rethinking courtship, marriage and population growth in eighteenth-century England', *Past and Present* 215 (2012), 125–164, pp. 153–154.

[13] Ibid., p. 162.

apprenticeship placed fewer constraints on courtship. Indeed, Griffin suggests that it was this increase in 'improvident' marriers that contributed to the fall in the age of marriage, rather than improving real wages, problematising the implied 'universal' national picture of marriage behaviour.[14]

Recent studies of irregular and clandestine unions also unsettle the picture of placid convention by revealing more diversity. For one thing, Scotland was somewhat different. Eleanor Gordon's overview of irregular marriage in Scotland challenges Probert's claim that clandestine marriages were a largely London phenomenon and shows that exchange of consent was enough to make a valid union in Scotland.[15] Gill Newton's study of clandestine marriage in London from 1610 to 1753 argues that Probert downplays the impact of clandestine marriage before 1753 – especially in London, where it was the rule, rather than the exception, and carried no stigma.[16] Newton finds that these London couples chose not to marry in their own parishes – seeking private unions not to hide secrets, but to emulate wealthy marriage habits. Moreover, they were not saving money, since the venues were not necessarily cheaper than church weddings, and they preferred to marry in locations that also offered entertainments and food and drink.[17] Although Londoners took advantage of the freedoms to marry at times and venues that suited their needs, she concludes that 'this did not mean behavioural constraints dissolved'.[18] While Gordon notes that, in Scotland, the majority of people conformed to marital law, she found that they adopted 'a more flexible definition of marriage than the official one'.[19] Perhaps what is emerging is an overall picture of limited flexibility, rather than rigid conformity. As Newton remarks, however, we still know very little about the identities and motivation of people who married clandestinely.[20]

This rest of this chapter offers a detailed, individualised and regional case study to tease out people's conformity to marital law. In 1758, Thomas Whitaker, a gentleman of Symonstone, in the parish of Whalley, Lancashire, brought an action of 'Jactitation of Marriage'

[14] Ibid., passim.
[15] Gordon, 'Irregular marriage', p. 515.
[16] Newton, 'Clandestine marriage', pp. 151, 152.
[17] Ibid., p. 153–155.
[18] Ibid., pp. 176–176.
[19] Gordon, 'Irregular marriage', p. 522.
[20] Jennifer McNabb, 'Fame and the making of marriage in northwest England, 1560–1640', *Quidditas* 26 (2005), 9–33.

against Ann Lee at the consistory court in Chester. Plaintiffs initiated such an action to stop a defendant declaring that a marriage existed between the two. Ann Lee claimed that, on 11 May 1737, when she was aged 22 and pregnant, she married Thomas, then aged around 35. They were wed, she said, by a priest, Christopher Bulcock, at the public house of Allen Edmundson, in Pendle Forest, Lancashire, and while they did not cohabit, the community knew they were husband and wife, and she bore him two daughters. Thomas denied that he had married her, since she was his father's servant, but admitted that she had been his mistress. The case turned on proving whether Ann and Thomas were legally wed. The clandestine nature of the ceremony did not invalidate it, since it was performed by a priest of the Church of England. Thus the status of the clergyman, Christopher Bulcock, came under scrutiny, because Thomas alleged that he was an 'idiot' and incapable of performing a wedding ceremony. In 1763, the consistory court decided in favour of Ann, so Thomas appealed the case to York; it was appealed again in April 1767 to the High Court of Delegates. Many deponents were called to give evidence about the marriages that Bulcock performed and so the several hundred pages that this protracted case generated offer insights into couples' motivations for marrying clandestinely.

Bulcock acted as the celebrant for couples marrying from the 1720s through to the 1750s. The deponents in the case refer to at least twenty-five weddings and several mentioned that they had also witnessed Bulcock performing numerous clandestine unions. Certainly, Michael Snape's study of the Anglican church in Whalley notes that twenty-seven couples were presented to the diocesan church courts between 1712 and 1753 for marrying without banns or licence.[21] The numbers may well have been substantial; one deponent estimated that he officiated as clerk at more than a hundred marriages across thirteen years, so one could speculate that Bulcock may have married 200 or more couples in his time. These marriages are analysed for what they indicate about the ways in which local circumstances shaped couples' decisions about marriage ceremonies. What emerges is that even in cases of near marital 'conformity' in clandestine unions, where couples were married outside their home parish by an Anglican priest, non-conforming behaviour is evident. The findings also inform the chronology of marital conformity over the eighteenth century. Emma Griffin argues that, by the late eighteenth

[21] Michael Snape, *The Church of England in Industrialising Society: The Lancashire Parish of Whalley in the Eighteenth Century* (Woodbridge, 2003), p. 115.

century, couples 'were not applying the old logic of marriage formation to a new, more favourable economic climate; they were jettisoning the old logic altogether'.[22] This case study implies that the old logic was not necessarily pervasive everywhere between the 1720s and 1750, owing to some of the structural factors that Griffin identifies as shaping behaviour later, such as social dislocation resulting from new economic conditions, which weakened the social forces that controlled access to marriage.

After all, as Michael Snape shows, Whalley was an area that underwent significant social and economic upheaval in the period studied. It was the largest parish in England, covering approximately 61 square miles.[23] The extensive parish was situated at the western edge of the Pennines, mostly south of the River Ribble, with much of it in the old royal forests of Pendle, Trawden and Rossendale – all areas that had undergone enclosure and settlement in the early modern period, resulting in a large population of smallholders and cottagers. Whalley was so extensive that it was divided into chapelries, with one parish church and seventeen chapels of ease. Eleven of the chapels were parochial, enabling them to perform christenings and burials, with the other four reserved for praying and preaching. The size of the parish is indicated by the fact that the chapelries were larger than many parishes elsewhere in England. Thus few residents were near the parish church and many chapels were unable to provide a full range of services. Inhabitants also faced the challenges of the topography – particularly in the smaller north-western chapelries, which combined rough terrain and poor communications. There were no turnpike roads until the mid-century and even afterwards roads were often inadequate. Michael Snape shows that the population in Whalley was rapidly growing, estimating that it experienced a three-fold increase between 1720 and 1780. This was mostly from natural increase, rather than migration, because of the expansion of textiles manufacture. Certainly, where deponents' employment was stated, these included shalloon weaver, cotton weaver, weaver, dyer, piece-maker, stuff-maker, winder of worsted yarn and tailor, as well as collier, carrier, cooper, lime-burner, gardener, inn-keeper, labourer, husbandman and yeoman.

As such, kinship ties were strong, and local customs and practices were not dissolved by industrial migration. Indeed, Jennifer McNabb observes more broadly that the north-west's remoteness and political and

[22] Griffin, 'A conundrum resolved?', p. 163.

[23] This paragraph is informed by Snape, *Church of England*, pp. 5–15.

economic autonomy in the early modern period 'allowed for the flourishing of distinctive cultural values and practices'.[24] Her work on cases disputing matrimonial contracts from 1560 to 1640 leads her to conclude that there was a 'distinct regional culture of matrimony in the northwest', with marriage practices, such as spousals, surviving in the region long after they were discontinued elsewhere in England.[25] The next section considers these distinctive marriage practices in Whalley in more detail for the subsequent century up to the 1750s.

## *Thomas Whitaker of Symonstone, Parish of Whalley,* vs. *Ann Lee*

Thomas Whitaker's jactitation suit denied that he was married to Ann, and claimed that her children were not his and illegitimate, although he eventually conceded that he had given a bond for £40 as security for the maintenance of the first child. He admitted only that he had promised to marry Ann to pacify her father, a miller in Padiham, a village a mile from Symonstone, who discovered the relationship and threatened Thomas that if he did not marry his daughter, he would expose him to Thomas Whitaker Sr. Interestingly, Whitaker Sr maintained the pretence that he was unaware of his son's union with Ann. In 1748, Whitaker Sr wrote to Robert Parker of Alkincoats, noting:

> [It] is some concern to me that the late Miller of Padiham John Lee's daughter Ann should run about the country with a child borne I think before last Christmas near Haworth & says to every body that she is my son's wife, but it must not be known whilst I am living, altho' 'tis said 'tis 10 years since they were married . . . .[26]

There is little doubt that Thomas did not see himself as legally wed to Ann, given that he married Ann Willion in May 1759 (with whom he went on to have two sons), during the suit's deliberation and fifteen months after he began the jactitation suit in February 1758.[27] He further alleged that Ann boasted that they were married for financial reasons alone. He stated that she rambled in the north of England after bearing her first child in 1737 (she claimed she worked industriously as variously

[24] McNabb, 'Fame and the making of marriage', pp. 12, 15.

[25] She defines such unions as lacking some component of the church's requirements for a formal marriage: ibid.

[26] Lancs. RO, DDB 82 Acc. 7886 Wallet 6, Thomas Whitaker to Robert Parker (23 May 1748), cited in Henry French and Mark Rothery, *Man's Estate: Landed Gentry Masculinities, 1660–1900* (Oxford, 2012), p. 224.

[27] Bigamy was a felony.

a servant, teacher and housekeeper in the locality) and returned to Symonstone only when Thomas's father died in 1757.[28] At that point, she was persuaded by 'ill-minded people who have long been endeavouring to set up a pretended marriage between Thomas and Ann' to publicly claim the union's existence.[29] Thomas's father's will left him a considerable entailed estate for life. On his death, it would pass to Thomas's sons, although his father stipulated that these must be offspring by any woman other than Ann. He further insisted that Thomas must always deny being married to Ann, otherwise the estate would go to the male heir of Ellen Baron, Thomas's sister. In Thomas's opinion, therefore, the Barons were keen to prove a valid marriage between Thomas and Ann so that his sons with Ann Willion were unable to inherit, thereby enabling the Barons' son to inherit the estate.[30] Ann did admit to living with the Barons, although she denied that Mrs Baron supported her financially.[31]

Ann's defence depended upon proving a valid marriage to Thomas. The odds were stacked against her, however. There were a couple of witnesses, but no record in Bulcock's marriage register. The couple had not cohabited, and she was obliged instead to offer evidence that they were reputed to be husband and wife.[32] For example, Elizabeth Bridge confirmed that, after the wedding, they 'were commonly esteemed a man and wife', although the wedding was kept secret during Thomas's father's lifetime.[33] To strengthen her case, Ann also brought evidence in the form of Thomas's letters written in 1737 and 1740. In one, dated April 1737, he conceded that he would 'make good my promise that I made yw [*sic*] the other night I do now assure then in writing that I do intend to marry you in case a method can be found out to do it privately and that they [Ann's parents] will promise me that they will use their utmost endeavour to conceal it'.[34]

[28] BIA Trans. CP. 1764/1, Answers of Ann Lee to the Exceptive Allegation, f. 517.

[29] BIA Trans. CP. 1764/1, Exceptive Allegation on the part of Thomas Whitaker, ff. 447–448.

[30] BIA, CP. I/1462, Positions Additional to an Allegation admitted on part of Thomas Whitaker (no date given, although probably 1763 or early 1764).

[31] BIA, CP. I/1463, Personal Answers of Ann Lee to Allegation (July 1765).

[32] Probert, *Marriage, Law and Practice*, pp. 104–105.

[33] Thomas's interrogatories asked deponents to comment on whether Thomas Whitaker and Ann Lee were known to be married: BIA Trans. CP. 1764/1, Elizabeth Bridge, f. 356. For reputation and co-residence, see Probert, *Marriage, Law and Practice*, pp. 180–181.

[34] BIA Trans. CP. 1764/1, Positions Additional on behalf of Ann (7 November 1758), exhibits 1, 2, 3, ff. 237.

The letters reveal the secrecy surrounding their relationship. Thomas was terrified of anyone, especially his father, discovering their intimacy, and their meetings were secret and organised under cover of his going fishing. Thomas would meet Ann at the back of her house and leave letters in hiding places.[35] When Thomas Whitaker Sr died in 1757, Ann said that she tried and failed to contact Thomas. On discovering that he was publicly denying their union, she sought advice from Mr Oddy, an attorney at law in Burnley. He communicated with Thomas's attorney, Mr Aspinall, who offered her £100 or £200 to stay quiet.[36] When Oddy failed to honour a meeting, she paid him off and applied to another lawyer, Mr Baldwin, who advised her to go to see Thomas to request a separate maintenance.[37] She alleged that, when she did this, Thomas beat her. He then brought the jactitation suit to prevent her from initiating a case for restitution of conjugal rites. Perhaps her answer to Thomas's exceptive allegation is most revealing of her motives in considering a restitution suit: she had heard 'that in courts of Law or Equity have been several suits or litigations touching the validity of such marriages', which were all determined in the plaintiffs' favour. Importantly, she understood that this meant that the issue of the unions did not suffer under any legal impediments.[38] As this indicates, for couples like Whitaker and Lee, much depended upon the status of their union. Yet, as the following section reveals, couples seem to have been willing to be wedded in circumstances that could be considered somewhat ambiguous.

## The Status of Christopher Bulcock

Throughout the suit and its appeal, Thomas's proctors focused on proving the inadequacy of the marriages that Bulcock performed. As Probert's analysis of the ingredients for a regular marriage makes very clear, the 'crucial element' for a valid union was an ordained clergyman. She shows that discussions of marriage assumed that an Anglican clergyman was essential, as did all contributors to the parliamentary debates about the Clandestine Marriages Act. The fact that the ceremony was clandestine did not invalidate the union, after all. Indeed, a marriage celebrated

[35] Ibid.

[36] Ann seems to have sought a regular maintenance, rather than a one-off payment. She alleged that Thomas negotiated with a friend to offer her £600 to deny the marriage, but she refused.

[37] Ann shows the ease with which people employed lawyers, as Brooks's scholarship demonstrates.

[38] BIA Trans. CP. 1764/1, Answers of Ann Lee to the Exceptive Allegation, ff. 558–559.

without the rites of the Book of Common Prayer and carried out in a location that was not prescribed could still be good if it was performed by a clergyman.[39] Deponents for both litigants agreed that Christopher Bulcock was a clerk in holy orders, licensed around 1712, and that, early in his career, he was officiating curate to the chapel of Accrington, in the parish of Whalley.[40] William Robinson, a gentleman of Newchurch-in-Pendle, remembered Bulcock returning from university and going into orders.[41] What made Buclock more problematic was whether he was in a fit state of mind and whether he could read the service. According to the *Codex Juris Anglicana*, candidates for ordination were to be sufficiently qualified to undertake ministry, which required knowledge of Latin and Greek, as well as testimonials of good behaviour.[42] Presumably, Bulcock met these requirements at the time, although Robinson stated that Bulcock officiated only three or four times before he went 'crazy'; hence Thomas alleged that Bulcock was an 'idiot' and thus incapable of acting as a minister.[43]

Deponents agreed that Christopher Bulcock suffered from some degree of mental infirmity, but not on its extent. Deponents on behalf of Thomas declared that he was unfit for the duties of a minister. Many referred to him as an 'idiot'. James Folds said that, when someone had done something foolish, it was common to tell them, 'thou art as mad as the Vicar of Blackow'.[44] Susanna Sutcliffe described him as 'the mad Vicar' when recalling him preaching forty years earlier at Newchurch-in-Pendle Chapel (c. 1721). Even at that point, she said, he would stop in his sermon so that people thought him 'crazy or short of learning'.[45] Thomas mustered deponents who knew Bulcock's habits and living conditions. One noted that he was frequently 'badly beshit' and stole food from children – although it should be noted that the same man acted as

39 Probert, *Marriage, Law and Practice*, pp. 56–58.

40 There is no listing on the Clergy of the Church of England Database (CCED) of Bulcock as curate of Accrington; indeed, the CCED shows another man named as curate in 1712 at Accrington. Nevertheless, assistant curacies are sometimes missed on the CCED owing to deficiencies in the diocesan records: Daniel Reed, 'Digital pitfalls: Laurence Sterne and the "Clergy of the Church of England Database"', *The Shandean* 28 (2017), 129–137.

41 Although some deponents deposed that Bulcock was educated at university, he is not listed in either Foster or Venn's accounts of Oxford or Cambridge alumni, suggesting that he perhaps qualified as a literate candidate without a university education.

42 *Codex Juris Anglicana*, p. 147.

43 BIA Trans. CP. 1764/1, Thomas Whitaker's Exceptive Allegation, ff. 451–452.

44 BIA Trans. CP. 1764/1, James Folds, of Trawden, Chapelry of Colne, Esquire, aged 50.

45 BIA Trans. CP. 1764/1, Susannah Sutcliffe's deposition.

Bulcock's clerk at the weddings he performed for the previous twelve or fourteen years.[46] Ann Walsh was put as a town apprentice to Bulcock's father and was in his service for fifteen years, during which time she cared for Christopher, since he was unable to wash and dress himself. He dirtied himself, she stated, rubbing his hand in his excrement.[47] Neighbours of the Bulcocks also reported that Christopher would chase women and children around the fields with his 'yard' hanging out.[48] Unsurprisingly, given the adversarial nature of this litigation, those who deposed for the defendant were more circumspect. They had heard him called the 'Vicar of Blacko', but not the 'mad' vicar, and they denied that he was completely irrational or impaired.[49] Typical was Richard Slater, who had been married by Bulcock twenty-eight years earlier and who admitted only that Bulcock was 'a little disordered in his senses', although capable of reading the ceremony.[50]

The emphasis on Bulcock's ability to read the ceremony was therefore critical for Thomas's case. He stated that the clergyman was incapable of 'transacting any publick or private concerns whatever especially performing a reading over the office of holy matrimony'.[51] The 1763 appeal to York described Bulcock as a 'Lunatick Clergyman then and at all times thereafter without any Lucid Intervals to render him capable to Marry any persons whatsoever or to do or perform any binding or Lawful Act whatsoever as being totally devoid of all mind memory reason or understanding'.[52] Memory was essential because there is some evidence that a candidate could be ordained if blind, despite the inability to read. An exchange of letters in 1730 between the Archbishop of Canterbury, the Bishop of Lincoln and their advisers sought to establish whether a blind candidate could be admitted to holy orders. The conclusion was that he could be if he was able to perform prayers and duties from memory. It was also noted that it was possible for an assistant to be kept to supply any defect in the

[46] BIA Trans. CP. 1764/1, John Titherington, of Dolehouse, Forest of Pendle, Shaloon Weaver, ff. 691–693.

[47] BIA Trans. CP. 1764/1, Ann Walsh, wife of Joshua Walsh, Mile Smithy, Chapelry of Colne (June 1761), f. 656.

[48] For example, BIA Trans. CP. 1764/1, William Folds, of Admiregill, parish of Barnoldswick, shalloon weaver (June 1761).

[49] BIA Trans. CP. 1764/1, Wife of Fishwick, f. 961.

[50] BIA Trans. CP. 1764/1, f. 1020.

[51] BIA Trans. CP. 1764/1, Thomas Whitaker's Exceptive Allegation, ff. 451–452.

[52] BIA CP. I/1464, 1763 appeal to York.

clergyman's performance of public service.[53] In the circumstances of a clergyman suffering from the impairments of old age, for instance, a curate could be paid to fulfil the duties of the parish.

What is clear from the depositions is that Bulcock's father and brother assisted him in performing weddings; later, after Robert Bulcock's death, Christopher's nephew took over. Indeed, William Cowper reported that Robert Bulcock, Christopher's father, was known as the 'Old Parson' because of the belief that Robert officiated at the marriages, since his son was incapable of reading the ceremony.[54] John Sutcliffe, who recalled witnessing the marriage of one couple in 1730, stated that Bulcock was fed 'Wynburys and Milk and Gingerbread' and coaxed like a child to say the service. Following the treat, his father then handed him the prayer book, said some words and asked him to repeat them. Christopher would repeat one word, then 'immediately fly of[f] into some rambling expressions', laughing, so that it took two hours before they could finish.[55] William Edmundson deposed that, owing to Bulcock's talking nonsense, he 'never did look upon it that he was right married to his said first wife'.[56]

As such, it was particularly crucial for Thomas's jactitation case to determine the extent to which Bulcock was able to read the marriage service without assistance. Ann's deponents stated that he was able to read the ceremony. Allan Edmundson ran the public house in which Bulcock had performed weddings; Edmundson was aged 78 when he was examined in 1760 and, by that point, had known Bulcock for forty years. Edmundson claimed that Bulcock was 'a little crack'd (with hard studying)', but 'was not an Idiot or incapable of performing his office', and said he heard him read the ceremony plainly.[57] Edmundson's daughter, Mary Ratcliffe, remembered many couples being married at her father's pub and stated that Bulcock performed his office word by word as the parsons do in the Church of England.[58] George Yates, a yeoman, went so far as to

53 Cornwall Record Office, PB8/8, Letter book of William Wake, 1730–1735, letters dated 11 May and 14 May 1730.
54 BIA Trans. CP. 1764/1, Allen Edmundson, ff. 397–398.
55 BIA Trans. CP. 1764/1, John Sutcliffe of Padiam, Shalloon Weaver (June 1761), ff. 611–612.
56 BIA Trans. CP. 1764/1, William Edmundson, of Whitemore Bottom, Chapelry of Colne, husbandman (June 1761), f. 546.
57 BIA Trans. CP. 1764/1, Allan Edmundson, ff. 397–398.
58 BIA Trans. CP. 1764/1, Mary Ratcliffe, f. 412.

declare that Bulcock could read the marriage ceremony without help and that he saw Bulcock sign a certificate.[59]

The other important fact to be determined was whether the couples who had been wed by Bulcock were forced to remarry later. To some extent, the depositions again fell into two camps. Several of Ann's deponents stated that they were not aware of couples remarrying after one of his ceremonies. Of course, Thomas's allegations declared that Ann's deponents were not competent to judge, since their own marriages were clandestine, and they needed to prove such unions legitimate and their children not base. He also alleged that clandestine marriers were debauched, profane and disorderly, and therefore likely to be bribed. Clearly, clandestinity itself could be used to symbolise deviance.[60]

Unsurprisingly, many of the deponents that Thomas called offered accounts of marriage ceremonies that were carried out again. Some said that they remarried because they felt Bulcock was too 'crazy' to have wed them properly.[61] Some couples were obliged to remarry after the first clandestine ceremony because their local clergyman thought the service irregular. Margaret Bateson married William Bateson in April 1738; they were 'immediately asked in Church at Gisborn on the Sunday next following and twice after successively' about the wedding and therefore were married in church on 10 May. Margaret stated that they had not felt married after Bulcock's service, so that they lived and lay together only after the church ceremony.[62] Such remarriages were recorded in the marriage register. In 1727, the parish of Downham noted in its register: 'John Bevern of Blackburn, carpenter, and Margaret Banks of Downham, spinster, Married February ye 15th, having been, as they pretended, married ye Day before by Christopher Bulcock, a Man non compos mentis, or not in his right senses. By James Cowgill, Cur[ate].'[63]

However, Thomas's deponents' situations were not without some ambiguity. Not all of the couples who deposed on behalf of Thomas were instructed to remarry immediately. It was four years after his marriage to his first wife that John Sutcliffe was called before the spiritual

59 BIA Trans. CP. 1764/1, George Yates, Windy Bank, Parish of Blackburn, yeoman (September 1762), f. 967.

60 BIA Trans. CP. 1764/1, Allegation on part of Thomas, f. 1131.

61 BIA Trans. CP. 1764/1, Margaret Bateson, f. 1237.

62 BIA Trans. CP. 1764/1, Margaret Bateson, f. 1237. For being 'asked' in the home church, see also Catherine Suddell, who married at about the age of 16, f. 1251.

63 Published in *Notes and Queries*, vol. 10, 5 December 1908, p. 447. Cowgill was curate at Downham from 1724 to 1747.

court in Padiham Chapel about his union. Afterwards, he was married again by James Fishwick, Padiham's curate. He stated that he had done this after being worn down by the Reverend Mr Fishwick frequently telling him that he and his wife lived like rogue and whore. On one occasion, the curate pointed at a nearby dog and declared, 'Mr Bulcock could no more marry you than that Dog', blaming such incapacity on Bulcock's want of understanding.[64] Not everyone was certain of Bulcock's inadequacies. James Folds, Esquire, for instance, declared that he could not tell if Christopher Bulcock's marriages were good or valid, although he knew that 'many' of those married by him were married over again at Colne or elsewhere.[65] Another of Thomas's deponents, Robert Nowell, gentleman, opined that he had heard it said that Bulcock's marriages 'would stand', although he never knew 'instances of a trial of it'.[66] Others specified that it was only after the Marriage Act 1753 that any people had been married over again, usually at the instruction of a clergyman.[67]

Even some clerics were ambivalent.[68] William Nabbs, curate of Newchurch in Pendle, had heard that Bulcock was in deacon's orders, but was not sure if he was licensed. He had not witnessed any weddings, which, given his clerical position, is not surprising, but thought Bulcock was not capable of going through the service by himself, since he was not rational and was melancholic. Nevertheless, in response to Ann's interrogatory, he stated that the many persons who had been married by Bulcock had 'lived together as Husband and Wife without being married again and such he supposes looked upon their marriages as good'. He insisted that he did not know if these unions were valid, referring this question to those more learned than him in law.[69] Most confusingly, perhaps, the Reverend Mr Fishwick deposed on behalf of Ann Lee. In contradiction to his reported

[64] BIA Trans. CP. 1764/1, John Sutcliffe's deposition, f. 625. Indeed, there is a marriage certificate for John Sutcliffe to Susan Brotherton: Lancashire Online Parish Clerk: Marriage, 10 October 1750, St Leonard, Padiham, Lancashire, England, John Sutcliff, of Padiham, and Susan Brotherton, of Padiham: LDS Film 1040343.

[65] BIA Trans. CP. 1764/1, James Folds, ff. 729–730. Another, a clerk of the Chapel of Harwood, declared his marriage was proven not valid: William Hindle, Great Harwood, Parish of Blackburn, Clerk of Chapel of Harwood (16 May 1763).

[66] BIA Trans. CP. 1764/1, Robert Nowell, of Altham, Gent (June 1761), ff. 785–786.

[67] BIA Trans. CP. 1764/1, George Yates, f. 971; see also Ann Pomfret, ff. 984–985.

[68] BIA Trans. CP. 1764/1, John Holmes, curate of Haslingdon, f. 50.

[69] BIA Trans. CP. 1764/1, William Nabbs, clerk, curate of Newchurch in Pendle (June 1761), f. 725. According to the CCED, he was ordained deacon in 1728, priest in 1730 and appointed curate at Newchurch in Pendle in 1735.

haranguing of Sutcliffe and others, he supported Lee's good character and claimed never to have seen Christopher Bulcock or to know anything of him personally. He admitted only to hearing that Bulcock had preached well when first appointed curate at Accrington, but then became affected in his head, possibly by intense study.[70]

## Clandestine Marriers' Motivation

So how far do these clandestine marriages demonstrate their Lancashire protagonists' conformity to canon law? In the first instance, it is worth noting that, in some respects, people who were married by Bulcock experienced a reasonably conventional service. The couples clearly believed that a clergyman was essential.[71] When acting as celebrant, Christopher Bulcock wore a clerical band and used the *Book of Common Prayer* to conduct the ceremony, just as with a regular Church of England service.[72] Tamor Crossley, who was married to her first husband by Bulcock and to her second husband by Reverend Mr. Fishwick, emphasised that Bulcock did exactly the same as Fishwick.[73] Many wives received a ring; Ann Lee's, it was recalled, was silver.[74] This was not universal, however. Susanna Sutcliffe, deposing for Ann, noted that there was no ring or joining of hands at her wedding. She remembered that her husband asked Bulcock's nephew whether 'they never used a "ring" and he said sometimes we do and sometimes we do not'.[75] The spouses received a certificate of marriage following the ceremony and presumably were recorded in a book, since Bulcock's nephew was requested to find an entry for Thomas's and Lee's union (although he failed to do so).[76] Of course, these marriages deviated in many ways from

[70] BIA Trans. CP. 1764/1, James Fishwick, Clerk of Padiham (13 September 1762). He was minister at Padiham from 1740. Michael Snape concludes that Whalley's clergy were a non-graduate clerical proletariat, often poor, ignorant and immoral, so Fishwick's status is perhaps questionable.

[71] A study of matrimonial suits shows that north-west inhabitants increasingly used the services of a minister in their unions in the seventeenth century: McNabb, 'Fame and the making of marriage', p. 26.

[72] BIA Trans. CP. 1764/1, Elizabeth Bridge, f. 353. According to Probert, most clandestine marriages used the *Book of Common Prayer*: Probert, *Marriage Law and Practice*, p. 198.

[73] BIA Trans. CP. 1764/1, Tamor Crossley, ff. 1087–1088.

[74] BIA Trans. CP. 1764/1, Elizabeth Bridge, f. 353.

[75] BIA Trans. CP. 1764/1, Susanna Sutcliffe, f. 631.

[76] BIA Trans. CP. 1764/1, John Titherington, f. 699. For Ann Lee's agent's failure to find the register in 1757 and 1759, see BIA CP. I/1463, which consists of a document aiming to show why the sentence for Ann should be declared null (November 1764).

marital law. They were not conducted in a church, but in a public house, after all.[77] The locations named included a parlour below stairs in Allen Edmundson's public house in Pendle Forest, the Cross Gates, a public house on Coalpit Road, a mile and a half from Brownhill where Bulcock lived, and the Robin Hood, in Barrowford, near Colne.

In short, then, the couples were not operating in ignorance of conventional forms of union and were likely aware that there were deterrents in place against this type of marriage. In 1750, for instance, four couples from the Chapelry of Burnley were fined by the visitation court for being married in secret by Bulcock.[78] Indeed, what is perhaps remarkable is that the couples who chose to use Bulcock did so in the full knowledge of his mental impairment. Even those who deposed on behalf of Thomas, confirming that Bulcock was unable to make his way through the service without rambling, were often those who had already seen him in action and still chose to use him for their own wedding. John Sutcliffe, for instance, witnessed one of Bulcock's weddings (and noted his impairment), but then used Bulcock for his own marriage two years later. Thirteen years after this, having been widowed, he married again, once more happily using Bulcock, who was encouraged to say the service by his nephew offering him a piece of pie.[79] Susannah, John Sutcliffe's second wife, had also seen Christopher struggle through wedding ceremonies, persuaded once by sweet pie and once by roast beef.[80] William Edmundson, a husbandman, initially refused to be married by 'such a fool' in 1720, but was eventually persuaded by his betrothed to proceed. This young woman went on to be a servant to the Bulcocks for two years up to 1730, with the duty of washing the clergyman like a child and changing his dirty bed.[81]

Some commonalities in motivation emerge from the depositions. Flexibility was important. John Sutcliffe explained that he had the banns called in church at Padiham when he planned to marry Isobel Whitehead. But, since he was in service, he was prevailed upon to put it off and to let his master stop the banns. About three or four months later,

[77] The making of marriages in public houses waned over the seventeenth century in the north-west, although private houses remained popular: McNabb, 'Fame and the making of marriage', p. 25.

[78] Clearly, Hardwicke's Marriage Act was successful, since there were no presentments after 1753: Snape, *Church of England*, p. 116.

[79] BIA Trans. CP. 1764/1, John Sutcliffe's deposition, ff. 613–614.

[80] BIA Trans. CP. 1764/1, Susanna Sutcliffe, f. 633.

[81] BIA Trans. CP. 1764/1, William Edmundson, Whitemore Bottom, Chapelry of Colne (9 June 1761).

the master repented, but the parson refused to marry him 'upon once asking[,] insisting upon asking him three times over again'. In other words, he wanted the banns called three times again. This was not speedy enough for the couple and John used Bulcock to marry Isobel.[82] For most, privacy, in the sense of secrecy, was crucial, much as Brian Outhwaite suggested. Indeed, the phrase most deponents use to describe Bulcock's business was marrying people 'privately'. For Thomas Whitaker and, less willingly, Ann Lee, marrying clandestinely kept their union secret. Secrecy was essential because his father had discovered the relationship between his son and his servant, and had warned his son he would disinherit the son and his offspring if he were to marry her.[83] William Edmundson simply stated that the young woman he courted agreed to have him, 'but would be married privately'. Thus they went to an alehouse where this was available, one and a half miles from Brownhill, Pendle.

Convenience was a factor, in terms of location, speed and cost. Those with more means had more choice when seeking a quick union. Thomas married Ann Willion in May 1759 in Scotland, because she was under the age of 21 and he did not want to wait for the Court of Chester to appoint a guardian, since her father was deceased; instead, they were married by a clergyman in Edinburgh.[84] Other studies have shown that couples might choose not to marry in their home parish for reasons that were not deliberately irregular. In London, it could be because many were recent migrants; elsewhere, some couples followed the incumbent of a parish who had more than one living or sought out another parish church because their own had no permanent incumbent. In some cases, as Probert observes, particular churches, such as a cathedral, became fashionable.[85] As stated earlier, Whalley was a large parish divided into chapelries and thus many of the population were not in reach of the chapels, only some of which provided a full range of services in any case. Couples may therefore have used Bulcock because he was convenient and there were few regular options. Ann Walmslay, for instance, was married by Bulcock twenty-six years before she deposed, in Robert Bulcock's

[82] BIA Trans. CP. 1764/1, John Sutcliffe's deposition, ff. 613–614.

[83] BIA Trans. CP. 1764/1, exhibit 2, second letter. Thomas Senior pre-empted him by writing a will that would disinherit Thomas Jr if he were to marry Ann Lee and denied that any issue of the marriage could inherit his estate.

[84] BIA CP. I/1463, Christopher Bridge of Padiham, innholder (January 1765), deposing on behalf of Thomas Whittaker.

[85] Probert, *Marriage Law and Practice*, pp. 173, 202–204.

house in Blacko.[86] Given the size and location of Blacko, where the marriages were performed, it was also perhaps easily accessible. The Cross Gates public house, where some of the marriages were celebrated, seems to have sat at the intersection of three roads.

It is difficult to establish whether cost was a factor. Probert and Newton found that this was not particularly important in London, where church marriages could be cheaper than clandestine ones, since marriage by banns incurred parish fees and ancillary costs.[87] The description of costs charged by Bulcock varied. Allen Edmundson, the landlord of the public house where some of the ceremonies occurred in the 1720s, remembered that a couple paid Bulcock 6*d.* for the service, which would be an incentive to use him. Others, however, mentioned costs of 2*s.*, and 5*s.* in the 1750s, which compared less well with marriages by banns, which tended to cost from 3*s.* 4*d.* to 5*s.* and more.[88] Newton shows that the clandestine marriage venues in London offered food and entertainment too, and it is feasible that a wedding carried out in a public house might have taken advantage of the alcohol and food that was available.

Couples' accounts of remarrying after being wed by Bulcock are also revealing and do not necessarily reveal any specific desire to conform to marital law. Many did so for pragmatic reasons rather than because they felt that the clandestine union was inadequate. William Hindle remarried his wife at the advice of John Smith, the curate of Harwood, the Sunday following the Whit Sunday after his marriage. Reading further, however, it becomes clear that, at the time of his marriage, William's wife was a minor. Her 'friends' in Yorkshire therefore refused to release her portion to him when he visited them following the clandestine ceremony. They stipulated that he would get part of her fortune only if they were remarried in church.[89] Tamor Crossley was married three times in total, twice to her first husband. They remarried after a wedding presided over by Bulcock simply to make a point. Having married outside their own parish, the Reverend Mr Fishwick still demanded his dues for the wedding. Therefore Tamor's husband indignantly informed the parson that

[86] BIA Trans. CP. 1764/1, f. 1017.

[87] See Jeremy Boulton 'Itching after private marryings? Marriage customs in seventeenth-century London', *The London Journal* 16 (1991), 15–34, pp. 17–18.

[88] Probert, *Marriage, Law and Practice*, pp. 197–198. Susannah Sutcliffe deposed that, when she used Bulcock to marry her husband, he paid Bulcock's nephew 2*s.* for the service: BIA Trans. CP. 1764/1. Snape found that some couples in 1750 were charged 5*s.* each: Snape, *Church of England*, p. 116.

[89] BIA Trans. CP. 1764/1, f. 1234.

'if he would have his dues he must do the work for it for which reason only they were married again for she thought nothing to the contrary but that she was well married by Mr Bulcock'.[90]

Even parish authorities conformed over marital arrangements only when it suited them. It seems that clandestine marriage was a quick solution to longer-term financial problems for some parish officers. William Cowper, Doctor in Physic, who lived in Colne, three miles from Blacko, was in the Commission of Peace for the West Riding of Yorkshire and County Palatine of Lancaster for twelve years. He deposed that Bulcock was notorious because of the 'great numbers of loose and mean persons being married at his residence'. What troubled Cowper most was that parochial officers frequently applied to bind over putative fathers, but would then reapply to have the recognisance superseded, because they had since prevailed upon the man to marry the pregnant woman at Blacko. When Cowper admonished the officers, telling them that they should not be aiding and abetting 'illegal and clandestine pretended nuptials', they informed him 'that it was done for expedition and cheapness for that if they could get the Old Parson or Old Vicar who married what marrying there was, in a good humour he was then moderate in his demands and would treat them with drink out of the fees either at the Hole or the Cross Gates'.[91]

## Conclusion

There are several points to be drawn from this analysis of the clandestine marriages of couples between the 1720s and 1750s in Whalley, Lancashire. Most obvious is that the union at the centre of the jactitation case reveals the fundamental problem of such marriages: proving their existence and the legal rights that marriage afforded spouses and heirs could be extremely difficult when the parties were in dispute. Thomas did not live to see his case resolved. He died in May 1766 and Ann Willion took over the suit as his 'widow', appealing to the High Court of Delegates. In January 1767, the judge decreed that the cause was 'ill-appealed' and should be remitted to the judge from whom it was appealed, condemning Ann Willion to the costs of the suit. Nevertheless, by April, the High

90 BIA Trans. CP. 1764/1, Tamor Crossley, ff. 1090–1091.
91 BIA Trans. CP. 1764/1, William Cowper, ff. 833–842.

Court had issued an inhibition to York. There is evidence of continued negotiations between all of the parties over the estate into the adulthood of Whitaker's sons with Willion and his nephew, Ellen Baron's son. It is clear that couples were safer ensuring that their union adhered to all of the regulations if they wished to ensure the security of their children's inheritance and status.

Next, the clandestine marriers' actions nuance our account of clandestine marriages. Their unions did not adhere to Probert's definition of clandestine marriages conforming, to all intents and purposes, to regular marriage; as we have seen, they were performed by a clergyman of dubious status in a public house.[92] Several of the couples ignored Bulcock's mental state to satisfy their needs, which revolved around privacy, cost, and ease of access and timing. They possessed a pragmatic attitude towards marriage law, simply marrying elsewhere when informed thereafter that their initial union was problematic. Probert may well be correct that such couples are exceptions who prove the rule of matrimonial conformity. Yet they do suggest that more diversity could coexist at local level. In the north-west, the combination of a pre-existing and fairly long-standing regional culture of matrimony was combined with specific economic, social and geographical conditions from the later seventeenth century, which together meant that the social forces that controlled access to marriage elsewhere were less powerful.

Finally, the examples offered by these couples offer a way of producing a slightly more joined-up approach to the making of marriage over the long eighteenth century. Currently, scholarship tends to address types of union discretely: the early modern irregular marriage; the clandestine unions of the first half of the eighteenth century; and the 'imprudent' marriages in industrialising areas in the late eighteenth century. Yet there are similarities underlying people's marriage practices, influenced by social, economic and religious factors that could allow a *longue durée* view of marriage that does not force us to assume that couples' behaviour must either conform or not conform to marital law. In the north-west, for example, as the toleration of irregular marriage declined, clandestine marriage, which facilitated easier unions that side-stepped some of the rigidities or hurdles of regular marriage, offered a convenient way of entering matrimony. Some people, at least, seem to have been satisfied to

92 Probert, *Marriage Law and Practice*, p. 177.

be wed by a clergyman who was assisted in saying the service by his father, who concluded ceremonies by announcing: 'So now you are wed enough.'[93] These nascent families certainly knew the religious and legal ideas underlying matrimony, but they applied them to suit their own ends.

[93] BIA Trans. CP. 1764/1, William Cowper, ff. 833–842.

11

# 'Blunderers and Blotters of the Law?'

## The Rise of Conveyancing in the Eighteenth Century and Long-Term Socio-Legal Change

CRAIG MULDREW

In his 1989 article 'Interpersonal conflict and social tension' Christopher W. Brooks posed the question, 'what happened to the common law in the Age of Reason?' – a theme he returned to in his subsequent articles 'Litigation and society in England, 1200–1996' and 'Litigation, participation, and agency in seventeenth- and eighteenth-century England'.[1] After witnessing a spectacular rise from 5,278 cases per year in 1560 to 28,734 in 1640, the central courts of Common Pleas and King's Bench saw the number of cases in advanced stages fall six times from about 30,000 to 5,000 cases during the period 1670–1750.[2] In his 1989 article, Brooks also noted that a similar decline could be traced in the town courts of Newcastle.[3] In his first book, *Pettyfoggers and Vipers of the Commonwealth*, he had already dealt with the rise of litigation in the Westminster courts, and the resultant expansion of the 'lower branch' of solicitors, attorneys and clerks who formed a 'legal bureaucracy' needed

[1] Christopher W. Brooks, 'Interpersonal conflict and social tension: civil litigation in England, 1640–1830', first published in A. L. Beier, David Cannadine and J. M. Rosenheim (eds), *The First Modern Society: Essays in English History in Honour of Lawrence Stone* (Cambridge, 1989), pp. 357–399, reprinted in Christopher W. Brooks, *Lawyers, Litigation and English Society since 1450* (London, 1998), pp. 27–62; Christopher W. Brooks, 'Litigation and society in England, 1200–1830', in *Lawyers, Litigation and English Society since 1450* (London, 1998), pp. 63–128; Christopher W. Brooks, 'Litigation, participation, and agency in seventeenth- and eighteenth-century England', in David Lemmings (ed.), *The British and Their Laws in the Eighteenth Century* (Woodbridge, 2005), pp. 155–181.

[2] These figures are based on three-year averages: Brooks, 'Interpersonal conflict', pp. 31–33; Christopher W. Brooks, *Pettyfoggers and Vipers of the Commonwealth: The 'Lower Branch' of the Legal Profession in Early Modern England* (Cambridge, 1986), pp. 51, 68.

[3] Brooks, 'Interpersonal conflict', p. 40.

to process lawsuits.[4] Brooks noted that most litigation in King's Bench and Common Pleas was over debt, and he postulated that economic reasons lay behind so many tens of thousands of suits, most of which were cases of debt, much more than neighbourly quarrels. Real vexatious litigation, he argued, was only 'flotsam and jetsam which floated in on the flood tide of litigation' in the central courts.[5] These economic causes were confirmed by my subsequent study of the economics of credit and its relation to litigation. Cases in the borough court of Great Yarmouth, for instance, rose from an annual average of 475 in the period 1545–1560, to 970 between 1569 and 1575 (an increase of 4 per cent per year). In Chester, the rate of litigation went from 77 suits in 1545 to 3,500 suits by 1585.[6] Almost overnight, litigation expanded to reach a per capita level that has never been matched since. If we add litigation from all jurisdictions together, by c. 1606 this results in 1,102,367 cases per year – or one suit for every household in the country![7] In comparison to this, the rate of litigation in the advanced industrial economy of England in 1975 was only about a quarter of this. In my work, I have explored how this was precipitated by the rapid expansion of credit, which caused disputes to explode because of the pace at which market transactions increased. Bottlenecks of credit created liquidity problems for individuals, leading them to recover their own debts, which then had a domino effect on others. The majority of the increase in suits was a result of the expansion of the market economy, in which about 90 per cent of transactions were done on credit. As chains of obligation grew longer, late payment became more of a problem and creditors turned to litigation to try to force payment when they needed liquidity. Although interpersonal conflict certainly played a role in some disputes being brought to court, in King's Lynn only 17 per cent of complaints resulted in an arrest on mesne process and only 4 per cent went all the way to judgment.[8] My study of urban litigation also found a general decline that roughly matched that in the central courts. In King's Lynn, for instance, complaints dropped from 1,500 to about 100 per year between

[4] Brooks, *Pettyfoggers*, ch. 2.

[5] Ibid., p. 111.

[6] This is discussed at more length in Craig Muldrew, *The Economy of Obligation: The Culture of Credit and Social Relations in Early Modern England* (London, 1998), pp. 216–236.

[7] Ibid., p. 236.

[8] Ibid., p. 255.

1650 and 1750, and the situation in Great Yarmouth and Exeter was similar.[9]

In examining the possible reasons for this sudden decline after such a massive rise, although Brooks certainly noted that changes in the practice of credit might well have had an effect, as a legal historian he focused on the possible social and institutional factors that might have affected decisions to take suits to court.[10] In 1989, he was sceptical of Lawrence Stone's thesis that the rise in litigation was a result of increasing interpersonal tension and that eighteenth-century bourgeois family life gave rise to more 'affective' values, which led to a decline in contentiousness.[11] Instead, Brooks focused on the rising proportion of central court litigation brought by middling-sort tradesmen and artisans as gentry debt litigation declined. This, he explained, was a result of a social difference in attitudes towards lengthy legal procedures and costs. Tradesmen much preferred efficient low-cost summary jurisdictions in new courts of requests to recover small debts to the much more participatory and egalitarian civic courts in which decisions had to be made by a jury.[12] Although juries were defended by senior judges such as Blackstone, as Brooks pointed out, the overall costs of litigation in the central courts doubled between 1680 and 1750 from less than £10 to between £20 and £30 for the same kind of work.[13] Later, in his 2005 article, he explored this theme, elaborating upon the argument of W. A. Champion that this was part of a realignment of an 'old' regulatory regime based on manorial courts, local borough courts and civic institutions such as guilds, whereby all creditors in society had equal access to sue over broken contracts based on equality before the common law and a jury of one's peers, to summary justice. This was based on arbitration forced on poorer debtors by justices of the peace and what legal historians studying the nineteenth century have called the 'class law' of the courts of requests. In the nineteenth century, county courts were developed based on similar principles.[14] I have also argued more generally that

[9] Ibid., pp. 230, 237–242. See also W. A. Champion, 'Litigation in the Boroughs: the Shrewsbury *Curia Parva*, 1480–1730', *Legal History* 15 (1994), 201–222, pp. 208, 216–217.

[10] Brooks, 'Litigation, participation and agency', p. 162.

[11] Brooks, 'Interpersonal conflict', pp. 49, 60.

[12] Margot C. Finn, *The Character of Credit: Personal Debt in English Culture, 1740–1914* (Cambridge, 2003), pp. 202*ff*.

[13] Brooks, 'Interpersonal conflict', pp. 45–49.

[14] Brooks, 'Litigation, participation and agency', pp. 162*ff*; W. A. Champion, 'Recourse to the law and the meaning of the great litigation decline, 1650–1750: some clues from the Shrewsbury local courts', in C. W. Brooks and Michael Lobban (eds), *Communities and*

there was a move from what I termed a 'juridical' society based on public legal dispute resolution to one that stressed more private personal self-control.[15]

In his local study of Shrewsbury, W. A. Champion showed that, after the 1630s, there was a gradual decline in the rate of litigation, which involved rising fees and the decline of very small-scale litigation under 10*s*. He noted that, at the same time, there was also a similar decline in quarter session activity and suits at the town's court leet.[16] Robert Shoemaker has also shown how litigation in the church courts over public insult declined as well in this period.[17] However, the evidence of indictable offences at the quarter sessions and assizes in Essex, Surrey and Sussex does not indicate any obvious decline in the late seventeenth or early eighteenth centuries.[18] Thus it seems that the litigation decline was concentrated in suits about credit in both senses of its meaning – that is, as both obligation and reputation. At the same time, a similar proportion of thefts, assaults and other crimes continued to be brought forward by victims for public resolution after c. 1700 as before – even though, as Peter King has shown, the majority were resolved outside of court.[19]

In this chapter, rather than focusing on the nature of litigation, I will argue that the changes in how credit was negotiated continued to involve the legal profession, but in a different way. In the period before the early eighteenth century, most credit was oral and unsecured. It was maintained by the paramount nature of reputational credit, which was universal, interpersonal, and based on one's ability to pay debts in good time

*Courts in Britain, 1150–1900* (London, 1997), pp. 192–198; Paul Johnson, 'Small debts and economic distress in England and Wales, 1857–1913', *Economic History Review* 46 (1993), 65–87.

15 Craig Muldrew, 'From a "light cloak" to the "iron cage": an essay on historical changes in the relationship between community and individualism', in Alexandra Shepard and Philip Withington (eds), *Communities in Early Modern England* (Manchester, 2000), pp. 156–177. How this was related to credit networks and the economy is something I am still working on, but see Craig Muldrew, 'Happiness and the theology of the self in late seventeenth-century England', in Michael Braddick and Joanna Innes (eds), *Suffering and Happiness in England 1550–1850* (Oxford, 2017), pp. 65–86; Craig Muldrew, 'Self-love, religion and the transformation of obligation to self-control in early modern British society', unpublished paper.

16 Champion, 'Recourse to the law', pp. 192–193.

17 Robert B. Shoemaker, 'The decline of public insult in London 1660–1800', *Past and Present* 169 (2000), 95–131.

18 J. A. Sharpe, *Crime in Seventeenth-Century England: A County Study* (Cambridge, 1983), p. 183; John Beattie, *Crime and the Courts in England 1660–1800* (Oxford, 1986), pp. 182, 202–203.

19 Peter King, *Crime, Justice and Discretion in England: 1740–1820* (Cambridge, 2000), ch. 2.

and not to overspend. In the early eighteenth century, this changed, and credit became focused more on local solicitors and scriveners, whose reputation relied on their good book-keeping and their honest writing of small bills and notes of hand, which could replace oral credit. They also facilitated the securitisation of credit by arranging local mortgages and lending on bond. In short, the role of the legal profession in credit networks went from handling litigation, which was used to ensure liquidity in *already existent* chains of oral credit, to creating forms of securitised interest bearing credit and creating local short-term paper credit/currency.

The significance of moves towards more stable credit networks in relation to the decline in litigation can be seen if we break down the nature of that decline in the central courts by type of case. As Brooks noted, the great rise there was in suits of debt. Actions of debt, together with actions on the case (which also concerned broken obligations, but focused on broken contracts rather than restitution of property), rose fifteen times by 1640, with over 80 per cent of suits being actions of debt by that year. Other actions such as ejectment and trespass, which tended to involve land rather than credit, barely increased at all.[20] Then, when the decline occurred, suits of debt went down by a multiple of fifteen between 1640 and 1750, while all other forms of action remained roughly the same.[21] In borough courts, actions on the case formed the great majority of suits by the late sixteenth century and it was these that declined there.[22]

In my *Economy of Obligation*, I noted that, in *per capita* terms, the volume of credit litigation had begun to decline from c. 1650.[23] However, in *absolute* terms, the volume of litigation remained very high after 1650 – if not as high as it had been at the beginning of the seventeenth century.[24] According to Brooks, the combined level of litigation in King's Bench and Common Pleas was actually at its highest c. 1670, before then dropping to only half of this level by 1700.[25] Looking at borough courts, in Great Yarmouth in 1686, the level of litigation was still as high as it had

20 Brooks, *Pettyfoggers*, p. 69.
21 Brooks, 'Interpersonal conflict', pp. 31, 52.
22 Muldrew, *Economy of Obligation*, pp. 207–210.
23 Ibid., pp. 237–241.
24 E. A. Wrigley, R. S. Davies, J. E. Oeppen and R. S. Schofield, *English Population History from Family Reconstitution, 1580–1837* (Cambridge, 1997), p. 614.
25 Brooks, 'Litigation and society', p. 68. The sample periods for counting were the three years around 1606, 1640, 1670 and 1700.

been in the early seventeenth century. In King's Lynn, as well, there was no decline between 1650 and 1685. In Exeter, by 1690, the number of suits was only about 15 per cent less than in 1625, while in Bristol there was a decline of about 20 per cent. Although the national population dropped and stagnated after 1650, because the urban population began to grow more strongly in the Restoration, per capita rates of urban litigation began to drop in this period, but in all of these jurisdictions around 25 per cent of litigants lived outside towns, as did most of the litigants using the central courts. Since all of this litigation was of a very similar nature, it makes sense to examine it as a national phenomenon – and here it seems an *overall* decline for the period after c. 1630 really started around 1690.[26]

This is important to locate, even if we can do so only quite roughly owing to the different sampling dates required by the sheer volume of counting involved. That litigation should begin to decline at this point in time quite strongly suggests that the reason can be linked to changes in the way in which credit markets worked. Since much of the initial boom in litigation was caused by the very informal oral nature of sales credit and reckonings, it would stand to reason that if credit were to start to become more formal, this would lead to a reduction in litigation. In his book *Casualties of Credit*, Carl Wennerlind has shown how there was a whole body of economic writing originating in the period of the English civil war arguing that England's system of local informal credit was a barrier to economic growth – most importantly, because poorer individuals could not be trusted to pay back their debts owing to low wages, which also limited their role as consumers.[27] Many proposals for different sorts of banks that would issue paper currency to speed up circulation were put forward, including land banks, which would register land to issue currency based on its value, and banks that could hold material wealth as collateral to back up the issuing of currency. But, in the end, the only successful institution was the Bank of England, which, although it initially issued some £5 banknotes, thereafter rarely issued anything less than £20.[28] But note issue was not its major function; rather, it was to issue shares, which were initially purchased mostly by a wealthy metropolitan clientele before spreading to provincial towns. Few beyond the middling sort held shares.

[26] Muldrew, *Economy of Obligation*, pp. 211–232.

[27] Carl Wennerlind, *Casualties of Credit: The English Financial Revolution, 1620–1720* (Cambridge, MA, 2011), pp. 54–79.

[28] Sir John Clapham, *The Bank of England*, two vols (Cambridge, 1970), vol. I, p. 146.

However, changes were happening in credit networks below the radar of the very well-established history of the financial revolution. It was proposed by Dr Hank McCurdy in his 2007 Cambridge PhD thesis on the 'Social incidence and economic significance of the growth of transferable paper instruments in seventeenth-century England' that informal written bills and notes were taking the place of unwritten obligations.[29] McCurdy looked at legal cases and, although there were enough cases for him to establish with confidence that such notes were being transferred after the Restoration and had filtered down to be used in local transactions by ordinary tradesmen, it was difficult to say how common they were. By 1684, it is clear that bills were negotiable by endorsement: in his legal manual on bills of exchange, John Scarlett noted that endorsements could be made as many times as there was room in the bill.[30] Surviving actual bills are almost non-existent, because they were not meant to store value like a sealed bond or a banknote or a stock; and they were destroyed as soon as they were no longer needed for circulation, to prevent future fraudulent use.[31] It is probable that the currency shortage caused by the combination of the Nine Years War and an overly clipped money supply led to a more rapid acceptance of negotiable bills, and, by 1697, a London merchant claimed that notes had been circulating with endorsements for thirty years.[32] The legality of transferable endorsed notes was enshrined in statute law in 1706 by Anne 3 & 4 ch. 8.

In John Money's *Chronicles of John Cannon*, a poor Somerset husbandman's son who became an Excise man, and then a local schoolteacher and scrivener for the less wealthy of the small town of Glastonbury, we have an excellent source with which to trace the transformation of a very rural credit market far away from the stocks and shares of metropolitan finance. In the period during which he recorded most of his financial transactions, from 1734 to 1742, Cannon listed more than 800 involving bills, notes, bonds and mortgages, sometimes of great complexity, although only a tiny minority were done for significant amounts of money.[33] The great detail available in Money's *Chronicles* is

[29] Hank McCurdy, 'Social incidence and economic significance of the growth of transferable paper instruments in seventeenth-century England', PhD thesis, University of Cambridge (2007), chs 3, 6.

[30] Ibid., ff. 70, 76, 83, 128, 161.

[31] Ibid., ff. 122, 236–263, especially 251.

[32] Ibid., ff. 127, 148.

[33] John Money (ed.), *The Chronicles of John Cannon Excise Officer and Writing Master*, two vols (Oxford, 2010), p. cxxiv ('Reading').

vital in that it enables us to identify the links between the circulation of small-scale paper credit and the security provided by mortgaging in one small community. Cannon moved to Glastonbury in 1731, where he spent the rest of his life, and almost all of the mortgages, bonds, bills and notes of hand that he wrote up were for parties within a radius of less than 4 miles, including the villages of Street and Meare, Butleigh, Baltonsborough and Pennard.[34] West Lydford, Cannon's place of birth and the residence of both his extended family and, after 1732, his wife and children, was about 10 miles distant, so required an overnight journey, but he still visited often. When working out the networks of credit in which Cannon participated, we are dealing only with an area about 4 miles in radius, containing probably fewer than 1,000 households.

Cannon also mentioned thirty-three different local attorneys within 20 or so miles of Glastonbury, in villages as small as Queen's Camel, Catcutt and West Lydford itself, although many are mentioned only a few times.[35] Both Wells and Shepton Mallet were also places where Cannon had dealings with other attorneys. If all, or even some, of these individuals performed similar services to those of Cannon, we can see how local paper credit/currency could have expanded to involve tens of thousands of bills and notes of hand. The attorneys whom Cannon mentioned by far the most were Thomas and William Nicholls, brothers resident in Glastonbury, and much of the work he mentions was done for these two men. We will never know how many self-trained individuals like Cannon were around at the time, but his level of education for someone poor must have been fairly rare.

In the previous period, individuals turned to the courts to create liquidity with almost no institutional clearing facilities available below the level of merchant's exchanges and, after 1660, London scrivener and goldsmith bankers. With the rise in the issue of paper notes, having a safe

[34] Craig Muldrew, 'The social acceptance of paper credit as currency in eighteenth-century England: a case study of Glastonbury c. 1720–1742', in Marcella Lorenzini, Cinzia Lorandini and D'Maris Coffman (eds), *Financing in Europe: Evolution, Coexistence and Complementarity of Lending Practices from the Middle Ages to Modern Times* (London, 2018), pp. 133–159; Money, *Chronicles of John Cannon*, pp. 196–197. Because of the great length of the manuscript, Money's edition has had to summarise some of the material. Here, all references to the *Chronicles* are to Cannon's original pagination. Where quotations are given, they have been taken from Money's transcription, where available, and from the original manuscript where Money has been able to provide only a summary. The manuscript is in the Somerset Record Office, DD/SAS/1193/4.

[35] Money, *Chronicles of John Cannon*, pp. 699–700 (index).

store of capital that could be verified with the evidence of stocks, bonds, mortgages, bills, notes or the word of a solicitor must have reduced the need to sue someone for a debt they owed to pay someone else simply for the purposes of liquidity.[36] A shortage of liquidity could now be ridden out or, in extreme cases, assets such as bonds could be liquidated with a local solicitor. This is undoubtedly one crucial reason why litigation over credit declined once the use of such notes became more common, which, if the example of Cannon's activity was being duplicated elsewhere, must have happened in the decades after 1690 and before 1730 – exactly the period when the number of suits was declining most steeply.

If it had simply been the case of changes in the credit market causing a decline in litigation, however, we would expect that the numbers of attorneys to have fallen almost as precipitously. Indeed, Brooks noted, the decline in central court litigation was accompanied by a similar decline in the number of attorneys, solicitors and barristers enrolled in the courts of Common Pleas and King's Bench. The number of barristers dropped by 50 per cent by 1770 when compared to the mid-seventeenth century, while by 1698 the number of enrolled solicitors and attorneys was already less than it had been in 1640 and 1673.[37] However, as a result of public concern about the quality of legal services, the 'Act for the Better Regulation of Attorneys' was passed in 1729, which required all would-be attorneys and solicitors first to have served a five-year clerkship, and then to be interviewed by a judge, before being enrolled. For both 1730 and 1731, we have published lists of enrolments that show that there were 4,825 attorneys enlisted for all of the Westminster courts at that time.[38] But these were only those individuals who practised in London and there had always been others who practised only in local courts. According to Brooks, there might have been 500 attorneys employed by local borough courts who were not active in the Westminster courts, and another 500 employed by regional councils and palatinate courts, around 1640.[39] A

[36] This was the subject of my book, *The Economy of Obligation*.

[37] Christopher W. Brooks, 'Law, lawyers and the social history of England, 1500–1800', in *Lawyers, Litigation and English Society since 1450* (London, 1998), pp. 179–198, pp. 182–185; David Lemmings, *Professors of the Law: Barristers and English Legal Culture in the Eighteenth Century* (Oxford, 2000).

[38] Penelope J. Corfield, *Power and the Professions in Britain 1700–1850* (London, 1995), p. 79. Brooks has also noted that many of these new London enrolments might have been articled clerks who took advantage of the legislation to become enrolled on easy terms: Brooks, 'Law, lawyers and social history', p. 183.

[39] Brooks, 'Law, lawyers and social history', pp. 182, n. 15, 184. Larger estates might also have employed attorneys for their extensive legal business: Brooks, *Pettyfoggers*, pp. 38–41.

larger borough court like King's Lynn had about ten attorneys in the 1680s, although only half of these were very active and at least two also practised in Westminster.[40] In her book on professions in the eighteenth century, Penelope Corfield has argued that the figure of 4,825 should be expanded to perhaps 5,500–6,000 to take into account smaller local members of the lower branch scattered around the country.[41] There would have been an increasing number of clerks working for attorneys, towns and tradesmen who also had writing and numerical skills, as we saw in the example of Cannon in Glastonbury. If we take that example, an area with a radius of 10 miles represents an area of about 314 square miles, which, if multiplied by the total agricultural area estimated for England in 1700, would produce an estimate of about 4,000 local clerks, scriveners and attorneys in England in 1750.[42] This is actually higher than Corfield's estimate and is further evidence of the increase in small practitioners like Cannon, who would never have been registered in London.

What this shows is that the number of attorneys, solicitors, legal clerks and small scale scriveners actually *increased* as litigation declined. The reason for this increase is also linked to another fundamental change in credit markets. Simply writing bills and notes, as well as keeping accurate accounts, may have required excellent written literacy skills, but did not require extensive legal training. The rise of the large-scale mortgaging of land for the first time in England, which also occurred in the late seventeenth century, however, did. It was such mortgages that actually underpinned much of the security of small-scale transfer of notes, which is also demonstrated in Cannon's *Chronicles*. But, as the number of people borrowing on the security of mortgages rose, more money could be made by what is generally termed 'conveyancing' – that is, the formal transfer of rights of property. This involved investigating any possible entails or other encumbrances and charges on land to help the lender to judge whether the amount borrowed could be repaid through the rental income of the land, while still satisfying other claims on the land. In 1670, the year that saw the peak of central court litigation, when local suits were still extremely numerous, conveyancing was conspicuous by its absence

[40] Muldrew, *Economy of Obligation*, p. 245.

[41] Corfield, *Power and the Professions*, p. 79.

[42] This uses an estimate of the agricultural land of 24 million acres in 1750: Mark Overton, *Agricultural Revolution in England: The Transformation of the Agrarian Economy 1500–1850* (Cambridge, 1996), p. 76.

in the standard manual for attorneys, *The Practique Part of the Law*; by 1724, when William Bohun's *Practicing Attorney* was published, it was discussed as one of four main aspects of an attorney's business. A guide to the professions published in 1747 provided a definition of conveyancing as:

> ... the drawing of Deeds, Mortgages and Conveyances of Estates. This is the most profitable Branch of the Law; for to that of Drawing Deeds they commonly add the Trade of a Money-Scrivener; that is, they are employed to find out Estates to purchase, or have Money to lay out for some, and borrow for others, and receive Fees from Borrower and Lender; and of course are employed to draw the Securities.[43]

In contrast to much of the rest of western Europe, there had been very little mortgaging in medieval England, because the general terms of mortgage law in England contained too much risk of forfeiture for the borrower and not enough flexibility for the lender in terms of renegotiation. This changed in terms of legal doctrine in the sixteenth century, with the development of what came to be termed 'the equity of redemption'. The equity of redemption allowed the mortgagor to remain the true owner of the property despite lacking legal title, while the mortgagee's interest was mere security, and forfeiture had to be declared by a court.[44] What this meant in reality was that mortgages became a convenient way of creating a long-term debt bearing legal interest, which provided an income for the lender and capital for the borrower. The 'family land bond' was now not threatened by all but very extensive overborrowing. The law also allowed the mortgagor and mortgagee a great deal of freedom to arrange their methods of repayment privately, with the knowledge that, at some point, the level of interest payments, if they came close to exceeding the value of the rent, could lead to foreclosure – but, at interest rates of around 5 per cent, this required huge amounts of borrowing. A number of individual studies show an impressive rise in the number of mortgages taken out over the course of the seventeenth century – especially in the Restoration (specifically, the 1680s), when it is usually said that the doctrine of the equity of redemption became fixed by

[43] M. Miles, '"Eminent practitioners": the new visage of country attorneys c. 1750–1800', in G. R. Rubin and David Sugarman (eds), *Law, Economy and Society, 1750–1914: Essays in the History of English Law* (Abingdon, 1984), pp. 470–503, p. 475.

[44] David Waddilove, 'Why the equity of redemption?', in Chris Briggs and Jaco Zuijderduijn (eds), *Land and Credit: Mortgages in the Medieval and Early Modern European Countryside* (London, 2018), pp. 117–149.

Lord Nottingham.[45] It has been argued that the key change in promoting the wider acceptance of the equity of redemption was the activity of indebted royalist families raising money to buy back confiscated lands after the civil war.[46] But, while this undoubtedly played a role in making conservative land holders more accepting of legal change, the acceleration of mortgaging took place much lower down the social scale, as local studies have shown.[47]

The move towards the acceptance of mortgaging should be seen as one reaction to part of the larger debate about the nature of credit in England, as outlined by Wennerlind [48] During the interregnum, there had been calls for the setting up of registries of deeds, so that the value of property could be more easily established by prospective lenders and borrowers or purchasers; during the Restoration, many pamphlets were produced advocating the setting up of land banks, based on the Dutch model, to convert landed wealth into transferable credit.[49] But such schemes would have required the 'rationalisation' of landholding, to some degree, which was made very difficult by the legal nature of customary tenure and the importance of equity procedure, which was so important to the working of the English law of property. Each manor had its own customs of inheritance for copyhold land, which generally was the most common form of tenure. These could also change over time as they were remembered by village elders. The equity of redemption made the capitalisation of property feasible within this system by placing responsibility for the negotiation of repayment in the case of default with local attorneys.

[45] H. R. French and R. W. Hoyle, 'The land market of a Pennine manor: Slaidburn, 1650–1780', *Continuity and Change* 14 (1999), 349–383, p. 371; David Sugarman and Ronnie Warrington, 'Land law, citizenship, and the invention of "Englishness": the strange case of the equity of redemption', in John Brewer and Susan Staves (eds), *Early Modern Conceptions of Property* (London, 1995), pp. 111–143.

[46] B.L. Anderson, 'The attorney and the early capital market in Lancashire', in F. Crouzet (ed.), *Capital Formation and the Industrial Revolution* (London, 1972), pp. 223-255.

[47] Imogen Wedd, 'Mortgages and the Kentish yeoman in the seventeenth century', in Chris Briggs and Jaco Zuijderduijn (eds), *Land and Credit: Mortgages in the Medieval and Early Modern European Countryside* (London, 2018), pp. 81–115; Juliet Gayton, 'Mortgages raised by rural English copyhold tenants 1605–1735', in Chris Briggs and Jaco Zuijderduijn (eds), *Land and Credit: Mortgages in the Medieval and Early Modern European Countryside* (London, 2018), pp. 46–80.

[48] Wennerlind, *Casualties of Credit.*

[49] Jaco Zuijderduijn, 'The other fundamental problem of exchange: mortgages, defaults, and debtor protection in sixteenth-century Holland', in Chris Briggs and Jaco Zuijderduijn (eds), *Land and Credit: Mortgages in the Medieval and Early Modern European Countryside* (London, 2018), pp. 281–307; J. Keith Horsefield, *British Monetary Experiments 1650–1710* (London, 1960).

In addition, the very complicated development of uses and trusts helped to make freehold land with tenurial incidents more freely mortgageable.[50] The rules relating to trusts were being worked out in the Court of Chancery in Lord Nottingham's era (1675–1682). In addition, the rules of what has come to be called 'strict settlement' of aristocratic estates also led to the need for mortgaging. Under the 'rules' of strict settlement, the current proprietor had only a life interest in the property, which was entailed to the eldest son and then a series of other male heirs, and which had to be put in a trust to meet these requirements if no son was of majority at the time of the death of the title holder.[51] Although it is impossible to measure, these developments almost certainly raised the amount of land being mortgaged.

Cannon's memoirs make clear that, by the 1730s, there was an extremely active mortgage market even for small closes, houses and stints on common land. Since conveyancing could involve accounting for different claims on a piece of land, it was more complicated than drawing bills and notes or bonds, and Cannon started by doing conveyancing work for the two local attorneys, the Nicholls brothers, although he does mention an early deed he made out in which he made an error that he had to correct (because they were written out on parchment sheets, so expensive to redo entirely). From 1736, however, Cannon's conveyancing activity expanded rapidly, as can be seen in Table 11.1.[52]

In just the last three years recorded in the *Memoirs*, Cannon facilitated about £8,682 worth of credit in a small area. This not only earned him significant fees, but also added capital to the local economy, which would have made indebtedness much less precarious. Previously, if someone had debts they owed to others called in and were unable to collect their own, then they could easily go broke. But, by the 1730s, if that same person held even a few acres of land, this could provide them with extra capital of up to £50. Cannon does not often describe the motivations behind the deeds he was hired to write, but he clearly describes the

[50] D. C. E. Yale (ed.), *Lord Nottingham's Chancery Cases* (London, 1954), vol. I, pp. xxxvii–cxxiv; D. C. E. Yale (ed.), *Lord Nottingham's Chancery Cases* (London, 1961–1962), vol. II, pp. 7–207.

[51] A good definition can be found here: www.nottingham.ac.uk/manuscriptsandspecialcollections/researchguidance/deedsindepth/settlements/terms.aspx

[52] Although there are some instances in which he mentions a mortgage without stating a value, these figures represent the great majority of the work mentioned in Cannon's *Chronicles*.

Table 11.1 *Yearly value of mortgage deeds transacted by John Cannon, 1736–1742.*

| Year | Amount (£) |
|---|---|
| 1736 | 110 |
| 1737 | 539 |
| 1738 | 340 |
| 1739 | 581 |
| 1740 | 1,005 |
| 1741 | 3,299 |
| 1742 | 4,418 |
| Total | 10,326 |

Data drawn from John Money (ed.), *The Chronicles of John Cannon Excise Officer and Writing Master*, two vols (Oxford, 2010)

complexities of mortgages themselves, presumably to provide information in the case of potential future disputes.

Table 11.2 lists those mortgages in which Cannon set out the number of acres being mortgaged and, here, it can be seen that different people borrowed differing amounts when calculated per acre, although the land must also have been of differing quality, which is impossible to know without any rental valuations. With an average value of about £18 an acre, there could easily have been over £100,000 of capital released in even such a small area as that around Glastonbury. According to Charles Davenant, mortgages were already worth £20 million in 1696, but, by the 1730s, if there were approximately 21 million acres of arable and pasture in England, at £18 an acre, this potentially could represent £378 million worth of new capital.[53]

Cannon's activity shows that, by the eighteenth century, the lower unregulated part of the lower branch now had a role to play in conveyancing, whereby they were offered work if they proved themselves to be accurate scriveners, and the rise of the mortgage market shows that there

[53] Charles Davenant, 'On credit, and the means and methods by which it may be restored', in *The Political and Commercial Works of that Celebrated Writer Charles D'Avenant, LL. D. Relating to the Trade and Revenue of England* (London, 1771), vol. I, pp. 150–167, pp. 161–162.

Table 11.2 *Estimated value per acre of mortgage loans arranged by John Cannon.*

| Amount (£) | Acres | Loan per acre(£) |
|---|---|---|
| 120 | 15 | 8.00 |
| 153 | 18 | 8.50 |
| 30 | 5 | 6.00 |
| 143.25 | 5 | 28.65 |
| 80 | 10 | 8.00 |
| 40 | 4 | 10.00 |
| 100 | 18 | 5.56 |
| 1,741.4 | 80 | 21.77 |
| 300 | 26 | 11.54 |
| 50 | 2.5 | 20.00 |
| 750 | 33.5 | 22.39 |
| 60 | 20 | 3.00 |
| 40 | 5 | 8.00 |
| 800 | 88 | 9.9 |
| 26 | 2 | 13.00 |
| 44 | 8 | 5.50 |
| 6,377.65 | 340 | 18.76 |

Data drawn from John Money (ed.), *The Chronicles of John Cannon Excise Officer and Writing Master*, two vols (Oxford, 2010)

was very likely a rise in the number of very local legal writers who did not need to engage in litigation.[54]

The importance of the mortgage as a source of credit in eighteenth-century society had already been identified by the economic historian B. L. Anderson by the late 1960s. Anderson was one of the first historians to point out the importance of credit in English society at the time. He investigated this issue because he was interested in capital formation during the Industrial Revolution rather than changes in the credit system of the seventeenth century (which had yet to be analysed). But, crucially for our purposes, the majority of the evidence for Anderson's study came from attorney's records from Lancashire, and their link to investment in

[54] Miles, 'Eminent practitioners', p. 476, n.10; Brooks, 'Law, lawyers and social history', p. 183.

new industry and trade through Liverpool.[55] He used the specific examples of attorneys Isaac Greene (1679–1749) and John Plume (1670–1763), who were actively engaged in arranging credit in the first half of the eighteenth century. Both of these individuals came from yeomen families. Greene drew most of his clients from landed society, arranging mortgages for them – but, with his earnings, he also bought land himself and invested in glassmaking.[56] Plumbe, whose accounts survive, was more involved in lending, both on his own account and for others to individuals from a wide range of society. Although, in terms of numbers, the majority of his activity was done using long-term lending on bonds, his business was secured by a number of larger mortgages. In 1732, Plumbe's lending on bonds was worth £739 12*s*. 2*d*. compared to four mortgages worth £318. However, by 1757, the value of his mortgage lending had risen to £2,990 – still only for four mortgages, but now with one for £2,190 on an entire estate. At the same date, his lending on bonds was worth slightly less at £2,700.[57] Most importantly, although Anderson noted that while Plume was also active in earning fees from the 'more orthodox' practice of the law as an attorney in Liverpool, representing clients in lawsuits, his business activities were founded on land ownership and, through the purchase of estates and other land, rent became his chief source of income.

Anderson's findings were forcefully confirmed in two important articles published by M. Miles in the early 1980s on the role of country attorneys and the money market by the mid-eighteenth century.[58] Miles's studies of two West Riding attorneys shows that one made 47 per cent of his profits from conveyancing and the other, 40 per cent, in comparison to 25 per cent and 13 per cent, respectively, derived from litigation. Also in an examination of the securities held by John Howarth on behalf of his clients from 1762 to 1796, the amounts of mortgages were consistently between two and ten times as valuable as those on bonds.[59] In 1789, for instance, John Howarth held £12,800 worth of clients' mortgages and £2,140 on his own behalf. In addition to this, Henry Horwitz and Patrick

[55] B. L. Anderson, 'Provincial aspects of the financial revolution of the eighteenth century', *Business History* 11 (1960), 11–22, B. L. Anderson, 'Money and the structure of credit in the eighteenth century', *Business History* 12 (1970), 85–101; Anderson, 'Early capital market', pp. 223–255.

[56] Anderson, 'Early capital market', pp. 229–230.

[57] Ibid., pp. 236–240.

[58] M. Miles, 'The money market in the early Industrial Revolution: the evidence from two West Riding attorneys, c. 1750–1800', *Business History* 23 (1981), 127–146.

[59] Ibid., pp. 136–137; Miles, 'Eminent practitioners', p. 474.

Polden have found that, in the court of Chancery between 1627 and 1735, the number of suits over debts and bonds dropped, while those concerning estate matters and other business contracts rose.[60] Rural estates could be mortgaged for thousands and urban properties, for hundreds of pounds.[61]

This demonstrates how lawyers played a crucial role in shifting the way in which local credit was organised. Lawyers had always played a role in credit because they had the enormous advantage of knowing more about most people's credit than anyone else in their communities owing to their involvement in credit litigation, and hence they were in an excellent position to be able to judge the creditworthiness of borrowers. This allowed them to act as local brokers, helping people with their financial transactions by lending on bond. In King's Lynn in the 1680s, lawyers sued far more than any other group: an average of 17.6 times each, or almost twice as often as any other occupation. Most of this litigation was initiated by only two men: Thomas Pepys and Thomas Selfe. Pepys sued seventy-six times, more than any other plaintiff, while Selfe sued on forty-six occasions. Thomas Pepys was also probably taking money in on bond, and lending it out again, also on bond, for a small commission, but perhaps in different amounts to various people at the legal rate of interest.[62]

But such lending was subsidiary to the earning they made from litigation. The account book of Hitchin attorney George Draper for 1671–1694 shows how active he was in prosecuting suits for litigants. In just one year, he was engaged in 1,954 transactions; in the index to his account book, there were 1,286 clients listed from Hitchin and much of the surrounding countryside around the town who owed him amounts as small as a few shillings.[63] Certainly, lawyers could grow very wealthy on such fees, as well as their lending, but, as the business of conveyancing expanded, it offered better opportunities for earning

[60] But there was legislation in 1697 that allowed the common law to give the kind of relief on penal bonds that was previously available only in Chancery, so the fall in litigation over such matters was not necessarily indicative of a decline in overall litigation: Henry Horwitz and Patrick Polden, 'Continuity or change in the court of Chancery in the seventeenth and eighteenth centuries?', *Journal of British Studies* 35 (1996), 24–57, p. 35.

[61] Anderson, 'Provincial aspects', pp. 16–19; Anderson, 'Money', pp. 237–239, 245.

[62] The account books of attorneys Thomas and William Harvey of Taunton demonstrate that they were doing just this in the 1660s and 1670s: Somerset Record Office, DD/SP/363.

[63] George Draper's Day Book 1671–1694, Hawkins and Co., 7/8 Portmill Lane Hitchin; Brooks, *Pettyfoggers*, pp. 105, 248.

more through fees. In addition, it encouraged lawyers to actively participate in the land market both as lenders and purchasers of land. Lending offered opportunities to purchase land from those who became too indebted to become rentiers.[64] Almost all conveyancing was made complicated by the land law and this could be used to justify high fees. A good example can be drawn from Cannon. In 1736, he recorded that he was sent for by another clerk of the solicitor William Nicholls, Thomas Merriot, who was lending £50 (actually the money of his wife) to one William Payne through a mortgage on 2 acres of meadow. To facilitate the transfer, Cannon needed to consult both the deed of transfer to a former mortgagee, one John Giblet (which Cannon had written up), and a copy of the will, dated 19 September 1721, of Benjamin Payne of Huntspill, who was the father of William Payne. According to Cannon, it was by this will that the title of said meadow was conveyed. Both Cannon and Merriot acted as witnesses to the new deed of transfer, and Cannon noted that Merriot's legal bill was £3 11*s.* 2*d.*, although he did comment that this 'was looked on as a price extravagant and unreasonable'.[65] Compared to the fees that an attorney, as opposed to a mere clerk, could charge, however, it seems quite small. In 1741, Cannon reported drawing up two large bills for William Nicholls to be paid by one Mr Cadby of Shapwick, in which were noted many days out on business for which he charged a guinea a day. In addition, a bill for 100 guineas was made for Nicholls's work in negotiating a marriage contract with his wife, which involved payment through a mortgage![66]

Miles also argued that, by the mid-eighteenth century, the court fees that could be earned from litigation were low in comparison to earnings from conveyancing. Even though fees had risen, litigation in local courts might earn between £2 and £5 for the few cases that went all the way to trial.[67] For most other suits resolved in the early stages of litigation, fees of less than £1 would have been earned. In the central courts, fees were greater, but suits could take months or years before they could be realised, whereas fees could be charged immediately for conveyancing work. As one attorney wrote as early as 1707, 'I confess there are many other gainful Businesses fall in a Practiser's Way, as Conveyancing,

64 Miles, 'Money market', p. 137.

65 Money, *Chronicles of Cannon*, p. 268.

66 Ibid., p. 616.

67 Champion, 'Recourse to the law', pp. 184–185; Craig Muldrew, 'Credit, market relations, and debt litigation in late seventeenth-century England, with particular reference to King's Lynn', PhD thesis, University of Cambridge (1990), pp. 371–384.

Court-Keeping, the Opportunity of picking good Bargains out of the many Estates he sees sent to Market, & c. by which some gain great Wealth; but these . . . arise not by Fees as an Attorney or Sollicitor'.[68] The average earnings of Yorkshire attorney John Eagle in 509 High Court actions between 1748–1758 and 1768–1780 was less than £3.[69] In Chancery, earnings were much higher, but in one such suit (where Eagle was owed £120), which lasted from 1759 until 1772, he complained that, 'if I am paid no more than common fees, I shall have nothing for my Trouble, but be more a looser than gainer by ye Cause'.[70] By the late eighteenth century, there were so fewer precedents in the precedent books kept by Yorkshire attorneys that those attorneys became unsure how to proceed.[71] From the point of view of supply and demand, this suggests that lawyers put up their fees for litigation to make the value of the time spent in that activity more closely match the earnings from time spent on conveyancing. Thus, as the number of suits started to fall, poorer clients and smaller suits no longer became worthwhile, and litigation was increasingly engaged in only by wealthier plaintiffs who could pay higher fees, as Brooks and Champion suggested.[72]

Conveyancing was also business done for those wealthy enough to have extra capital to lend and those with property to mortgage. Between 1768 and 1780, John Howarth, another West Riding attorney studied by Miles, did conveyancing work for 55 gentry clients, 201 clients from the upper middling sort, such as yeomen clothiers and shopkeepers, 61 clients of the lower middling sort, such as weavers and craftsmen, and only 9 clients from poorer occupations. Such work consisted of: searching for titles; leases to tenants; mortgages; marriage settlements; wills and trusts; buying and selling of property; money-scrivening; partnership agreements; settlements of estates; settling partnership accounts; releases; deeds of feoffment; bonds; transfers of property and mortgages; petitions to enclose land; deeds of appointment; fines; and indentures of apprenticeship.[73]

In addition to conveyancing, there was also a lot of work created by the parish 'state' in the operation of the settlement laws, and justices of the

68 Miles, 'Eminent practitioners', p. 492.
69 Ibid., pp. 498–499.
70 Ibid., p. 494.
71 Ibid., pp. 489–490.
72 Brooks, 'Litigation, participation and agency', pp. 164, 167–168, 180; Champion, 'Recourse to the law', pp. 184–186, 190.
73 Miles, 'Eminent practitioners', pp. 478, 500.

peace often consulted an attorney. In addition, already active employments such as estate stewards and bailiffs who ran manorial courts became more demanding with the enlargement of capitalist farming in the south, which involved the work of keeping accounts and dealing with legal matters necessary to improve land with customary rights, such as drainage or the transformation of waste, would have required more legal work. Also, new legal work emerged in the post-1750 period with parliamentary enclosure and the establishment of navigation and turnpike trusts and schemes. Much litigation now actually concerned new situations, such as the valuing of lands through which canals were to be cut. It also became more common for an attorney to offer paid advice. The Day books of John Howarth reveal some 579 instances of giving advice between 1768 and 1780, but, of this, fully 40 per cent concerned conveyancing, and 24 per cent on parish business and business for justices of the peace. Only 18 per cent related to potential litigation that might involve debt.[74]

Michael Birks, in *Gentlemen of the Law*, and Robert Robson, in *The Attorney in Eighteenth-Century England*, also both looked very generally at some eighteenth-century attorneys through surviving papers to provide examples of the social role of their subject.[75] They also both noted the importance of conveyancing and other scrivening work over litigation. One good example is Robert Hobbes of Stratford-upon-Avon, who left a diary covering 1800–1803. The diary opens when he was then aged nearly 27. Besides his legal work, he rented some land, which he cultivated to provide food for his family and fodder for his horses. He was a churchwarden and clerk to the local justices, and he became town clerk as well. Without doing very much work, he was earning just over £200 a year. As Birks put it, 'with a gig in his stable and a cellar stocked with port and other wines he managed to live a life which most solicitors would envy today'.[76] Conveyancing formed the greater part of Hobbes's business. Occasionally, he negotiated a loan, such as when he procured £200 for a Miss Ruding, and lent his name to the bond that secured it. But, by 1800, there was a local bank that now looked after the financial affairs of most people in Stratford, including Hobbes himself, much reducing the need for attorneys to lend on bond rather than through conveyancing. Sometimes, he engrossed his own conveyances, as well as

[74] Ibid., pp. 480–490.

[75] Michael Birks, *Gentlemen of the Law* (London, 1960); Robert Robson, *The Attorney in Eighteenth-Century England* (London, 1959).

[76] Birks, *Gentlemen of the Law*, pp. 199–200.

drafting them; on other occasions, he sent the drafts to stationers for engrossing on parchment. The tedious job of drafting deeds, which often ran to sixty folios, was compensated by the knowledge that the size of his fee depended on the length of the document. Arranging transfers of shares in the new Birmingham and Warwick Canal Company was also profitable. Drawing up wills might bring in as much as two guineas, which he looked upon as 'a very handsome fee'. Two entries from the dairy give an indication of his lifestyle:

> *Monday, April* 28. Very fine morning – paid Harrison for shaving me 8s. od. paid Jeffs for jobs is. 6d. Kempson called this morning and executed his mortgage to me for £100 and I included my bill of £8 9s. i d. in the amount. Worked at Richardson's case. Went out with new horse in the gig on Warwick Road and he performed well. Uxor and I to Dr. Brees to tea and cards and I won 9s. 6d. at commerce. The Doctor gave me his note for £44 on settling Beansale Exchange.
>
> *May* 2. Very busy in garden sticking pease. Saw Bellamy at Charles Taylor's and drank wine and tea with them. Sent case and letter to Richardson in his business. Went to Morris's to supper ... after went to Goate's and stayed till 12. Made Walker's will and attested Execution of it.[77]

Life was not always so bucolic and peaceful, however. The practice of lending on mortgage led to increasing complaints about lawyers. These had previously been about stirring up vexatious and costly suits to earn more fees, but now they became charges of sharp practices concerning mortgaging. Attorney John Plume, mentioned earlier, was able to use his arrangement of mortgages to gain land as payments for debts. As an example, Plume lent one Alexander Hesketh of Aughton £2,400 in 1715; by 1718, Hesketh had agreed to purchase manorial rights of two estates as payment. At the same time, Hesketh mortgaged a number of properties to Plume, who was eventually able to foreclose between 1724 and 1744, although only after the former put up a long legal defence and presumably after he became so indebted that it was difficult for him to continue annual interest payments.[78] John Cannon, on more than one occasion, complained of the 'treacherous and foul practice in the law' of his employer, attorney William Nicholls, and also accused him of making up a mortgage 'full of gross blunders and erasures' in 1729.[79] This bad

[77] This is a summary of the description given in Birks, *Gentlemen of the Law*, pp. 200*ff*.

[78] Anderson, 'Early capital market', pp. 242–243.

[79] Money, *Chronicles of Cannon*, pp. 557, 618. When discussing the parish accounts, Cannon further claimed that 'Mr. William Nicholls had undertook to erase, alter, put

reputation seems to have come to a head in the case of the complicated mortgage of one Henry Scrace. Scrace seems to have been continually in debt and, although he had come into the possession of quite a large farm of 86 acres, he mortgaged it to various people for increasing amounts from £260 to £1,300 over the years, paying interest of 5 per cent, until it was eventually foreclosed upon in 1747, after his death.[80] In the very last entries in his *Chronicles* from 1742, Cannon reported that William Nicholls had negotiated a bond of £200 to help Scarce out, but had run off without delivering the money, leaving Scrace at the hands of creditors:

> He has left a strong rumour of many vile practices by him acted of late, especially concerning the affair of Henry Scrace and the Clarks . . ., that he had drawn the said Scrace and one of the Clarks into a bond of £200 to one Mr. Thomas Cooth of Shepton Malet, and to colour the matter made himself a surety in the said bond, and as soon as it was executed swept the money into his hat and kept it for his own use, which act proved of great damage to Scrace. For the mortgagees and his creditors levyed execution on his estate and goods, the latter of which one Richard Creed, a sheriff's officer, sold at low value; but the said Scrace and others took up their asylum at the house of one Pearl.[81]

At the end of the *Chronicles*, Scrace was holed up in:

> . . . the house of one Pearl in Glaston who sold spirituous liquors and was also under a cloud; and keeping firearms dared any to attempt the taking them and that the said Nicholls pretended they had a design on his life because in the evening they fired pistols and guns etc. Besides the aforesaid several others loudly exclaimed against him for his unjust dealing. Also at this time he was indebted to me in above £3 for engrossing and writing which he had at several times employed me to do for him.[82]

They remained there for a number of days, playing cards and 'living in a riotous manner, not regarding how the world went or how their just debts ought to be satisfied, but on the contrary gaming, cheating and shuffelling every person that came into their company'.[83]

This example demonstrates that credit secured on mortgage could provide temptation both in the form of going further into debt while

out and set in several matters and things (especially his own unjust and extravagant bills, etc.) that had been denied at Easter last and also had blotted and defaced the book in a very shameless matter with tallow grease and dirt': ibid., pp. 289–290.

80 Money, *Chronicles of Cannon*, p. xci (index).

81 Ibid., p. 695.

82 Ibid.

83 Ibid.

the security of land was there and, for a lender, especially a sharp attorney like Nicholls, encouraging more lending until the equity of redemption would no longer hold. When describing his own family lineage, Cannon noted how his great-uncle had lost his substance in the last half of the seventeenth century by committing all of his money not to his family, but:

> ... to the hands of one John Hole a neighbour, by some called Broker Hole, an appellation given him from his Calling who made it his Sole business to put out other person's moneys on security to himself & in his own name as if really his own making them to give Releases to himself for their own money by which indirect practice he got great substance and ill name and odious to all knew him. This Hole had his deserved End, for falling from his horse at a gate in the road (since called Hole's Gate) he break his neck ... which gave our Author to reflect that a secret Curse goes with goods ill-gotten, and as the proverb *What is gotten upon the devil's back is spent under his belly.*[84]

By the 1730s, as Cannon's memoirs show, the country attorney had become a central fixture of local middling-sort village life, participating in the rounds of sociability that went together with parish administration, conveyancing and giving advice.[85] Although the centre of legal culture remained the Inns of Court and Westminster, and important jurists such as Blackstone and Lord Mansfield published legal treatises and gave important decisions, in many other ways there was a shift in the gravity of legal life away from the metropolis and major towns towards the wider nation, including the countryside and small towns like Glastonbury. The two attorneys studied by B. L. Anderson, for instance, were from Wavertree Hall and Childwell Hall in Lancashire. From being litigators centred on borough courts of record doing moneylending on the side, attorneys could really now be said to be proto-bankers, leveraging mostly rural land to create capital and a larger money supply. Also, in the previous century, the poor were quite active in making complaints in courts such as that of King's Lynn for a fee of 4*d*., which would have been done though one of the town attorneys. In contrast, by the eighteenth century, an attorney focusing on conveyancing would now be more likely to deal only with a poor client who was being evicted from a parish or petitioning a justice of the peace over a pension, or to be consulted by

84 Ibid., p. 8.

85 Craig Muldrew, 'The "middling sort": an emergent cultural identity', in Keith Wrightson (ed.), *The Cambridge Social History of England, c. 1500–c. 1750* (Cambridge, 2017), pp. 290–309, pp. 301–304; Henry French, *The Middle Sort of People in Provincial England 1600–1750* (Oxford, 2007), ch.4.

a justice engaged in summary justice for disagreements and small debts, not through litigation or negotiating a mortgage.[86]

In this way, the shift to conveyancing can certainly be seen as a part of a shift from the old communal regulatory regime, which stressed equality before the law, to a much more class-based system, secured by either landed property or buildings that could be mortgaged, or stored capital in the form of annuities bonds and shares. Such security meant the local small-scale credit could be turned into a form of paper currency that was trusted within small areas, which would have been an advantage to poor wage earners, who could then have become less dependent on oral trust or household goods, of which they had only a little. But it could also mean that they had less opportunity to sue over unpaid wages if an employer did not have enough credit to write bills that would be accepted in the community. At the same time, however, courts of requests evolved in towns with minimal legal involvement to allow a cheaper process to recover small debts without litigation, which was largely used by shopkeepers against poorer debtors.[87] The great variety of small-scale credit still common in eighteenth-century Birmingham can be seen in the descriptions of suits in the town's court of requests, written up by its most prominent judge, William Hutton. Hutton was a bookseller, not trained in the law, and the fact that this court was attacked and burned, along with Hutton's house, during the riots against non-conformists in 1791 is also testimony to an underlying resentment of such law.[88]

Christopher W. Brooks was always a historian who felt deeply that legal history was a part of social and political history.[89] This can equally be said of economic history. Rising court fees and the desire of shopkeepers for a cheaper, more expeditious, means of debt collection were certainly part of the decline in litigation, but since litigation had been the result of the expansion of informal oral credit, the decline in litigation was, first of all, a result of the shift towards different forms of written credit – informal bills, notes of hand and mortgages. Since attorneys could earn more from providing these services, the cost of litigation was

[86] Gwenda Morgan and Peter Rushton (eds), *The Justicing Notebook (1759–64) of Edmund Tew, Rector of Boulton* (London, 2000); Peter King, 'The summary courts and social relations in eighteenth-century England', *Past and Present* 183 (2004), 125–172.

[87] This is discussed in Finn, *Character of Credit*, pp. 202–227.

[88] William Hutton, *The Courts of Requests: Their Nature, Utility and Powers Described, with a Variety of Cases* (Birmingham, 1789), pp. 30–31; Finn, *Character of Credit*, pp. 202*ff.*

[89] This was the subject of his second monograph: Christopher W. Brooks, *Law, Politics and Society in Early Modern England* (Cambridge, 2008).

driven up. Credit was increasingly secured by the practice of the equity of redemption, which made mortgaging land much more attractive and common. This inevitably pulled much legal business into the countryside. Complex trust settlements and marriage contracts on the part of wealthier landholders also required expensive legal services, as did canals, turnpikes and parish business. Mortgages could, of course, also be raised on urban property and buildings, but with the rise of the courts of requests, much ligation over unpaid urban credit was now done outside strict common law pleadings of debt and assumpsit. Credit might have been more secure, but it was a security denied to the propertyless. The degree to which this process contributed to the formation of a middle 'class' identity, as opposed to the 'sorting' of the early modern period, is a pertinent one. To be middling sort in the sixteenth and seventeenth centuries was to have a reputation for trustworthiness in an insecure world of chains of debts. The question now needs to be asked: how much did security contribute to new personal and group identities based on the security of capital in addition to, or rather than, good credit? Any answer will obviously involve the role of legal practitioners in society.

12

# England and America

## The Role of the Justice of the Peace in County Durham, England, and Richmond County, Virginia, in the Eighteenth Century

GWENDA MORGAN

Between the Restoration of the Stuart monarchy and the American Revolution, the 'Old Dominion', as Virginia was known, developed a self-perpetuating county magistracy that dominated every aspect of the province's life through 'the structural mechanism of the county court' and 'the careful tending of its faithful magistrates'. Virginia, England's oldest and largest colony in North America, not only prospered during the eighteenth century, but also came to be considered 'the most English of all of British North American colonies'.[1] Although frequently asserted, the extent to which this was true has not been seriously examined by historians or legal scholars on either side of the Atlantic. One way of exploring this question is to examine the comparative experience of justices of the peace in the two different places.[2] This is possible thanks to the existence of two contemporary sources: one Virginian, *The Diary of Colonel Landon Carter of Sabine Hall 1752–1777*; and the other English, *The Justicing Notebook (1750–64) of Edmund Tew, Rector of Boldon.*[3]

Landon Carter's diary was a lengthy and broad-ranging diary, recording many aspects of his life and especially his fractious relationship with

[1] A. G. Roeber, *Faithful Magistrates and Republican Lawyers: Creators of Virginia Legal Culture, 1680–1810* (Chapel Hill, 1981), p. xv.

[2] Justices of the peace in England and lesser officials in London have received close attention from Norma Landau and Bob Shoemaker: Norma Landau, *The Justices of the Peace, 1679–1760* (Berkeley, 1984); R. B. Shoemaker, *Prosecution and Punishment: Petty Crime and the Law in London and Rural Middlesex, 1650–1725* (Cambridge, 1991).

[3] Jack P. Greene (ed.), *The Diary of Colonel Landon Carter of Sabine Hall, 1752–1778*, two vols (Charlottesville, 1965); Gwenda Morgan and Peter Rushton (eds), *The Justicing Notebook (1750–64) of Edmund Tew, Rector of Boldon* (Woodbridge, 2000).

his son, Robert Wormeley Carter. Jack P. Greene, the foremost historian of colonial America, argues that the diary (little of which survives for 1773–1774) is 'neither so complete as that of George Washington nor so light and entertaining as that of William Byrd II of Westover', but adds that 'it is more intimate and more revealing than either'.[4] By contrast, Edmund Tew's journal contains little reference to his family, although he was married twice and had a number of children – but it gives much detail about his life as a justice of the peace. Landon Carter of Richmond County, Virginia, and Edmund Tew of County Durham, England, resembled each other in some ways, but not in others. Both held high office on either side of the Atlantic, serving as justices of the peace and at roughly the same time. These 'gentlemen justices', as they were known, served in momentous times – a fact clearly recognised in Carter's journal, but missing in Tew's writings. Members of the landed gentry *did* serve as justices in County Durham, but, as Norma Landau has observed, they became less prominent in judicial activities, despite being sworn in as justices.[5] Tew noted with regret that his colleague John Burdon had retired from being an active justice to his country estate in the south of the county (at Hardwick Hall) and that other gentry justices, such as George Baker, essential to policing the growing seaport town of Sunderland, nevertheless lived some miles outside in his country house.[6]

Before turning to the diaries and their authors, something needs to be said about the communities in which they worked. Tew regularly attended quarter sessions held in the county seat of Durham. Although Durham was nominally a city, it was in reality rather a small town. Nonetheless, it was home to a cathedral, and held court sessions and frequent markets – features that were absent in Richmond County, Virginia. Towns such as Newcastle, Sunderland, South Shields and Darlington were significant urban centres, and urbanisation was an ongoing and dynamic process in the north-east of England. The population of Richmond County, Virginia, was also undergoing rapid population growth during the eighteenth century. Urbanisation was not part of the process, but the growth of slavery was significant. Half the population of the county were slaves at the time of the Revolution. Although the

4 Greene, *Diary of Landon Carter*, vol. 1, pp. ix–x; Rhys Isaac, *Landon Carter's Uneasy Kingdom: Revolution and Rebellion on a Virginia Plantation* (New York, 2004), p. 40.

5 Landau, *Justices of the Peace*.

6 C. S. Sydnor, *American Revolutionaries in the Making: Political Practices in Washington's Virginia* (New York, 1952), originally published as *Gentlemen Freeholders*, p. 63; Tew, *Notebook*, p. 74; Landau, *Justices of the Peace*, pp.140–144.

urban development of County Durham was limited, non-nuclear settlement characterised Richmond County, making the centrally located courthouse a convenient meeting place for the transaction of all types of business.[7] In this respect, it could be argued that court day, with its multiple functions, was much the same in County Durham as Richmond County. In both places, the days of the court's meetings were also times of great social gathering and interaction. As one dean of Durham Cathedral and justice of the peace, Spencer Cowper, recalled, when he entertained at the quarter sessions meetings, he had, counting his family, around a hundred people attending.[8]

In Virginia, the justices of the peace were 'the most numerous and widespread of the officeholders'.[9] Their power was vested in the county court – a judicial body that possessed legislative, executive and electoral power. Every variety of governmental power was lodged in the county court. Describing one such court, Sydnor identified it as the place that embodied local power, and in which indentures of bargain and sale and deeds of mortgage were executed.[10] Guidance was available to Virginia justices not only from the more experienced members of the bench, but also from publications such as George Webb's *The Office and Authority of a Justice of Peace*,[11] which offered them advice on a much wider variety of subjects that came before them than was available in English manuals.

The most significant difference between the powers of the two justices was that the Richmond County court on which Carter sat could try capital crimes. When the accused faced a charge of felony and was a slave, that person could be tried under a special commission, with justices acting as judge and jury. If the accused were found guilty and sentenced to death, execution could take place at the county courthouse. Virginia counties had received the power of life and death in relation to slaves as a consequence of a legislative Act of 1692.[12] In the counties of colonial Virginia, there was an assumption that these individuals' fate would be an example to others.[13] The power of English justices in county

[7] For the importance of county courthouses in Virginia, see Rhys Isaac, *The Transformation of Virginia, 1740–1790* (Chapel Hill, 1982).

[8] Edward Hughes (ed.), *Letters of Spencer Cowper, Dean, 1746–74* (London, 1956), p. 65.

[9] Sydnor, *American Revolutionaries in the Making*, p. 63.

[10] Ibid., p. 80.

[11] George Webb, *The Office and Authority of a Justice of Peace* (Williamsburg, 1736).

[12] W. Hening (ed.), *Hening's Statutes at Large, 1684–1710* (Philadelphia, 1823 [1692]), vol. III, pp. 102–103.

[13] Virginians who were free and white were still conveyed to the capital Williamsburg for felony trials, whose records are no longer extant.

courts was limited to hearing misdemeanours, such as assaults, and minor felonies, such as petit larceny, for which the convicted could be whipped, imprisoned or, after 1718, transported to the Americas. English justices also served as adjudicators in many kinds of Poor Law cases, in disputes between parishes over their responsibilities towards the poor or in answering appeals from the poor themselves. They also regulated public assets such as roads and bridges, jails and houses of correction. With regard to serious crimes, the felonies making up the capital cases went to the assizes, which, although held locally and tried before local juries, were under the control of itinerant judges, well trained in the law, who were sent on circuit either once or twice a year dependent on the size of the population being visited and the distance from London.[14] Although colonial Virginia briefly experimented with circuit judges in the seventeenth century, the practice was abandoned after a short time. The power of Virginia's eighteenth-century justices of the peace exceeded that of their English counterparts, in large part because of the need to ensure their power over slaves in a society in which slavery was widespread and there was a constant fear of slave insurrections.[15] Apart from the tobacco riots in the 1730s, social cohesion among Virginia's white population was strong.[16] There was no counterpart in English society to the phenomenon of slavery, but social unrest was pronounced. Local authorities were quick to request the presence of troops in towns in cases of local unrest, but anxious to see them depart just as quickly once a problem was resolved, since their presence could be a source of tension.[17] It could be argued that while the court system in Virginia was in the hands of the local gentry, that of England was controlled from the centre.

The county court in Virginia met monthly and sat for several days at a time, while the quarter sessions in England, its nearest equivalent, met for more limited periods and did much less. Virginia had no church courts, their functions being absorbed by the county courts, so matters relating to religion and the church could be brought before the county

[14] In the intervals between meetings of the assize courts, accused men and women could be detained in somewhat inadequate prisons: J. M. Beattie, *Crime and the Courts in England 1660–1800* (Oxford, 1986).

[15] Some punishments in the counties would have made little sense. Prisons were inadequate, being little more than small holding tanks, and likely to be burnt down often by their inmates.

[16] *Dublin Evening Post*, 22 July 1732.

[17] Gwenda Morgan and Peter Rushton, *Rogues, Thieves and the Rule of Law: The Problem of Law Enforcement in North-East England, 1718–1800* (London, 1998), pp. 191–213.

court. The Anglican church in Virginia was the established church. Its ministers had to be ordained by the Bishop of London and there were no native-born ministers in the colony until shortly before the American Revolution. The grand jury, an institution common to both England and Virginia, met twice a year in Richmond County in the early eighteenth century, but only once later in the century, and presented residents of the county for various infractions of the moral code. Carter himself was presented to the Richmond County court by the grand jury for swearing, was fined for the offence and found the prosecution shameful.[18] Residents of Richmond County were not inhibited in calling men such as Carter to account despite their wealth and status.

## Landon Carter

Born in 1710, Landon Carter was a key figure on the Richmond County bench. He was one of the sons of Robert 'king' Carter of neighbouring Lancaster County, reputedly one of the wealthiest planters, if not the wealthiest planter, in Virginia, with extensive connections to London and along the Atlantic coast. He was sent to school in England at the age of 9 and returned to Virginia aged 16, when his father determined on his career as a planter. The Carters were among the oldest and wealthiest families in the colony of Virginia. At the age of 22, Carter married Elizabeth Wormeley from a neighbouring county and of a status similar to himself. She was the first of his three wives, each of whom enhanced his possessions. His father made large grants of land to him in 1724 and again in 1730. He settled in Richmond County c. 1733–1734 and was appointed to the county bench in 1735, at the tender age of 25. Youth was no barrier to advancement in colonial Virginia. When vacancies occurred on the county bench, members of the quorum forwarded the names of their preferred candidates for replacements to the governor. Carter was impatient with dereliction of duty.[19] He quarrelled with some of his fellow justices and refused to sit with them for lengthy intervals (1742–1748, 1756–1758 and 1762–1769). He was easily offended and would withdraw from the bench if he believed the behaviour of others warranted it, although he remained a member. Carter continued to serve, albeit intermittently, until he withdrew from public life following his

[18] Roeber, *Faithful Magistrates and Republican Lawyers*, p. 89.
[19] Isaac, *Landon Carter's Uneasy Kingdom*, pp. 256–257.

failure to be re-elected to the House of Burgesses, the Virginia legislature, in 1768.

Appointment as a parish vestryman and colonel of the county militia followed in due recognition of Carter's status, giving him the opportunity to use 'his' militia, as he put it, to hunt for runaway slaves.[20] However, wealth and status were not guarantees of popular success in other areas. Election to the legislature, the House of Burgesses, proved elusive. He was rejected by the voters in successive elections in 1735, 1742 and again in 1748, but finally won a seat in 1752, with the public support of John Tayloe, the wealthiest planter in the county and a member of the Governor's Council. Carter sat in the legislature for significant periods of time, until he was unseated in 1768. He was a supporter of the Revolutionary movement and the author of a number of political tracts in support of opposition to British colonial policy. Carter prided himself on the quality of his tobacco, as did others of his status, displaying what T. H. Breen called a 'tobacco mentality'.[21] Carter died in 1778, at the age of 69, one of the '10 or 12 wealthiest planters in Virginia',[22] leaving an estate of over 50,000 acres, more than 500 slaves and 7 children. Such wealth was on a scale far beyond the reach, and doubtless the imagination, of a clerical magistrate such as Edmund Tew. Although Carter claimed that moderation was the guiding principle of his life, the distinctive characteristic of his personality was 'an intense and abiding distrust of men'. Carter, it would seem, became increasingly sensitive year by year. By the 1770s, the smallest slight 'deeply wounded his ego'. In 1747, the Reverend William Kay wrote to the Bishop of London, complaining about Carter's character:

> I found to my sorrow that I had one wealthy, Great, powerful Colonel named Landon Carter, a leading Man in my vestry, whom I could not reasonably please or oblige . . . I soon perceived that he wanted to extort more mean, low, and humble obedience, than I thought . . . consistent with the office of a clergyman, all his [boasts] and insults I little noticed, until he publicly declared that I preached against him (which I did not), cursed and attempted to beat me, saying my Sermon was aimed at him, because I preached against pride. I replied that I was glad he had applied it, for it was against every one that was proud. After this he was my

[20] Greene, *Diary of Landon Carter*, p. 291 (27 April 1766).

[21] T. H. Breen, *Tobacco Culture: The Mentality of the Great Tidewater Planters on the Eve of Revolution* (Princeton, 1985).

[22] Isaac, *Landon Carter's Uneasy Kingdom*, p. xvii.

> implacable Enemy and swore Revenge, that if he ever got a majority against me, he would turn me out of the parish . . . .[23]

A majority having been secured against him, Kay was declared dismissed and the two churches in his parish were nailed up to prevent him from entering. Kay sued Carter in the courts and won, even though Carter's resources were such that it was difficult to get the better of him. Furthermore, when Carter appealed the case to the Privy Council in London, he lost again. In 1764, Carter published a pamphlet entitled *The Rector Detected*, which opposed the Two Penny Act, an attempt to improve the pay of Virginia's Anglican minsters that was destined to fail. Carter fared better with a subsequent minister, the Reverend Isaac Giberne, for whom he provided accommodation until Giberne and his wife had a plantation of their own – but when Carter wanted a grandchild christened at Sabine Hall, Giberne refused.[24]

Landon Carter kept an extensive and wide-ranging diary, in which he recorded many facets of his life. Jack P. Greene has written that there was little 'in the general pattern of [Carter's] life to distinguish him from any number of his contemporaries among the Virginia gentry'.[25] Many of his entries dealt with farming; others, with domestic affairs, with the affairs of his children, with relatives and neighbours, with the climate, and, most importantly, with the various stages in the cultivation, harvesting and packaging of tobacco for export. Rhys Isaac found Landon Carter's farm journal highly informative: 'In the quality of his daily entries, and in his sustained recording over 22 years, Landon penned the most elaborated and revealing English-language farm journal coming down to us from the eighteenth-century age of agricultural improvement.'[26] Carter perceived himself, according to Isaac, to be a 'merciful father' of an extended family, in which Carter included servants and slaves.[27] Following the death of his third wife, he resolved not to marry again. The dispersed nature of settlement in Virginia left Carter a lonely and disappointed man. 'In Virginia,' he wrote in his diary, 'a man dyes a month sooner in a fit of any disorders because he can't have one soul to talk to.'[28] Although Carter

[23] Ibid., p. 249.
[24] Ibid., p. 250; Greene, *Diary of Landon Carter*, vol. 1, p. 261, n. 29.
[25] Jack P. Greene, *Landon Carter: An Inquiry into the Personal Values and Social Imperatives of the Eighteenth-Century Virginia Gentry* (Charlottesville, 1965), p. 10.
[26] Isaac, *Landon Carter's Uneasy Kingdom*, p. 57; Greene, *Diary of Landon Carter*, vol. 1, p. 4.
[27] Rhys Isaac, 'A discourse on the method: action, structure, and meaning', in *The Transformation of Virginia, 1740–1790* (Chapel Hill, 1982), pp. 323–256.
[28] Greene, *Diary of Colonel Landon Carter*, vol. 1, p. 242 (23 November 1763).

made references to meetings of the county court and to special called courts, he provided little information about the business of the court. Virtually nobody came to Sabine Hall, Carter's mansion in Richmond County, Virginia, to bring a complaint or to seek justice and his presence on the bench was variable.

## Edmund Tew

Born in Northamptonshire in 1700, Edmund Tew was the son of a rector, educated at Christ's Hospital, London, and the University of Cambridge. Although from the Midlands, he was appointed to the commission of the peace for County Durham in the north of England in 1750, having become Rector of Boldon in 1735. Clerical magistrates were not unusual in England and, in County Durham, took an increasingly prominent part in county business after 1750. By contrast, in Virginia, where anticlericalism had been particularly strong in the seventeenth century, clergymen were not eligible to serve on the bench. In many ways, Carter and Tew were very different. Whereas Landon Carter was a local man, belonging to a prominent and wealthy family with strong ties to the region, Tew was a newcomer in the north of England. Whereas Carter held a seat in the colonial legislature, Tew had not been elected by his local constituency nor (as far as is known) had he put himself forward to represent it at a national level.

Although his schedule could hardly be compared with that of Carter, Edmund Tew kept a record of summary justice as he exercised it in County Durham, which also suggests how busy a life he led. As an Anglican minister, Tew would have regular access to a local constituency. He would also meet with his fellow justices at the quarter sessions. He was therefore regularly visible on two public stages, as well as on special occasions when invited to preach in Newcastle. Compared with Carter, Tew's personality is more difficult to read, but his public record, while by no means complete, is far easier to trace. Morgan and Rushton have described how Tew acted as an arbitrator in many of the cases that came before him. He imposed solutions, levied penalties and ordered compliance. While Tew was resident in Boldon, many of his clients came from nearby Sunderland and South Shields. He was remarkably accessible, a few miles' easy walk from South Shields to the north and Sunderland to the south, so many may have sought him out as their first choice in the quest for justice or a resolution of local differences, even though other justices of the peace were available in the area. As noted, however, there were few magistrates easily accessible in these towns and some had retreated to their country estates. Presumably, Tew had established a sound reputation. Eighteenth-century magistrates had much to do, especially in the areas of conflict over employment, settlement and welfare.[29] English magistrates had enjoyed advice from manuals for justices of the peace since the early seventeenth century and, by Tew's time, the most favoured author was a magistrate from the north-west of England, Richard Burn, whose work had grown to three volumes after several editions: a copy is listed in the inventory of Tew's library at his death. This comprehensive guide offered technical details of the law, recommendations as to how justices should proceed and make their judgments, and advice on how they should carry out their administrative duties in their counties. Although he dealt extensively with criminal matters, Burn covered everything from the Poor Law, vagrancy and crime to the assize of bread and licensing of alehouses. He had become indispensable.[30]

Edmund Tew joined the bench of County Durham in 1750, when he was 50 years old. The appointment of clergymen to serve as magistrates was not unusual at this time. Tew took an active part in the magistracy, but what distinguishes him for modern historians was the record of summary justice he dispensed in his parlour and which survives in his justicing notebook. The notebook contains sketchy details of 1,400 warrants he swore out in the face of complaints brought to him in his house (the rectory, attached to the church at Boldon) from surrounding communities, between 1750 and 1764. Most complaints coming to him related to personal matters. Of these, there were 678 (that is, 46.3 per cent of the total), many of which (375, or 26.7 per cent) related to problems with the employment of servants.[31] Entries in Tew's notebook were as brief as Carter's were long, but they were confined to relevant details, such as when he issued a general warrant against James Young of South Shields for deserting his wife, or when he committed James Weddell for beating and chaining down his wife for two hours to a log (Weddell being persuaded 'to go into the king's service').[32]

[29] Gwenda Morgan and Peter Rushton, 'The magistrate, the community and the maintenance of an orderly society in eighteenth-century England', *Historical Research* 76 (2003), 54–77.

[30] Richard Burn, *The Justice of the Peace and Parish Officer*, three vols, 6th edn (London, 1758).

[31] Morgan and Rushton, 'The magistrate, the community', p. 61, table 1.

[32] Tew, *Notebook*, p. 183 (29 October 1763).

Although plaintiffs sought remedies at law and secured verdicts in their favour, more was at stake than the resolution of specific cases. It was the authority of the law that was paramount. Although Tew was not without his critics, it was the authority of the law that needed to be upheld. When John Bridon complained that he had not had justice from Tew in a dispute with a village constable, Bridon was locked up in the county jail and not released until he formally apologised in a dispute with a local constable, 'falling upon his knees and paying 10 shillings'. Disparaging the law was not to be tolerated any more than was insulting its local representative. John Bell, like Bridon, was confined in the county jail 'for calling me *fool etc.*, and afterwards insulting me and threatening me with the King's Bench'; two local businessmen, one engaged in loading the coal ships, interceded for Bell, and Tew forgave him 'upon his asking pardon upon his knees before all my parish and the constable', and paying a guinea to the funds for the poor of the parish.[33] In this way, Tew harnessed his authority as a Church of England minister to that of his role as magistrate to defend his dignity and public standing – a clear demonstration of how close church and state could be in practice, as well as theory, in this period in England.

These last examples suggest a crucial difference between the two justices: in both cases, their authority could be supported by extra-judicial sources, in that Carter, to put it rather crudely, had class and Tew had the church. They both operated in societies that were grossly unequal, but, ironically, the disparities were greater, and the rich elite smaller, in colonial Virginia than in northern England. Landon Carter was part of a very small set of families whose huge land- and slave-holding gave them dominance in the colony. There were aristocratic and grand gentry families in the north-east region of England, but Tew and others like him worked with a broader range of local people in business, shipping and farming who made up a practical population of employers and landholders who were deeply engaged in their local communities. Tew could rely on their support in times of difficulties, although, as in the case of John Bell, they could also act as peacemakers in disputes between the magistrate and local people. Carter seems to have behaved in ways more resembling his English aristocratic contemporaries in that he did not get his hands dirty with the everyday business of the law. They were all conducted on the bench and, to his credit, Carter did serve his time, but his private life did not record any judicial activities. The other major

33 Ibid., pp. 63, 72.

contrast between the two men's lives as justices lies in the institutional settings – particularly in the role of the Church of England. This can be exaggerated: both Virginia (and other colonies such as South Carolina) and England relied on the unit of the parish to administer financial and other assistance to the poor.[34] Despite this similarity, the church in Virginia had no system of ecclesiastical justice through which to prosecute immorality and neglect of religious duties. In fact, prosecutions for breaking the Sabbath had been common in the county courts of seventeenth-century Virginia. In England and Wales, the church courts retained some influence well into the eighteenth century and beyond (see Chapter 9 by Rushton, in this volume), and the church retained jurisdiction over crucial areas of people's personal lives, such as the proving of wills and testaments, and the validation of marriages. In most of the colonies, such matters had been secularised early in their history. As such, although Carter no doubt played a part in his parish – not least in choosing to quarrel with its priest, as mentioned – he was not embedded in it as an integral part of its everyday functioning as was Tew. The dual role of minister and magistrate was therefore typical of England – and, to some extent, in New England towns and communities, at least during the seventeenth century – but it had no counterpart in Virginia.

[34] Howard Mackey, 'The operation of the English old Poor Law in colonial Virginia', *The Virginia Magazine of History and Biography* 73 (1965), 29–40.

13

# Law and Architecture in Early Modern Durham

ADRIAN GREEN

This chapter explores the connections between law and architecture to illuminate the relationship between law and society as a lived experience. Christopher W. Brooks's scholarship demonstrated the myriad ways in which law entered the interstices of social life in early modern England. My approach focuses on the materiality of social relations and how buildings are embedded in cultural behaviour. The present volume offers an opportunity to discuss the legal dimension of early modern England's built environment. It should be possible to analyse the ever-evolving common law judgments, royal proclamations, parliamentary statutes, borough by-laws, manorial customs and church court procedures that touched upon building. Brooks showed the way towards such a study.[1] Contract and custom framed construction as much as materials and craft skills, while moral codes policed behaviour in and around buildings. Routinely respected and often communally agreed, legal rules were frequently the subject of dispute in England's diverse range of courts. Law structured the built environment wherever legalities constrained individual agency over how and where to build or live. The present chapter, however, focuses on buildings used directly for the conduct of the law.

The city of Durham, in the north of England, provides an apposite case study. As a palatinate, Durham had a unique cluster of ecclesiastical, common law and Exchequer courts, including its own court of Chancery. Civil and common lawyers, circuit judges and bishop's chancellors, along with their officials and clerks, created a unique legal milieu around Durham's great cathedral church and bishop's castle. When robed for court, the common and civil lawyers would have been distinguished by their professional dress from the gowned clergy and cloaked gentry in the same arena. Members of the region's middling sorts had cause to visit

[1] Christopher W. Brooks, *Law, Politics and Society in Early Modern England* (Cambridge, 2008), chs 11 and 12.

Durham on legal business, because its courts, lawyers and document makers provided vital services for inhabitants and propertied men and women with interests in the palatinate and diocese. No longer a place of pilgrimage for saints' shrines, post-Reformation Durham was a site of religious controversy, and had lost the Corpus Christi processions that brought together the town's trades in the tollbooth and the cathedral community. It was Durham's legal functions that provided a regional focal place after the Reformation. The diocese included the industrialising coalfield on the rivers Tyne and Wear, and Durham's relationship to the town of Newcastle upon Tyne was in some ways a provincial version of Westminster's relationship to the City of London.

Attorneys and solicitors built offices in the vicinity of Durham's courts, while civil lawyers worked and lodged within the cathedral complex, and circuit judges received hospitality from the bishop in his castle. Kenneth Emsley and Constance Fraser became familiar with this cast of characters while researching *The Courts of the County Palatine of Durham*: 'Having "lived" with the personnel of the bishop's courts for fifteen years we can virtually see them bustling around the Palace Green, riding to Westminster on appeals to the King's courts, or in the case of the bailiffs, warding off the brickbats of indignant wives resisting attempts to arrest their husbands.'[2] This chapter takes that imaginative potential seriously. To comprehend the social experience of architecture, we first need to establish its context.

## I

As a palatinate granted autonomy from the Crown after the Conquest, Durham had done justice in the name of the bishop rather than the king throughout the Middle Ages. Durham's peculiar palatinate functions remained in place between the great reforming decades of the 1530s and 1830s. Acts of Parliament substituted the name of the king for the bishop in 1536, but only ended the bishop's temporal authority (except in his court of Chancery) in 1836.[3] This apparent continuity was interrupted by the civil wars and interregnum in Crown authority between 1644 and 1660. Durham's courts collapsed following the Scots occupation in the summer of 1644 and resumed only from 1648. By 1654,

[2] Kenneth Emsley and Constance M. Fraser, *The Courts of the County Palatine of Durham from Earliest Times to 1971* (Durham, 1984), p. vii. See also G. T. Lapsley, *The County Palatine of Durham: A Study in Constitutional History* (Cambridge, MA, 1900).

[3] Emsley and Fraser, *Courts of the County Palatine*, p. 32.

Durham was operating like any other county under centralised authority and it remained more like a regular county integrated with the Westminster courts after the Restoration in 1660.[4] There was thus a contrast between law in Durham before the civil wars and after.

The palatinate courts operated in relation to the Council in the North before 1642, which served as the executive court for England north of the Trent. Durham Castle was designated one of its seats in 1537, with Bishop Tunstall as its president, although the King's Council generally met in the King's Manor at York. There, the former prior's lodgings of St Mary's Abbey were remodelled for the Council. Tunstall, a former diplomat, altered Durham Castle – adding a long gallery, smart dining chamber, bedchambers and chapel – possibly with the Council in mind.[5] In Elizabeth's reign, there were disputes between Durham and York over the authority of the palatinate versus the Council, but the bishop's prerogatives endured. By 1599, justices on the northern circuit operated within the palatinate by commission under the bishop's great seal; in 1610, 'after years of dispute and a charter which seemed to point in another direction', the Westminster Exchequer 'confirmed the bishop's exceptional sway over the city of Durham'.[6] Bishop Matthew's charter of 1601 had ceded episcopal supervision over the bishop's borough around the marketplace to a new mayor and common council with their own court. This charter was interpreted differently by Bishop James, whose bailiff, Edward Hutton, and steward, John Richardson, were physically prevented from opening a court in the tollbooth by the townsmen in September 1609. Action in the king's Court of Exchequer in 1610 favoured Bishop James over the Corporation. Henceforth, Durham's borough court remained much like the bishop's halmote courts on rural manors; all of which looked to the bishop's Exchequer for executive authority.[7]

[4] Durham University Library, Mickleton MS 38, f. 19; Durham Cathedral Add MS 244, ff. 1A and 17–21, Bishop's warrant to commission William Wall as attorney in temporal courts (20 September 1661), and Pardon to Thomas Davison, sheriff, re. restoration of temporalities to Bishop Cosin (16 May 1662).

[5] Nikolaus Pevsner and Elizabeth Williamson, *The Buildings of England: County Durham* (London, 1985), pp. 212–218; Martin Roberts, *Durham: 1000 Years of History* (Stroud, 2003).

[6] W. J. Jones, 'Palatine performance in the seventeenth century', in P. Clark, A. G. R. Smith and N. Tyacke (eds), *The English Commonwealth 1647–1640: Essays in Politics and Society Presented to Joel Hurstfield* (Leicester, 1979), pp. 189–204, at pp. 199–200.

[7] Emsley and Fraser, *Courts of the County Palatine*, pp. 20–23; Jones, 'Palatine performance', p. 192.

Freeholders sought to qualify the power vested in the bishop by representation in the House of Commons. The enfranchisement of Durham was initiated repeatedly in parliaments before the civil wars, but never passed; members of Parliament were granted under Lord Protector Cromwell from 1656, but denied by Bishop Cosin after 1660 and only permanently gained in 1674. Copyholders meanwhile sought to defend their rights with the aid of local lawyers. Brooks tells us that:

> [I]n the 1620s, a group of inhabitants from Weardale in county Durham petitioned the House of Commons asking that they be allowed to try a case concerning their tenant rights in any court in the realm rather than within the palatine jurisdiction of the Bishop of Durham, who was also their landlord', noting that 'the advice of local lawyers who helped them to use the royal courts at Westminster was of considerable aid in achieving these aims.[8]

Durham was thus connected to London via its legal community. Attorneys sought the advice of lawyers at the Inns of Court and Durham's legal year began in early September to enable judges to return in time for the Westminster law term. In 1638, Richard Matthew, attorney at Durham, sought the opinion of Edward Wright, counsellor at law of Gray's Inn, about his client Ralph Claxton's dispute over land with Richard Lilburne. Claxton had 'offered to prove the truth of his claim by trial by battle'; in August 1638, champions for Claxton and Lilburne 'appeared in array and cast into the court their gauntlets with five small pence in each. Their weapons were batons with sand-bags attached.'[9] The matter reached the Privy Council, which struggled to intervene once the mode of trial by battle had been initiated in Durham's ancient county court. By the late 1630s, however, such procedures were outmoded and, as Mervyn James argued, Durham had become a 'civil society'.[10] An important aspect of civility in early seventeenth-century Durham was the reforms made to the palatinate courts by common law judge Sir Richard Hutton. Educated at Cambridge and Gray's Inn, Hutton served as the bishop's temporal chancellor from 1608 to 1639. Appointed justice of the Common Please in 1617, 'he could not always be present in

[8] Christopher W. Brooks, *Pettyfoggers and Vipers of the Commonwealth: The 'Lower Branch' of the Legal Profession in Early Modern England* (Cambridge, 1986), p. 279; Alan Heesom, 'The enfranchisement of Durham', *Durham University Journal* 80 (1988), 265–285.

[9] Emsley and Fraser, *Courts of the County Palatine*, pp. 32–36.

[10] Mervyn James, *Family, Lineage and Civil Society: A Study of Society, Politics, and Mentality in the Durham Region, 1500–1640* (Oxford, 1974).

Durham, and sometimes held sittings in London', but remained 'to the community of Durham what an Ellesmere or a Coventrye were to England'.[11]

Tensions over authority vested in the church remained a subject of dispute throughout the seventeenth century. Durham lawyer Anthony Pearson, who presumably trained in London, although there is no record of him at the Inns of Court, set forth *The Great Cause of Tythes Truly Stated, Clearly Opened and Fully Resolved* (1657). In *A Few Words to All Judges, Justices, and Ministers of the Law* (acquired by bookseller George Thomason in 1654), Pearson asserted that if tithes continued, they should be used to relieve the poor.[12] An early Quaker, Pearson managed the sequestrated bishopric lands purchased by Sir Arthur Haselrig, but did little to resolve copyholders' grievances over 'tenant right'.[13] The bishop's rights to Durham borough were meanwhile confiscated by Parliament and sold to London aldermen, who in turn sold the tollbooth court to the Corporation for £200.[14] In 1660, Bishop Cosin resumed control of Durham city and became lord lieutenant of the county, denying representation in the House of Commons. Pearson returned to the Anglican fold and was appointed under-sheriff in 1664. He died the following year, presumably from plague, and was buried in St Mary-the-Less in South Bailey, in the heart of Durham's learned legal and clerical community within the outer bailey fortifications of Durham Castle.

Durham's law courts were heavily used before the civil wars, especially to resolve broken contracts and pursue suits of equity in Chancery. Just as Brooks found to be the case for civil litigation in King's Bench at Westminster, this surge in litigation was followed by declining use of the courts after the Restoration. Inhabitants of the palatinate increasingly favoured Westminster over Durham Chancery and, from the 1720s, wealthy estates were more often registered for probate at the Prerogative Court of Canterbury at Doctors' Commons in London rather than in Durham. In the eighteenth century, Durham's court of pleas

[11] Jones, 'Palatinate performance', pp. 194–195.

[12] See Richard L. Greaves, 'Pearson, Anthony (bap. 1627, d. 1666)', *Oxford Dictionary of National Biography* (ODNB).

[13] J. Linda Drury, '*Sir Arthur Hesilrige* and the Weardale chest', *Transactions of the Architectural and Archaeological Society of Durham and Northumberland* 5 (1980), 125–137; J. Linda Drury, 'More stout than wise: tenant right in Weardale in the Tudor period', in David Marcombe (ed.), *The Last Principality: Politics, Religion and Society in the Bishopric of Durham, 1494–1660* (Nottingham, 1987), pp. 71–100.

[14] Emsley and Fraser, *Courts of the County Palatine*, pp. 19–20, citing DUL Mickleton MS 37, ff. 137–140.

'became little more than a court for the recovery of petty debts', while 'Durham Chancery sat for only a few days in the year and its records were in a terrible state'; its judges, 'no longer of national standing', were reputed to be work-shy – 'one it is said, tried to apprehend John Doe and Richard Roe because of their litigious habits'.[15]

Common lawyers compensated for the litigation decline by specialising in conveyancing, aiding the region's buoyant industrial and agricultural economy with its rising rents.[16] Durham's attorneys and solicitors were a vital dimension of the commercial property market in north-east England, which, from 1711, advertised in the *Newcastle Courant* newspaper. In 1712, the Mickleton family of lawyers advertised 'CROOK HALL, near Durham, being pleasantly situated, with all manner of Conveniences, and good Gardens is to be Let. Enquire of Mr Robert Spearman or Mr Christopher Nicholson, Attorneys at Law in Durham'.[17] This shift in legal business from litigation to conveyancing was reflected in architecture, as well as print. Whereas Durham's court buildings were rebuilt through to the 1660s, newly built lawyers' offices were a more imposing presence from the later seventeenth century. Whether attending court or visiting the solicitor's office, Durham's legal dimension was at least as significant to visitors as the religious and political purposes of its architecture. Traders objected to proposals for the abolition of the palatinate in 1688 on the grounds that business would decline if people did not travel to Durham for court days.[18]

## II

Durham's courts were ranged along the west side of the bishop's palace green – the piazza between the bishop's castle on the north and cathedral to the south. In the early modern period, the entire bishopric complex had a legal function – from the bishop's consistory court in the cathedral to the bishop's Chancery court in the Exchequer, county court house on Palace Green and circuit judges lodged in Durham Castle. A spiritual

[15] Emsley and Fraser, *Courts of the County Palatine*, p. 3; Jones, 'Palatinate performance', p. 203; Brooks, *Pettyfoggers and Vipers*.

[16] David Levine and Keith Wrightson, *The Making of an Industrial Society: Whickham, 1560–1765* (Oxford, 1991); Adrian Green and Barbara Crosbie (eds), *Economy and Culture in North-East England, 1500–1800* (Woodbridge, 2018).

[17] *Newcastle Courant*, 27 August 1712.

[18] Gwenda Morgan and Peter Rushton, *Rogues, Thieves and the Rule of Law: The Problem of Law Enforcement in North-East England, 1718–1800* (London, 1998), p. 20.

chancellor oversaw the diocesan consistory court and registry, while a temporal chancellor oversaw the palatinate courts, which met in the county court house and Exchequer next to Durham Castle. Writs were issued from the Chancery court in the Exchequer for cases held in the courts of pleas (for civil matters) and gaol delivery (for criminal cases) in the county court house. Although the bishop continued to appoint the gaoler, sheriff, under-sheriffs and coroner, and could pardon felons, the palatinate courts fell into line with national patterns. In Elizabeth's reign, most court of pleas business concerned real estate, but – as part of the boom in credit across England's expanding economy – credit and debt were predominant after 1600. Criminal cases overseen by the sheriff and coroner became the responsibility of commissions of assize and justices of the peace, meeting as quarter sessions, with parties represented by attorneys.[19]

Across from the courts, to the east of Palace Green, were the lawyers' offices. Hearth tax records for 1674 record fifteen single-hearth households in 'High Bailey', likely documenting junior lawyers and clerks in lodgings.[20] The common lawyers occupied streets and courts in what was originally the outer bailey of Durham Castle, just as the Inns of Court in London arose on land occupied by medieval episcopal palaces. The great hall of Lincoln's Inn was a rebuilding of the bishop of Chichester's hall.[21] The parallel endured and the rebuilding of London's Inns after the Great Fire of 1666 generated a form of brick house closely matched in the detailing of brick-built lawyer's offices in Durham.

What is less obvious from the architecture is that the concentration of common and civil lawyers would have involved a degree of local training. The civil lawyers had their own apparatus for educating officials within the cathedral, but Durham never became institutionalised as a provincial Inn of Court. Yet it might have done so. When the cathedral fell vacant in 1644, it was immediately proposed as the home for a northern university. New College was begun in 1653 and, according to the statutes drawn up

[19] Emsley and Fraser, *Courts of the County Palatine*, p. 34.

[20] Adrian Green, Elizabeth Parkinson and Margaret Spufford (eds), *County Durham Hearth Tax Assessment Lady Day 1666* (London, 2006), p. cxxxiv.

[21] David Rollason, Margaret Harvey and Michael Prestwich (eds), *Anglo-Norman Durham, 1093–1193* (Woodbridge, 1994); Margaret Bonney, *Lordship and the Urban Community: Durham and Its Overlords, 1250–1540* (Cambridge, 1990); Mark Girouard, 'The halls of the Elizabethan and early Stuart Inns of Court', in J. E. Archer, E. Goldring and S. Knight (eds), *The Intellectual and Cultural World of the Early Modern Inns of Court* (Manchester, 2011), pp. 138–156, pp. 141–142.

in 1657, was to have included a faculty of civil law.[22] Oxford vigorously defended its teaching of civil law against this northern rival, which was effectively stifled before the Restoration in 1660. Had this Puritan university succeeded, further colleges would have been established. Durham Castle – with its hall, lodging chambers, chapel and gardens already resembling an early modern Inn of Court – might have become a law school for the North.[23]

## III

It is an intriguing question how far the common and civil lawyers got on in early modern Durham. Legal historians usually cite derisory attitudes among the common lawyers, but there remains a whiff of Whig history in the notion that common lawyers had the better arguments after the Reformation and through the civil wars. At Durham, the confluence of civil and common lawyers must have created a more fluid legal community. There were nevertheless differences in jurisdiction and differences in income. While civil lawyers – who were sometimes ordained clergy – were provided with accommodation as part of their sinecures within the church, common lawyers enjoyed higher incomes from fees, and were able to build and furnish houses as their own premises and property.[24] Despite their differences, common and civil lawyers worked together when cases crossed jurisdictions – such as an inheritance dispute originating in the consistory court, contested at common law in the county court, resolved as a suit of equity in Chancery. When Durham attorney Thomas Kinge leased the tithes of St Oswald's parish church in Durham, he was accused in the court of pleas of accepting payment in kind rather than cash and began a suit in the consistory court over withheld tithes.[25] In reading up on cases or tracking down documents, attorneys and solicitors would have used the cathedral library and diocesan registry, as well as, from 1670, the law books added to Bishop Cosin's library. Durham's legal community may even

[22] Durham Cathedral Library, Hunter MS.47, Durham College 1657 Statutes Cap. 22, specifies professors, tutors and fellows 'in Divinity Phisick Civill Law or other Faculty'.

[23] Charles Webster, *The Great Instauration: Science, Medicine and Reform, 1626–1660* (London, 1975), pp. 232–242 and 528–532; Blair Worden, *God's Instruments: Political Conduct in the England of Oliver Cromwell* (Oxford, 2012), pp. 153–154.

[24] Brooks, *Pettyfoggers and Vipers*, pp. 227–262.

[25] Emsley and Fraser, *Courts of the County Palatine*, p. 34.

have felt solidarity in the face of superior secular and ecclesiastical jurisdictions at York. Common lawyer Christopher Mickleton kept a book of precedents on the ecclesiastical jurisdiction between York and Durham, together with a list of painted windows in the cathedral, in which he baptised his sons and was buried in 1669.[26] The clergy, however, were not always sympathetic to rule by law. Bishop Cosin expressed an aversion to legal procedure, remarking to his secretary Myles Stapylton in March 1670: 'I cannot endure troubles at law, wherein I have been so badly used.'[27]

## IV

Before and after the interregnum, and at a time when the industrial and agricultural revolutions were taking place in Durham and Northumberland, the bishop's consistory court in Durham provided an amenity for the entire diocese, including the growing city of Newcastle upon Tyne and the lead mining parish of Alston in Cumberland, but excepting Hexhamshire and other peculiars under York.[28] Consistory courts handled the legal business of the church, and licensed midwives, surgeons and schoolmasters, as well as regulating matters relating to marriage. English bishops also had the right to charge a fee for registering wills for probate, which, in other European countries and English colonies, fell under secular notarial systems.[29] The leading authority on England's probate procedures was a civil lawyer active in Durham, Henry Swinburne (c. 1551–1624). Born in York and trained at Oxford, Swinburne spent the majority of his career at Durham and York. His *Treatise of Testaments and Last Wills* (1591) and *Treatise of Spousals, or Matrimonial Contracts* (1686, 1711) were based on his experience in the probate and marriage registry, and an unpublished manuscript on marriage survives among the Mickleton legal papers at Durham. Swinburne's

[26] DUL, Mickleton and Spearman MS 42, ff. 2r–5v and 7r–10v; Sheila Doyle, 'Christopher Mickleton (bap. 1612, d. 1669)', ODNB.

[27] Adrian Green, *Building for England: John Cosin's Architecture in Renaissance Durham and Cambridge* (Toronto, 2016), p. 88.

[28] Greg Finch (ed.), *A Pack of Idle Sparks: Letters from Hexham on the Church, the People, Corruption and Scandal, 1699–1740* (Hexham, 2013).

[29] J. G. A. Pocock, 'Schools and schoolmasters in some Durham episcopal records', *Durham Research Review of the Institute of Education* 3 (1952), 15–23; T. Arkell, N. Evans and N. Goose (eds), *When Death Do Us Part: Understanding and Interpreting the Probate Records of Early Modern England* (London, 2000).

printed works remained authorities on testaments and matrimony through to the nineteenth century.[30]

The bishop's spiritual chancellor sat as judge for the consistory court – a judicial appointment requiring legal training and not always an ordained cleric. The bishop's temporal chancellor, also a qualified lawyer, headed his palatinate courts. Surrogates acted as deputies to the spiritual chancellor, overseeing marriage licences and probate administrations in conjunction with the registrar, who administered the court and diocese. As the bishop's legal officer, the registrar required legal training, keeping a record of the bishop's formal acts in 'act books' and maintaining the registry, as well as providing legal advice.

The court met in the Galilee chapel of Durham Cathedral. Among its many responsibilities were the appointing of bedesmen to clean this sacred building. The architectural association of consistory courts to the fabric of English cathedrals suggests a spiritual connection. Administration of marriage, adultery and illegitimacy, and settling affairs at death, was perhaps more readily accepted by the populace as more appropriate for the church than for common lawyers jealous of the civil lawyers' jurisdiction.[31] Brooks tells us that Sir James Whitlocke, 'speaking in Durham Cathedral in 1628 before an audience that doubtless included many clergymen', 'argued that it was a mistake for anyone to think that the Reformation had greatly reduced the reach of the ecclesiastical courts. On the contrary, the fact that the jurisdiction now flowed from the king rather than the pope made it stronger than ever.'[32]

Even the door to the cathedral had a legal significance. Its sanctuary knocker symbolised the benefit of clergy available within, although the bishop's attorney-general could deny felons refuge.[33] Inside, the cathedral was a site of religious controversy. Puritan Peter Smart preached a sermon against his fellow cathedral canon John Cosin in assize week 1628, which became a national *cause célèbre* as Smart pursued Cosin over illegal innovations in worship in the church's Court of High

[30] Sheila Doyle, 'Henry Swinburne (c. 1554–1624)', ODNB; Sheila Doyle, 'An uncompleted work by Henry Swinburne on matrimony', *Journal of Legal History* 19 (1998), 162–172.

[31] Peter Rushton, 'Women, witchcraft and slander in early modern England: cases from the church courts at Durham, 1560–1675', *Northern History* 18 (1992), 116–132; Peter Rushton, 'The broken marriage in early modern England: matrimonial cases from the Durham church courts, 1560–1630', *Archaeologia Aeliana* 13 (1985), 187–196; Rebecca King, 'Rape in England, 1600–1800: trials, narratives and the question of consent', MA dissertation, Durham University (1998).

[32] Brooks, *Law, Politics and Society*, p. 225. Whitlocke also touched on tithe disputes.

[33] Emsley and Fraser, *Courts of the County Palatine*, p. 34.

Commission. Smart considered Cosin a bad influence and referred to Durham attorney Hugh Wright as 'the Arminian Hugh Wright', a 'disciple' of Cosin, who had erected a painted glass window of the crucifix in St Nicholas's church on Durham marketplace. Earlier, in 1614, Wright had been accused in the county court of overcharging his client Thomas Pearson, a Durham mercer.[34] Thus tensions over religion spilled into the micro politics of the city. Yet Smart and Cosin's bitter controversy over religious truth – focused on the installation of a font canopy, choir stalls and high altar, which offended Calvinist tenets of plain worship and double predestination – did not affect the business of the consistory court. Meeting in the Galilee at the west end of the cathedral, the court was accessible from the churchyard without needing to pass through the nave. Even so, the presence of Bede's tomb in the Galilee must have stirred memories of the Reformation, when king's commissioners removed the bejewelled shrine. Symbolically righting a wrong, Cosin placed a new tombstone with a Latin inscription on the occasion of the king's visit in 1633.[35] We can only wonder how the arcaded Romanesque architecture of the Galilee was regarded by users of the room. The plainness of Bede's tomb amid whitewashed walls covering pre-Reformation wall paintings were surely inescapable signs of the post-Reformation character of the church and its courts.

Public entrance to consistory courts was separate from religious space in English cathedrals. While officials passed from the cloisters through the cathedral into the Galilee, people on business to the court used the public entrance facing Palace Green. At York, the consistory court met in the south transept of the minster, but was accessed via the Galilee porch without passing through the church. At Chester, the consistory court was entered via a porch on the south side of the cathedral. Durham's diocesan court was presumably arranged similarly to the surviving court fittings installed at Chester in 1636 – with a central table enclosed by panelling, headed by a raised bench for the chancellor, and further benches for officials and clerks.[36]

Throughout the diocese, local officials known as apparitors were responsible for reporting matters to the registrar, including estates

[34] Ibid., p. 17; Green, *Building for England*, p. 42.

[35] Green, *Building for England*, pp. 48–49; inscription printed in George Ornsby (ed.), *The Correspondence of John Cosin D. D. Lord Bishop of Durham, Part I* (Durham, 1869), pp. 296–297.

[36] Historic England, *Law Courts and Courtrooms 1: The Buildings of the Criminal Law* (Swindon, 2016), p. 7.

eligible for probate. Given the low proportion of estates entered, it was evidently left to executors to register wills and provide inventories and accounts. But the jurisdiction mattered: intestate inheritance followed the rules of the civil law, whereby children (or siblings of the unmarried) received equal portions and widows were entitled to a third of the goods. By 1500, this no longer applied in the province of Canterbury, where a man had freedom over his goods, but it remained active in the province of York up until 1692.[37] By the eighteenth century, Durham was integrated with national practice.

The oddity of the English inheritance system was that bishops had a jurisdiction only in moveable goods, while real estate came under the common law. The tide of probate registration rose in Elizabeth's reign and continued to flow through ecclesiastical registries up until the early eighteenth century, when the need to settle debts and hence estates apparently normalised without the need for formal enforcement. Paralleling the rise and fall in civil litigation over contract and credit, few probate inventories were registered at Durham after 1720. Despite proposals to standardise the process by Thomas Cromwell in the 1530s and in the 1650s, probate remained with the church up until 1858.[38]

Durham's consistory court preceded the standardisation of time. Legal terms followed the festivals of Hilary, Easter, Trinity and Michaelmas, according to the calendar of saints' days. But the men involved in making documents submitted to the court were agents of rationalisation. One Durham scrivener, Ralph Tailor, provided a service to the dying in Newcastle upon Tyne during the 1636 plague by submitting their wills to the registry at Durham.[39] Later, the registry archive was kept in a stone lean-to built on to the exterior of Durham Cathedral between the north porch and western tower next to the Galilee. Shown on an undated eighteenth-century painting now in Durham Castle, and engravings published in 1786 and 1801, this single-storey structure with a central door, two windows and a stone slate roof was a smart addition to the cathedral fabric. Its architecture indicates a late seventeenth- or early eighteenth-century date of construction. Its public prominence

[37] A. L. Erickson, *Women and Property in Early Modern England* (London, 1993), p. 28.

[38] Arkell et al., When Death Do Us Part; Craig Muldrew, *The Economy of Obligation: The Culture of Credit and Social Relations in Early Modern England* (Basingstoke, 1998), pp. 22, 103–104; Durham probate records calculated from the North-East Inheritance Database (http://familyrecords.dur.ac.uk/nei/).

[39] Keith Wrightson, *Ralph Tailor's Summer: A Scrivener, His City and the Plague* (New Haven, 2011).

underscores the value attached to documents generated in association with the cathedral and its court; these documents were removed to a new Gothic Revival diocesan registry on the site of the county court house in 1820.[40]

## V

The colonnaded county court on Palace Green – 'one of the city's major architectural losses' – provided Durham with its 'sessions house', serving the county palatine of Durham, including its detached portions in Northumberland and Yorkshire.[41] Not all English counties had a dedicated court house and many made do with pragmatic arrangements in town halls or even judges' houses.[42] In Virginia, where there were no church courts, county courts were integral to the process of colonisation, and a key component of legally sanctioned settlement and slave-holding. Hanover County court house (1735) bears a resemblance to Durham's early modern county court (built 1588 and rebuilt 1664).[43] The two buildings share an architectural form that followed their function. Both were imposing buildings: an exaggerated single storey beneath a hipped roof at Hanover; attic windows and a roof lantern lighted a large central hall within the Durham court house. Both were fronted by an open arcade providing a public space outside the court for people to wait, converse and make deals.[44] The columns on Durham's Elizabethan court

[40] Durham University DURUC.1924.80, 'North Prospect of Durham Cathedral'; Peltro, 'The cathedral church of Durham', in Henry Boswell (ed.), *Complete Historical Descriptions . . . of the Antiquities of England and Wales* (London, c. 1786); J. Carter, 'Elevation of the north front of the cathedral church at Durham (1801)'; Pevsner and Williamson, *County Durham* (London, 2002), p. 244. Probate registry documents are now held by Durham University, with digital images on the North-East Inheritance Database.

[41] Roberts, *Durham*, p. 116; Green, *Building for England*, pp. 86–87; Emsley and Fraser, *Courts of the County Palatine*, pp. 12–20.

[42] Christopher Chalkin, *English Counties and Public Building, 1650–1830* (London, 1998); Historic England, Law Courts and Courtrooms 1; Clare Graham, *Ordering Law: The Architectural and Social History of the English Law Court* (Burlington, 2003), pp. 127–128, 145, 353.

[43] Durham University Library, Mickleton & Spearman MS 20, ff. 231–232, details erection of new sessions house with measurements; printed in George Ornsby (ed.), *The Correspondence of John Cosin D. D. Lord Bishop of Durham, Part II* (Durham, 1872), pp. 382–383.

[44] See A. G. Roeber, 'Authority, law and custom: the rituals of court day in Tidewater, Virginia, 1720 to 1750', *William & Mary Quarterly* 37 (1980), 29–52; Carl R. Lounsbury, '"An elegant and commodious building": William Buckland and the design of the Prince

house loggia were repeated in the 1664 rebuilding for Bishop Cosin.[45] Applying Renaissance architectural orders to a court house signified learning in a place of justice. Bishop Cosin referred to the windows as being in the Italian manner, while its interior 1660s woodwork may well have resembled the town court fittings in Newcastle upon Tyne's guildhall, built in 1655 with a double hammerbeam roof.[46] Durham's county court house was architecturally symbolic of the law inside and out.

County courts were held fortnightly before the sheriff as sole judge, with business concentrated on three court days called 'jury days'. The law diary of John Spearman, court officer and under-sheriff from 1674, indicates that the court continued to meet fortnightly before the sheriff and under-sheriff after the Restoration. Judges were of national standing when the session of the court of pleas coincided with the circuit assizes. More often, the bench was a panel of local gentlemen, including the bishop's legal officers. Justices of the peace on Durham's magisterial bench were likewise legally trained and university-educated officials from the palatinate administration alongside county gentry.[47]

Tensions between the city and bishop surfaced over rebuilding the Durham county court (or sessions) house on Palace Green and the guildhall (or tollbooth) on Durham marketplace in the 1660s as part of Bishop Cosin's programme for restoring Durham as an exemplar of episcopal authority. Bishop Tunstall had moved the tollbooth (previously a free-standing timber-frame building) to the western side of the marketplace c. 1535 and the county court house had been built in 1588. Both buildings were rebuilt at Bishop Cosin's behest in the 1660s. Tensions between the guildsmen, craftsmen and bishop are documented in the case pursued in Chancery in 1669 against York bricklayer Huira Marshall

William county courthouse', in *Essays in Early American Architectural History: A View from the Chesapeake* (Charlottesville, 2011), pp. 97–109.

[45] Courthouse illustrated in Durham University DURUC.1924.80, undated painting of the 'North Prospect of Durham Cathedral'; Bodliean Library, Gough Maps 7, f. 2B, Bok engraving of Durham, c. 1665; Durham Cathedral Library, Thomas Forster and James Mynde, View of Durham Cathedral and the Bishop's Palace Green (1754). Roberts, Durham, p. 116, provides a reconstruction drawing.

[46] Green, *Building for England*, pp. 69, 71–73, 87–88; Nikolaus Pevsner, I. A. Richmond, John Grundy, Grace McCombie, Peter Ryder and Humphrey Welfare, *The Buildings of England: Northumberland* (London, 1992), pp. 443–445.

[47] Emsley and Fraser, *Courts of the County Palatine*, pp. 19–20 and 37, citing William Hutchinson, *History of Durham* (London, 1789), vol. II, pp. 278–279; Ushaw College Library, Durham, MS VII A 1 17, ff. 9, 18r–v; Durham University Library Mickleton MS 78; Diana Newton, *North-East England 1569–1625: Governance, Culture and Identity* (Woodbridge, 2006), pp. 53–65.

for working in Durham without being a freeman, at Bishop Cosin's instigation, and in the guilds' refusal in 1664 to contribute to the costs of rebuilding the county court on Palace Green. Bishop Cosin's mason, John Langstaffe, was a practising Quaker – prosecuted in the court he was contracted to rebuild and fined for holding meetings at his house in Auckland, he was even held in the bishop's gaol located in the Great North Gate of Durham Castle that marked the divide between the outer bailey of the castle and bishop's borough around the marketplace.[48]

The ancient county court was abolished in 1846 when a new court for petty claims moved to join the assize courts in front of the new prison in Elvet. The court building was completed by Ignatius Bonomi in 1811, with four giant attached columns continuing the association of the architectural orders with justice.[49] Bonomi's court house bears a resemblance to Inigo Jones' 1617 design for Star Chamber at Whitehall, which also had four giant attached columns beneath a pediment and a rusticated base. If built, Jones's Star Chamber design would have matched his iconic banqueting house. Drawing upon ideas of imperial authority and justice in Palladio's reconstruction of the Roman basilica and the temples of Venus and Rome, Whitehall Palace was intended to be symbolic of monarchical divine authority. For the royal law court meeting in Star Chamber, Jones drew upon the temples of Venus (the sun) and Rome (the moon) as 'allegorical personifications of the sovereign, the crowned image of God, the very source of justice', and King Charles I took King Solomon's palace as the model for his vision of a rebuilt palace of Whitehall as 'the ultimate symbol of divinely inspired authority'.[50] The execution of the king in front of the banqueting house in 1649 proved beyond doubt that architecture and authority were intimately related in early modern England. Continuing a preoccupation with architecture and the sources of authority, after the Restoration Bishop Cosin fitted out Durham Castle with portraits of the late king and a tapestry of the 'Story of Solomon' in the low dining room next to the judge's lodgings.[51]

48 Roberts, *Durham*, p. 121; Green, *Building for England*, pp. 85–87.

49 Pevsner and Williamson, *Durham*, p. 227; Durham County Record Office, Prints (T) DU/Dur/M2, floor plans of the New Assize Courts, c. 1870.

50 Giles Worsley, *Inigo Jones and the European Classicist Tradition* (New Haven, 2007), pp. 95, 124, 171 and 180–181, citing Per Palme, *Triumph of Peace: A Study of the Whitehall Banqueting House* (Stockholm, 1956).

51 Green, *Building for England*, pp. 84, 116; Adrian Green, 'Auckland and Durham castles in John Cosin's time', in David Rollason (ed.), *Princes of the Church: Bishops and Their Palaces* (London, 2017), pp. 332–347.

Bishop Cosin might have wished to create a columned Exchequer building in the 1660s, but made do with the existing architecture. First erected for Bishop Neville between 1438 and 1457, this administrative building was modified internally in the sixteenth and seventeenth centuries, presumably in parallel with administrative reforms. Despite the modernisation of the building, ancient procedures were memorialised in the document chest bearing the arms of Bishop de Bury (1333–1345) and Ralph Neville (d. 1367).[52] Improvements in document keeping were akin to rebuilding, especially under Chancellor Hutton, who was presumably involved in reordering the Exchequer building in tandem with revising the practice and procedure of the palatinate courts from 1608. An overmantel with the arms of King James (1603–1625) and Bishop James (1607–1617) (now in the Senate Suite in Durham Castle) was part of a Jacobean refurbishment – perhaps commemorating King James's visit to Durham in 1617. The c. 1680 stair may relate to Chancellor Otway (1673–1693) revising procedures in the court of pleas, whereby Durham followed proceedings in the court of Common Bench at Westminster.[53] Major reforms in procedure and record-keeping might be coordinated with architectural changes.

Although the building was technically part of Durham Castle, it was located outside the moat and barbican, with direct public access from Palace Green. An entrance corridor led past service rooms in the basement to a spiral staircase rising to a first floor landing with two doors – one wider than the other. The wider door gave access to the courtroom, while the narrower door let into the office behind. Above the court was the cursitor's room – an office, as at Westminster, where writs were made out for the county. Printed *Tables of Fees to be taken by The Cursitor of the Court of Chancery, & The Prothonotary of the Court of Pleas, at Durham* survive from 1775.[54] In Durham, as in the king's Chancery court at Westminster, chancellors exercised an equitable jurisdiction that supplemented common law procedures in the court of pleas.[55]

The Exchequer was also responsible for the bishopric estate regulated by manorial halmote courts held twice a year in May and October, often in the house of the grieve. The copybook of a seventeenth-century grieve, John Kay, survives, as does his house at West Auckland, with a canted bay

[52] Now in the Burrell Collection, Glasgow.

[53] Jones, 'Palatine performance', p. 195; Emsley and Fraser, *Courts of the County Palatine*, p. 37.

[54] Printed by T. Slacks, Newcastle, 1776. Copy on display in Durham Museum.

[55] Emsley and Fraser, *Courts of the County Palatine*, p. iii.

window lighting the parlour, in which village legal business was conducted.[56] County Durham has no surviving local court houses like the seventeenth-century building and fittings for the wapentake court at West Derby, Lancashire.[57]

A sketch plan of the courtroom in the Exchequer is shown in Figure 13.1.[58] George Orsmby's sketch, seemingly made in 1907, shows an area for the public separated by rails from the court. Seats for solicitors were set against a large square table, across which the raised chancellor's seat faced the barrister's benches. Armorial paintings of King James and Bishop James (1606–1617), along with the arms of the palatinate, were placed over the chancellor's bench for Chancellor Hutton. The arms and barrister's bench facing the chancellor survives.[59] Orsmby suggests that on the ground floor of the Exchequer were housekeeper's rooms, privies and a coal house; on the first floor is found the courtroom, alongside offices for the registrar, auditor and receiver general; on the top floor, four offices for the prothonotary, cursitor, bishopric halmote courts and county court.

Bishop Cosin installed new windows in 1668, designed by John Langstaffe to match the episcopal library being built onto the Exchequer. Gothic windows and a battlemented roof maintained the traditional architecture of the bishopric. The nineteenth-century Gothic Revival door to the Exchequer, however, presumably replaced a 1660s door that surely matched the library's classical doorcase with broken arched pediment and acanthus leaf brackets. Bishop Cosin's public library was relevant to Durham's legal community. Completed in 1669, the main room was filled with works on theology, philosophy and history. Possibly responding to reader demand, Cosin immediately added an annex in the gap between the L-shaped Exchequer building and library in 1670, where he installed the law books. A series of canonical authors were painted over the book presses to signal subjects. For the law, Cosin selected Justinian, Emperor of the East, King Alfred the Great, Sir John Fortescue and Sir Edward Coke. The law library at Durham thus traced the development of Roman civil law, as codified by Justinian, to

[56] Ibid., pp. 4–8; DUL, Halmote Court Miscellaneous Books No. 95; East Oakley House, West Auckland.

[57] Graham, Ordering Law; Christopher Chalkin, *English Counties and Public Building 1650–1830* (London, 1998).

[58] DUL, Add.MS.199, interleaved in a copy of J. T. Fowler, *Durham University: Earlier Foundations and Present Colleges* (London, 1904).

[59] Bench now in Durham Museum.

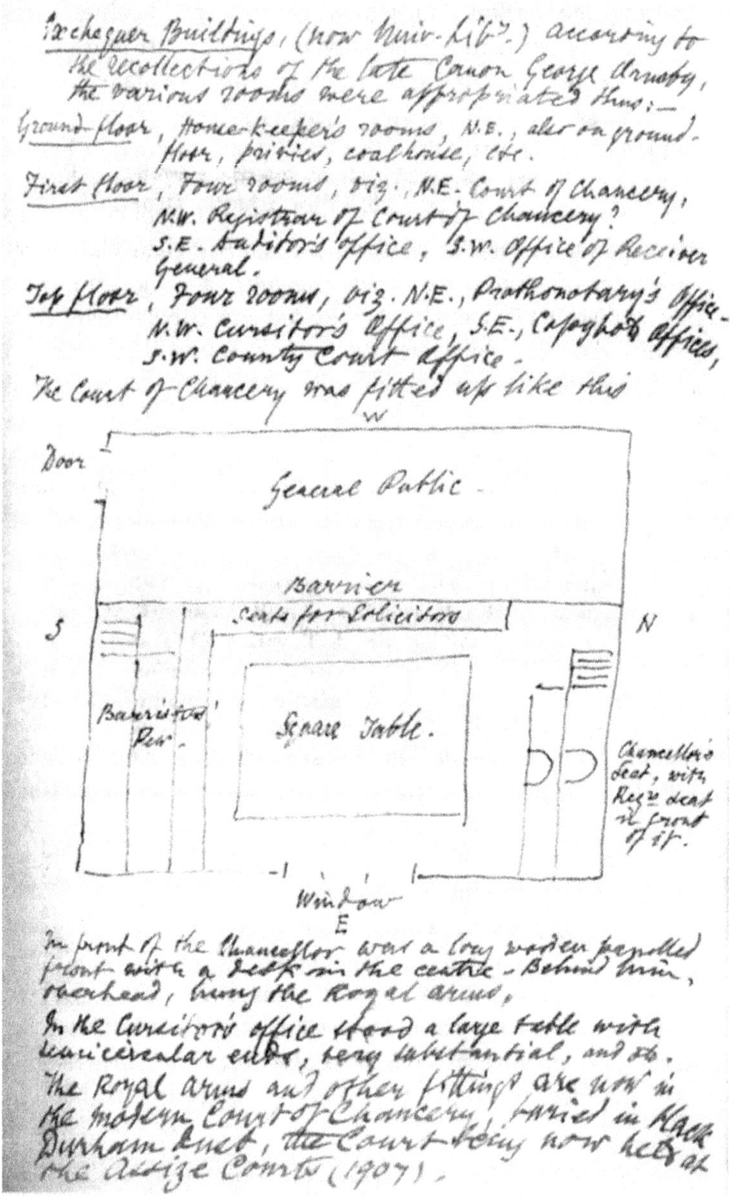
Exchequer Buildings, (now Univ. Lib.) according to the recollections of the late Canon George Ornsby, the various rooms were appropriated thus:—
Ground floor, House-keeper's rooms, N.E., also on ground-floor, privies, coalhouse, etc.
First floor, Four rooms, viz., N.E. Court of Chancery, N.W. Registrar of Court of Chancery? S.E. Auditor's office, S.W. Office of Receiver General.
Top floor, Four rooms, viz. N.E., Prothonotary's Office. N.W. Cursitor's Office, S.E., Copyhold Offices, S.W. County Court Office.
The Court of Chancery was fitted up like this

In front of the Chancellor was a long wooden panelled front with a desk in the centre. Behind him, overhead, hung the Royal arms.
In the Cursitor's office stood a large table with semicircular ends, very substantial, and etc.
The Royal arms and other fittings are now in the modern Court of Chancery, buried in black Durham dust, the Court being now held at the Assize Courts (1907).

Figure 13.1 Sketch plan of Durham Chancery court by George Ormsby, 1907. © Durham University Library, Add.MS.199.

the Anglo-Saxon law codified by Alfred and subsequent English common law tradition, formulated in the modern age by Fortescue and Coke.[60]

Durham Chancery usually convened once a year and sat for only a few days, but was extremely well used in the decades before the civil wars. There were 100–150 major orders per annum between 1600 and 1640, and the entry book for 1633–1642 comprises 700 pages.[61] The reason for this upswing in business was that the palatinate's equity court proved an extremely useful means for resolving conflicts arising over industrial and agricultural interests. Early industrialisation on the basis of the coal trade and a vigorous commercial agriculture were transforming the landscape of County Durham through the rapid enclosure of townfields and coal-pits. J. U. Nef argued that Durham Chancery was instrumental in the scale of the coalfield's exploitation, since no pre-existing body of law existed to regulate the mines, to enable access rights or to compensate for damages.[62] Durham Chancery ceased to meet in the Exchequer building in 1855, but continued to function until 1971, when it was absorbed into the High Court.[63]

## VI

The barbican and moat to Durham Castle were filled in by Bishop Cosin and replaced with gardens in the 1660s. Inside the castle, the common law judges travelling the northern circuit were given splendid lodgings. Bishop Neile added the suite of chambers for the judges in the 1620s, which were refurbished by Bishop Cosin at the Restoration. Both Neile and Cosin were committed to the political purposes of episcopacy and its architectural expression. An inventory taken at the end of Neile's episcopate in 1628 itemises the sequence of rooms comprising the judge's chambers. The inventory made after Cosin's death in 1672 is more detailed, recording the luxurious furnishings of 'Judge Huttons Chamber. 'In the Chancellor's Chambre, 5 pieces of green forest Hangings, A French Bedstead Cloathe Bed lined with Sarcanet Silk Quilt, 2 Elbow Chairs, 4 back stoole, 2 Tables & Carpets', among other things – indicating a bedchamber that doubled as a reception room for

[60] Green, *Building for England.*

[61] Jones, 'Palatine performance', p. 192.

[62] Marcus Knight, 'Litigants and litigation in the seventeenth-century palatine of Durham', PhD thesis, University of Cambridge (1990); J. U. Nef, *The Rise of the British Coal Industry*, two vols (London, 1932).

[63] Durham Chancery court was relocated to a new Exchequer building (1851) on Owengate.

the bishop's temporal chancellor and these lodgings remained at the disposal of the circuit judges up until the 1930s.[64]

Given that the Latin origin of the term 'palatinate' means 'of the palace', it was entirely fitting that the judges lodged in the episcopal palace. The bishop's hospitality was no mere gesture, but a manifestation of the law in space and place. Figure 13.2 shows the judges' lodgings, which gave onto the castle mound. The mound was terraced into brick-faced circular walks for exercise and contemplation by Bishop Cosin in 1665. Similar garden mounds for scholarly male communities were created at New College, Oxford, in 1594 (given steps in 1649), Marlborough College, Wiltshire, and at Gray's Inn, where the mount was built at Sir Francis Bacon's direction in 1608.[65] Durham Castle's formal gardens doubtless provided a reassuring sense of order and beauty for the powerful, which necessarily resulted in a subaltern experience for those labouring to make and maintain the gardens, and for the local populace, who witnessed the learned elites pacing the castle terraces from Palace Green and the bishop's borough below. Meanwhile, for the learned, these gardens were a source of consolation and contemplation – like the 'bookish' gardens created at the Inns of Court.[66] Aligned with his library, Bishop Cosin built a tall brick tower on a garden walk, with brick parapet overlooking the river. Reminiscent of Michelle Montaigne's tower in France and Bacon's garden mount at Gray's Inn, Cosin's gardens were all about immersion in study. As Bacon wrote, a garden 'is the purest of human pleasures. It is the greatest refreshment to the spirits of man, without which, buildings and palaces are but gross handy-works.'[67] The bishop's chancellor and circuit judges thus had access to gardens as a reflective amenity integral to learned culture.

[64] Green, *Building for England*, pp. 112–143; Green, 'Auckland and Durham castles'. 'Judge Hutton's Chamber' appears to commemorate Richard Hutton (d. 1639), unless it refers to an unidentified Restoration judge.

[65] Green, *Building for England*, pp. 82–85; Jennifer Sherwood and Nikolaus Pevsner, *The Buildings of England: Oxfordshire* (London, 1974), p. 174; Paula Henderson, 'The evolution of the early gardens of the Inns of Court', in Jayne Elisabeth Archer, Elizabeth Goldring and Sarah Knight (eds), *The Intellectual and Cultural Worlds of the Early Modern Inns of Court* (Manchester and New York, 2011), pp. 179–198.

[66] Elizabeth Goldring, 'Introduction: the art, architecture and gardens of the early modern Inns of Court', in Jayne Elisabeth Archer, Elizabeth Goldring and Sarah Knight (eds), *The Intellectual and Cultural Worlds of the Early Modern Inns of Court* (Manchester and New York, 2011), pp. 124–137, p. 134.

[67] Francis Bacon, 'Of gardens', in *The Essays, or Counsels Civil or Moral* (Oxford, 1999 [1625]), p. 104.

**Figure 13.2** Durham Castle, in Bishop Crewe's time (1674–1721), showing the judges lodgings (first built by Bishop Neile, 1617–1627) facing the terraced walks cut into the keep mound by Bishop Cosin (1660–1672).


The legal community at Durham must also have gathered in the castle hall on occasion, for feasts and entertainments, as well as bishopric formalities. This hall resembled those at the Inns of Court, as well as those of Oxford and Cambridge colleges.[68] Given that the open hall was largely redundant in domestic contexts by the seventeenth century, its continuity in institutions central to English learned culture indicates the importance of hierarchy within the legal and clerical elite – spatially articulated in terms of learning on the basis of life cycle and age rather than social status. Even so, for all its refined Renaissance gardens and furnishings, Durham Castle was equipped with an armoury to defend the rule of law by force if necessary.

68 Girouard, 'Halls of the Inns of Court', pp. 138–156.

## VII

In the later seventeenth and eighteenth centuries, Durham's lawyers built handsome houses not unlike the chambers at the Inns of Court. Houses containing offices combined with domestic accommodation were distinct from tradesmen's and gentry houses on the same street. When not engaged in the law, Durham lawyers often retired to a semi-rural suburban house a short ride from the city. Jacob Bee records the marriage in 1695 of Mr George Dixon of Akeley-heads and Durham, attorney, to Betty Gray; the Dixons presumably resided at Aykley Heads just outside Durham, with offices combined with domestic accommodation in town.[69] The pre-eminent legal dynasty in Durham – the Mickletons – had a suburban residence at nearby Crook Hall, as well as legal offices on Palace Green and North Bailey.

The architectural detailing of the Mickletons' law offices connects to the post-Fire Inns of Court. London's speculative builder, Nicholas Barbon, was involved in the new houses built for the Inns after 1666.[70] The Mickletons had chambers in London and were linked to the Inner Temple.[71] Christopher Mickleton (1612–1669), the founder of the antiquarian-minded lawyer dynasty at Durham, purchased Crook Hall in 1657. He transferred it to his son, James, as a wedding gift in 1660, although they subsequently litigated over use of the property. James was disinherited and it was presumably Christopher's second son, Michael (1663–1711), who built the brick house facing Palace Green in the 1690s. Christopher's grandson, James Mickleton (1688–1719), inherited in 1711; mainly resident at Gray's Inn in London, he fell into debt and drinking, and he drowned in the Thames. Crook Hall was let in 1712 to bolster his income, but subsequently reoccupied by the family and rebuilt with a handsome brick facade. The Mickletons' seven-bay house facing onto Palace Green was originally two storeys with projecting string courses, resembling brick houses at the London Inns. Figure 13.3 shows the building known today as Cosin's Hall. It was raised to three storeys in the eighteenth century, when sash windows and a Rococo doorcase were inserted and the facade was rendered.

[69] J. C. Hodgson (ed.), *Six North Country Diaries* (London, 1910), p. 57.

[70] Geoffrey Tyack, 'The rebuilding of the Inns of Court, 1660–1700', in Jayne Elisabeth Archer, Elizabeth Goldring and Sarah Knight (eds), *The Intellectual and Cultural Worlds of the Early Modern Inns of Court* (Manchester and New York, 2011), pp. 199–213; see also Elizabeth McKellar, *The Birth of Modern London: the Development and Design of the City, 1660–1720* (Manchester, 1999).

[71] Sheila Doyle, 'The Barrington Manuscripts: from Durham to the Inner Temple', *The Law Librarian* 23 (1992), 66–74.

**Figure 13.3** The Mickletons' great house, Palace Green. Originally two storeys when first built c. 1695.
© Historic England photo.

Removal of the render has left a somewhat dog-eared appearance. When in use as lawyer's offices, the smart house on Palace Green was connected to the Mickleton and Spearman offices on North Bailey from 1697. In addition to rebuilding 43–45 North Bailey, 46 North Bailey was newly built early in the eighteenth century on the site of a coffee house.[72] Immaculately proportioned offices off a central staircase were accessed from a passage at the side of the building, with no front door to the street. The facade presented regularly spaced windows over three floors, lighting generous offices within. Orange rubbed brick, over white painted sash-window frames, created an aesthetic reminiscent of chambers at the Inns. Its

[72] DUL, GB 033 HUD, Huddleston papers; UND/CH1/A11C/2, 12 April 1697, Lease from Archdeacon Booth to John Spearman of 43–45 North Bailey, refers to 'great house'; UND/CH1/B3 re. 46 North Bailey, previously a coffee house. See also Durham Probate Registry, wills or administration bonds for James Mickleton, 1694 (DPR/I/1/1694/M7/1–2), John Mickleton of North Bailey, 1710 (DPR/I/3/1709/B175), Christopher Mickleton of North Bailey, 1719 (DPR/I/1/1719/M4/1–2), James Mickleton of Crook Hall, 1723 (DPR/I/3/1719/B162/1–2); John Mickleton of Crook Hall, 1723 (DPR/I/1/1722/M8/1–2), and Abigail Mickleton, widow, 1723 (DPR/I/1/1723/M9/1–2).

**Figure 13.4** 1 South Bailey, Durham. Lawyer's house and office, built for William Pye, 1735.


smart brick facade with string courses was nevertheless distinctive to Durham – being built with bricks made from brick earth excavated with the coal measures and window panes using glass made in Newcastle. One early eighteenth-century window survives *in situ* on the staircase – its wide glazing bars, like the ramped handrail to the stair, indicating a c. 1720 date. Thus the architectural detailing of these legal offices connects Durham to fine chambers in London, while the materials of the house were generated in regional context.

Lawyer William Pye built himself similar premises in South Bailey in 1735.[73] Figure 13.4 shows Pye's house, which combined an office with domestic accommodation. Built mainly of brick, the street facade is in dressed stone, with touches of classicism including string courses. Like the Mickletons' great house on Palace Green, Pye's house at 1 South Bailey was a broad building of seven bays. Both houses have two entrances. The main door accessed the lawyer's offices, with generous

[73] Canon Greenslade, 'No. 1 South Bailey', *St. Chad's College Magazine* 7 (1948), 12–18; DUL, Durham Probate Registry, will of William Pye of South Bailey, 1753 (DPR/I/1/1753/P8/1–4).

hallways enabling clients to wait. A separate service entrance was provided on the far side of both facades for servants and deliveries to the kitchen. Both houses thus had off-centre main entrances, although the architects sought to disguise this lack of symmetry by horizontal banding articulated in string courses and diminutive secondary entrances to the far side of both facades. Architecture exemplifies cultural connections – with the same requirements for the Mickletons' brick house of the 1690s and Pye's stone house of the 1730s generating buildings with the same form, despite being built by different generations in contrasting materials. The specific context in which buildings arose explains the patterning of architecture.

These houses were distinct from other genteel houses in Durham and differed from the clergy housing in Durham Cathedral College – not that the clergy and gentry residing in Durham's cathedral close were unfamiliar with the law. On 8 January 1684, Jacob Bee noted the death of 'Robert Hilton, esquire, justice of the peace in Westmorland', who had recently retired to this genteel enclave, having 'came to Durham and lived in the Coledge: he died very suddenly, having been abroad at supper the night before, and went very well to bed'. Bee also recorded the deaths of local lawyers: in April 1696, 'Lawyer Davison of Elvet' 'dyed very suddainly at Hardwick' near Sedgefield; in March and April 1690, 'Mr George Barkas, attorney at law, clarck to every mayer in Durham during his time', then 'Mr Francis Crosby, junior, being attorney at law and merchant' died.[74] Weather, along with mortality and political events, filled Bee's diary. On 3 August 1683, he wrote: 'The assesses begun, and such an inundation of watter that the judges was forcet to come down Gillygate, and come in about 8 at night, and read their commission. Judges names, Jones and Strut.' In March 1685, Mr Charles Montague and Sir Richard Lloyd were 'chosen burgesses for the citty of Durham, being elected without opposition'. Lloyd was a distinguished lawyer – a fellow of All Souls Oxford, admitted to Gray's Inn in 1655 – who had been spiritual chancellor of Durham since 1676 and who had represented the City of Durham in Parliament from 1679 to 1685, succeeded by Montague as member of Parliament from 1685 to 1710. Durham's clerical-legal establishment thus dominated the politics of the city, even after enfranchisement. Finally, Bee's diary demonstrates familiarity with the full range of office-

[74] Greenslade, *Six North Country Diaries*, pp. 47, 53, 56–57, which also notes, in October 1714, Mr Pexel Padman of St Nicholas parish, attorney, buried in St Oswald's churchyard.

holders in this small society, from cathedral registrar to bishop's porter. Having recorded on 7 December 1690 that registrar 'Mr. William Wilson in the Bailey was drowned', found and buried in the cathedral, Bee noted in 1694 the death 'on 25 Feb. My Lord of Durham's porter, Mitcholl by name'.[75]

## VIII

Durham's palatinate status made it distinctive, although its assize week and consistory court were much like other county towns and cathedrals, and the city participated in provincial England's urban renaissance. Greater integration with Westminster from the mid-seventeenth century fits with Michael Braddick's account of state centralisation. Durham also connected to English colonial contexts – not least in providing precedent for the charter of Maryland, the native place of Christopher W. Brooks.[76]

Brooks spent his career at Durham University from 1980 to 2014. As professor of history, he occupied a book-lined study in the North Bailey house built as offices for Mickleton and Spearman early in the eighteenth century, and enjoyed a fellowship at Durham's Institute of Advanced Study in their great house on Palace Green in Michaelmas term 2008. Studying the Mickleton and Spearman papers aided Brooks's understanding of English legal history and of Durham's place within it. He concluded that while the palatinate courts 'had a strong sense of corporate identity and self-interest', 'from at least the 1620s some notable local practitioners, including the local antiquary and attorney Christopher Mickleton, combined London training and practice with work in the palatinate'.[77] The architecture of their Durham offices embodied their connection to the Inns of Court.

Human culture's built manifestation can create enduring legacies. In 1953, Nikolaus Pevsner observed that the University of Durham is 'the oldest of the provincial universities of England, and thanks to certain

[75] Greenslade, *Six North Country Diaries*, pp. 46, 49–50, 54, 56.

[76] Adrian Green, 'The big house in the English provincial town', in Catherine Armstrong and John Hicks (eds), *The English Urban Renaissance Revisited* (Cambridge, 2018), pp. 116–143; Michael J. Braddick, *State Formation in Early Modern England, c. 1550–1700* (Cambridge, 2000); Tim Thornton, 'The palatinate of Durham and the Maryland Charter', *American Journal of Legal History* 45 (2001), 235–255. Jones notes that the 'short-lived palatinate of Avalon in Newfoundland, designed in partial imitation of Durham, inspired the proprietary charter of Maryland': Jones, 'Palatinate performance', p. 190.

[77] Brooks, *Pettyfoggers and Vipers*, pp. 37–38.

reasons, aesthetic as well as otherwise, is the only one which has achieved the creation of a *milieu* that can compare with Oxford and Cambridge. Create is perhaps not the right word; for the milieu was there before the university.'[78] Brooks (with his gentle Princeton manner and acerbic Oxford wit) maintained that milieu in his own generation. Originating in the monastic community before the Reformation, this learned culture endured thanks to the lawyers on the Durham peninsula in the early modern era. Between the dissolution of Durham Priory in 1539 and the creation of Durham University in 1832, Durham's legal dimension was to the fore. Pevsner had an astute eye for architecture's relationship to culture: 'Wandering along North and South Bailey to call on members of the university, one may well feel transported into the streets of Oxford or Cambridge. Birmingham or Manchester could never even try to achieve that.'[79] While England's civic universities aimed at other purposes, Durham was, from its inception, a 'tiny Anglican outpost' of Oxford and Cambridge.[80] Before 1832, however, Durham's links to England's 'third university' at the Inns of Court were manifest in its architecture, helping to make early modern Durham a place of law. The palatinate's courts provided an amenity that doubtless buttressed the authority of the church before 1640, even while suppressing the rights of citizens and representation in Parliament. After 1660, Durham's lawyers increasingly served the propertied. Analysing the materiality of architectural settings for the conduct of the law can only deepen our appreciation of the social significance of the law for all who had cause to engage with it.

[78] Nikolaus Pevsner, *The Buildings of England: County Durham* (London, 1953), pp. 128–129.

[79] Ibid.

[80] Stefan Collini, *What Are Universities for?* (London, 2012), p. 27.

# 14

# Law and Revolution

## The Seventeenth-Century English Example

CHRISTOPHER W. BROOKS

## I

This paper is best seen as a research exploration rather than a definitive statement. I have written it in order to focus my thoughts about how to organise the research and writing of a 350,000-word book on the history of English law between 1625 and 1689 that will appear in a series called the *Oxford History of the Laws of England*, which traces the development of English law from Anglo-Saxon times till the end of the nineteenth century.[1] I am still actively engaged in the research on a number of different fronts, but from time to time I find myself bobbing up from the archival work with general questions about how I want to characterise this particular segment of English legal history, and this is not as easy as might at first be supposed.

There are, in connection with English law, particularly testing questions about change and continuity, not to mention causality. The principal court records and many of the concepts still current in the mid-nineteenth century can be traced back in a remarkably unbroken fashion as far as the reigns of Henry II or Edward I, and from at least the late sixteenth century onwards the invocation of the 'law' in political argument has frequently stressed its unbroken longevity as a principal validation of its authority. Change, let alone 'modernisation', have rarely been put forward as positive values, and even where change has been detected, legal historians have been inclined to write about a process of internal 'evolution' of writs, remedies and doctrines that does not always align all that closely, if at all, with external social, political or cultural transformations.[2] Indeed, the weight of continuity is beautifully summed

[1] The *Oxford History* is designed to replace the classic, but outdated, W. S. Holdsworth, *History of English Law*, seventeen vols (London, 1903–1966).

[2] A classic, if extreme, restatement of this approach is offered by S. F. C. Milsom, *A Natural History of the Common Law* (New York, 2003), said to be 'the dominant voice in English

up (in all senses of the words) by the Sterling Law School building at Yale University, which was completed in 1931. Based on the English Inns of Court, it recalls the Victorian Great Hall at Lincoln's Inn (1843), which is itself an imagined recreation of what such a building might have been like in the later sixteenth century. There is in this a recognition of the importance of history, but, it seems, a distinct ambiguity about the nature and impact of historical change. There might be alterations, but what you see remains essentially the same.

Continuity in the Anglo-American legal tradition has to be taken seriously, not least because law and its institutions have been constants in social, economic and political life that transcend many of the traditional chronologies separating the medieval, early modern and modern periods, however they are described.[3] Indeed, from the perspective of the social or political historian, this is an advantage insofar as it makes it possible to plot changes in practices and ideas (doctrine) within the comfort of a relatively static framework and without being enslaved to preconceived temporal points (or arcs).[4] Yet this still leaves unanswered the question of how that legal history should be characterised in terms of change over time and what questions should be asked. The chronological divisions associated with the volumes commissioned for the *Oxford History* have been devised largely to create manageable chunks signposted (in the best common law tradition) by changes from one monarch to the next and many aspects of the legal history of the post-medieval, and especially post-Restoration (1660), periods remain seriously under-researched. In fact, to complicate things even further, at least in the United Kingdom, historical approaches to law, or historical jurisprudence, and indeed historical studies of it as a social phenomenon have remained relatively marginalised at least in part because of the dominance of legal 'positivism' (essentially, the idea that law is what is declared law by the sovereign) and the kind of (philosophical) analytical jurisprudence epitomised by H. L. A. Hart's

legal history for the last fifty years' (Lesley Dingle and Daniel Bates, 'Professor Stroud Francis Charles (Toby) Milson', online at www.squire.law.cam.ac.uk/eminent-scholars-archive/professor-stroud-francis-charles-toby-milsom),

[3] This general problem has been explored recently by Phil Withington, *Society in Early Modern England: The Vernacular Origins of Some Powerful Ideas* (Cambridge, 2010).

[4] For example, we now know that court usage has oscillated in interesting ways over the past 600 years or so: Christopher W. Brooks, *Lawyers, Litigation and English Society since 1450* (London, 1998), ch. 5. Developing this story is what I saw myself doing in Christopher W. Brooks, *Law, Politics and Society in Early Modern England* (Cambridge, 2008).

famous book *The Concept of Law*, which argues in terms of abstract, rather than *real*, legal systems.[5]

Following the lead of Sir John Baker, the general editor of the *Oxford History*, who has written about the first half of the sixteenth century in terms of 'English law and the Renaissance',[6] I have seriously considered thinking of my period in terms of 'English law in the Baroque'. It is novel, but essentially non-committal, and the association with a style that was ostentatious, elaborate and sometimes beautiful, but ultimately both vapid and authoritarian, has its appeal. But, of course, the immense political upheavals of the period from 1642 to 1660 and the ongoing turmoil that persisted at least until the so-called Glorious Revolution of 1689 constituted a series of events in which law and lawyers were deeply involved, and which, in any case, I am obliged to negotiate to tell my story. Furthermore, a minor strain in twentieth-century social science has in the past been devoted to the investigation of the relationship between the big three Western European Revolutions, the British, the French and the Russian, and large-scale legal innovation and change. Influenced by Marxian ideas about the evolution of Western societies from feudalism to capitalism, the attraction of the idea is that it provides a way to describe the pre-Revolutionary structure, and then to examine their fate when there was an opportunity to remake them in order to better fit the new social and economic relationships that engendered the revolution in the first place.[7] At the very least, a consideration of change over time is essential, and there is an opportunity to consider the impact, or lack of impact, of a major political and social discontinuity – to examine consequences, as well as causes.

There was quite a bit of work on England along these lines in the 1960s, but this approach became so conflicted so quickly that it has been largely neglected for nearly half a century. The reasons for this, which include doubts about how we define revolutions and what caused them, as well as questions about how to describe the interactions between a society and its

5 H. L. A. Hart, *The Concept of Law* (Oxford, 1961), recently discussed in a posthumous book by Brian Simpson, *Reflections on the Concept of Law* (Oxford, 2011). The issue is of some personal importance to me because I was a research fellow at Brasenose College, Oxford, in the mid-1970s when Hart was principal of the college and because Simpson was the person who originally suggested the idea of the new *Oxford History* to Oxford University Press.

6 J. H. Baker, *The Oxford History of the Laws of England, Vol. VI, 1483–1559* (Oxford, 2003), ch. 1.

7 Michael Burrage, *Revolution and the Making of the Contemporary Legal Profession: England, France and the United States* (Oxford, 2006).

institutions, are sufficiently convincing that I have no objection to listening to suggestions that I change the title and approach of my paper altogether.[8] I am, from the outset, going to play fast and loose with some of the terms of the argument. I am not prepared, at least at the moment, to undertake elaborate comparisons with other times and places. Nor do I want to get tangled up with definitions of revolution or involved with examining how events on the ground match up with categories of analysis, particularly those relating to class, that originate with Marx. This, it seems to me, can only detract from the attempt to provide some kind of coherent account of what actually happened (which is what is clearly needed) and lead to sterile conclusions which may suggest that the questions themselves were badly formulated. Rather than defining a revolution, I am simply going to assert that the mid-seventeenth-century events that led to the execution of King Charles I in 1649 and the establishment of the only republic the British Isles have known prior to the twentieth century constituted a major discontinuity that affected all levels of society from the top to the bottom, and I would also posit that one reason for arguing for a new-found social depth to the impact of these events is the fact that a much, much larger proportion of the population was involved with legal institutions (from courts to Parliament) than previous writers on the subject were aware. Finally, as some recent historical work has suggested, far from being resolved by the Restoration of the Stuart monarchy in 1660, England's troubles continued for at least another twenty-five or thirty years up to, and maybe after, 1689.[9]

## II

In terms of immediate antecedents for this kind of approach, there are only a couple of specific titles worth mentioning, alongside a much larger body of more disparate work that, on the whole, points strongly towards continuity rather than change and which provides my principal point of departure. In 1912, the influential Christian socialist historian R. H. Tawney published a book called *The Agrarian Problem of the*

[8] Although I note that some early modern historians are beginning to call for a re-evaluation of the place of the events of 1640–1660 in most general accounts of the history of the period.

[9] Jonathan Scott, *England's Troubles: Seventeenth-Century English Political Instability in European Context* (Cambridge, 2000); Steven Pincus, *1688: The First Modern Revolution* (New Haven, 2009).

*Sixteenth Century*, which probably comes closest to a classic Marxist case for something like revolutionary legal change in the seventeenth century. Interested in the struggles between the landed gentry and smaller land-holders (especially those known as copyholders) over the control of the landed wealth of the country, and the communal life that went with it, Tawney cast his argument in terms of land tenure and the role of the courts in determining winners and losers in connection with it. Furthermore, in a series of articles he wrote some years later, he launched a major historical controversy by asserting that the English Revolution of the mid-seventeenth century marked the triumph of the landed gentry over English economic and political life that was still having an impact in his own day.[10] In his view, the courts and the common law remained an integral element in establishing this hegemony. According to Tawney, '[f]or a century and a half after the Revolution [the gentry had] what power a Government can have to make and ruin England as they please'. If economic conditions made the new agrarian regime profitable, 'it is none the less true that legal causes decided by whom the profits should be enjoyed'.[11] Most agrarian (and legal) historians now disagree with nearly all of the detail of Tawney's interpretation, but he was at least asking meaningful questions about how far law was involved in the distribution of resources and social structure. Indeed, his assertion that developments in the civil wars enabled the gentry to rule England more or less as they liked for the following two-and-a-half centuries has perhaps been dismissed more casually than it should have been.

More recently, the late Harold Berman, a distinguished law professor, wrote a series of books called *Law and Revolution* that attempted to reconceptualise the history of the Western legal tradition, and the last volume he published in this series contains quite a lot of material on England in the seventeenth and eighteenth centuries. Berman appears, in this work, to have been concerned primarily with the development of history as a source of legal authority, which he sees being advanced through mid-to-late seventeenth-century figures such as Sir Matthew Hale and in the gathering together of a rather disparate common law learning into more authoritative texts. Nearly all of this seems to me so

[10] R. H. Tawney, *The Agrarian Problem in the Sixteenth Century (with an Introduction by Lawrence Stone)* (New York, 1967 [1912]); R. H. Tawney, 'The rise of the gentry', *Economic History Review* 11 (1941), 1–38. The subsequent 'storm over the gentry' is discussed in L. Stone, *Social Change and Revolution in England 1540–1640* (London, 1965).

[11] Tawney, *Agrarian Problem*, p. 407.

deficient in terms of what is now known about early modern English law and in terms of causality that it seriously lacks analytical purchase. However, although Berman's detailed analysis is unsatisfying, another distinctive feature of his approach is an insistence that religion – in particular, the religious changes associated with the Protestant Reformation – need to be taken seriously as a principal dynamic in early modern legal change, and here, as I will suggest later, he has a point.[12]

Apart from Tawney and Berman, work on 'law and revolution' in the seventeenth century has been thin on the ground. Historical understanding of the 'revolutionary' events themselves has moved away from looking for social, or even political, causes. It is hard, for example, any longer to see the English civil wars as a bourgeois revolution of the classic type imagined by Marx. Furthermore, in terms of consequences, most modern work on the period has tended to stress continuity, rather than change, and this is true no matter what perspective is taken on the actual character of the 'revolution' itself. In this view, everything is explained by the fact that we describe the years after the Stuarts returned to the throne in 1660 as the Restoration. The previous two decades were troubled ('bad') times – a discontinuity best forgotten.

Indeed, by the time scholars stopped thinking seriously about the matter (*c.* 1975), you could put together quite a coherent demonstration of how the persistence into the nineteenth century of the unreformed common law was a perfect example of the survival of the *ancien régime* in England through the upheavals of the seventeenth century, as well as the monumental changes of the late eighteenth century. A 1960s statement of the case would go something as follows: English law before the civil war was blood-thirsty,[13] oppressive, impossibly prolix and complex, and of use only to the rich – and by that we would mean the gentry. Elaborating on the theme, distinguished historian Gerald Aylmer wrote in 1961:

> None of the common law courts had adapted themselves to meet changes in the conditions under which property was held, or in economic activities

[12] H. Berman, *Law and Revolution, Vol. II: The Impact of the Protestant Reformations on the Western Legal Tradition* (Cambridge, MA, 2003); cf. H. Berman, *Law and Revolution: The Formation of the Western Legal Tradition* (Cambridge, MA, 1983).

[13] Mainly because of problems of exposition, I am not giving much consideration in this paper to the criminal law, which has received considerable scholarly attention. There is a vast bibliography, which would have to begin with the seminal collection of essays edited by Douglas Hay, Peter Linebaugh, John G. Rule, E. P. Thompson and Cal Winslow, *Albion's Fatal Tree: Crime and Society in Eighteenth-Century England* (London, 1975).

> generally. All were intricate in procedure, dreadfully slow and expensive, and archaic, if not sometimes unpredictable and arbitrary in judgement. In these respects, King's Bench was only less unsatisfactory than Common Pleas. But, as so often in human affairs, the bad helped to stand in the way of the worse; the common law was undoubtedly a barrier of sort against arbitrary government.[14]

Although Aylmer's authoritative verdict was based on astonishingly little evidence, it was credible at the time, at least partly because there is no doubt that a pretty active genre of pamphlet literature associated with the subject of law reform emerged during the 1640s and 1650s, especially in the wake of the execution of Charles I in 1649.[15] It seems that everyone from the Levellers to Lord Protector Oliver Cromwell maintained that legal change was one of the objectives that had made the war worth fighting. The Rump Parliament and Cromwell both appointed high-level committees to investigate the possibilities, and the Protector retained William Sheppard as a legal adviser responsible for formulating detailed plans for reform that got as far as being presented to the House of Commons.[16] Yet, so the story goes, those who had the power to make changes put the process into the hands of the lawyers and, consequently, little was achieved. In his book on the interregnum civil service, Aylmer noted that the bureaucratic sector least affected by the new regime, 'alike as to men and measures' was the legal side of government, including the courts.[17] Even changes made in the 1650s, such as the translation of common law proceedings from Latin into English, were reversed (with remarkably little comment) in 1660. The entire ramshackle business was easily restored with the monarchy, not least because monarchy and the common law had a powerful co-dependency. Civil-war-era change was an opportunity missed. Consequently, the *ancien régime* persisted until the nineteenth century, when a period of real law reform finally addressed some of the worst abuses. Medieval English legal history ended at just about the same time as a Gothic Revival mausoleum, the Public Record Office, was erected in Chancery Lane to house its remains.

[14] G. E. Aylmer, *The King's Servants: The Civil Servants of Charles I, 1625–1642* (London, 1961), p. 65.

[15] There are no footnote reference for the passage cited. Aylmer apparently assumed that what he wrote was common knowledge.

[16] D. R. Veall, *The Popular Movement for Law Reform* (Oxford, 1970), remains a comprehensive starting point for the literature, although the analysis is outdated and now seems unsophisticated.

[17] G. E. Aylmer, *The State's Servants: The Civil Service of the English Republic, 1649–1660* (London, 1973), p. 328.

## III

Unfortunately, there has been little research over the past thirty years on the period from 1640 onwards that sheds much fresh light on these assertions, but a quite considerable amount of work has now been undertaken on the sixteenth and early seventeenth centuries. This alters the picture of the *status quo ante bellum*, and therefore should, I think, be taken to have created a new starting point for approaching the law reform movement and the apparent continuity in the history of English law across the political upheavals of the later seventeenth century. On this account, a combination of innovation in the procedures connected with getting defendants to appear in court and the development of a capacious form of action, the action on the case, plus the first real pulse of demographic growth since the Black Death, created, by the end of the reign of Elizabeth in 1603, a very distinctive institutional and cultural bloom for English law. Nearly all courts, from the secular to the ecclesiastical, from the central to the local, were bursting with business. The numbers of qualified lawyers increased manyfold. The Inns of Court and Inns of Chancery in London, the places where they trained, achieved institutional and architectural high-water marks.[18]

Perhaps even more significantly, the demographic and economic developments of the sixteenth and early seventeenth centuries appear to be reflected in the increase in litigation, and the majority of those involved in it resided within the urban and rural middling sort rather than aristocracy and gentry. In their well-known books on the development of the early modern state, both Mike Braddick and Steve Hindle stress the importance of access to and use of the law in developing ties between individuals and communities and the state, as well as contributing to participation in government by a much broader social spectrum of people than had previously been taken to be the case.[19] By contrast, there has been less work devoted to questions about the relationship between law and economic developments of the kind Gerald Aylmer hinted at, although enough has been done to make problematical his conceptualisation of the question. Most of what we currently know about early modern economic and social history, including land-holding, comes

[18] Brooks, *Lawyers, Litigation and English Society*, especially chs 2–4; Brooks, *Law, Politics and Society*.

[19] M. J. Braddick, *State Formation in Early Modern England, c. 1550–1700* (Cambridge, 2000); S. Hindle, *The State and Social Change in Early Modern England c. 1550–1640* (Basingstoke, 2000).

from court records or non-litigious documents such as deeds to land or trading agreements.[20] The common law courts, no less than other legal institutions, were already deeply involved in economic life before 1640, however modern or non-modern it may have been. Indeed, it is precisely the centuries-old interaction between the common law and English society that makes it difficult to disentangle the relationship between the two.

It is important to stress that much of this legal activity appears to have been associated with creditor and debtor relationships of various degrees of complexity, but the ground-breaking published reports of Sir Edward Coke, which cover the later years of Queen Elizabeth and the early parts of the reign of James I, show the development of case law (cases determined by the common law judges in courts such as King's Bench and Common Pleas) in a number of different directions. For example, lawyers and judges acted remarkably quickly to develop a common law approach to customary tenure, which eventually meant that copyhold land became much like freehold in terms of inheritability and alienability. This is important because, as historians have long been aware, customary tenures of this type traditionally carried obligations to lords, as well as certain entitlements, such as the right to pasture animals on common land. Copyholds were part of the web of social, as well economic, life in a primarily agricultural economy and the security of tenure of copyholders was an important consideration in understanding the distribution of landed wealth in the country. By the end of the 1620s, moreover, the analogy between the rights of customary tenants as against their landlords, and the rights of the subject as against the king, had become a predominant metaphor in national political life: 'a people whose property could be taken from them at the will of the monarch were slaves, not subjects ... they were serfs or villeins, rather than free tenants whose rights to property were protected by law'.[21]

Next, something like a law relating to the liberty of the subject was being developed. You can read about it in a lecture Francis Ashley gave at the Middle Temple in 1616, in which he drew heavily on cases reported by Coke to outline the ways in which the common law offered remedies against oppressions committed by churchmen, overzealous justices of the peace, rapacious landlords.[22] This is also the thrust of Paul Halliday's

[20] A point made by Keith Wrightson, *Earthly Necessities: Economic Lives in Early Modern Britain* (New Haven, 2000).

[21] Brooks, *Law, Politics and Society*, p. 190. See further ibid., chs 8, 9, 11, 13.

[22] Ibid., pp. 420–422.

work on the emergence of the widespread use and development of the writ of habeas corpus at about the same time, although I attribute more significance to evolving ideas of personal liberty than he does.[23] Furthermore, in the case of legal matters associated with tenures, and indeed economic relationships more generally, there does seem to have been a degree of judicial instrumentalism at work. The famous decisions reported by Coke on the position of copyholders, the rights of guilds or companies to control trades, or the willingness of the courts to uphold contracts in the form of verbal or informal written agreements all contain elements of a political economy that actively valued small farmers and acknowledged the need for the regulation of trades and the education of young tradesmen, as well as the need for individuals to be able to earn a decent living to support themselves and their families. Yet it is also important to remember that pre-revolutionary law remained essentially reactive. It was up to litigants and their lawyers to bring cases to be heard, which they did in large numbers, and although Coke and others frequently referred to reason, there was a consistent willingness to accept customary and prescriptive rights if these could meet standards of proof.[24]

There were problems associated with this legal regime. The lack of public notoriety for conveyances and an effective way of registering, or otherwise recording, transactions made questions about titles to land extremely complicated. Resolving them frequently involved hiring lawyers to study deeds, marriage agreements and other documents going back over decades, and, since possession gave an advantage in law, the practice of making 'forcible' entries in order to establish a physical interest in a house or a piece of land evidently still persisted right up to 1640. At the same time, there was also an unresolved tension at the heart of the law relating to obligations. The most basic legal instrument of the time was the conditional bond, in which one party agreed to carry out some action or repay a debt within a specified period of time, or else to pay their creditor a sum of money that was usually twice the amount involved in the transaction. According to the common law, such agreements, which were formally written (usually using a set text of words) and sealed, involved a very high degree of liability and enforceability.

[23] P. Halliday, *Habeas Corpus: From England to Empire* (Cambridge, MA, 2010).

[24] Brooks, *Law, Politics and Society*, pp. 277, 424. For reasons of space, I have not said anything about gender, but these general points can be applied to women, and to some extent married women, as well as men: see T. Stretton, *Women Waging Law in Elizabethan England* (Cambridge, 1998).

There was no defence against non-payment; indeed, you could be in deep trouble if a nasty creditor were to sue you on a bond that you had failed to have cancelled when you paid the debt due. Hence, from one perspective, this seems to have been a legal regime in which there was a high degree of freedom in making contracts, backed up by severe measures of enforcement, including the fairly widespread scourge of imprisonment for debt. Yet, in English law, there was also an important concept, known as equity, which could offer some relief to debtors of this kind, as well as to other people whose paperwork was not in order or who could point to extenuating circumstances that prevented them from honouring their obligations. Since disputes in equity were, in theory, decided by a judge on the basis of his conscience as it applied to the facts before him rather than according to the letter of common or statute law, there could be no precedents and hence no real body of the law as it was normally understood. Nevertheless, there were well-known jurisdictions, such as the courts of Chancery and Requests, which entertained lawsuits in equity and many of the rapidly growing number of cases they heard in the period up to 1640, and indeed thereafter, involved debtors who were claiming relief from obligations such as those enshrined in bonds. Although chancellors tried to be strict in enforcing bonds, they frequently encountered claims of fraud of various kinds in making the instruments, theft of them, deceit and other kinds of dishonesty that made the cases seem worth looking into. Furthermore, as litigants had long been aware, starting a lawsuit in Chancery was a good way of frustrating an opponent who had the upper hand in another court, and since it involved hiring lawyers to enter lengthy bills, which stated the case, and, if it came to that, the taking of depositions from witnesses that could be used by the court to reach its decision (without the use of a jury), litigation was notorious for being costly.[25] Hence the English system seemed, on the one hand, to insist on the most draconian penalties for failure to honour obligations and, on the other, to be extremely meticulous about making sure that any plausible excuse for failing to do so could get a hearing.

This was the legal side of the social and economic world that Craig Muldrew so convincingly recreated in his *Economy of Obligation*, yet while it evidently depended heavily on trust, the court records inevitably

[25] Although there is a good book on the Elizabethan Chancery by W. J. Jones, *The Elizabethan Court of Chancery* (Oxford, 1967), the only guide to the seventeenth century I can suggest is Brooks, *Law Politics and Society*, pp. 310–318.

leave one struck just as often by claims about hard dealing, fraud and interpersonal conflict.[26] Nevertheless, taken as a whole, the evidence of legal change over the hundred years prior to the civil war would seem to point towards a society that used legal institutions on a level not matched before, or indeed afterwards, and a body of law that had responded to social and economic change to the extent that it could be claimed that the laws of England helped to make the liberty of the subject under the law a social value. According to the common lawyers themselves, if England had ever been a feudal society, it had evolved over the fifteenth and sixteenth centuries into one of land-holdings of various different sizes and according to a bewildering array of tenures, but in which no man, however lowly, had to do homage to another just because he paid rent to him. The rise of the yeomanry and the urban middling sort are at least as important a feature of social, economic and legal life as the rise of the gentry.

## IV

On this reading of the evidence, what is most conveniently described as the legal culture of the pre-civil-war years contributed significantly to the political idiom in which the mid-century conflicts were argued nor was it in any obvious way out of touch with the interests or aspirations of most sections of the population. The painfully legalistic quality of the conflict, which culminated with the unique event of a trial of a king for treason against his people, was a reflection of the politico-legal culture in which it occurred and, for most of the 1640s, there were not many signs that lawyers and the courts were liable to come under attack. While the Church of England and its institutions, including bishops and the ecclesiastical courts, were either abolished or collapsed, the two sides in the civil wars, king and Parliament, competed with each other for control of the courts and the appointment of judges to ride the assize circuits; some lawyers, such as Oliver St John or Bulstrode Whitelocke, became leading figures in the parliamentary cause. Once the worst of the fighting was over in the later 1640s, litigation rates returned to levels at least as high as they had been in 1640, and in most respects, the existing secular legal institutions and ideas survived the transition from monarchy, to republic, to the lord protectorship of 'His Highness' Oliver Cromwell with

[26] C. Muldrew, *The Economy of Obligation: The Culture of Credit and Social Relations in Early Modern England* (Basingstoke, 1998).

relative ease.[27] Many lawyers, like many laymen, were reluctant to participate in the trial that led to the execution of the monarch, Charles I, but the fact that this trial became a kind of non-event in legal history can be attributed partly to the fact that the case that was easiest to prove against the king was that he had participated in the murder of his own subjects. More importantly, since the king refused to plead to charges of misgovernment that were drawn up against him, there was no legal argument on these points, and since his conviction was based on a default verdict, it generated no case law that could be referred to in the future.[28]

Yet, once the deed was done, even though there were some who refused to serve, the Rump Parliament was able to find perfectly distinguished lawyers to act as judges. The most important of these at the time, Sir Henry Rolle, led the way by successfully insisting that he would not serve the republic unless he could take an oath of office that allowed him to swear that he would continue to judge according to the ancient fundamental laws of England.[29] It is true, and perhaps significant, that there were very few important justifications of the establishment of the republic written from the perspective of English law,[30] but although

[27] Brooks, *Lawyers, Litigation and English Society*, especially pp. 30–31. My more recent work in the court records of the 1650s suggest that, if anything, I previously underestimated the volume of business in the interregnum, especially in Chancery and King's Bench.

[28] S. Kelsey, 'The trial of Charles I', *English Historical Review* 118 (2003), 583–616. The political case drawn up by the prosecutor at the trial was published as John Cook, *King Charles his Case . . . Being for the most part that which was intended to have been delivered at the Bar, if the King had Pleaded to the Charge, and put himself upon a fair trial* (London, 1649). Reaching back to the beginning of the king's reign in the 1620s, it reads much like twentieth-century 'Whig' constitutional accounts of the conflicts between king and people.

[29] B. Whitelocke, *Memorials of the English Affairs, or an Historical Account of what passed from the beginning of the Reign of Charles to King Charles the Second* (London, 1682), pp. 363, 368, 372, 432; Ruth Spalding, 'Whitlocke, Bulstrode (1605–1675)', *Oxford Dictionary of National Biography* (ODNB).

[30] I am referring to the works written in connection with the so-called engagement controversy – in particular, those by Thomas Hobbes and Marchmont Needham. One possible exception is a two-volume work by barrister Nathaniel Bacon: Nathaniel Bacon, *A Historical Discourse of the Laws and Government of England from the first times to the end of the Reign of Elizabeth* (London, 1649); Nathaniel Bacon, *The Continuation of an Historicall Discourse, of the Government of England, Untill the end of the Reign of Queene Elizabeth. With a Preface, being a Vindication of the ancient way of Parliaments in England* (London, 1650). I am uncertain about its impact in the 1650s, but an 'Advertisement' by John Starkey that was included in a reprint published in early 1689 says that it had become popular after Charles II endeavoured to extend the prerogative, and attempts to republish it in 1672 and 1682 were severely prosecuted. The 1689 edition

lawyers wrote a lot in various different ways, they had rarely been producers of polemical literature on the scale of the clergy either before or during the civil wars. Surviving speeches given by judges, or other senior lawyers, in the localities at meetings of assize tended to stress how fortunate it was that the people could continue to rely on their home-grown legal system, which was distinctive from, and better than, those in other countries. Indeed, in 1649, Sergeant Thorpe, who was soon to become a baron of the Exchequer, used the occasion of a speech he gave on the northern assize circuit to praise the abolition of the House of Lords because it marked a definitive end to the pretensions to rule of the 'over-mighty', and overbearing, aristocracy and gentry.[31]

Thorpe's speech could be said to reflect perfectly the vulgar Marxist typology of long-term historical change, but it is no less important that it does not seem to have involved making a very dramatic imaginative leap from more populist legal rhetoric of the pre-civil-war years. Equally, I am not sure I can agree with Alan Cromartie's thought-provoking suggestion that the monarchy and the law were so mutually dependant that monarchy could never be completely transformed into another form of government so long as the traditional law survived. It seems that Bulstrode Whitelocke, a parliamentarian Chancery commissioner, was involved in drawing up new forms of legal writs during the king's trial rather than after the verdict.[32] Subsequently, court records were adapted almost immediately to reflect the series of changes at the head of the state and the wording makes some interesting reading. During the republic, legal process went out in the name of the keepers of the liberties of England by the authority of Parliament. In the court of Exchequer, whose jurisdiction had traditionally been limited to those who could show they were debtors to the king, it quickly became established that it was open to anybody, apparently on the basis that since everyone was obliged to pay taxes, everyone was, in theory, a debtor to the 'public exchequer'. Litigants in actions of slander in the King's Bench and

was also explicitly associated with the work of John Selden, at whom we look later in the paper.

31 Bodleian Library, Oxford, MS Rawlinson C. 182, ff. 101*ff* (charges by John Glynn and Matthew Hale in 1656); Samuel Johnson and William Oldys (eds), *A Collection of Scarce, Curious, And Entertaining Pamphlets And Tracts, as well In Manuscript As In Print, Found In The Late Earl Of Oxford's Library, Interspersed With Historical, Political, And Critical Notes (or the Harleian Miscellany)* (London, 1744–1753), vol. 2.

32 Whitelocke, *Memorials*, p. 363.

Common Pleas were described as 'honest citizens', and the word 'state' occurs occasionally in ways that are familiar to us today.[33]

To the modern ear, these changes of wording are intriguing, even appealing. What contemporaries made of them is much more difficult to say, but the fact is that the old legal system continued under new management. Furthermore, given the high levels of civil strife and the desolation of war, what people evidently wanted more than anything else from it was 'assurance' about their goods, landed interests (large or small) and family settlements, including an effective means of proving wills and managing the estates of the deceased. What is somewhat surprising about the nature of civil war and interregnum litigation is that while the dislocation and costs of war can be found in the court records, there is a much more pronounced impression of business-as-usual. The major exceptions to this were an increased visibility of disputes over tithes, which appear to reflect the use by parishioners of the religious uncertainty of the period to escape an ancient and undoubtedly irritating obligation, and the much greater recourse to the court of Chancery in connection with matters associated with the probate of wills that was directly due to the abolition of the ecclesiastical courts. On the whole, furthermore, the lawyers made a fair fist of delivering in terms of 'assurances'. Think, for example, of the development of the strict family settlement in the 1650s – a process that was closely associated with finding more effective ways of putting estates into trusts that would avoid, as far as possible, the costs of confiscations of land associated with political delinquency, particularly on the royalist side.[34] At the same time, this period can be associated with the further development of a distinctive view of property in land that began to allow the concept of land ownership as a natural right to enter the picture and hence to make way for the kind of theory of political obligation that the non-lawyer John Locke subsequently developed in his famous *Two Treatises on Government*.

None of these developments appear to have contributed directly to an atmosphere that would have actively encouraged radical legal change or grass-roots movements for reform that had either weight of numbers or a clearly identifiable focus. Nevertheless, there were attacks on the legal profession in Parliament, and, perhaps more notably, there is evidence from the popular press of a wide-ranging law reform movement that

[33] C. H. Firth and S. R. Rait, *Acts and Ordinances of the Interregnum*, three vols (London, 1911), vol. ii, pp. 6–9.

[34] L. Bonfield, *Marriage Settlements, 1601–1740: The Adoption of the Strict Settlement* (Cambridge, 1983).

called for changes in a range of institutions and practices. There was clearly a significant amount of smoke. The problem lies in discovering the exact location of the fire.

In 1645–1646, John Cook, a barrister of Gray's Inn, who became the prosecutor at the trial of Charles I, evidently felt compelled to write a defence of law and lawyers. The immediate cause was a pamphlet that advocated excluding lawyers from standing in by-elections, or indeed acting as members of Parliament altogether. In addition, Cook seems to have been aware that 'antinomianism' and other religiously inspired calls for further reformation were leading some people to think in terms of a world ruled only by the laws of God, in which secular lawyers would not be needed at all – an expression of anti-professional feeling that was to become a feature of radical sectarianism in general. In response, Cook identified some areas, such as the taking of excessive fees, in which reform would be advisable, but he defended the court of Chancery and made a strong case for the need for the continuation of the rule of law as it had generally been known.[35] In 1649, after Pride's Purge and the execution of Charles Stuart, there were sufficiently vocal criticisms in Parliament of the number and influence of the lawyers for Bulstrode Whitelocke to speak at length in defence of them, largely by drawing on a fairly traditional argument that it was, in fact, the sophistication of English society that caused so much recourse to law. According to Whitelocke, one reason for the deluge of litigation was the capacity of English people to dispose of their property by will; another was 'the freedom of our Nation where every one hath equal right and title to his estate' and where there 'is as full a propriety, to the meanest as to the greatest person, which causeth our countrymen to insist upon their right'.[36]

This parliamentary hostility to lawyers may well have owed something to the easily observed influence of lawyer members of Parliament, such as Whitelocke, Oliver St John, John Glynn and John Maynard – particularly since some of them had been amongst those who were in favour of

[35] John Cook, *The Vindication of the Professors and Profession of the Law: So farre forth as Scripture and right Reason may be Judge, and speedy Justice (which exalts a Nation) may be advanced . . .. Occasioned by way of Answer to a printed Sheet, intituled, Advertisements for the new Election of Members for the House of Commons* (London, 1645–1646). In the 1630s, Cook served in the discredited Irish administration of Thomas Wentworth, the earl of Strafford. In the 1650s, Cook served as a judge in Ireland after its re-conquest by Oliver Cromwell.

[36] BL, MS Additional 37345, f. 24$^{v}$.

demobilising the New Model Army after its victories in the first Civil War – and, despite Whitelocke's intervention, a committee headed by the future judge Sir Matthew Hale was appointed by the Rump Parliament to investigate and come up with reform proposals. Meanwhile, outside Parliament, the soldiers of the New Model Army, which effectively took power in 1648, were seriously concerned about being indemnified for offences against people and property committed during the course of the war, and there were also issues associated with demobilisation, such as the demand that veterans be permitted to take up the freedom of corporate towns even if they had not been able to complete apprenticeships as a result of war service. But none of this can be associated easily with calls for more general law reform that came near matching the intensity of the debates between the soldiers and the military grandees over property and the franchise that took place in Putney Church in 1647. While some members of the loose association of mainly London activists known as the Levellers contributed to the law reform debate, John Lilburne, one of the principal leaders and a record-breaking escape artist from charges of treason, was frequently depicted with a copy of Magna Carta in his hands. In the late 1640s, he became good friends with David Jenkins, a royalist Welsh judge and another thorn in the side of Parliament, when they did time together in the Tower of London.[37] Equally, while there were individuals who linked common law and monarchical tyranny as the twin embodiments of the Norman yoke that had oppressed the people since the time of the conquest, there were not all that many of them, and law reform was certainly not advanced by the parliamentary apologist Marchmount Needham as a reason for supporting the newly created republic. There were some calls for the abolition of the manorial system and copyhold tenure, but these were invariably accompanied by proposals about how landlords might be compensated and were probably non-starters largely because it would not have been obvious to copyholders that they would have radically improved the terms under which they held their land.[38]

In fact, once the evidence is sifted, the most dynamic, and effective, agitator for law reform in the period was almost certainly Oliver Cromwell (and perhaps some of his confederates in the Army) and there was also a significant amount of pressure from within the various

[37] See Andrew Sharp, 'Lilburne, John (1615?-1657)', ODNB; Christopher W. Brooks, 'Jenkins, David (1582–1663)', ODNB.

[38] Veall, *Popular Movement*.

branches of the legal profession itself.[39] Cromwell probably saw legal reformation as a corollary of godly reformation, but in the only significant speech in which he mentioned law reform in general, he also seems to have seen it as part of the process of healing and settling the nation that was such a political necessity after the dissolution of the Rump Parliament in 1653 and the establishment of the Commonwealth.[40]

Paradoxically, the single institution around which debate about reform was most intense was the court of Chancery – the debtor's, and indeed the copyholder's and married woman's, friend – in which conscience supposedly ruled the strict letter of the law. In fact, the role of the Chancery in the legal system had, for a number of reasons, long been a matter of debate amongst the lawyers themselves, but on the whole the need for some kind of 'equity' as a part of English law does not seem to have been questioned in the interregnum. Instead, contemporaries repeatedly expressed concerns about the fact that the existence, and accessibility, of a court like the Chancery encouraged what was normally referred to as a multiplicity of suits by allowing litigants subject to a hearing in one court to delay proceedings by taking their case into another one. Moreover, complaints about the court's large bureaucracy were accompanied by aspersions on the honesty of its officials, including the judges, and a suspicion of decision-making by single judges sitting behind closed doors with nothing more than their consciences to guide them.[41]

[39] See now B. Worden, *God's Instruments: Political Conduct in the England of Oliver Cromwell* (Oxford, 2012).

[40] T. Carlyle, *Oliver Cromwell's Letters and Speeches* (London, 1845), vol. VIII, pp. 29–30 (4 September 1654). In a speech in 1656, Cromwell made his famous remarks criticising the application of the death penalty to trivial matters such as petty theft (ibid., pp. 185–186). As the work of Cynthia Herrup is showing, this does seem to have been associated with the emergence of transportation as an alternative to the death penalty in some cases of felonious crime. (ED. See Cynthia Herrup, 'Punishing pardon: some thoughts on the origins of penal transportation', in Simon Devereaux and Paul Griffiths, (eds), *Penal Practice and Culture, 1500–1900: Punishing the English*, Basingstoke, 2004, pp. 121–137.)

[41] Veal, *Popular Movement*; Philostratus Philodemus, *Seasonable Observations on a late book intitled A System of the Law* (London, 1653); Anon., *Observations concerning the Chancery (1655); The Continuance of the High Court of Chancery vindicated, to be absolute necessary (the abuses and corruptions being removed) and the removal thereof, and the perfect Reformation of the proceedings in that Court, Proposed in several Bills weekly, or more, often, intended to be Published* (London, 1654), p. 3; Anon., *Certaine Assayes Propounded to the consideration of the Honourable [Hale] Committee for regulating the proceedings at Law, Whereby it is made evident that most cases now determined in*

There were therefore calls for courts that fused common law and equity – something that was not formally accomplished across the English legal system until the 1870s. While proposals for new courts of this kind came to naught, the opening up of the court of Exchequer to all-comers in 1649 meant that there was an increasingly important jurisdiction, staffed by common law judges, which further developed procedures that in effect allowed litigants to choose within the same jurisdiction whether they would be tried before the barons in equity or before a jury in the country at assizes. But the reforms actually introduced for the court of Chancery fell far short of anything so adventurous, perhaps largely because of the way in which they were managed. A notorious ordinance of 1654 that was introduced through the Council of State by Cromwell for the reform of the Chancery reiterated the long-familiar mantra that suits that could, or should, be tried at common law ought to be kept out of the Chancery. But, alongside this, the ordinance also introduced some procedural changes, including, most importantly, a call for a reduction in the number of under-clerks in the office of the Six Clerks – the people who, in essence, acted as attorneys for litigants in the court.[42] Evidently drawn up without consulting widely in the profession, the specific provisions of this ordinance were sufficiently objectionable for several of the common lawyers who served as commissioners of the Great Seal to resign on the grounds that they undermined the liberty of the subject,[43] and the prominent lawyer Matthew Hale, no doubt like others, was incredulous that there should be proposals to reduce the number of lawyers associated with the court when its principal problem was a massive overload of business that was exacerbated by the atrophy of the ecclesiastical court jurisdiction over marriage and testamentary matters.[44] There is still more that needs to be learned about the actual impact of this measure, which in any case lapsed with the death of the Protector in 1658, but the more significant point is that the longest serving and most politically radical of the Chancery commissioners, John Lisle, left behind a massive manuscript abridgment of Chancery cases that integrates fairly seamlessly dicta

*Chancery and other Courts of Equity may be reduced to Tryall at Law to the great ease and benefit of the Commonwealth* (London, 1652).

42 *Acts and Ordinances of the Interregnum*, vol. ii, pp. 946–967.

43 R. Spalding (ed.), *The Diary of Bulstrode Whitelocke, 1605–1675* (London, 1990), pp. 402, 407–409; Whitelocke, *Memorials*, pp. 602–603.

44 Willam Andrew Clark Library, Los Angeles, CA, 'Sir Matthew Hale's Cases and Opinions' (three vols), vol. ii, ff. 71–72, 87. Responding to a technical query about limiting the numbers of attorneys according to the ordinance, Hale commented that, in truth, the business of the court warranted more, rather than fewer.

from before 1640 with those he collected until he was forced into exile in 1659.[45] The Chancery did not need to be restored in 1660; it never went away. It had not changed all that much during the civil wars, but at the same time the process of trying to produce a predictable law of equity, which began around the turn of the seventeenth century, was already well established by the time the earl of Nottingham, who is often credited with the final 'settlement' of the court, took the Great Seal in the 1670s. In terms of actual business, my impression is that the really significant development, which may well have been associated with the social and economic costs of the civil wars, was a distinctly growing number of cases in which the law of mortgages was developed largely as a way of securing the payment of debts and as a way of raising ready money. In fact, if there is a single area I would point to as distinctive of the period stretching from 1650 to 1689, it is the association of legal instruments and lawyers with the emergence of what appears to be the origins of early forms of deposit banking and a closer integration of land into the market for credit.[46]

Apart from the Chancery ordinance, the other set of radical reform proposals that had some support in high places, and therefore some chance of implementation, were those associated with William Sheppard, a relatively obscure barrister from Gloucestershire, who was granted a substantial salary to act as a legal adviser to Protector Cromwell.[47] Probably the most prolific author in English legal history, Sheppard published a large number of works about different aspects of the law and, with the encouragement of Cromwell, he also produced *England's Balme*, a lengthy manifesto for general law reform, which touched on some of the usual contemporary concerns about the number and honesty of lawyers, while making some novel proposals – most notably, for the creation of a new type of local jurisdiction that would include the appointment of lay invigilators in local courts.[48] While

45 Spencer Research Library, University of Kansas, Lawrence, MS D87, 'Abridgement of Chancery Causes'.

46 See Christopher W. Brooks, 'The agrarian problem in revolutionary England', in Jane Whittle (ed.), *Landlords and Tenants in Britain, 1440–1660: Tawney's Agrarian Problem Revisited* (Woodbridge, 2013), pp. 183–199. See also Christopher W. Brooks, R. H. Helmholz and P. G. Stein, *Notaries Public in England since the Reformation* (London, 1991), pp. 73–75 and the references therein.

47 There is a good biography by N. L. Matthews, *William Sheppard, Cromwell's Law Reformer* (Cambridge, 1985).

48 W. Sheppard, *England's Balme; or proposals by way of grievance and remedy; humbly presented to his highness and the parliament: towards the regulation of the law and the better administration of justice* (London, 1657).

Sheppard's technical professional works are mostly conventional in their approach and content, *England's Balme* is more radical and clearly inspired to some degree by notions of Godly reformation (the lay invigilators in courts seem to have been inspired by the role of lay elders in presbyterian or congregationalists churches). Even so, Sheppard himself appears to have been aware that proposals to return justice to the localities were just what nobody wanted in a time of partisanship and political factionalism. When he went round the Inns of Court in an effort to generate support amongst lawyers, he was accused of being nothing more than the mouthpiece of the 'swordsmen'. Members of the protectorate Parliament apparently laughed out loud when they were given a brief chance to consider the proposals in *England's Balme* in 1657.

The 'failure' of law reform in the 1650s is perhaps best epitomised by the short-lived conversion of the record of court proceedings into English in 1654 and then the return to Latin in 1660. The changes apparently amounted to little more than the translation of older books of entries into English, followed shortly thereafter by the reissue of the Latin ones; people could not fail to have noticed, but hardly anyone commented. Nevertheless, it is also wrong to dismiss the more modest proposals for change, such as those put forward by Matthew Hale's committee for law reform (appointed by the Rump) as nothing more than minimalist measures promoted by the lawyers in an effort to forestall root-and-branch change.[49] In his *History of the Common Law*, Hale described the period from 1485 down to his own day in roughly similar terms to those I used earlier in this paper. He was aware of the stresses that had been caused by the boom in litigation, the introduction of a limitless form of action and the use of fictions to facilitate more effective processes. Civil war agitation over law reform perhaps provided an occasion for the consideration of matters that would not have happened otherwise, but in the event the political uncertainties did little to facilitate effective implementation. Hence, despite the talk even from this more lawyerly perspective, things look much the same after 1660 as they did before 1640. Hale himself seems to have carried the issues he was most

[49] The proceedings of the commission, which began in 1651, are preserved in a minute book: BL, MS Additional 35863. The proposals are printed in the Somers Tracts, and the committee received some scholarly attention in the 1960s – most notably, in M. Cotterell, 'Interregnum law reform: the Hale Commission of 1652', *English Historical Review* 83 (1968), 689–794.

concerned about – the need for a registry for all transactions in connection with land and a way of dealing more effectively with the regular resort to equity in cases that essentially involved debts – into the Restoration as matters that still needed reform. Some of the technical changes considered by his committee, such as the elimination of the need to pay for original writs at the start of actions in the court of Common Pleas and measures for the more effective summonses of defendants, actually had the support of some of the lawyers and they eventually came into effect through a quiet process of evolution that often involved legal fictions.[50]

Perhaps not surprisingly in the wake of the civil wars, it seems that both for Hale and for another prominent judge, Francis North, an epidemic outbreak of fraud was the most serious problem confronting legal and economic life in the post-Restoration era,[51] and while this might easily be associated with a general decline in moral standards following the free-for-all of war, it was also, from the juridical point of view, a problem engendered by the high premium placed on the right of people to keep private (secret) the details of their affairs, whether these had to do their business interests, their landed interests or, indeed, their family.[52] At the same time, in the commercial sphere, late-seventeenth-century lawyers and judges successfully incorporated what is sometimes known as the law merchant into the common law, particularly by enforcing the negotiability of promissory notes and inland bills of exchange – legal instruments that became vital in the way in which 'money' and goods changed hands between people who lived and worked in different places within England, and between England and the rest of the world.[53]

[50] Christopher W. Brooks, *Pettyfoggers and Vipers of the Commonwealth: The 'Lower Branch' of the Legal Profession in Early Modern England* (Cambridge, 1986), pp. 129, 131, 144–145.

[51] See the discussion of the Statute of Frauds of 1677 in M. R. T. Macnair, *The Law of Proof in Early Modern Equity* (Berlin, 1999), pp. 149*ff*; see Holdsworth, *History*, vol. vi, appx I, p. 375 for Nottingham's draft of the measure.

[52] Lambeth Palace Library, London, MS Fairhurst 3475, ff. 150–153, 172–181, 186, 240 [Hale]; BL MS Additional 32518 [North], 'Notes on the establishment of registration', ff. 51*ff*. There is a telling comment on the reasons why secrecy was so important in the commonplace book of Henry Powle, Beinecke MS 75, f. 130. Registers of men's debts, mortgages and securities were said to be likely to produce great inconveniences by ruining men's credit, especially those that dealt in trade, which subsist most in credit, by 'laying open their debts to the view of all ye world', which will 'make people afraid to trust'.

[53] J. S. Rogers, *The Early History of the Law of Bills and Notes: A Study of the Origins of Anglo-American Commercial Law* (Cambridge, 1995).

## V

To cut a long story short, there were some demonstrably significant changes associated with the civil wars, including, for example, the abolition of the court of Star Chamber and the provincial Councils of the North and Wales.[54] Equally, the doubt cast on the viability of the ecclesiastical courts by their suppression during the civil wars (and the rise of Protestant dissent afterwards) began a swing of the pendulum towards domestic patriarchy that was such a feature of the next 200 years. Nevertheless, the structure of the system as a whole, and the volume and general nature of the business in the courts in the 1680s, were so similar to what they had been before 1640 that it is hard to see a compelling reason for describing the civil wars as a watershed. The reason for this was not the hostility of the lawyers to reform, but rather the fact that the 'revolutionary' early modern changes in English law had already occurred before 1640 and these constituted a legal regime that most sides to the conflict, and most social groups within the population, were content to preserve. Indeed, you could go so far as to say that the laws of England, formulated over the centuries in an ongoing dialogue between litigants and the courts, were a source of stability during a period of internecine strife, religious fanaticism and military dictatorship. Yet this is a judgement made in relation to the kinds of everyday business for which ordinary people of all sorts used courts and it has been delivered with hardly any reference to political thought or the intellectual content of the law. In the remainder of the paper, therefore, I want to link a consideration of two subjects, law and religion, on the one hand, and legal education, on the other, to suggest that the period of political discords, especially if they are stretched up to 1689, did mark the end of an old legal order that made way for the emergence of a new, or at least an altered, one in the 1690s and the early decades of the eighteenth century. Later seventeenth-century politics have traditionally been seen as the 'Triumph of the Lawyers', but I am arguing instead that they contributed measurably to the relative decline of the traditional judge-made common law as an influential player in the English state.

It is hardly surprising that there is something to say about the relationship between law and religion in a period that saw a reformation and the eventual advent of a kind of *de facto* religious pluralism, but it is harder to

[54] See J. P. Kenyon (ed.), *The Stuart Constitution, 1603–1688: Documents and Commentary* (Cambridge, 1966). The downfall of the Council in Wales is well documented in the papers of the first earl of Bridgewater in the Huntington Library, San Marino, CA.

tell the complete story in a short space.[55] As everyone knows, the English Reformation began with an Act of Parliament that created a jurisdictional breach between England and Rome, and made the king the head of the church. However, regardless of the theological direction taken by the new church over the years, it retained hierarchical (bishops) and juridical (church courts) structures that were arguably identical to those of the pre-Reformation (Roman Catholic) era.[56] Throughout the early modern period, bishops became increasingly important political players and the church courts seem to have been as busy as every other jurisdiction in the realm. Indeed, because they handled the probate of wills, as well as the making and unmaking of marriages, English church courts appear to have had a wider jurisdiction than many of their continental counterparts. However, the church courts also used procedures (including those for summonsing defendants, taking evidence and rendering verdicts by judges rather than juries) and approaches drawn from the Roman and canon law traditions that were, once again, in place before the Reformation. They were different from those of the common law and they could plausibly be described as 'popish'.[57]

Jurisdictional conflicts between the common lawyers and the churchmen over a range of issues stretching from questions about tithes and the fate of deprived ministers to the validity of procedures such as the notorious oath *ex officio* in the ecclesiastical courts arose pretty quickly. From the very early 1550s, there were calls, particularly from Protestant lawyers, for the creation of a unified legal system. Since this did not materialise, a body of law emerged in a haphazard way about what was sometimes described as the ecclesiastical polity, and, within this, lawyers began to think in terms of a spirituality (which was the province of the church), and the temporality (which was the remit of the common law, as determined by the judges sitting in Westminster Hall). Conflicts arising in connection with this issue include those associated with Puritan clergymen in the 1580s and 1590s, and those involving disputes between Sir Edward Coke, Archbishop Bancroft and James I in the first two decades of the seventeenth century, which eventually led to the appointment in 1621 of John Williams, bishop of Lincoln, to the lord keepership

55 I have, in fact, written a long paper on the subject, from which much that follows is drawn. My feeling at the moment is that it will take a book to tell the full story. (ED. See Chapter 15 in this volume.)

56 Much of the general context is explored in Jacqueline Rose, *Godly Kingship in Restoration England: The Politics of the Royal Supremacy, 1660–1688* (Cambridge, 2011).

57 See Brooks, *Law, Politics and Society*, chs 5–8.

of the Great Seal and hence chief judgeship in the court of Chancery.[58] However, although the contemporary personal and political evidence is rich, I think it is helpful to appreciate that this kind of conflict between the spirituality and the temporality in fact had deep roots in European history. Developments in post-Reformation England recapitulated the conflicts between monarchs and popes, and civilians and canonists, that lay at the heart of the so-called Investiture controversy of the Middle Ages, and, by 1640, there were common lawyers who not only knew it, but were also saying it.[59]

The substance of the conflict in England involved the consideration of the relative validity of claims to temporal versus spiritual authority and, of course, questions about where supreme authority over the spirituality lay: was it in the king, the king in Parliament, or indeed, as some argued, the bishops and ecclesiastical hierarchy? At the same time, it is critical that theology or divinity of the kind engaged in by university-trained clergymen figured hardly at all in everyday professional legal thought. Although the study of canon law at Oxford and Cambridge was banned in the 1530s, later writers on the English ecclesiastical courts regularly referred to their traditional jurisdiction within the country and developed their arguments by reference to the Roman civil law tradition, which continued to be taught at the universities.[60] More general theological and clerical writing, including that involved in debates over the structure of the church, tended to be based on the scriptures, and on the ancient and modern commentators on them.[61] Meanwhile, although common lawyers did not often publish much on theology or church government, they were as profoundly affected on a personal level by evangelical Protestantism as any other section of the population. They took notes on sermons and had friends amongst the clergy. But their law books constituted another sphere, in which arguments were based on the positions put forward in previous cases and the accumulated dicta of judges, as well as statutes passed by Parliament, and old deeds and charters, including, of course, grants by the Crown. All of these points can be summed up through a brief account of the extensive archival

[58] The last prominent clerical Lord Chancellor was Cardinal Wolsey in the 1520s. Williams was the last cleric to head the court of Chancery.

[59] P. Stein, *Roman Law in European History* (Cambridge, 1999), pp. 40–41, 49–50, 59, 64.

[60] B. Levack, *The Civil Lawyers in England 1603–1641: A Political Study* (Oxford, 1973); Richard Cosin, *An Apologie for Sundrie Proceedings by Iurisdiction Ecclesiasticall, of late times by some chalenged, and also diuersly by them impugned* (London, 1593).

[61] For example, Joseph Hall, *Episcopacie by Divine Right Asserted* (London, 1640).

remains of the important Restoration judge Sir Matthew Hale. A remarkably prolific writer, Hale bequeathed a number of devotional works, all bound in white vellum, to his wife. His posthumously published *Contemplations Moral and Divine* (1676) almost certainly sold more copies in the late seventeenth century than his legal works, which in any case appeared only some years after his death.[62] However, Hale left his most important legal collections to his son and to the library of Lincoln's Inn, his Inn of Court. These consisted of a very complete collection of manuscript law reports – in fact, probably the best one to survive from the period – and a massive legal commonplace book that was very similar to that known to have been made by other lawyers, except that it is obviously much more comprehensive than most.[63]

As intellectual disciplines, law and divinity were remarkably incommensurate. Common lawyers were hard-wired with a type of anticlericalism that transcended personal religious beliefs in a period in which figures such as Bancroft, Williams and Archbishop William Laud were exercising an enormous influence on the king. The conflict that arose created a powerful dynamic that ultimately impacted on the development of the common law itself. The way in which this was worked out in connection with the jurisdictional relationships between the ecclesiastical and common law courts prior to 1640 has been greatly illuminated by the work of R. H. Helmholz, which shows that the church courts continued to thrive in many respects, but were increasingly paranoid about sniping at their jurisdiction by the common lawyers, largely because litigants were aware that they could use the jurisdictional conflict to their own advantage.[64] In the 1640s, the demise of the church courts seems to have taken place without much comment in the extensive pamphlet literature of the period. But there were other intellectual and

[62] A. Cromartie, *Sir Matthew Hale 1609–1676: Law, Religion and Natural Philosophy* (Cambridge, 1995), especially chs 9–11.

[63] Hale's devotional works have mostly ended up in Lambeth Palace Library: 'The Black Book of the New Law, collected by me and digested into alphabetical titles, written with my own hand' is in Lincoln's Inn Library, London, MS Hale CXXI (CXCI). There is fair copy (presumed to have been made for his son?) in the Yale Law Library, New Haven, CT, MS G.C73.1, along with mostly fair copies of Hale's extensive collection of manuscript law reports from his own time. There are also important Hale papers at the Clark Library in Los Angeles, CA.

[64] R. H. Helmholz, *The Oxford History of the Laws of England, Vol. I: The Canon Law and Ecclesiastical Jurisdiction from 597 to the 1640s* (Oxford, 2004). See also R. A. Houlbrooke, *Church Courts and the People during the English Reformation 1520–1570* (Oxford, 1979); M. Ingram, *Church Courts, Sex and Marriage in England, 1570–1640* (Cambridge, 1987).

political consequences as well. The historical articulation of the place of the common law in the English polity, which modern writers associate with Coke and the so-called ancient constitution was worked out in the late sixteenth century largely in parallel to, and in conjunction with, the history of the English church. Much of the language of liberty that emerged from this same period was generated in connection with conflicts between the ecclesiastical and temporal courts. By 1640, the hostility between the lawyers and the clergy in the age of Archbishop Laud led to an onslaught by lawyer members in the Long Parliament that was directly responsible for the exclusion of bishops from the House of Lords, which led consequently to the collapse of the Church of England and its juridical institutions.[65]

The implications of these developments are personified in the life and thought of John Selden. A lawyer by training, historian by vocation and moderate parliamentarian member of Parliament during the civil wars, Selden was widely recognised as one of the most learned men in Europe, and his life's work was devoted largely to understanding the relationship between temporal and spiritual authority.[66] His first major intervention in this field was the highly controversial *History of Tithes* (1618), which is sometimes described as a pioneering work of social history because Selden insisted that tithes and the obligations to pay them were human, rather than divine, in origin – points that could be established only through the study of legal records, rather than on the authority of clerical claims. In the 1640s and 1650s, he researched the place of episcopal authority in the English church, and its relationship to temporal power by tracing the history of Christianity back to the legal practices of the early Hebrews, the point being that if you wanted to know what the primitive Christian church was like, then it was essential to understand the political and legal context in which it arose rather than relying on (or believing) the facile claims to divine authority made by the clerics from reading what Selden described as their 'fancy gilt-edged Bibles'.[67]

Given these views, Selden and many other common lawyers were not notably concerned about the atrophy of the ecclesiastical court system

[65] Brooks, *Law, Politics and Society*, ch. 8.

[66] Our understanding of Selden has increased immeasurably as a result of the publication of G. J. Toomer, *John Selden: A Life in Scholarship*, two vols (Oxford, 2009).

[67] John Selden, *The History of Tithes* (London, 1618), pp. iii, xiii, 478–491. An accessible store of Selden's views on religion in the 1640s and early 50s is S. W. Singer (ed.), *The Table Talk of John Selden* (London, 1860), pp. 171, 151, 240–245. There is a seventeenth-century version of the manuscript in the Beinecke Library.

that accompanied the eventual abolition of episcopacy during the 1640s. Some, like Edward Hyde, earl of Clarendon, and later Matthew Hale, were perhaps coming to see ecclesiastical discipline primarily in terms of control over the clergy rather than laymen.[68] In any case, the old argument about the jurisdictional superiority of the temporal over the spiritual courts was a well-established trope by the mid-seventeenth century.[69] In practice, during the 1640s and 1650s, matters previously handled by the church courts began to find their way into temporal jurisdictions to the extent that they created pressures because of the sheer weight of business.[70] One of the major practical problems – how to handle the proving of last wills and testaments – was addressed, although not altogether successfully, by the creation of a probate court in London: a scheme that had antecedents in failed projects from the time of James VI and I, and which in fact brought England in line with other European countries.[71] At the same time, if, as Selden thought, marriage was essentially a civil contract between two people, then there was no great conceptual leap involved in handling litigation regarding it in the secular courts. Although marital discord resulting in domestic violence had long been heard in the localities by justices of the peace, there were other important issues, such as the questions regarding the validity of marriages made outside the established church, and the enforcement of the payment of alimony in connection with marriage breakdowns, which began to come before the royal courts during the interregnum, and some of the issues continued to have an impact in the 1660s and 1670s.[72] On the one hand, the secular-contract view of marriage helped to protect Protestant non-conformists from the full impact of legal disabilities that

[68] W. Dunn Macray (ed.), *The History of the Rebellion and Civil Wars in England begun in the year 1641, by Edward earl of Clarendon*, six vols (Oxford, 1969), vol. i, p. 407.

[69] Brooks, *Law, Politics and Society*, p. 123.

[70] Helmholz, *Canon Law and Ecclesiastical Jurisdiction*, pp. 308–309, describes the atrophy, but many of the details of the consequences remain to be worked out in detail.

[71] C. Kitching, 'Probate during the civil war and interregnum, part I: the survival of the prerogative court in the 1640s', *Journal of the Society of Archivists* 5 (1976), 283–293; C. Kitching, 'Probate during the civil war and interregnum, part II: the court for probate, 1653–1660', *Journal of the Society of Archivists* 6 (1976), 346–356; *Reformation in Courts and Cases Testamentary* (London, 1650), which is attributed to Henry Parker, makes the case for the creation of a secular registry. Much of the litigation connected with wills, as opposed to their authentication, was already being handled by the secular courts.

[72] In 1653, the commissioners of the Great Seal complained to Oliver Cromwell that cases concerning the payment of alimony were clogging the dockets of the court of Chancery: Spencer Library, University of Kansas, MS D. 87, John Lisle's Chancery Abridgment, f. 103.

might have fallen on them if their marriages and the legal documents associated with them (marriage settlements, legacies) had been invalidated.[73] On the other hand, the lapse in the ecclesiastical jurisdiction may also have disadvantaged married women by leading common law judges to invest more authority in husbands as heads of their households.[74] The revolution appears to have had a negative effect on the legal rights of married women.

It is true, of course, that the church courts, along with bishops and the monarchy itself, were restored surprisingly quickly after the return to London of Charles II in the spring of 1660, but their general importance in social life never again appears to have been the same.[75] Selden probably deserves to be considered one of the godfathers of the kind of hostility to 'priest craft' that is associated mainly with the eighteenth-century Enlightenment, but which can be found in Restoration lawyer-politicians such as Harbottle Grimston and Sir John Maynard, and which conflicted many others when questions were asked about the place of the restored episcopal church in the polity, or how dissenters, ranging from Presbyterians to Quakers, should be dealt with.[76] It is through Selden, furthermore, that we can see most clearly a connection between legal thought and the wider world of English and European political thought in the form of Grotius, Thomas Hobbes, and, later on, Pufendorf and Locke. It is also clear that Selden had a profound influence on other major figures of the time such as Hale, Henry Rolle, Bulstrode Whitelocke and John Vaughan (a prominent Restoration judge).[77] Yet while these intellectual developments might be considered revolutionary, it is important to keep in mind that Selden did not write often on contemporary legal problems (apart from church/state) nor did he contribute directly to the science of common law reasoning. In what is thought to have been

[73] C. W. Horle, *The Quakers and the English Legal System 1660–1688* (Philadelphia, 1988), pp. 234–238; Cromartie, *Sir Matthew Hale*, pp. 134–135.

[74] See, e.g., the arguments of Sir Robert Hyde in *Manby* v. *Scott* (1674) 1 Mod. Rep. 124 (86 *English Reports* 781).

[75] I. M. Green, *The Re-Establishment of the Church of England 1660–1663* (Oxford, 1978), ch. 6; R. B. Outhwaite, *The Rise and Fall of the English Ecclesiastical Courts, 1500–1860* (Cambridge, 2006), pp. 80–81; Barry Till, *The Church Courts 1660–1720: The Revival of Proceedings* (York, 2006).

[76] M. Goldie, 'Danby, the bishops and the Whigs', in T. Harris, P. Seaward and M. Goldie (eds), *The Politics of Religion in Restoration England* (Oxford, 1990), pp. 75–105, pp. 84–85, 87, 93.

[77] Hale and Vaughan were executors of Selden's will. Whitelocke sought him out as soon as he became a law student.

a redaction of his thought by Matthew Hale, Selden (and Hale's) theory about the nature of law stipulated that the one and only law of nature was that promises should be kept, and that human positive laws were essential to ensure human beings honoured this obligation. Indeed, such was Hale's scepticism about abstract theories that he comprehensively endorsed the rather introverted, or closed, tradition of common law thought typified by Coke in a short manuscript treatise that he wrote in response to an attack on the common law by Thomas Hobbes.[78]

Thus, while Selden's influence is, in some respects, everywhere after 1640 and, indeed, 1660, it remains a frustratingly ambiguous one,[79] and while there were doubtless several reasons for this, what I want to stress here is that one of the most important of these may well be the fact that he was an intellectual giant working in a pedagogic vacuum. Before the civil wars, the Inns of Court and Inns of Chancery in London, England's law schools, were bursting with students; although some have doubted their efficacy, the fact remains that the learning exercises at the Inns, such as lectures and moots, have left a mass of manuscript student notes that dwarf equivalent kinds of material at the ancient universities.[80] But the learning exercises at the Inns collapsed at the time of the outbreak of the war, and although the governing bodies of the Inns attempted to revive them in the 1650s and thereafter, these attempts were so unsuccessful that the entire system was still in desperate need of resuscitation in the nineteenth century.[81] Although still imperfectly understood, the immediate causes appear to be obvious ones, associated with the practical problems caused by war, including the exclusion of political delinquents

[78] Printed in Holdsworth, *History*, vol. v, pp. 500–513. '[I]f the most refined Braine under heaven would go about to enquire by speculation, or by reading Plato or Aristotle, or by considering the laws of the Jews or other nations to find out the principles of English land law', he would be wasting his time, because those laws were simply positive laws made either through customary judgments in court or as a result of explicit parliamentary statute. (ED. See now M. Hale, *Of the Law of Nature*, ed. David S. Sytsma, Grand Rapids, 2015; Gerald J. Postema, ed., *Sir Matthew Hale on the Law of Nature, Reason and Common Law: Selected Jurisprudential Writings*, Oxford, 2017.)

[79] There is a discussion in Cromartie, *Sir Matthew Hale*, ch. 2.

[80] The proof is listed in J. H. Baker (ed.), *Readers and Readings in the Inns of Court and Inns of Chancery* (London, 2000), which is a catalogue of readings with a guide to where copies and notes can be found.

[81] The story is touched on in several chapters in Brooks, *Lawyers, Litigation and English Society*. See also W. Prest, *The Inns of Court under Elizabeth and the Early Stuarts* (London, 1972); D. F. Lemmings, *Gentlemen and Barristers: The Inns of Court and the English Bar 1680–1730* (Oxford, 1990). The detailed history of the Inns between 1640 and 1688 is still unwritten.

from their chambers. By the time of the Restoration, twenty years later, students evidently did not want to put up the extra fees required to stay in London during the learning vacations rather than returning to the country where their legal and other interests had apparently become centred. Even the development of the post between London and the provinces may have been a contributing factor, since there was, from the 1670s onwards, a tendency for local practitioners to work through London agents rather than coming up to London themselves, as had been the case prior to 1640. After the Glorious Revolution and during the first two decades of the eighteenth century, becoming a member of a legal Inn went so far out of fashion that the institutions at times teetered on the verge of bankruptcy for lack of income from fees and because of the lack of new entrants.[82]

These changes in the Inns of Court and legal education are the most obvious consequences of the revolutionary period, and a measure of their significance is that the quality of legal education in the United Kingdom, and in particular the deficiencies of British law schools in comparison with those in the United States, are still a matter of public debate. However, the explanations that historians have thus far offered for them have pointed towards the causes mentioned above, along with a growth in printed legal literature that rendered attendance at the learning exercises unnecessary, as well as the cost and expense that lecturers had come to expect they would have to pay (not only did you have to give the lectures, but you also had to pay for elaborate feasts afterwards).[83] While certainly plausible, it is worth noting that these explanations fit comfortably with a long-standing assumption, which probably dates from this period, that law is a vocation best mastered through forms of apprenticeship and that anything written independent of practice or with little regard to what was actually being decided in the courts was not relevant. Furthermore, the legal literature of the post-Restoration period is not all that impressive. Sheppard's massive output by and large seems to have been marginalised because of his association with Cromwell and the 'bad times'. Matthew Hale wrote a great deal, and he no doubt had in mind a broader project that involved a comprehensive analysis of the history, structure and principles of English law, but hardly any of his legal works were published in his lifetime. It is true that there

[82] See Lemmings, *Gentlemen and Barristers.*

[83] Most recently argued by W. Prest, 'Readers dinners and the culture of the early modern Inns of Court', in J. E. Archer, E. Goldring and S. Knight (eds), *The Intellectual and Cultural World of the Early Modern Inns of Court* (Manchester, 2011), pp. 107–123.

was, during the civil war period and thereafter, a very significant increase in the availability of printed law reports, but many of these in fact put into print manuscripts collected by dead (pre-civil-war lawyers), such as the judge Sir George Croke. The random, almost accidental, quality of published reports in the post-Restoration period itself has led scholars to conclude that those that were not printed are, in many cases, better than those that were.

Even if all of the circumstantial factors involved in the decay of the learning exercises are accepted, however, the attempts by the governing bodies of the Inns to revive them at the time of the Restoration would probably not have been such abject failures if they had had the consistent support of the judiciary, but this, evidently, was lacking. In a preface probably written by Hale for the publication of the *Abridgment* of Sir Henry Rolle, for example, the author recommended the course of hard work and independent study that he and Rolle had undertaken in their pre-civil-war student days as part of a circle of up-and-coming lawyers surrounding John Selden (who had refused to take a turn as a lecturer at his Inn of Court in the 1610s); the author did not suggest that it was essential to participate in the formal learning exercises.[84]

There is not enough evidence to support a conspiracy theory, but it is worth comparing one of the last readings given before the outbreak of war with one of the first made afterwards. On the eve of the Bishops' Wars against Scotland, a barrister called Edward Bagshaw planned a series of readings that recapitulated nearly all of the by-then-familiar arguments about the relationship between the common law and the churchmen. In an unprecedented measure, Archbishop Laud convinced the king to suppress the lectures and threatened Bagshaw with prosecution by High Commission. Bagshaw rode out of London towards Northampton, accompanied by forty members of the legal Inns. He was subsequently elected a member of Parliament for the London borough of Southwark, who later asked him to present the Root and Branch Petition to the House of Commons, and he was one of the principal architects of the exclusion of bishops from the House of Lords.[85] By comparison, when the solicitor general, Sir Heneage Finch, gave a lecture on the royal prerogative at the Inner Temple in August 1661, Charles II, the duke of York and various other dignitaries arrived on a barge and were treated to a lavish dinner, with music, that was served by no fewer

[84] H. Rolle, *Un Abridgment des plusieurs cases et resolutions del common ley* (London, 1668).
[85] Described in Brooks, *Law, Politics and Society*, pp. 218–220.

than fifty junior members of the Inn. Yet, so far as is known, only one manuscript copy of Finch's lecture actually survives.[86]

William Dugdale, a high church Anglican, who published a history of the Inns in 1666, stressed the ceremonial, and the lavish eating and drinking that accompanied readings, but he said very little about their content, and herein may have been one of the key problems. Although they allowed plenty of scope for digression into case law, or indeed legal history, readings were traditionally supposed to be about statutes and, in the years before the civil war, it had become increasingly common for lawyers to talk about recent legislation, as well as ancient statutes such as Magna Carta. But who would want to run the risk of giving a series of lectures on, say, one of the constituent parts of the Clarendon Code (which introduced harsh penalties on non-conformists), when whatever one said was liable to generate hostility from sections of the House of Commons, bishops, the Crown or dissenters? Whatever the causes, the collapse of readings and the other learning exercises inevitably undermined the world of 'common learning' that had arguably characterised the legal Inns in their heyday, and which seems to have been such an integral part of the peculiar system of judge-made (or judge-found) law that was the essence of the English system. The collapse of lectures limited discussion of the law outside the courts and made the profession more dependent on the published opinions of the sitting judges. Furthermore, the publication of a few works (which, of course, made them widely accessible), along with the decline in the previously widespread practice of taking personal notes in court, in fact limited the range of materials to which students had access, as well as the ways in which they might be interpreted.

This state of affairs would have been important in any circumstances, but it was particularly critical during the 1670s and 1680s, when the English judiciary became openly politicised on an unprecedented (and never repeated) scale over the question of the relationship between the church, the king, and Parliament. One series of judicial sackings and reappointments followed another as Charles II, and in particular James II, sought support for their policies of offering dispensations to Catholics and non-conformists.[87] Contrary to what is sometimes written, this was possible not simply because of the weakness or malleability of the judges,

[86] W. Dugdale, *Origines Juridiciales* (London, 1666), p. 157; Harvard Law School, MS 5125.

[87] The best account is still two articles (in three parts) written in the 1950s: A. Havinghurst, 'The judiciary and politics in the reign of Charles I', *Law Quarterly Review*, 66 (1950), 62–78 and 229–252; A. Havinghurst, 'James II and the Twelve Men in Scarlet', *Law*

but because there were perfectly good common law arguments in favour of licensed indulgences for those outside the Church of England. The most telling single example I can give of this is the fact that the best brief in favour of any of the four dispensations granted by Charles II and James II (in 1662, 1672, 1687 and 1688) was written at the request of the king by Bulstrode Whitelocke, a loyal servant of both the republic and protectorate, who was, for the most part, seriously out of favour after 1660. Following Selden, Whitelock argued that control of the church had always been a matter for temporal authority and, in England, that authority was vested by the Reformation statutes in the King, who, with the help of his common law, controlled the church in England. If the king was head of the church, he was perfectly entitled to grant dispensations to people who wanted to practise their religion outside of it. However, in this same treatise, Whitelocke openly torpedoed his own argument by pointing out that since the royal dispensations over the church in question were statute laws, questions about their legality would ultimately have to be determined by Parliament.[88] Like Selden and Hale, the lesson Whitelock had learned from the civil wars was that the supreme source of legal authority was Parliament, and Restoration parliaments were, so we are told, dominated primarily by country squires driven by powerful support for the Church of England.

My suspicion is that, even amongst many Tory lawyers, there was a recognition from the 1660s, if not the 1650s, that religious pluralism was a fact of life that needed to be accommodated, and that the longstanding animosities between the lawyers and churchmen in fact meant that this could be relatively easily conceived within the context of traditional common law thinking.[89] Whitelocke himself acknowledged that he was able to write his treatise quickly because he had assembled most of the relevant notes in the 1630s.[90] Polemical writers such as Whig propagandist William Petyt collected relevant materials from amongst the old controversies stretching back to Elizabethan times; writing about the famous test case of *Godden* v. *Hales*, another lawyer, the Tory Roger

*Quarterly Review* 69 (1953), 522–546. As has often been noted, Restoration legal history in general has been remarkably neglected.

88 BL, MS Additional 21,099, 'The King's Right to graunt Indulgence in matters of Religion asserted by [Sir] B[ulstrode] W[hitelock]'; Spalding, *The Diary of Bulstrode Whitelocke*, pp. 663–664.

89 See also M. Goldie (ed.), *Roger Morrice and the Puritan Whigs. The Entering Book of Roger Morrice 1677–1691*, six vols (Woodbridge, 2007), vol. i, especially p. 283.

90 BL, MS Additional 37343, ff. 78*ff.*

North, rehearsed all of the old arguments, which took him far into the murky depths of English legal history, but without finding a very satisfying conclusion.[91] The problem was that the lawyers failed to come up with a new argument, let alone a decisive one, and the re-established power of Parliament meant that they were not, in any case, going to be given much scope for having a say in the matter. Instead, the profession was no doubt as fractured into factions, and then parties, as the rest of the country at the time. From the point of view of the judiciary in particular, revolutionary, or at least political, turbulence became much more corrosive in the period between 1660 and 1689 than it had been during the civil wars. Playing musical chairs with the judiciary was no way of encouraging respect for the law. Ironically, while the bishops of the Church of England, who had been the villains of 1642, became, at least for a time, the heroes of 1688, every single one of the judges of James II was dismissed in the wake of the Glorious Revolution. A judicial bench was, of course, restored, and stabilised, by William and Mary, and by subsequent regimes. But while the legal system as a whole survived largely intact, the old common law world of judge-made law, and the educational practices that had evolved over the centuries with it, were never thereafter the same – nor was the role of law and lawyers in political thought and life. The rise of partisan politics effectively put an end to the kind of juridical state that had existed before 1640. Within a couple of decades, furthermore, there was a massive decline in litigation, and ultimately a contraction in the numbers of lawyers, which eventually created a legal regime that was driven much more decisively by statute law, and hence political interests, than by the cases that litigants brought before the courts and by judicial cogitations about them. This has recently been associated with a more general shift in social and micro-political life away from the kinds of popular legalism and participation that characterised the sixteenth and seventeenth centuries, and a greater emphasis on the command of the state, and indeed social patriarchy.[92] It was also, of course, this legal regime, not the one that survived the civil wars, that was subject to the reforms of the nineteenth century.

[91] BL, MS Additional 32520, ff. 34–35.

[92] I addressed this in Christopher W. Brooks, 'Litigation, participation and agency', in D. Lemmings (ed.), *The British and their Laws in the Eighteenth Century* (Woodbridge, 2005), pp. 155–181. The idea has been developed further in D. Lemmings, *Law and Government in England during the Long Eighteenth Century: From Consent to Command* (Basingstoke, 2011).

15

# Religion and Law in Early Modern England

CHRISTOPHER W. BROOKS

Although the Church of England was established by statute law in the sixteenth century and secured as a national church at the time of the Glorious Revolution of 1688, considerably more is known about its conflicted doctrinal history than about its legal and constitutional characteristics. Historians of the English church, its clergy and theology, along with those of Catholics, non-conformists and post-Restoration dissenters, have taught us an enormous amount. They have examined conformist theology and apologies for the episcopal structure of the church, as well as the deeply held criticisms of both expressed by generations of individuals who questioned current orthodoxies. They have debated whether it was Archbishop Laud's drive for more effective management of the Church of England or the ongoing agitation of those 'Puritans' who thought the sixteenth-century reformations had not gone far enough that best deserves the dubious distinction of being the most dynamic 'cause' of the mid-seventeenth-century civil wars.[1]

Yet, while it is inevitable that the religious history of post-Reformation Britain should be written from the perspective of the clergy, or particularly committed laymen, this can lead us to overlook the fact that the spiritual side of life coexisted with a more secular one. Equally, although religious writers of all persuasions often debated the institutional shape of the English church and its relationship with temporal authority, the

[1] There are so many works to choose from that it is pointless to do more than mention a few of the most recent and influential here; other relevant work is noted in the course of the paper. See N. Tyacke, 'The Puritan paradigm of English politics, 1558–1642', *Historical Journal* 53 (2010), 527–550; Polly Ha, *English Presbyterianism, 1590–1640* (Stanford, 2010); C. W. A. Prior, *Defining the Jacobean Church: The Politics of Religious Controversy 1603–1625* (Cambridge, 2005); D. Como, *Blown by the Spirit: Puritanism and the Emergence of an Antinomian Underground in Pre-Civil War England* (Stanford, 2004); P. Lake, *The Antichrist's Lewd Hat: Protestants, Papists and Players in Post-Reformation England* (New Haven, 2002); A. Walsham, *Providence in Early Modern England* (Oxford, 1999).

language in which they discussed these issues rarely coincided with that used in secular legal and constitutional thought, even though questions about the place of the church, or religion, within the broader polity nearly always had temporal consequences. The purpose of this paper is to open up another perspective by investigating the way in which English lawyers and English legal thinking interpreted, and reacted to, developments in the ecclesiastical polity. It gives some consideration to the legal dimensions of religious heterodoxy, but the primary concern is to identify the differences between clerical and legal thought, and to uncover the ways in which questions about the church helped to shape the development of secular legal ideas and institutions. On one level, there are questions about the English ecclesiastical court system, which was structured on bishops and their dioceses, and which used Romano-canonical procedures, and its relationship with the common law courts at Westminster, where law was made, or 'found', on a case-by-case basis by royal judges acting in the king's name. But these issues frequently became tied up with broader questions about the relationship between temporal and spiritual authority, the place of the Crown and, indeed, the nature of law itself. The discussion begins with some general observations about law and religion, taking the one to be primarily that body of thought and practice associated with common lawyers and the Inns of Court in London, and identifying the other largely, although not exclusively, with the clergy (both conformist and non-conformist) and the institutions of the Church of England, including its courts. The paper then moves on to examine a series of critical episodes between the 1530s and the introduction of limited religious toleration for Protestant dissenters at the end of the 1680s.

## I

It is a commonplace that the distinction between church and state as it is known today only arose in the wake of the American and French Revolutions of the late eighteenth century, but questions about the relationship between the 'spirituality' and the 'temporality' are in fact amongst the oldest in European history. From the time of Charlemagne, emperors and popes disputed the right to make laws that were binding on all of the peoples within their dominions. Papal lawyers argued that the divine mission of the church made it superior to the secular empire, so that imperial law was valid only if it conformed to that of the pope. The long-running Investiture Controversy of the eleventh and early twelfth centuries, which had reverberations in England, as well as on the Continent, concerned the contested powers of popes and secular rulers over the appointment of bishops and the jurisdiction over which they presided. The resolution of the dispute in the Concordat of Worms (1122) made a distinction between the temporal position of prelates as feudal vassals of the Crown, and their spiritual authority and jurisdiction, which was derived from the pope as head of the church. Over time, two legal regimes developed throughout most of Western Europe and, although both owed a great deal to the Roman law tradition, secular civil lawyers and canon lawyers who worked within the ecclesiastical jurisdiction were as aware of the differences between them as they were of some of the procedural similarities. Canon lawyers claimed a superiority for their law because it claimed to be the law of God, while secular civil lawyers complained that the ecclesiastical courts used their self-proclaimed jurisdiction over sin to justify their right to meddle in all kinds of affairs, either temporal or spiritual. Furthermore, although the two laws were frequently taught together, secular lawyers maintained that jurists did not need to study theology – that, in other words, everything they needed to know was contained in the *Corpus Iuris Civilis*.[2] It is hardly surprising that there was a sixteenth-century adage, perhaps originating with Martin Luther, to the effect that good lawyers made bad Christians.[3]

Many aspects of this medieval background remained strikingly relevant to early modern perceptions of English legal history, and it also helps to explain the broad contours of clerical and legal learning in the sixteenth and seventeenth centuries. Although the study of canon law at Oxford and Cambridge was banned in the 1530s, later writers on the English ecclesiastical courts regularly referred to their traditional jurisdiction within the country and developed their arguments by reference to the Roman civil law tradition, which continued to be taught at the universities.[4] More general theological and clerical writing, including that involved in debates over the structure of the church, tended to be based on the scriptures, and the ancient and modern commentators on

[2] P. Stein, *Roman Law in European History* (Cambridge, 1999), pp. 40–41, 49–50, 59, 64.

[3] W. R. Prest, *The Rise of the Barristers: A Social History of the English Bar 1590–1640* (Oxford, 1986), p. 218.

[4] B. Levack, *The Civil Lawyers in England 1603–1641: A Political Study* (Oxford, 1973); see also Richard Cosin, *An Apologie for Sundrie Proceedings by Iurisdiction Ecclesiasticall, of late times by some chalenged, and also diuersly by them impugned* (London, 1593).

them.[5] Meanwhile, although common lawyers did not often publish much on theology or church government, they were as profoundly affected on a personal level by evangelical Protestantism as any other section of the population. They took notes on sermons and had friends amongst the clergy. They composed private religious meditations and other works of personal piety. Some, like Thomas Norton, who was the first English translator of Calvin's *Institution of the Christian Religion*,[6] or James Morice, who defended deprived late Elizabethan clergymen, were passionately religious men with impeccable links to the first and second generations of evangelical Protestantism.[7] The Restoration judge, Sir Matthew Hale, a prolific legal writer, left a number of devotional works, all bound in white vellum, to his wife. His posthumously published *Contemplations Moral and Divine* (1676) almost certainly sold more copies in the late seventeenth century than his legal works, which in any case appeared only some years after his death.[8]

Nevertheless, theology or divinity of the kind engaged in by university-trained clergymen figured hardly at all in everyday professional legal thought. As intellectual disciplines, law and divinity were remarkably incommensurate. For example, the Puritan martyr Henry Barrow spent some time at Gray's Inn and may therefore have been at least an able 'barrack-room lawyer',[9] but his principal work, *A Brief Discovery of the False Church*, which attacked both bishops and presbyters, cannot be evaluated as a piece of constitutional or legal writing. It is based almost entirely on arguments from scripture and, although there is one passage that mentions an era of 'primitive defection' when 'the ministrie began to vsurpe and grow into unlawfull supioritie and iurisdiction',[10] the gap between Barrow's sensibility and that of common lawyers who interrogated him was, for the most part, unbridgeable. Barrow's remark that 'that nation or common welth, Prince, magistrate, estate, degree, person

[5] For example, Joseph Hall, *Episcopacie by Divine Right Asserted* (London, 1640).

[6] John Calvin, *The Institution of Christian Religion* (London, 1561).

[7] Christopher W. Brooks, *Law, Politics and Society in Early Modern England* (Cambridge, 2008), pp. 67–68, 99–101, 208–209.

[8] A. Cromartie, *Sir Matthew Hale 1609–1676: Law, Religion and Natural Philosophy* (Cambridge, 1995), especially chs 9–11.

[9] Patrick Collinson, 'Barrow, Henry (c. 1550–1593)', *Oxford Dictionary of National Biography* (ODNB). Barrow is also discussed in Michael P. Winship, 'Freeborn (Puritan) Englishmen and slavish subjection: popish tyranny and puritan constitutionalism, c. 1570–1606', *English Historical Review* 124 (2009), 1050–1074.

[10] Henry Barrow, *A Brief Discoverie of the False Church* (London, 1590), pp. 96, 188–189, 220.

whosoever that submittth not to our Lord *iesus christ* to be wholy gouerned by his word both bodie & soule in all things whatsoever without exception . . . shall be utterlie destroyed amongst Christ's enemies' raised problematic questions that were not easily framed, much less resolved, within the discourse of secular law.[11] Time and time again, religious claims of access to divine authority resulted in animosities between the clergy and the lawyers as professional groups, even where there was a general agreement on points of practical divinity or on what constituted a Christian way of living.

It is true that the concept of natural equity – a legal mechanism that, in theory, permitted a judge to take account of moral values in situations in which the strict letter of the law would likely lead to injustice – had an institutional expression within the secular legal system in the form of the high court of Chancery. Up until the mid-sixteenth century, moreover, the office of Lord Chancellor or Lord Keeper, was normally held by a cleric. But Christopher St German, the most influential writer on equity in the period, argued in the 1520s that it was essential for the effective rule of law that the discretion of chancellors should be limited. In addition, although St German maintained that the laws of England were consistent with the laws of God, he also pointed out that most positive human laws were laws merely because someone said they were and, in his opinion, this included most of those associated with the Church of England, which were largely the product of human, rather than divine, agency.[12] Writing over 150 years later and undoubtedly influenced by the chill wind of philosophical scepticism, Sir Matthew Hale captured the self-contained nature of English common law in his reply to an attack on it by Thomas Hobbes. '[I]f the most refined Braine under heaven would go about to enquire by speculation, or by reading Plato or Aristotle, or by considering the laws of the Jews or other nations to find out the principles of English land law', he would be wasting his time, because those laws were simply positive laws made either through customary judgments in court or as a result of explicit parliamentary statute.[13] Despite the devotional works and alongside a number of (mostly unpublished) legal treatises, Hale evidently thought that his most important professional source of

[11] J. Payne Collier (ed.), *The Egerton Papers: A Collection of Public and Private Documents, chiefly illustrative of the Times of Elizabeth and James I* (London, 1840), p. 168.

[12] Christopher St German, *Doctor and Student*, ed. T. F. T. Plucknett and J. Barton (London, Selden Society vol. xci, 1974), pp. 44–45; Brooks, *Law, Politics and Society*, pp. 25–26, 46.

[13] Printed in W. S. Holdsworth, *A History of English Law* (London, 1966), vol. 5, pp. 500–513, at p. 505.

knowledge was a massive manuscript commonplace book that was organised according to the common law forms of action and which recorded judicial dicta in connection with them, going back to the time of Henry VII. The original was the only one of his works that he left to Lincoln's Inn Library for the benefit of law students and he had a fair copy made for the use of his son.[14]

There was also a more mundane, but nonetheless significant, reason why common lawyers did not feel the need to integrate whatever theological opinions they may have had into courtroom arguments. There was, after all, a parallel set of institutions within the polity: the English ecclesiastical courts, whose jurisdiction was explicitly founded on the notion that decisions should be made for the good of litigants' souls, and which served to discipline the clergy, adjudicate in the important fields of marriage and the probate of wills, and punish immoral or uncharitable behaviour amongst parishioners.[15] Thanks to this jurisdictional partition, common lawyers did not normally have to think in terms of incorporating the spiritual and temporal spheres. The ecclesiastical courts were institutional proof of a long English tradition of enforcing spiritual discipline. Indeed, after the break from Rome, the charges delivered by judges and other lawyers at meetings of local secular courts such as quarter sessions and assizes regularly called on the inhabitants of the localities to make sure that the ecclesiastical laws of the realm were obeyed and enforced.[16] Nevertheless, the existence of two parallel legal jurisdictions was also a potential source of conflict. Sixteenth- and seventeenth-century lawyers invariably traced the friction back to the late fourteenth-century statutes of Provisors and Praemunire, which made it an offence, enforced ultimately by penalty of death, for any case to be taken before the pope's courts at Rome if it could be heard in an English royal court. Furthermore, during the late fifteenth century, common lawyers began using a prerogative writ, the writ of prohibition, to stay actions in the ecclesiastical courts in certain types of case (including debts and slander), where the issues could be said to involve

[14] Lincoln's Inn Library, London, MS Hale CXXI (CXCI): 'The Black Book of the New Law, collected by me and digested into alphabetical titeles, written with my own hand.' The fair copy is in the Yale Law Library, New Haven, CT., MS G.C73.1.

[15] R. A. Houlbrooke, *Church Courts and the People during the English Reformation 1520–1570* (Oxford, 1979); M. Ingram, *Church Courts: Sex and Marriage in England 1570–1640* (Cambridge, 1987); R. H. Helmholz, *The Oxford History of the Laws of England, Vol. I: The Canon Law and Ecclesiastical Jurisdiction from 597 to the 1640s* (Oxford, 2004).

[16] Brooks, *Law, Politics and Society*, pp. 87–88.

a temporal consideration – a factor that, in their view, meant that it should be tried in a secular, rather than a spiritual, court.[17]

Not surprisingly, the standard post-Reformation narrative of English church history could inflame this way of thinking. Although Elizabethan apologists for the ecclesiastical courts plausibly defended them as institutions that had existed for so long that they enjoyed a customary role in the polity no less venerable than that of the common law itself, it was easy enough to retort that all English ecclesiastical law had been introduced against the prerogative of the king and the will of the people. Since God never explicitly gave the clergy power to make laws within the realm, those in existence were based on the usurped authority of the bishop of Rome. Equally, following the religious legislation of 1559, which vested the spirituality in the monarch, it could be argued that ecclesiastical law became the king's law – that is, common law – and that it should therefore be subject to review by the common law judges, and that practices within the ecclesiastical courts that failed to adhere to the general principles of English common law were invalid.[18]

As some contemporaries were quick to appreciate, one way of resolving these issues was to pass legislation in Parliament that would in effect recodify English canon law and adopt it formally as a part of the law of England. Addressing himself to Henry VIII in the early 1540s, for example, the well-known Commonwealth's man John Hales of Coventry advocated the written codification of all English law, including that of the temporal, as well as the spiritual, jurisdictions, and there are two other features of his thought that later emerged as commonplaces amongst lawyers. First, there was an unmistakable distaste for the institutional clericalism of the pre-Reformation period, which Hales described as being distinctly hostile to the common law and its practitioners. Second, he was clear that any new law code should be devised by common lawyers and should be based on the common law of England, rather than on foreign importations such as the Roman civil or canon law.[19]

While it is not known what, if any, direct impact Hale's treatise had on policy, at least one part of the programme he outlined was eventually realised. In 1550, Parliament appointed a commission, headed by Archbishop Cranmer and including common, as well as civil, lawyers,

[17] Ibid., pp. 45–47.

[18] Ibid., pp. 97*ff*.

[19] British Library, London, MS Harleian 4990, 'An oration in commendation of the laws', ff. 14–18; Brooks, *Law, Politics and Society*, p. 52.

which was charged with the task of sorting through English ecclesiastical law and coming up with agreed titles that could be formally adopted, presumably through parliamentary statute. The commissioners actually did the work, but although the reformed code they produced, the *Reformatio Legum Ecclesiasticarum,* contained very little in the way of radical innovation, it was apparently suppressed by the Duke of Northumberland's government in the early 1550s. The *Reformatio* was published by John Foxe in 1571, and promoted by Thomas Norton, a lawyer and 'man of affairs', in Parliament at around the same time. But the project had so little traction that it is difficult to recover the precise reasons for its lack of appeal.[20] Most likely, a new code of ecclesiastical law was simply something that very few people wanted to see implemented in legislation, regardless of how they felt about the place of the spirituality in the English polity. The commissioners appear to have presumed that the ecclesiastical courts would continue to use their traditional Romano-canonical procedures, which would not have satisfied common lawyers with the cast of mind of John Hales. However, by creating a statutory ecclesiastical jurisdiction, the adoption of the *Reformatio* (or something like it) would have unambiguously subjected the church courts to constant review by the common law judges at Westminster and may have opened them to common lawyers, neither of which was likely to appeal all that much to the churchmen, or indeed to a monarch like Elizabeth I. No less important, the *Reformatio* and the thorny questions it raised threatened to upset a perfectly satisfactory institutional *status quo*. People evidently found the ecclesiastical courts useful and resorted to them in increasing numbers during the late sixteenth century. At the same time, the common lawyers apparently saw little to gain from becoming involved in the kinds of intractable issues associated with the ecclesiastical jurisdiction over marriage or, more surprisingly that over the probate of wills, which was unique in Europe. Indeed, leading common lawyers sat on the ecclesiastical courts of High Commission, a species of supreme church court that was created by letters patent from the Crown on the basis of statutory powers vested in it by the 1559 religious legislation, and which was intended originally to deal with serious matters of church discipline up to and including heresy.

[20] Gerald Bray (ed.), *Tudor Church Reform: The Henrican Canons of 1535 and the Reformatio Legum Ecclesiasticarum* (Woodbridge, 2000), pp. xl, xliv, lix, lxxiii, lxxxi, xcvii, cv.

The passage of legislation along the lines of the *Reformatio* would almost certainly have had a profound impact on a number of areas in English law – most notably, that relating to marriage and the family, including widening the scope of divorce. In mid-sixteenth-century France, for instance, lay legislation on marriage has been credited with instituting more profound patriarchal family relationships and it coincided with a decline in the significance of a separate ecclesiastical jurisdiction.[21] Whether it would have fully resolved the conflicts between English churchmen and the secular lawyers is a matter for speculation. In the event, the last early modern attempt to resurrect the *Reformatio* came with its republication in 1640, when it attracted only a modest amount of attention.[22]

## II

The argument here is emphatically not that there was a widespread or systematic juridical dissatisfaction with the Elizabethan religious settlement of the sort expressed by Henry Barrow.[23] Yet the firmly entrenched, but uneasy, relationship between the spiritual and temporal jurisdictions became a powerful dynamic in public life in the years up to 1640 and then again after 1660. The ongoing ambiguities reflected in it lay at the heart of significant developments in common law thought, and were central to many of the political and constitutional controversies of the period.

The most long-running issue – one that clearly delineated the terms of the argument – was that concerning how far the common law courts should be involved in the adjudication of cases arising out of the payment of tithes, the principal means of remunerating the parish clergy. In a series of lectures at the Inner Temple in 1568, for example, Richard Gwynne hit almost every relevant point in what became a standard line of argument. The examination of English history showed that kings and people had evolved into a polity in which the king and the common law controlled the ecclesiastical sphere. Kings had always appointed bishops. All ecclesiastical power and jurisdiction had been granted to the churchmen by either the king or Parliament. Canon law

21 S. Hanley, '"The jurisprudence of the arrêts": marital union, civil society and state in France 1550–1650', *Law and History Review* 21 (2003), 1–40.

22 Bray, *Tudor Church Reform*, p. cv. It is mentioned in Edward Bagshawe, *Two Arguments in Parliament, the first Concerning Canons, the second praemunire* (London, 1641), p. 11, a work discussed later in the paper.

23 For the variety and content of the religious thought of lawyers, see Prest, *Barristers*, ch. 7.

had never been law in England and provincial constitutions of the English church were valid only insofar as they had been approved by the common law. It was clear that tithes had always been tried in temporal, as well as ecclesiastical, courts, and this was proof that the payment of the tenth part grew to the clergy of England by a positive and political law made for the ease of the realm, and not *jure divino* only or by virtue of any foreign law.[24]

Although never published, the synoptic preface of Gwynne's lecture seems to have circulated widely amongst lawyers. Even so, a well-documented campaign by James Morice and Robert Beale, two second-rank Crown officials, to challenge the attempt by John Whitgift, the archbishop of Canterbury, to use the ecclesiastical courts to enforce conformity on Puritan clergymen in the early 1580s generated more controversy and was, in the long run, more significant.[25] Morice's thinking about some of the issues can be traced back to the late 1570s, when he gave a series of lectures at the Middle Temple on the royal prerogative that outlined a version of English church history involving centuries of struggle between monarchs and the English people against clerical pretensions and 'usurpations'. Focusing on the role of the writ of prohibition, Morice stressed that the ecclesiastical jurisdiction had always been subject to the 'customs of the land', or English common law, and that it had therefore always been regulated either by the judges of the common law courts or by legislation passed in Parliament.[26]

Robert Beale was clerk of the Crown to Queen Elizabeth and something of an adopted son of John Hales, as well as a self-proclaimed legal auto-didact.[27] In a memorandum critical of Whitgift's policy, Beale warned that discord in the church would subvert the fight against popery, that the deprivation of 200–300 clergymen for failing to agree to every detail of the Book of Common Prayer would make it impossible to achieve the Protestant goal of maintaining an effective teaching ministry

24 BL, MS Additional 11405, ff. 5–13. There is a seventeenth-century commercial copy in University College, London, MS Ogdon 29, Papers of Timothy Turner, ff. 117*ff*. For further copies, see J. H. Baker, *Readers and Readings in the Inns of Court and Inns of Chancery* (London, 2000). Note that this reading is misdated in Brooks, *Law, Politics and Society*, p. 121.

25 Both are treated in more detail in Christopher W. Brooks, 'A Puritan collaboration in defence of the liberty of the subject: James Morice, Robert Beale and the Elizabethan campaign against ecclesiastical authority', in Paul Scott (ed.), *Collaboration and Interdisciplinarity in the Republic of Letters* (Manchester, 2010), pp. 3–16.

26 BL, MS Egerton 3376, f. 58$^{v}$; Brooks, 'A Puritan collaboration', pp. 6–7.

27 Brooks, 'A Puritan collaboration', pp. 5–6; BL, MS Additional 48039, ff. 48–49.

and that the queen would sacrifice public support if the church were to enforce conformity to ceremonies that were theologically 'indifferent'.[28] He argued that many points of Christian doctrine were a matter for individual conscience and hence not subject to the determination of either the monarch or the prelates, who sought to abuse royal authority in order to enforce practices that had not been authorised by legitimate legislation.[29] He maintained that the *ex officio* oath, a procedure used by the ecclesiastical authorities to make prosecutions in the court of High Commission and other ecclesiastical jurisdictions, was contrary to the basic principles of common law because it forced people to swear, on pain of imprisonment, that they would answer questions put to them before any specific charges had been made. In 1589, moreover, Beale became involved in the case of nine leading clergymen, including Thomas Cartwright, the leader of the English presbyterian movement, who were being prosecuted in the court of Star Chamber, as well as before the court of High Commission, at least in part because they refused to answer questions put to them or to swear the *ex officio* oath.[30] Far from accepting that their actions were illegal, Beale launched a comprehensive attack on the legal basis of the coercive power of the church. Referring to the failure to adopt the *Reformatio*, he maintained that the church was governed by an 'imperfect' law. The Elizabethan statutes on religion and the articles established by Parliament in 1559 allowed only for the prosecution of wilful, malicious acts against the church. They did not permit church court officials to ransack men's houses and studies to find evidence against them, or to compel those men to incriminate themselves on oath.[31]

The extent of James Morice's direct involvement in the defence of the presbyterian ministers is unclear, but he soon became an even more public critic of the practices of the ecclesiastical courts than Beale. In 1591, he acted as counsel for another clergyman, Robert Caudry, who had been deprived of his living in North Luffenham (Rutland) for defaming the Book of Common Prayer.[32] In late 1590 or early 1591, he published *A briefe treatise of oaths*, a learned and systematic attack on the use in the ecclesiastical courts of the oath *ex officio*, which argued that it was contrary to common law, as well as Roman civil and canon law

[28] BL, MS Additional 48039, f. 57.
[29] BL, MS Lansdowne 42, ff. 175–175$^{v}$.
[30] Patrick Collinson, *The Elizabethan Puritan Movement* (London, 1967), pp. 385–432.
[31] Brooks, 'A Puritan collaboration', pp. 8–9.
[32] Ibid., pp. 9–10.

itself.[33] Then, in 1593, he introduced two unsuccessful bills into Parliament which maintained that the practices of English ecclesiastical courts were against the due process clauses of Magna Carta, and which called for the outlawing of all oaths and subscriptions.[34]

Beale and Morice developed language that contrasted the ecclesiastical practices they opposed with what they described as the native legal and constitutional liberties of the English.[35] Furthermore, since the churchmen lent heavily on a high view of royal authority over the church, they stressed instead the role of Parliament in making the Reformation and hence a mixed-monarchical theory of the constitution.[36] But, although they had the tacit support of Lord Treasurer Burghley, their position was attacked in print by Richard Cosin,[37] a protégé of Archbishop Whitgift, and their immediate endeavours were largely unsuccessful. The judges' decision in *Caudry's case* confirmed the legitimacy of the court of High Commission and the oath *ex officio*. Morice's parliamentary initiative led to costly royal disfavour, as well as a brief period of imprisonment at the order of the Privy Council.[38]

Yet their efforts had a greater long-term impact than they might have expected.[39] The last person known to have been in possession of Morice's bills for the better enforcement of Magna Carta was Sir Edward Coke, the Speaker of the 1593 Parliament and a future Lord Chief Justice of England.[40] In the report that he published of *Caudry's case*, Coke acknowledged the judges' decision, but outlined the history of the ecclesiastical polity in exactly the same terms as Morice had done in his lecture of 1578.[41] It was this report, combined with the published attack on it by the Jesuit Robert Parsons, that led to Coke's clearest and most important

33 James Morice, *A briefe treatise of oathes exacted by ordinaries and ecclesiasticall judges, to answere generallie to all such articles or interrogatories, as pleaseth them to propound And of their forced and constrained oathes ex officio, wherein is proued that the same are vnlawfull* (Middelburg, *c.* 1590), pp. 10–12, 18–19, 24.

34 Brooks, *Law, Politics and Society*, pp. 108–109.

35 BL, MS Additional 48039, f. 49v.

36 Brooks, 'A Puritan collaboration', pp. 13–15.

37 Richard Cosin, *An Apologie for Sundrie Proceedings by Iurisdiction Ecclesiasticall, of late times by some challenged, and also diversly by them impugned*, 2nd edn (London, 1591).

38 Brooks, 'A Puritan collaboration', p. 15.

39 Not surprisingly, both figure in late seventeenth-century presbyterian histories: see M. Goldie (ed.), *Roger Morrice and the Puritan Whigs: The Entering Book of Roger Morrice 1677–1691*, six vols (Woodbridge, 2007), vol. i, p. 283.

40 Brooks, *Law, Politics and Society*, p. 108.

41 *Quinta pars relationum … The Fifth Part of the Reports of Sir Edward Coke* (London, 1604), pp. 42–45.

statements about the antiquity of English law. For Coke, as was indeed the case for Richard Gwynes in 1568, the history of the ancient constitution was framed largely in terms of the relationship between the common law and the church. Moreover, far from implying a lack of historical agency, as is sometimes suggested, it was a history full of political conflict that frequently pitted king, people and the common law against the churchmen.[42]

On his promotion to the judiciary, furthermore, Coke engaged in a long-running controversy with Whitgift's successor, Richard Bancroft, over the relationship between the ecclesiastical and the secular courts that centred once again on the common law writ of prohibition.[43] According to the clerics, at least, it was costing the church courts a lot of business. The juridical conflict led to a series of interpersonal clashes between the churchmen and James I, on the one side, and the judges, led by Coke, on the other, which arose during conferences the king held to resolve the matter and which, on one occasion, saw Coke down on his knees in front of the monarch. Coke maintained that since the church courts were the king's courts, the common law judges should be the ones to determine the relationship between the two. James, however, held that, as king and fountain of justice within the realm, as well as head of the church, he was the sole source of power for determining where the boundaries should be drawn between temporality and the spirituality. In this sense, the king was above the law, rather than created by it, as Coke maintained.[44]

This species of 'constitutional conflict' over the ecclesiastical polity also had a another dimension, since it was closely related in conceptual terms with attacks on secular 'equitable' jurisdictions that were based on the royal prerogative, such as those of Chancery, the Council in the Marches in Wales and the Council of the North. Since these courts, like the church courts, were based on the royal prerogative, they were potentially outside the jurisdictional scope of the Westminster judges and the common law. As many contemporaries pointed out, the most important of these courts, Chancery had always exercised its jurisdiction on this

[42] Brooks, *Law, Politics and Society*, pp. 118–123.

[43] Roland G. Usher, *The Rise and Fall of High Commission*, 2nd edn (Oxford, 1968); Stuart B. Babbage, *Puritanism and Richard Bancroft* (London, 1962). There are also a number of detailed papers on prohibitions in the papers of Lord Chancellor Ellesmere: Henry E. Huntington Library, San Marino (hereinafter HEHL), MSS Ellesmere 2007, 2008, 2011, 2013–2015.

[44] Brooks, *Law, Politics and Society*, pp. 109–117.

basis, but it was precisely because of this that Coke accused Lord Chancellor Ellesmere of committing the offence of *praemunire* for using Chancery subpoenas to prohibit cases from being resolved by the common law courts and thereby depriving the subjects of their right to be tried by the law of England. Although Coke was dismissed from office by James I in 1616 largely as a result, it made common lawyers even more sceptical than they had been previously of the kinds of abstract moral arguments made before a single individual sitting in judgment as chancellor and who had at his disposal the prerogative powers of the monarch.[45]

At about the same time, moreover, John Selden, who was emerging as one of the towering intellects in seventeenth-century Europe, wrote what proved to be an extremely controversial book on *The History of Tithes*. Having circulated initially in manuscript, the work was published in 1618 after Selden discovered that the clergymen were already writing refutations of it. Despite Selden's own, perhaps disingenuous, protestations, the clergy and lay readers alike took the book to be a refutation of the proposition that tithes were due to the church according to divine right. From a scholarly perspective, it was also a point of highest principle with Selden that the subject be addressed in terms of European legal history, rather than through the scriptures or the writings of the Church Fathers. If tithes were the subject of municipal law, there was no conceivable reason why their nature and history should not be interrogated by a common lawyer. Furthermore, in the 'Review' at the end of *The History*, Selden explained why neither canon or Roman civil law carried weight in municipal law courts, where the native legal learning of countries ranging from Scotland to Italy always ruled supreme. English common lawyers were therefore part of a much larger cadre of European legal professionals concerned with the articulation of the legal and constitutional relationships in the states in which they lived, including those that involved the church.[46]

The public humiliations that Selden suffered as a result the *History of Tithes*, including a citation before the court of High Commission, are said to have turned him forever against the bishops and the epistemological practices of the churchmen.[47] Although less personal, a similar blow was dealt to the common law profession as a whole when, following the

[45] Ibid., pp. 142–152.

[46] John Selden, *The History of Tithes* (London, 1618), pp. iii, xiii, 478–491.

[47] G. J. Toomer, *John Selden: A Life in Scholarship*, two vols (Oxford, 2009), vol. i, pp. 309–310.

disgrace of Sir Francis Bacon in 1621, James I appointed a clergyman, John Williams, as Lord Keeper and hence the principal judge in the court of Chancery. Williams, who had served as a chaplain in the household of Lord Chancellor Ellesmere, was a friend of Selden. But a telling insight into their relationship is the fact that Selden made Williams the dedicatee of his edition of the medieval chronicle *Eadmer*, a work that concentrated on the English version of the Investiture Controversy.[48] Promoted simultaneously to the see of Lincoln, Williams was the first churchman for seventy years to hold the Great Seal of England – and he was the last ever to do so.[49] Furthermore, although sniping from the common lawyers and political intrigue led to his dismissal from office in 1625, there were rumours at the time that Williams would be replaced by William Laud, the future archbishop of Canterbury.

## III

Looking back from the perspective of the Restoration, the barrister Francis North, a future keeper of the Great Seal, thought that the reign of James I represented the high-water mark in the hostility between the common lawyers and the churchmen, and in some respects he was clearly right.[50] Judging from the surviving records of King's Bench, the number of prohibitions issued by the court reached an early seventeenth-century high of ninety in 1610–1611, just as the churchmen claimed.[51] No less important, the potential juridical significance of the development of common law remedies that could be used against the churchmen was spelt out in a well-known reading on the due process clauses of Magna Carta given by Francis Ashley at the Inner Temple in 1616. Ashley, an active magistrate in his native Dorchester (Dorset) and a man of known Puritan sympathies, seems to have been predominately interested in the ways in which the common law – in particular, the writ of habeas corpus – could be used by individual subjects to resist all kinds of 'oppressions'. Nevertheless, he was particularly vehement in celebrating the protection that the Great Charter offered against the 'exorbitant pretensions of the clergy'.[52]

48 Ibid., pp. 334–335.
49 Brooks, *Law, Politics and Society*, pp. 150–152, 162–165.
50 BL MS Additional 32518, f. 219.
51 The National Archives, Kew, KB 165/1, Plea side *scire facias* rolls.
52 BL, MS Harleian 4841, ff. 4, 51; Brooks, *Law, Politics and Society*, pp. 156–157.

By the beginning of the reign of Charles I in 1625, by contrast, the number of prohibitions issued by King's Bench had dropped to roughly half that of the high point in the early 1610s, and systematic discussion of the relationship between the temporal and spiritual spheres is much harder to find between 1625 and 1635 than it had been in the time of James I.[53] Indeed, in 1620, the approach that Thomas Trist took to a reading at the Middle Temple on the Edwardian statute of tithes (2 & 3 Ed. VI, c. 13) was apparently less confrontational than Selden's book had been.[54] Yet, despite the different political circumstances of the 1620s, some of the issues raised by the Elizabethan conflicts about the oath *ex officio* remained in play. According to Sir Edward Coke, a bill proposed in the Parliament of 1621 for better securing subjects from unlawful imprisonment, which appears to have been directed mainly at justices of the peace, was based on the one that James Morice brought into the House of Commons in 1591.[55] The same measure also appears to have been in Coke's thoughts when he initially proposed a parliamentary reaffirmation of the Great Charter in the debates that eventually led to the Petition of Right in 1628.[56]

In the 1630s, as is well known, Laud stepped up the pressure on nonconformity through the use of High Commission[57] and maintained a high view of the royal prerogative, whilst at the same time asserting what he himself described as the *jure divino*, or divinely sanctioned, authority of bishops and their jurisdiction.[58] Although not all of them were a direct reaction to Laudian policy, the number of prohibitions issued by the King's Bench was already, in 1630, nearly double that of

[53] TNA, KB 165/5: Michaelmas 1 Charles I to Trinity 1 Charles I (forty-three prohibitions; five consultations).

[54] BL, MS Additional 25233, ff. 1–2. Although he repeated the by-now-old saws about the distinctions between the secular and ecclesiastical jurisdiction, and the historic encroachments of the clergy, the substance of his lectures consisted of a fairly dispassionate account of the law relating to tithes – in particular, those held by laymen – as it then stood.

[55] P. Halliday, *Habeas Corpus. From England to Empire* (Cambridge, MA, 2010), p. 221.

[56] Brooks, *Law, Politics and Society*, p. 174.

[57] S. R. Gardiner (ed.), *Reports of Cases in the Courts of Star Chamber and High Commission* (London, 1886).

[58] J. H. Parker (ed.), *The Works of the Most Reverend Father in God, William Laud, D.D., sometime Lord Archbishop of Canterbury*, seven vols (London, 1847–1860), vol. vi(i), p. 43. William Drake noted in his commonplace book early in the 1630s that 'Bishops press things of indifferency with so much eagerness because it is a means to uphold their courts, and because they think the preciser sort of men the greatest enemies to their riches and glory': HEHL, MS HM 55603, f. 4.

1625.[59] Laud complained throughout the decade about the deleterious effect these prohibitions might have on the church courts and on the professional fortunes of the civil lawyers who worked within them, even though there was apparently no precipitate decline in the fortunes of the ecclesiastical jurisdiction.[60] Certainly, none of the common law judges made anything like as dramatic a stand on the issues as Coke had done in the first decade of the seventeenth century. Instead, there was a series of clashes of greater or lesser notoriety that reflected the growing intellectual tensions between the lawyers and the churchmen.[61] Of these, the most famous was the sentence in Star Chamber against the barrister William Prynne and his co-defendants, Bastwick and Burton, for their intemperate attacks on episcopacy. But while the publicity surrounding this case is testimony to its immediate political importance, there were also lesser-known incidents that are even more revealing about the juridical issues at stake.[62]

In 1635, for instance, Bulstrode Whitelocke, a young barrister who was recorder of Abingdon (Oxfordshire), became involved in a dispute that began when some of the townsmen there complained about so-called non-conformists who, amongst other things, allegedly refused to stand up during the creed or to bow to the altar at the name of Jesus.[63] The town mayor, who was sympathetic to the non-conformists, refused to take any action. Whitelocke, who described himself as 'very much for liberty of conscience', supported him, and was evidently saved from the wrath of the Privy Council only through the intervention of the 'Puritan' earl of Holland, the high steward of Abingdon. In his diary, Whitelocke explained that he had not proceeded against the 'non-conformists' because the complainants had not preferred an indictment and he 'knew of no common law, nor statute, in force for the punishment of

[59] TNA, KB 165/5: Michaelmas 5 Charles I to Trinity Vacation 6 Charles I (seventy-six prohibitions; fifteen consultations).

[60] Helmholz, *Canon Law and Ecclesiastical Jurisdiction*, pp. 304–305, acknowledges the shadow of prohibitions, but shows that business declined only slightly right up to 1642.

[61] Brooks, *Law, Politics and Society*, pp. 208–220. In addition, there was an ongoing conflict between Laud and the Council of the Marches in Wales in the late 1630s over the claim of the Council to hear cases connected with legacies in wills and sexual incontinence: HEHL, MS Ellesmere 7482–3, 7508–9.

[62] Late seventeenth-century presbyterian Roger Morrice may, in fact, have exaggerated the extent to which the prosecution of Prynne on its own stirred up the hostility of the lawyers to Laud and Charles I: Goldie (ed.), *Roger Morrice and the Puritan Whigs*, vol. i.

[63] BL, MS Additional 37343, ff. 5*ff*. See also R. Spalding, *The Improbable Puritan: A Life of Bustrode Whitelocke, 1605–1675* (London, 1975); R. Spalding, 'Whitelocke, Bulstrode, appointed Lord Whitelocke under the protectorate (1605–1675)', ODNB.

them, especially by justices of the peace'. As he told the earl of Holland, the offences in question were 'spiritual matters' that should have been brought before the church courts. He even pointed out that he himself might well have been censured for encroaching on the jurisdiction of the church if he had done as the conformists had wished. As Whitelocke later described it, his overall view at the time was that government was a 'civil thing' and, in England, government, including that of the church, was a matter for the civil magistrate, the king and Parliament. In the 1630s, he did a lot of reading about the jurisdiction of the temporal courts in ecclesiastical matters, largely because, in 'these dayes', the 'spiritual men' began to 'swell higher then ordinary' and took it 'as an injury to the Church, that anything savouring of the spirituality should be within the cognisance of ignorant laymen'. Yet, aware that his inaction at Abingdon had cost him friends amongst the Oxfordshire gentry, Whitelocke became wary thereafter of expressing his views too openly in public speeches.[64]

While Whitelocke apparently aimed for a quiet life, Edward Bagshawe, another lawyer with Oxfordshire connections, came into much more direct conflict with the clerical establishment in early 1640, when he began a series of lectures at the Inner Temple on the ecclesiastical legislation of Edward III by explaining to his audience that he had hit on the topic because it enabled him to advance the common law above the civil and canon laws, and to prove that it was more 'agreeable' to the law of God than the other two.[65] Bagshawe later maintained that the lecture merely outlined the law as he had come to understand it after nearly thirty years as a student and practitioner, and in many respects there was indeed little in it that was new.[66] One of the few recent cases that Bagshawe specifically mentioned was that of George Huntley, a clergyman, who became involved with High Commission and was deprived of his living in Kent in 1629.[67] But although Bagshawe subsequently criticised the Caroline judges for failing to issue prohibitions to

[64] BL, MS Additional 37343, ff. 5–7.

[65] BL, MS Stowe 424, f. 3. There are several manuscript versions. See also Brooks, *Law, Politics and Society*, pp. 218–220.

[66] *A Just Vindication of the Questioned Part of the Reading of Edward Bagshaw, Esq., An Apprentice of the Common Law* (1660), pp. 16, 42.

[67] BL, MS Hargrave 206, ff. 43–44. Huntley, an MA from Oxford, was born about 1585. He was appointed rector of Stourmouth (Kent) in 1610 and deprived in July 1629: Clergy of the Church of England Database (www.theclergydatabase.org.uk). Notes on a petition that Huntley addressed to the judges concerning his case survive in Lambeth Palace Library, London, MS 3263, f. 17 (papers of Sir John Bramston, CJKB).

High Commission when they were warranted by law, or refusing writs of habeas corpus brought by those imprisoned, these issues were hardly the only ones on which he focused.[68] Providing an overview of the legal history of the English church, Bagshawe's division of the relationship between the clerical and secular jurisdictions into three phases was probably borrowed from a report of a well-known Irish case of *praemunire* published by Sir John Davies in 1615. In the first 500 years after the death of Christ, there had been in England virtually no distinction between temporal and ecclesiastical causes. In the next 500 years, the temporal authorities had allowed the clergy jurisdiction over marriage and testamentary matters on the grounds that they were purely spiritual concerns. For most of the final 500 years, roughly from the time of the Norman Conquest onwards, the clergy had accumulated greater and greater powers – a process that might well have continued had they not tried, during the time of Wolsey, to suppress the common law and establish the civil and canon laws, before being thwarted by king and Parliament.[69] Referring to the works of Selden, Bagshawe maintained that parish churches had originally been founded by laymen. Only later, as the clergy became great, did bishops secure control over the consecration of clergymen, which left patrons with nothing but a bare 'notion'.[70] He questioned whether there was any common or canon law that justified the burning of convicted heretics. He maintained that anyone who sued for a temporal thing in a spiritual court committed the offence of *praemunire* and that it was for the common law judges alone to interpret statutes relating to spiritual, as well as temporal, matters.[71] Referring to the Investiture Controversy, he noted at one point that the Constitutions of Clarendon (Henry II) were as famous as the Pragmatic Sanction, and he devoted considerable attention to a refutation of the views of the civilians Richard Cosin and Sir Thomas Ridley, who had argued that the English Reformation, and spiritual headship of the Crown, made the laws of *praemunire* redundant.[72]

Yet none of this was apparently the reason why Archbishop Laud enlisted the support of King Charles to suppress the lectures. On the

[68] *A Just Vindication*, pp. 4–5.

[69] BL, MS Hargrave 206, ff. 3v, 14, 24; Sir John Davies, *Le Primer Report des Cases & Matters en Ley* (Dublin, 1615), pp. 84*ff*.

[70] BL, MS Hargrave 206, f. 13.

[71] Ibid., ff. 44–48.

[72] Ibid., ff. 24, 44–49; Sir Thomas Ridley, *A View of the Civile and Ecclesiastical Law* (London, 1634 [1604]).

eve of the Bishops' War, Bagshawe was also arguing that beneficed clergymen should not exercise civil jurisdiction by acting as justices of the peace. Furthermore, he maintained that Acts of Parliament, including important legislation such as the Elizabethan Act of Supremacy, could be made legally even when bishops were not sitting in the House of Lords. Developing a point that he had argued recently in the Star Chamber case brought by Laud against Bishop Williams, Bagshawe in effect denied bishops any secular political authority as a result of their spiritual status.[73] Referring to Coke's report of *Caudry's case*, which had covered the history of ecclesiastical patronage, his position was that bishops held their seats in the House of Lords as a result of the temporal baronies that had been attached to their sees, rather than in respect of their ecclesiastical offices. Although Laud managed to prevent Bagshawe from completing his reading, it was sufficiently well known at the Inns of Court for some forty members of the Temple to ride alongside him as he left London in the spring of 1640. Along with another barrister, John White, author of *The First Century of Malignant Priests*,[74] Bagshawe was offered a seat in the Short and Long Parliaments by the (London) borough of Southwark, largely on the basis of the reputation his reading had established.[75] Once there, he and other lawyers were the leading figures in the movement that led eventually to the abolition of the court of High Commission, as well as a bill that excluded bishops from the House of Lords.[76]

[73] W. Cobbett and T. B. Howell (eds), *Cobbett's Complete Collection of State Trials and Proceedings for High Treason and Other Crimes*, thirty-four vols (London, 1809–1828), vol. iii, cols 770*ff*.

[74] *The first century of scandalous, malignant priests, made and admitted into benefices by the prelates, in whose hand the ordination of ministers and government of the church hath been. Or, A narration of the causes for which the Parliament hath ordered the sequestration of the benefices of severall ministers complained of before them, for vitiousnesse of life, errors in doctrine . . . and for practising and pressing superstitious innovations against law, and for malignancy against the Parliament* (1643).

[75] Brooks, *Law, Politics and Society*, pp. 220–221.

[76] Ibid., pp. 234–236; Edward Bagshawe, *Two Arguments in Parliament, The First Concerning Cannons, The Second Praemunire* (London, 1641). This speech refers extensively to the Investiture Controversy and also praised the *Reformatio*. It raises nearly every issue in the legal controversy with the churchmen going back to the reign of Elizabeth. For a recent account of some of the general religious and political issues, see W. M. Abbott, 'Anticlericalism and episcopacy in parliamentary debates, 1640–41: secular versus spiritual functions', in Buchanan Sharp and Mark Charles Fissel (eds), *Law and Authority in Early Modern England: Essays Presented to Thomas Garden Barnes* (Newark, 2007), pp. 157–185.

## IV

Writing many years after the fact, Edward Hyde, a barrister from Wiltshire, who became earl of Clarendon and a mainstay of the Stuart cause from 1641 until the late 1660s, claimed that the downfall of the Church of England would never have been accomplished without the help of the lawyers. Although clearly aware of the longer-term sources of discord, Clarendon maintained that the lawyers in the Long Parliament were motivated primarily by a desire to prevent the king from packing the House of Lords with new bishops appointed to fill existing vacancies and he concluded that they had used the law to 'wound the Church in its jurisdiction and at last to cut it up by the roots, and demolish its foundation'.[77] Yet, while the exclusion of the bishops from the Lords was the wedge that led eventually to the abolition of episcopacy and the atrophy of the ecclesiastical courts, lawyers appear to have been clearer about what they disliked in the existing church than about what they wanted to put in its place.[78] Few were as keen as Clarendon to support the traditional episcopal structure of the church, but, as the 1640s unfolded, the alternatives multiplied and ongoing political developments complicated the process of finding a settlement. The need of the two houses for support from the Scots resulted in the Solemn League and Covenant of 1643, which appeared to bind those who took it to support a closer convergence of the churches of England and Scotland by introducing some form of presbyterian church government into England. Meanwhile the growth of sectarianism lent a greater voice to Independents and Congregationalists, who were increasingly hostile to the idea that the power of the state should be used to enforce religious conformity, but who were also branded by their enemies as sources of religious and social disorder.[79]

The well-known gyrations of William Prynne from radical anti-episcopalian to anti-presbyterian and supporter of the re-established

[77] W. Dunn Macray (ed.), *The History of the Rebellion and Civil Wars in England by Edward, Earl of Clarendon*, six vols (Oxford, 1969), vol. i, pp. 401, 404–407.

[78] Writing in 1645 and in connection with the execution of Laud, Henry Parker covered much of the familiar ground regarding the dual jurisdiction, but focused on the way in which the churchmen had extended the royal prerogative to extend their own power: Henry Parker, *Jus Regum, or A Vindication of the Regall Power Against All Spirituall Authority exercised under any form of Ecclesiastical Government* (London, 1645), pp. 20–27.

[79] D. L. Smith, *Constitutional Royalism and the Search for Settlement c. 1640–1649* (Cambridge, 1994), pp. 143*ff*; A. Hughes, *Gangraena and the Struggle for the English Revolution* (Oxford, 2004).

Church of England may have been only an exaggerated example of a common trajectory.[80] As early as February 1641, Edward Bagshawe spoke in Parliament in favour of a return of episcopacy to its primitive state, but he explicitly rejected presbyterianism as an alternative for England, even though, he said, he might have favoured it if he had lived in a country such as France, Spain or Scotland, in which the civil law, the law of the pope, was in force as the national municipal law.[81] He refused to take the Covenant in 1643, served in the 'anti-parliament' at Oxford and was imprisoned by the two Houses on a charge of treason early in the summer of 1644.[82]

The only significant voice in favour of religious toleration was that of the regicide John Cook, the prosecutor of Charles I, who published *What the Independents Would Have* in 1647. Cook thought that the time was ripe for ensuring that the laws of England contained nothing contrary to the law of God, but his position was moderate. The Independents were asking for nothing more than what Elizabethan and Jacobean Puritans had been seeking: the complete freedom to pursue their religious practices without interference from the ecclesiastical authorities of the Church of England. Cook agreed that many of the radical religious ideas in circulation might be described as erroneous, or indeed heretical, but he argued that the best way of dealing with them and, at the same time, of ensuring adherence to civil authority was to allow them to interact in the marketplace of ideas. In this respect, he was against persecution, even though he accepted the idea of a state-sponsored moderate presbyterian church, and he agreed that it was necessary and legitimate to use coercive measures against non-Christians and Catholics.[83]

Well-known political figures such as Oliver St John and John Glynn, both of whom became interregnum judges, are harder to pin down. St John, who was a close friend of Oliver Cromwell and who may have shared some of his religious views, introduced the bill for the exclusion of

[80] See William Lamont, 'Prynne, William (1600–1669)', ODNB.

[81] *Mr Bagshaw's Speech in Parliament February the ninth, 1640, Concerning Episcopacy and the London Petition* (1641), p. 7.

[82] Bulstrode Whitelocke, *Memorials of the English Affairs: or, an Historical Account of What passed from the beinning of the Reign of King Charles the First, to King Charles the Second his Happy Restaurations* (London, 1682), p. 88; Edward Bagshawe, *The Rights of the Crown England as it is Established by Law* (London, 1660), Epistle, pp. 124–126.

[83] John Cook, *What the Independents Would have or, A Character Declaring some of their Tenents, and their desires to disabuse those who speak ill of that they know not* (London, 1647).

bishops from the Lords, spoke in favour of the Solemn League and Covenant, and was appointed a member of the Westminster Assembly of Divines. But he was also, of course, a leader of the political Independents in Parliament, even though there is no clear indication about where he stood ultimately on the fate of the English church.[84] John Glynn, the Recorder of London in the late 1640s, was associated with City presbyterianism and the so-called Peace Party that favoured the disbandment of the army, but in November 1644 he spoke effectively in Parliament against the introduction of *jure divino* presbyterianism. In the late 1650s, he became embroiled in controversies associated with the treatment of Quakers in the West Country and had his legal learning thrown back in his face with some vehemence when he prosecuted them for failure to remove their hats in court.[85]

As the 1640s progressed, John Selden wrote quite a lot about the government of the church, but the bulk of it was in Latin and it remains difficult to uncover exactly which solution he thought best for his own time. Although he remained a supporter of Parliament, Selden argued against the exclusion of bishops from the Lords in 1642 because he thought there was a need for the clerical estate to be represented in the secular polity.[86] He then spent the last decade of his life seeking a better understanding of the earliest government of the Christian church by investigating the ways in which the Hebrews had managed their ecclesiastical polity, the argument being that this must have been the political environment into which early Christianity was born and practised.[87] Like many lawyers, Selden was on friendly terms with the moderate episcopalian archbishop of Armagh, James Ussher, and he thought that the vilifications of bishops in the civil war period had been exaggerated.[88] On the other hand, Selden had a generally low opinion of clerical

[84] William Palmer, 'St John, Oliver (c. 1598–1673)', ODNB. St John's 'theological commonplace book', BL MS Additional 25285, refers frequently to Thomas Beard, *The Theatre of Gods Judgments or a Collection of Histories out of Sacred Profane and Ecclesiastical' Authors* (London, 1598), Beard having been Oliver Cromwell's schoolmaster.

[85] Anon., *A Letter of an Independent to His Friend Mr Glyn, Recorder* (London, 1645), pp. 4–7, maintained that Glynn had defected from independency, and now maintained oaths and covenants that were the new *ex officio* oaths; Whitelocke, *Memorials*, p. 105; George Fox, *The West Answering to the North in the fierce and cruell persecution of the manifestation of the Son of God* (London, 1657), pp. 17–28.

[86] Brooks, *Law, Politics and Society*, p. 235.

[87] Toomer, *Selden*, vol. ii.

[88] A. Ford, *James Ussher: Theology, History, and Politics in Early-Modern Ireland and England* (Oxford, 2007), pp. 228, 240, 268–270.

thought, especially when it threatened to meddle in secular affairs or matters of state. One of the most active parliamentary members of the Assembly of Divines, he ridiculed the way in which the clerics depended on the Bible to pontificate about early church history. Along with other leading lawyers in the House of Commons, he vehemently opposed the advice of the Assembly to Parliament that an English presbyterian church should be understood to have been based on the law of God.[89]

Selden's historical studies demonstrated that, in the time of the ancient Hebrews, the secular state had been the ultimate arbiter of moral law. While this might identify him as an Erastian, he did not embrace the label, and his position might better be described as one that interrogated the extent to which the state enforced sanctions such as excommunication, how it dealt with non-believers and indeed whether marriage was in origin a spiritual, as opposed to a temporal, relationship.[90] Suspected of atheism, Selden was devastatingly cynical about actual religious practices, but he nevertheless maintained that natural laws received directly from God formed the bedrock of legal obligation and civil society ('keep your promises').[91] A sense of the divine was profoundly important, but religious forms were evidently uncertain and, indeed, transitory. Judging from a typically cryptic remark that probably dates from the early 1650s – 'Religion is well enough settled already if we would let it alone' – he may have been content with the 'de facto' toleration that was emerging during the Republic, when penalties for failure to attend church were abolished by statute and a good deal of autonomy with regard to the appointment of ministers was left to people in the localities.[92]

Furthermore Selden, and other common lawyers, were not notably concerned about the atrophy of the ecclesiastical court system that accompanied the eventual abolition of episcopacy during the 1640s. Some, like Clarendon and later Matthew Hale, were perhaps coming to see ecclesiastical discipline primarily in terms of control over the clergy rather than laymen.[93] In any case, the old argument about the jurisdictional superiority of the temporal over the spiritual courts was a well-established trope by the mid-seventeenth century.[94] In practice, during

89 Whitelocke, *Memorials*, p. 68; Cromartie, *Sir Matthew Hale*, p. 161.
90 Toomer, *Selden*, vol. ii, pp. 569*ff.*
91 Ibid., 493–506; S. W. Singer (ed.), *The Table Talk of John Selden* (London, 1860), pp. 171, 151, 240–245.
92 Ibid., p. 245.
93 Clarendon, *History of the Rebellion*, vol. i, p. 407. For Hale, see later in the paper.
94 Brooks, *Law, Politics and Society*, p. 123.

the 1640s and 1650s, matters previously handled by the church courts began to find their way into temporal jurisdictions to the extent that they created pressures through the sheer weight of business.[95] One of the major practical problems, how to handle the proving of last wills and testaments, was addressed, although not altogether successfully, by the creation of a probate court in London – a scheme that had antecedents in failed projects from the time of James VI and I, and which in fact brought England in line with other European countries.[96] At the same time, if, as Selden thought, marriage was essentially a civil contract between two people, then there was no great conceptual leap involved in handling litigation regarding it in the secular courts. Although marital discord resulting in domestic violence had long been heard in the localities by justices of the peace, there were other important issues, such as the questions regarding the validity of marriages made outside the established church and the enforcement of the payment of alimony in connection with marriage breakdowns, which began to come before the royal courts during the interregnum, and some of the issues continued to have an impact in the 1660s and 1670s.[97] The secular-contract view of marriage helped to protect Protestant non-conformists from the full impact of legal disabilities that might have fallen on them if their marriages and the legal documents associated with them (marriage settlements, legacies) had been invalidated.[98] However, the lapse in the ecclesiastical jurisdiction may also have disadvantaged married women by leading common law judges to invest more authority in husbands as heads of their households.[99]

[95] Helmholz, *Canon Law and Ecclesiastical Jurisdiction*, pp. 308–309, describes the atrophy, but many of the details of the consequences remain to be worked out in detail.

[96] C. Kitching, 'Probate during the civil war and interregnum, part I: the survival of the prerogative court in the 1640s', *Journal of the Society of Archivists* 5 (1976), 283–293; C. Kitching, 'Probate during the civil war and interregnum, part II: the court for probate, 1653–1660', *Journal of the Society of Archivists* 6 (1976), 346–356. *Reformation in Courts and Cases Testamentary* (1650), which is attributed to Henry Parker, makes the case for the creation of a secular registry. Much of the litigation connected with wills, as opposed to their enrolment, was already being handled by the secular courts.

[97] In 1653, the commissioners of the Great Seal complained to Oliver Cromwell that cases concerning the payment of alimony were clogging the dockets of the court of Chancery: Spencer Library, University of Kansas, MS D. 87, John Lisle's Chancery Abridgment, f. 103.

[98] C. W. Horle, *The Quakers and the English Legal System 1660–1688* (Philadelphia, 1988), pp. 234–238; Cromartie, *Sir Matthew Hale*, pp. 134–135.

[99] See, e.g., the arguments of Sir Robert Hyde in *Manby* v. *Scott* (1663) 1 Mod. 124 (86 *English Reports* 781).

It is true, of course, that the church courts, along with bishops and the monarchy itself, were restored surprisingly quickly after the return to London of Charles II in the spring of 1660.[100] Yet even a few months earlier, this had not been inevitable. In September 1659, Bulstrode Whitelocke, a loyal Cromwellian and long-time friend of Selden,[101] presided over a series of meetings by the Council of State that discussed the role of sovereign temporal power in spiritual matters. The Council, which does not seem to have been all that well attended, began with a consideration of the simple proposition that 'The Supreame Delegated power is not intrusted to judge or make Lawes in matters of faith or worship of God so as to exercise coercive power therein'.[102] Over the next few days, this evolved into a longer and more complex statement that was evidently drafted, at least in part, by several Army officers:

> That the supreame Delegated power is not intrusted to restrain the profession of any person or persons who professe faith in God the father and in Jesus Christ God manifested in the flesh and in God the holy spirit . . . And doe acknowledge the holy scriptures of the Old and New testaments to be the revealed or written word or will of God . . . but ought to give due encouragement and equal Protection to them in the Profession of their faith and exercise of Religion whilst they abuse not their liberty to the civil injury of others, or disturbance of others in their way of worship.[103]

Articulating what would become familiar distinctions between the mass of Protestants and minorities such as Quakers, antinomians and Socinians, the final form of words apparently envisioned no alteration with respect to existing institutions and even went so far as to guarantee 'equal protection' for religious practices that fell within the broad theological prescriptions it outlined.

Although the Council of State, and Whitelocke himself, was soon afterwards swept from power, the recalled Long Parliament passed an ordinance in March 1660 that aimed to reinstate a form of presbyterian

[100] I. M. Green, *The Re-Establishment of the Church of England 1660–1663* (Oxford, 1978), ch. 6; R. B. Outhwaite, *The Rise and Fall of the English Ecclesiastical Courts, 1500–1860* (Cambridge, 2006), pp. 80–81; Barry Till, *The Church Courts 1660–1720: The Revival of Proceedings* (York, 2006).

[101] R. Spalding (ed.), *The Diary of Bulstrode Whitelocke 1605–1675* (Oxford, 1990), pp. 50, 354, 397, 403.

[102] Whitelocke Papers (Longleat), vol. xix, ff. 86–88 (consulted on microfilm at the Institute of Historical Research, London).

[103] Ibid., ff. 87–88.

ecclesiastical polity.[104] At about the same time, Matthew Hale, a protégé of Selden who was soon to become the most influential judge of the 1660s and 1670s, made some private notes on the religious question that reflect his sense of the choices that still remained to be made.[105] Hale maintained that ecclesiastical and civil government were God-given institutions, but he also thought that the ways in which these were articulated at different times and places depended on human choices made by particular communities of people.[106] The problem with clerical power was that it was hard to challenge because it relied ultimately on divine right (*jure divino*) authority, even though excessive claims to power had always been the undoing of the clergy from the time of popery to the recent ascendency of presbyterianism.[107] As for the laity, Hale credited thousands of his contemporaries amongst the 'middle sort of people' with sophisticated religious understandings that enabled them to argue learnedly over ceremonies and other aspects of religious practice. Indeed, men were inclined to think that the imposition of rigid rules about 'indifferent matters in religion' constituted an attack on their liberties.[108] Nevertheless, Hale rejected a polity of independent congregations or sects, because their wrangling would be a constant source of 'confusion' and conflict in civil society.[109] A presbyterian ecclesiastical polity, on the other hand, would be dangerous because it threatened to lead to a theocracy. Its independence from the Crown would cause the clergy to have an even greater influence over the people and would incline the state towards a 'democratical' government.[110] No less important, presbyterian jurisdiction would tend to draw all kinds of causes, temporal as well as spiritual, towards their consistory courts. All civil causes involving claims of injuries (trespasses) included scope for the idea of sin to be brought into the reckoning and this would threaten an extension of their jurisdiction. The consequence of all this would, 'of necessity', be a 'perfect subjection of all civil rights and government to the ecclesiastical'.[111] By process of elimination, therefore, Hale's reasons for supporting the re-establishment of an episcopal church of England were

[104] Nicholas Tyacke, *Aspects of English Protestantism 1530–1700* (Manchester, 2001), p. 71.
[105] Lambeth Palace Library, London: MS Fairhurst 3507, ff. 143–173. See also Cromartie, *Sir Matthew Hale*, p. 178.
[106] Lambeth Palace Library, London: MS Fairhurst 3507, f. 143.
[107] Ibid., ff. 159, 164v.
[108] Ibid., ff. 167v–168.
[109] Ibid., ff. 143–153.
[110] Ibid., ff. 156–157.
[111] Ibid., ff. 153–154.

largely pragmatic.[112] Bishops could, in theory, be just as troublesome as presbyters, but their dependence on the Crown made them tractable and more 'subordinate to the civil power'.[113] Furthermore, episcopal government in England by long use and accommodation had a double fitness to the English constitution. The exercise of ecclesiastical jurisdiction was woven into the fabric of civil administration and was manageable by civil power. If it broke its bounds, legislation and legal devices such as prohibitions would provide a means of restraining clerical excesses.[114]

## V

Judging from these notes and his later actions on behalf of comprehension, Hale apparently imagined a re-established episcopal church of England with sufficient latitude in its doctrine to permit presbyterians and other moderate non-conformists to join its ranks. Furthermore, although few of the details were outlined, the coercive power of that church, including excommunication, would have been defined by temporal authority and kept within bounds by the traditional means through which the common law had monitored the churchmen and the spiritual jurisdiction. What he did not foresee, however, was the failure of the 1662 church settlement to accommodate presbyterians, or the vehemence with which the Cavalier Parliament would introduce penal legislation (the so-called Clarendon Code), which explicitly banned those who failed to conform to the Church of England from holding public office and imposed severe sanctions, including imprisonment, on those found guilty of attending proscribed religious services.[115] Hence, as the post-Restoration period unfolded, non-conformists – most notably, the Quakers – established legal defence networks that developed strategies for evading the multidimensional legal disabilities they faced. In the case of spiritual sanctions, including the disciplinary powers of the church courts, the by-now-ancient remedies associated with prohibitions could be used to delay or evade the worst consequences of proceedings – a process aided by the failure to restore High Commission, which had

[112] Although he also accepted that the scriptural authority for episcopacy, including episcopal ordination, was better than that for presbyterianism: ibid., f. 159$^{v}$.

[113] Ibid., ff. 156–157.

[114] Ibid., f. 162.

[115] Paul Seaward, *The Cavalier Parliament and the Reconstruction of the Old Regime 1661–1667* (Cambridge, 1989), ch. 7.

been abolished in 1641.[116] By comparison, the parliamentary legislation was much more difficult to argue against, but its impact on individuals depended on the willingness of magistrates and juries in the provinces to convict, as well as the attitudes of the judiciary towards enforcement – a subject on which there were apparently differences of opinion. While some judges, including Sir John Kelyng and Sir Richard Rainsford developed reputations for being hard on dissenters, several others, including Hale and Sir John Vaughan, were noted instead for their leniency.[117] Furthermore, Parliament itself further weakened the ability of the judiciary to enforce the statutes it passed by insisting in 1667 that the judicial punishment of juries for giving verdicts against the evidence was an 'arbitrary and illegal power, which is of dangerous consequences to the Lives and Liberties of the people of England, and which tends to the introduction of an arbitrary government'.[118] This pressure on the judges led to a decision in 1672 in a trial involving the Quaker leader William Penn (known as *Bushell's case*), which declared the practice illegal and therefore made the 'pious perjury' of jurors a potential source of relief for non-conformists.[119]

Indeed, by the later 1660s, Sir Orlando Bridgeman, having been appointed Lord Keeper after the fall of the earl of Clarendon and perhaps the least likely of the Restoration judges to have any sympathy for religious non-conformity, was under pressure from both non-conformists (because of their sufferings) and from the government (probably in sympathy with Catholics) to support some kind of reform of the religious settlement.[120] Although Bridgeman had publically declared that he would live and die in the opinion that neither the king or people could live safely if the church, bishops and liturgy were overthrown, he also thought that if some remission of 'things indifferent' were

[116] Horle, *Quakers and the English Legal System.*

[117] J. Miller, *After the Civil Wars: English Politics and Government in the Reign of Charles II* (Harlow, 2000), p. 203.

[118] *Journals of the House of Commons 1547–1714*, seventeen vols (1742), vol. ix, pp 35, 37; A. Grey, *Debates of the House of Commons, from 1667 to 1694*, ten vols (London, 1763), vol. i, pp. 62–64. The bill was eventually laid aside.

[119] *The Reports and Arguments of that Learned Judge Sir John Vaughan, late Chief Justice of his Majesties Court of Common Pleas* (1672), pp. 135*ff.*

[120] John Spurr, 'The Church of England, comprehension and the Toleration Act of 1689', *English Historical Review* 104 (1989), 927–946, pp. 932–933, who also covers the involvement of lawyers in comprehension schemes in 1668. For Matthew Hale's involvement, see G. Burnet, *The Life and Death of Sir Matthew Hale, sometime Lord Chief Justice of His Majesties Court of Kings Bench* (London, 1681), pp. 68–69.

not given to peaceable dissenters, then the church itself would crack as a result of attempting to maintain too tight a grip on conformity.[121] At Bridgeman's instigation, a small group of 'presbyterian' ministers, including Richard Baxter, apparently negotiated with Hale for a revised Act of Uniformity that would have made it possible for them to conform to a state church more flexible in terms of certain doctrines and ceremonial practices about which they had scruples. But, because of parliamentary hostility and perhaps also because Hale was uncomfortable with the 'presbyterian' desire to give powers over excommunication to parish clergymen, the project ultimately collapsed.[122] Furthermore, although the circumstances associated with this bill provided some of the backdrop to the publication by Charles II of a Declaration of Indulgence in 1672, it is not clear what, if any, connection there was between the two initiatives. Bridgeman evidently refused to apply the Great Seal to the Declaration and left office soon thereafter.[123]

The Declaration of Indulgence of 1672 was, of course, the second of three such measures proposed by Charles II and James II: the first was issued in December 1662 and the last, in 1687. The key to all three was the idea that the king, as head of church and state, could grant an indulgence (licence or pardon) to either Catholic or Protestant non-conformists that would negate, or save them harmless, from any prosecution on statutes relating to religion, including the measures in the Clarendon Code and later legislation such as the Test Act of 1673. The Declaration of 1662 was, in fact, largely aspirational.[124] It referred to the promise Charles II had made at Breda, before returning to the throne, that he would grant liberty to tender consciences. In addition, it noted the practical difficulty of

[121] Staffordshire Record Office, Lichfield, MS D 1287/18/3, Bundle 1, Sir Philip Warwick to Bridgeman (10 July 1668); Bundle 8, William Troughton to Bridgman (27 February 1668/1669).

[122] J. Miller, *After the Civil Wars: English Politics and Government in the Reign of Charles I* (London, 2000), pp. 204–205, 208, 210.

[123] According to Baxter, Bridgman lost his nerve in the face of parliamentary opposition as early as 1670: Matthew Sylvester (ed.), *Reliquiae Baxterianae or Mr Richard Baxter's Narrative of the Most Memorable Passages of his Life and Times* (London, 1696), vol. iii, pp. 22–25, 36.

[124] *His Majesties Declaration to all his loving Subjects*, 26 December (1662). The circumstances are discussed by G. B. Abernethy, 'Clarendon and the Declaration of Indulgence', *Journal of Ecclesiastical History* 11 (1960), 55–73. Clarendon evidently failed to get the approval of the bishops or judges for such a measure in June 1662: ibid., p. 62. It is not clear where Clarendon himself stood on the matter, but his position may well have been much like that of Hale, which was that a law, once passed, had to be upheld: Smith, *Constitutional Royalism*, pp. 300–302.

securing the loyalty of subjects who were constantly threatened with persecution and stated the king's intention of going to Parliament to secure his power to grant dispensations against penal laws in matters of religion. Even so, the immediate result was a storm in Parliament that caused the Crown to back down. Furthermore, it seems that the king sought a fully worked-out legal argument in support of his position only several months later, when he commissioned Bulstrode Whitelocke to write a brief on the subject in March 1663. In the political wilderness and struggling to fend off prosecution as a result of his service to the interregnum regimes, Whitelocke's friendship with Selden and his familiarity with the issues over a long period may have made him a less surprising choice than might at first sight appear. According to his own reckoning, he was able to write a lengthy manuscript treatise within a month at least in part because he already had notes made in the 1630s that were relevant to the subject.[125]

Like Matthew Hale and Charles II himself, Whitelocke set his thinking within a contemporary context that was dominated by practical political considerations. It was clear that there were differences of opinion amongst Christians about matters of faith and church discipline, the truth of which were extremely difficult to resolve and which did not, in any case, relate to questions about whether something was sinful – that is, inherently wrong – or not. Persecution would serve only to harden opinion and to create sedition. It would cost the king the loyalty and economic contribution of the 'industrious' trading people, who were disproportionately represented amongst dissenters. It was wrong that men should be punished in their estates, liberties and lives for nonconformity when the points at issue were not in themselves sinful or seditious.[126]

Doubtless inspired by Selden, Whitelocke developed his argument by starting with a long-term historical view and then narrowing his focus to the law of England. Referring specifically to the Hebrews, he observed that they and most other nations lodged spiritual jurisdiction in the hands of lay magistrates.[127] He pointed out that the early Christians

[125] BL, MS Additional 21,099, 'The King's Right to graunt Indulgence in matters of Religion asserted by [Sir] B[ulstrode] W[hitelock]'; Spalding, *The Diary of Bulstrode Whitelocke*, pp. 663–664. See also Ruth Spalding, 'Whitelocke, Bulstrode (1605–1675)', ODNB. As Abernethy, 'Clarendon and the Declaration of Indulgence', p. 65, notes, Clarendon was severely incapacitated by gout in late 1662 and the first few months of 1663.

[126] BL MS Additional 21099, ff. 10–11, 29, 42–46.

[127] Ibid., ff. 19, 61.

had faced penalties for non-conformity in imperial Rome. By contrast, the chapters on English law drew largely on familiar arguments that Whitelocke had recorded in some seventy pages of manuscript notes made during the mid-1630s.[128] Following Sir John Davies, he pointed out that many issues that had come to be described as purely spiritual, such as those relating to testaments and matrimony, had originally been purely 'civil' or temporal. The religious legislation of the sixteenth century had vested the headship of the English church in the monarch and this included powers to grant dispensations.[129] Here, the key point – which was, in some respects, new to the argument – was that legislation relating to ceremonies or church discipline should be classed as prohibited wrongs (*mala prohibita)* rather than as self-evident wrongs manifestly sinful or contrary to the law of nature (*mala per se*). While the latter were beyond the reach of royal pardons or dispensations, it was an accepted and necessary part of the law of England that the King should have the power to issue them where the offence in question was merely *malum prohibitum.*[130]

One of the main differences between Whitelocke's argument in 1662 and what appears to have been his position in the 1630s was that, in 1662, his case depended on an assertion that the king was as much the head of the church as the pope had ever been.[131] In the 1630s, by comparison, Whitelocke vested authority over the church mutually in the hands of the king and Parliament,[132] and he himself seemed to realise that herein lay the critical problem about Crown-sponsored religious toleration after 1660. The Restoration Act of Uniformity was manifestly an Act of Parliament, and the subsequent legislation in the Clarendon Code and the Test Act involved statutes that mixed the temporal and the spiritual, and which also made claims to defending the public interest. The royal supremacy over the church was, in effect, colliding with the claims of Parliament to make binding positive law that was not subject to abrogation at the will of the monarch.[133] In the closing paragraphs of his treatise, Whitelocke admitted the impasse, noting that the opinion of

[128] BL, MS Additional 37343, ff. 78*ff.*

[129] Ibid., f. 58. Whitelocke even went so far as to argue that the supreme ecclesiastical jurisdiction had originally been in fathers and from hence had been transferred to kings.

[130] BL MS Additional 21099, ff. 58, 147.

[131] Ibid., f. 144.

[132] BL MS Additional 37343, ff. 78$^{v}$–130.

[133] As Lamont shows in his ODNB article, in the 1660s, William Prynne was arguing that the king embodied the patriarchal authority of Adam, and that distinctions between church and state were a popish invention.

the House of Commons was critical in resolving the question and that he felt obliged to 'submit' to whatever its judgment might be.[134]

Yet while Whitelocke appears to have conceded defeat for the argument he was trying to make, his treatise contained most of the elements that would be further developed, first in the 1670s and then in the 1680s, with regard to 'dispensations'. The problem was that while elaboration of this line of common law thinking led to greater complexity, it could not overcome the political realities of potential clashes between the positions of members of Parliament, on the one side, and the Crown, on the other. In notes he made for parliamentary debates on the second Conventicle Act in March 1670, Heneage Finch, then the king's solicitor general and a leading speaker in Parliament, drew a distinction between what he described as the king's headship of the church by common law as opposed to that given him by statute, which in effect downplayed the significance of sixteenth-century religious legislation and led Finch to deny explicitly that the king had the same powers as the pope.[135] Furthermore, since a measure such as the Conventicle Act was a law for the preservation of the public peace, Finch maintained that it would have been very 'unnatural' for the king to allow any privilege against its execution. On the other hand, speaking (reluctantly) amidst the parliamentary outcry against the Declaration of 1672, Finch maintained that the king did have the power to make dispensations of the kind it envisioned and therefore advised the Commons to petition humbly to the king that he revoke it, rather than to make a more direct challenge to its legality.[136]

Exactly who drew up the second Declaration of Indulgence is unclear, but it was much more tightly crafted than the first one. It proposed a system that would have allowed dissenters and Catholics to continue to practise their religion, but only if they took out licences from the Crown, which provided a means of separating out potentially seditious practices from those that were merely matters of conscience and which would also create a record containing more detailed information about those to whom licences had been granted. It was, in fact, little different in

[134] BL MS Additional 21099, ff. 195–199$^{v}$.

[135] Leicestershire Record Office, Wigston Magna, DG 7 (Finch Political Papers), P.P. 20 (30 March 1670).

[136] D. E. C. Yale (ed.), *Lord Nottingham's Chancery Cases*, two vols (London, 1954–1961), vol. ii, pp. 978–982. Finch's son, Daniel, proved in the 1680s to be a leading advocate of comprehension and toleration: H. Horwitz, 'Comprehension and indulgence in the Exclusion Crisis', *Journal of Ecclesiastical History* 15 (1964), 201–217.

conception from the Act of Toleration of 1689 – except, of course, for the critical difference that the Act was a piece of legislation (a positive law) agreed by the king and Parliament.

The other notable feature of the Declaration of Indulgence of 1672 is that the judiciary did not have an opportunity to offer an explicit opinion on it. According to Heneage Finch, members of the Commons were keen to know what the lawyers thought, but the actions of Lord Keeper Bridgeman, if nothing else, must have made the Crown aware that legal opinion on the measure was bound to be divided. There was, moreover, a long-running piece of civil litigation, a case known as *Thomas* v. *Sorrell*, which demonstrated that the judges were unlikely to speak with a single voice when it came to the question of how far the king might grant dispensations from a penal statute.[137] Begun in 1667, but not brought to judgment until the spring of 1673, the central issue in *Thomas* v. *Sorrell* was the validity of a dispensation granted in the Jacobean charter of the London Company of Vintners, which permitted its members to sell wine in London and within three miles of the City, notwithstanding a statute of Edward VI that prohibited the practice. Although it had nothing to do with religion, the issues, involving what contemporaries described indiscriminately as 'licenses and dispensations', so closely mirrored those in the Declaration of Indulgence that the terms of that measure may well have been fashioned out of the courtroom arguments. However, although two of the principal judgments in the decision, those by Hale and Sir John Vaughan, agreed that the Company of Vintners' licence was legal, they arrived at their conclusions in significantly different ways.

Hale's decision was apparently not widely, or fully, reported, but his autograph notes on the case show that he paid a great deal of attention to it.[138] He pointed out that it was better that a particular company should suffer by a limited construction of the power of dispensing with laws than that, by an extension of them beyond their due bounds, the just solemnity and security of Acts of Parliament should be shaken.[139] He was clear that the repeal or suspension of a penal law could not be undertaken without an Act of Parliament, and the example he used was that the king could not alter religion established by an Act of Parliament without an Act of

[137] The fullest printed report is 2 Keble 245, 322, 372, 790 (84 *English Reports* 152, 201, 233, 500). There is also a useful account in Middle Temple Library, London, MS Treby, f. 73*ff*; Cromartie, *Sir Matthew Hale*, pp. 126*ff*.

[138] LPL, MS Fairhurst 3478, ff. 3*ff*. There is a Law French fair copy in Yale Law School, New Haven MS G.R. 29/25, f. 368.

[139] Ibid., f. 3.

Parliament. Although the ecclesiastical supremacy had been vested in Henry VIII and had descended from him to King Edward VI, once a matter of religion had the 'signature and authority' of an Act of Parliament, only another Act of Parliament could alter it.[140] In the end, Hale ruled for the Company of Vintners by making what was apparently an unusual distinction between a dispensation and a licence. Dispensations were granted by the Crown, but licences were authorised by statute, and Hale's argument for the Company of Vintners was that it could show that it had such a licence.[141]

Although Hale was involved in drawing up bills for 'comprehension', he did not accept that the king, on his own, could license nonconformity. By contrast, Hale's colleague Vaughan, whose religious outlook is harder to fathom, was a friend of Thomas Hobbes, as well as an executor of Selden, who had staunchly refused to recognise any of the interregnum regimes.[142] But he argued the 'case of wine' in a way that opened the door to a unilateral royal grant of licensed toleration. Although Vaughan never mentioned the religious question directly, many of the steps in his argument suggest that he clearly had it in mind. He noted first of all that all penal laws were *pro bono publico* ('for the good of the realm') and he acknowledged that, for that reason, it could be argued that there was no scope for dispensation from any of them.[143] To overcome this obstacle, however, he developed two further distinctions. The first was between laws that prohibited offences that were *mala per se* (self-evident wrongs in themselves), which could not easily be dispensed with, and offences that were prohibited by public policy (*mala prohibita*), which could be dispensed with. Yet the real key to his argument came from his second distinction: that the power of dispensation – even in the case of a *malum prohibitum* by statute – could be used only where there was no danger that a grant of a licence to one of the king's subjects might cause damage to another that could be recovered by an action at law. If this rule was accepted, then it is possible to see how royal dispensations granted by the king, which affected only his own interests, might be considered legal. Indeed, it raised the very interesting question of which of the king's subjects were directly wronged as a result of licensed religious toleration that was prefaced with an assertion that

140 Ibid., f. 7.
141 Ibid., ff. 12–13, 21.
142 J. Gwynn Williams, 'Vaughan, Sir John (1603–1674)', ODNB.
143 *The Reports and Arguments of that Learned Judge Sir John Vaughan*, pp. 335, 358.

the peace and prosperity of the realm were damaged by the penal laws against non-conformists and Catholics.[144]

Of course, given the unprecedentedly complex confessional politics of the 1670s and 1680s, this position was not viable, but it was hardly out of line with the long-term relationship between the common law and the churchmen, or indeed with legal thinking since the 1640s that had questioned how far the 'sword of the king' should be drawn whenever the established church demanded it.[145] Furthermore, although the manipulation of the judiciary by Charles II and James II to secure a judicial bench that would support their policies of 'toleration' in the late 1670s and 1680s has become notorious, it was feasible only because the lawyers themselves were unable to argue with one voice about the relationship between the temporality and spirituality, or indeed the relationship between the power of Parliament and that of the Crown. During the exclusion crisis, Tory proposals to smooth the succession to the throne of the Catholic duke of York by restricting the power he would have over the church led to a recrudescence of legal anti-clericalism.[146] Veterans of the civil war years such as Sir Harbottle Grimston and Sir John Maynard opposed measures that might remove matters of faith, worship and the appointment of bishops from the control of sovereign power, because they were against putting it into the hands of the clerics.[147]

The Whig assault on the bishops of the Church of England was accompanied by the efforts of one of their leading antiquarian propagandists, William Petyt, to collect together a large number of papers relevant to the struggles between the churchmen and the lawyers dating back to the end of the sixteenth century.[148] The churchmen had not stopped making arguments about the divine origins of the spirituality,

144 Ibid., p. 348. Vaughan quoted Spanish jurist Suarez by way of illustrating that the learning surrounding dispensations had originated with the pope.

145 Anon., *The Judgment of A Good Subject upon His Majesties Late Declaration for Indulgence of Tender Consciences* (London, 1672), p. 15.

146 William Gibson, 'The limits of the confessional state: electoral religion in the reign of Charles II', *Historical Journal* 51 (2008), 27–47. For the use of excommunication by bishops for electoral purposes in the late 1670s and 1680s, see also Anon., *The case and cure of person excommunicated according to the present law of England, in two parts* (London, 1682).

147 M. Goldie, 'Danby, the bishops and the Whigs', in T. Harris, P. Seaward and M. Goldie (eds), *The Politics of Religion in Restoration England* (Oxford, 1990), pp. 75–105, pp. 84–85, 87, 93.

148 J. C. Davies (ed.), *Catalogue of Manuscripts in the Library of the Honourable Society of the Inner Temple*, three vols (London, 1972), vol. 1.

but in other respects the issues had moved on. The conflict between the 'temporality and the spirituality'[149] was construed into debates about the nature of legislation – indeed, law itself. Questions about the relative roles of the Crown versus Parliament in making laws were certainly important. But so too were questions about the power of law, whatever its temporal source, to supervise the consciences of English men and women. This point is most directly illustrated by reference to the thoughts of one of the leading Whig lawyers of the day, Sir Robert Atkyns, about the power of the Crown to grant dispensations. As a recently appointed judge of the Common Pleas in 1673, Atkyns had apparently agreed with the position of Sir John Vaughan in the Vintners case, going so far as to maintain that, even if it was correct that dispensations originated in Rome, not everything that came from 'thence' was bad.[150]

Having subsequently resigned his place on the bench in the 1680s, however, Atkyns published in 1689 an account of the argument he had made in the famous test case, *Godden* v. *Hales* (1686), a collusive action brought to confirm that a dispensation granted by the king could enable a Catholic (or Protestant non-conformist) to hold a commission in the army despite the Test Act of 1673, which established conformity to the Church of England as a criterion for holding a public office. In this, Atkyns declared instead that only the law-maker could dispense with a law and, in England, that meant that only Parliament could dispense with an Act of Parliament.[151] He addressed the question of whether judges might employ a notion of equitable relief from the letter of a harsh law by quoting Sir Francis Bacon for the view that the 'pretense of equity' could not be used to decree against express statutes of the realm.[152] Furthermore, although he avoided a clear formulation of the question of whether a dispensation might be good in those circumstances in which only the king's interests, as opposed to those of the public or common good, were at stake, he clearly had it in mind when he declared it self-evident that the realm was under threat by papists.[153] The Test Act had been made to keep out a foreign power, but dispensing with the Act

[149] BL, MS Additional 32520, f. 84$^{v}$ (the words of Roger North).

[150] *Thomas* v. *Sorrell* (1673) 1 Freeman 85, at 90 (89 *English Reports* 63). Atkyns is also said to have been connected with a failed 'comprehension' bill that was being floated in the late 1660s: Roger Thomas, 'Comprehension and indulgence', in G. F. Nuttall and O. Chadwick (eds), *From Uniformity to Unity 1662–1962* (1962), pp. 189–253, p. 197.

[151] Robert Atkyns, *An Enquiry into the Power of Dispensing with Penal Statutes* (London, 1689), pp. 4–5, 40–41.

[152] Ibid., p. 25.

[153] Ibid., pp. 4, 12–14.

seemed the most likely way of letting it in; the case therefore concerned the safety of government, the good of the people and maintaining true religion established by statute law.[154] Yet, in making this case for the enforcement of religious disabilities, Atkyns also (and perhaps inadvertently) made another argument that rings rather oddly for a student of common law reasoning in this period: a just law was no restraint of liberty; rather, it freed us from servitude to our wills and passions.[155] This is surely a point about men's souls, rather than their actions – a traditional distinction between the ecclesiastical and secular law – and a juridical echo of what Mark Goldie has described as late Restoration theological theories of religious intolerance.[156]

In conclusion, if 1688 represented the ultimate triumph of parliamentary authority, this was brought about in no little part as a result of the political, and legal, problems concerning the ecclesiastical polity. Part of the price paid was the continued establishment of the Church of England, a toleration of Protestant non-conformity that depended on a licence from Parliament rather than any clearly articulated theory of freedom of conscience and the maintenance of civil disabilities established by statute law against Catholics. Ever since the 1530s, the relationship between church and state had been far from straightforward. The peculiar characteristics of the post-Reformation religious settlement in England, including the continued vitality of the ecclesiastical court system, encouraged thinking about the spirituality and the temporality as separate spheres, and clashes between the two helped to restrain religious persecution, whilst being largely responsible for generating the 'language of liberty' that is so characteristic of the early seventeenth century. These also impacted on the development of the 'equitable' side of English jurisprudence and eventually generated arguments that contributed tangibly to the downfall of the episcopal Church of England in the 1640s. Yet the conflict between the temporality and the spirituality severely strained the credibility of the judicial bench and perhaps also the credibility of the judge-made law that had characterised the previous two centuries.[157]

[154] Ibid., p. 43.

[155] Ibid., p. 9.

[156] M. Goldie, 'The theory of religious intolerance in Restoration England', in O. P. Grell, Jonathan I. Israel and Nicholas Tyacke (eds), *From Persecution to Toleration: The Glorious Revolution and Religion in England* (Oxford, 1991), pp. 331–368, pp. 348, 356.

[157] Writing on the subject of *praemunire*, either Francis North or his brother Roger went over much of the material covered in this paper and concluded that it was a story in

Having been villains in 1642, the bishops were heroes in 1688, while James II's judges were discredited and replaced.[158] On 29 December 1688, Sir Richard Heath, a baron of the Exchequer, wrote an apologetic letter to the archbishop of Canterbury in which he affirmed that he had never, in any 'public or private discourse', proposed the repealing of the penal laws, or anything else, 'to the prejudice of the church of England'.[159] Nevertheless, he was dismissed from office and excluded from the Indemnity Act because he had allegedly supported James II's Declaration of Indulgence.

After having painstakingly gone through all of the arguments relating to dispensations at about the same time as *Godden* v. *Hales* was being heard, polymath lawyer Roger North complained that it was a very hard study and that the character of the common law itself tended to add to the difficulties inherent in the questions. There were no authoritative books on the subject. The principal sources, the law reports, often taken as manuscript notes in court, were frequently inaccurate or recorded only part of an argument. Individual cases were usually settled according to particular circumstances and with as little reference to general arguments as possible. Judges delivered decisions individually in court, so that it was frequently difficult to identify a clear line of thought that was critical to a judgment. The educational practices at the Inns of Court, which tended to encourage the discovery and elaboration of fine 'differences', exacerbated diversity of opinion and this early training tended to remain with lawyers all their lives.[160] Perhaps North exaggerated, but the conflict between the spirituality and the temporality exposed weaknesses in English law, as well as the English church.

which 'the Spirituality and temporality in England hath both strove for power and privilege . . .': BL, MS Additional 32520, f. 84v.

158 A. F. Havinghurst, 'James II and the Twelve Men in Scarlet', *Law Quarterly Review* 69 (1953), 522–546.

159 Middle Temple Library, London, 'Heath's notes on cases in King's Bench and the Exchequer', f. 80.

160 BL, MS Additional 32520, ff. 34–35.

# A BIBLIOGRAPHY OF THE WORKS OF CHRISTOPHER W. BROOKS

## Books

*Pettyfoggers and Vipers of the Commonwealth: The 'Lower Branch' of the Legal Profession in Early Modern England* (Cambridge University Press, 1986).

*Notaries Public in England since the Reformation* (co-authored with P. G. Stein and Richard Helmholz) (Society of Public Notaries of London, 1991); also published in Italian as *Notai in Inghilterra Prima e Dopo la Riforma* (Giuffrè, Milano, 1991).

*The Middling Sort of People: Culture, Society and Politics in England 1500–1800* (co-edited with Jonathan Barry) (Macmillan, Basingstoke, 1994); translated and published in Japanese by Showado Press, Tokyo, 1998.

*The Admissions Registers of Barnard's Inn 1620–1869* (Selden Society Supplementary Series 12, London, 1995).

*Communities and Courts in Britain, 1150–1900* (co-edited with Michael Lobban) (Hambledon Press, London, 1997).

*Lawyers, Litigation and English Society since 1450* (Hambledon Press, London, 1998).

*Law, Politics and Society in Early Modern England* (Cambridge University Press, 2008).

## Articles

'History, English law and the Renaissance: a comment', *Past and Present* 72 (1976), 133–146 (co-authored with K. M. Sharpe); reprinted in K. M. Sharpe, *Politics and Ideas in Early Stuart England: Essays and Studies* (Pinter, London, 1989), pp. 174–181.

'Litigants and attorneys in King's Bench and Common Pleas 1560–1640', in J. H. Baker (ed.), *Legal Records and the Historian* (Royal Historical Society Studies in History, London, 1978), pp. 41–59.

'The common lawyers in England 1560–1640', in W. R. Prest (ed.), *Lawyers in Early Modern Europe and America* (Croom Helm, London, 1981), pp. 42–64.

'Charles Willson Peale: painting and natural history in eighteenth-century North America', *Oxford Art Journal* 5 (1982), 31–39.

'Interpersonal conflict and social tension: civil litigation in England 1640–1830', in A. L. Beier, D. Cannadine and J. Rosenheim (eds), *The First Modern Society: Essays in Honour of Lawrence Stone* (Cambridge University Press, 1989), pp. 357–399.

'Common law', 'Uses and Wills, An Act Concerning' and 'Wills, Statute of', in R. Fritze and G. R. Elton (eds), *Historical Dictionary of Tudor England* (Greenwood Press, Westport, 1991), pp. 113–118, 520–522, 545–546.

'The place of Magna Carta and ancient constitution in sixteenth-century English legal thought', in Ellis Sandoz (ed.), *The Roots of Liberty: Magna Carta, Ancient Constitution and the Anglo-American Tradition of the Rule of Law* (University of Missouri Press, London and Columbus, 1993), pp. 75–114.

'Apprenticeship, social mobility and the middling sort, 1550–1800', in Jonathan Barry and Christopher W. Brooks (eds), *The Middling Sort of People: Culture, Society and Politics in England 1500–1800* (Palgrave, London, 1994), pp. 52–83, 233–242.

'Professions, ideology and the middling sort of people, 1550–1650', in Jonathan Barry and Christopher W. Brooks (eds), *The Middling Sort of People: Culture, Society and Politics in England 1500–1800* (Palgrave, London, 1994), pp. 113–140.

'A law-abiding and litigious society', in J. S. Morrill (ed.), *The Oxford Illustrated History of Tudor and Stuart Britain* (Oxford University Press, 1996), pp. 139–155.

'Le déclin et la recreation des organisations professionelles de barristers et de solicitors aux XVIIIe et XIXe siècles', in Jean-Louis Halpérin (ed.), *Les structures du barreau et du notariat en Europe du XVIIIe siècle à nos jours* (Presses Universitaires de Lyon, 1996), pp. 99–112.

'Apprenticeship or academy? The idea of a law university 1820–1860' (co-authored with Michael Lobban), in Jonathan Bush and Alain Wijffels (eds), *Learning the Law: The Teaching and Transmission of Law in England, 1150–1900* (Hambledon Press, London, 1999), pp. 353–382.

'Contemporary views of "feudal" social and political relationships in sixteenth and seventeenth-century England', in Natalie Fryde, Pierre Monnet and Otto Gerhard (eds), *Die Gegenwart des Feudalismus - Présence du féodalisme et présent de la féodalité - The Presence of Feudalism* (Vandenhoeck & Ruprecht, Göttingen, 2002), pp. 109–135.

'Les actes juridiques, le cycle de vie, et les relations sociales dans l'Angleterre de la période moderne', in S. Beauvalet, V. Gourdon and F.-J. Ruggiu (eds), *Liens sociaux et actes notariés dans le monde urbain en France et en Europe: XVIe–XVIIIe siècles* (Presses de l'Université Paris-Sorbonne, 2004), pp. 77–86.

'The longitudinal study of civil litigation in England 1200–1996', in W. R. Prest and Sharyn Roach Anleu (eds), *Litigation: Past and Present* (University of New South Wales Press, Sydney, 2004), pp. 24–42.

'Lawyers as intermediaries between people and courts: some reflections on the English experience (c. 1450–1800)', in C. Dolan (ed.), *Les auxiliaires de la justice: intermédiaires entre justice et les populations de la fin du Moyen Âge à la période contemporaine* (Presses Université Laval, Sainte-Foy, 2005), pp. 279–299.

'Litigation, participation and agency in seventeenth and eighteenth-century England', in David Lemmings (ed.), *The British and Their Laws in the Eighteenth Century* (Boydell and Brewer, Woodbridge, 2005), pp. 155–181.

'A Puritan collaboration in defence of the liberty of the subject: James Morice, Robert Beale, and the Elizabethan campaign against ecclesiastical authority', in Paul Scott (ed.), *Collaboration and Interdisciplinarity in the Republic of Letters: Essays in Honour of Richard G. Maber* (Manchester University Press, 2010), pp. 3–16.

'Being human, human rights and modernity', *Insights* 3 (2010), 2–12.

'The agrarian problem in "revolutionary" England 1640–1689', in Jane Whittle (ed.), *Landlords and Tenants in Britain 1440–1660: Tawney's Agrarian Problems Revisited* (Boydell and Brewer, Woodbridge, 2013), pp. 183–199.

'Paradise lost? Law, literature, and history in Restoration England', in Lorna Hutson (ed.), *The Oxford Handbook of English Law and Literature, 1500–1700* (Oxford University Press, 2017), pp. 198–218.

## Oxford Dictionary of National Biography Entries

Sir John Bankes (1589–1644); Sir Anthony Benn (1569/70–1618); Sir John Bramston the elder (1577–1654); Richard Brownlow (1553–1638); Sir Henry Calthorpe (1586–1637); Chaloner Chute (1595–1659); Sir George Croke (c. 1560–1642); Joseph Day (bap. 1758? d. 1832); Edward Drew (c. 1540–1598); William Fleetwood (1525–1594); Sir Gilbert Gerard (d. 1593); Sir Harbottle Grimston (1603–1685); Sir Thomas Hetley (c. 1570–1637); Sir Robert Houghton (1548–1624); David Jenkins (1582–1663); Sir William Jones (1566–1640); John Kitchin (d. in or before 1588); Edward Littleton (1589–1645); James Morice (1539–1597); Edmund Plowden (c. 1518–1585); Robert Powell (fl. 1609–1642); Sir Timothy Turner (1585–1677); Francis Wyndham (d. 1593); also revised entry for Christopher Tancred (1689–1754)

# INDEX

CPSIA information can be obtained
at www.ICGtesting.com
Printed in the USA
LVHW022126170121
676736LV00004B/13

9 781108 740647